Narratives of the Revolutionary and Napoleonic Wars

Also by Catriona Kennedy

SOLDIERING IN BRITAIN AND IRELAND, 1750–1850: Men of Arms (*co-edited with Matthew McCormack*)

Narratives of the Revolutionary and Napoleonic Wars

Military and Civilian Experience in Britain and Ireland

Catriona Kennedy
Lecturer, History Department, University of York

palgrave
macmillan

First published 2013 by
PALGRAVE MACMILLAN

Palgrave Macmillan in the UK is an imprint of Macmillan Publishers Limited, registered in England, company number 785998, of Houndmills, Basingstoke, Hampshire RG21 6XS.

Palgrave Macmillan in the US is a division of St Martin's Press LLC, 175 Fifth Avenue, New York, NY 10010.

Palgrave Macmillan is the global academic imprint of the above companies and has companies and representatives throughout the world.

Palgrave® and Macmillan® are registered trademarks in the United States, the United Kingdom, Europe and other countries

ISBN: 978–0–230–27543–0

This book is printed on paper suitable for recycling and made from fully managed and sustained forest sources. Logging, pulping and manufacturing processes are expected to conform to the environmental regulations of the country of origin.

A catalogue record for this book is available from the British Library.

A catalog record for this book is available from the Library of Congress.

Contents

Acknowledgements

This book is based on research conducted for the AHRC-funded project 'Nations, Borders, Identities: The Revolutionary and Napoleonic Wars in European Experience' in partnership with a Berlin-based project on the memory of these wars funded by the German Research Foundation. One of the great pleasures of this project has been the intellectual exchange afforded by and friendships developed through this British–German collaboration and the camaraderie that took us from 'Arbeitfrühstucken' in Berlin to hoedowns in North Carolina. My thanks to Karen Hagemann, the driving force behind the project, Alan Forrest, Etienne François, Arnd Bauerkämper, Richard Bessel, Wolfgang Koller, Ruth Leiserowitz, Lars Peters, Karine Rance, Kirstin Schäfer, Maria Schultz and Marie Cecile Thoral. My office mate Leighton James deserves a special mention for his good-humoured collegiality throughout. Particular thanks as well to Jane Rendall who with characteristic generosity read the full manuscript and provided judicious commentary and corrections: any errors which remain are of course my own.

The book has benefited from the insights and suggestions of colleagues at various seminars, workshops and conferences, but I'm especially grateful to the following current and former colleagues at the Centre for Eighteenth Century Studies at the University of York who, together, have provided an exceptionally stimulating and supportive environment in which to work: John Barrell, Mike Brown, Helen Cowie, Geoff Cubitt, Mary Fairclough, Natasha Glaisyer, Joanna de Groot, Harriet Guest, Nicholas Guyatt, Mark Hallett, Mark Jenner, Emma Major and Jim Watt. Thanks too to colleagues in the History department who read and commented on early chapter drafts: Alex Goodall, Hannah Greig and Mark Roodhouse. In York and Dublin, Alison O'Byrne, Anna Barnard, Helen Smith, Anouk Bradish, Siân Muldowney and Arran Murphy provided much appreciated friendship, laughter and support. I owe a particular debt of gratitude to Helen Smith, who generously and carefully proofread and commented on the complete manuscript.

I would like to thank the following archives and libraries for permission to quote from material in their collections in the epigraphs to the Introduction, Chapter 1, and Chapter 5 the Royal Irish Academy, the National Library of Wales, the National Army Museum.

I think my family has been mildly perplexed by how long it's taken to complete this book, so I'm grateful to them for trying to conceal their surprise each time I told them it *still* wasn't finished. Neil Armstrong has been there since this book's inception and his love and support have been vital to its completion. The book is dedicated to my mother, Kathleen Kennedy, and to the memory of my father, Seán Kennedy.

Introduction

> I have always been of the opinion that the most perfect and compleat idea of public manners & actions is better to be collected from circumstantial detail of particular facts & occurrences as they arise, than from any general relation of events & council...my purpose of making those understand what the scourge of war is, who have never felt it...cannot be done by describing calamity in the mass but in the particulars that compose it.
>
> *Revd James Little's Diary of the French Landing in Mayo, 1798*[1]

The British experience of war in the twentieth century is often encapsulated in the epithets attached to the two world wars: 'the lost generation' of 1914–1918 and the 'People's War' of 1939–1945. While neither term fully captures the complexities of these conflicts, they each convey something of their human and social impact: the tragedy and waste of the trenches in the case of the First World War and the cross-class unity and consensus that supposedly characterized Britain during the Second World War. The experience of the Revolutionary and Napoleonic wars (1793–1815), in contrast, cannot be evoked by any similarly resonant formulations. Although known as the 'Great War' until 1914, in recognition of the unparalleled scale and intensity of the conflict, this tells us little about the personal experience of these wars, or what they meant to those who lived through them. A sense that these earlier conflicts pressed only lightly upon the fabric of Britons' everyday existences is perhaps best captured in Winston Churchill's well-known reflections upon reading Jane Austen's *Pride and Prejudice* in 1943: 'What calm lives they lead, those people! No worries about the French Revolution, or the crashing struggles of the Napoleonic wars.'[2] For Churchill, Austen's novels portrayed a society cocooned from the contests raging outside its neatly trimmed hedgerows and gossip-filled drawing rooms: a domestic insularity which he implicitly contrasted with the sacrifices and mass civilian mobilization demanded by modern 'total' war.

1

Although the wars of 1793–1815 saw neither the technological innovation, nor, in Britain at least, the mass compulsory conscription that would mark out a new era of warfare in the twentieth century, they did see the massive expansion of the armed forces, the partial militarization of civilian society, and the deployment of a highly-charged patriotic rhetoric that proclaimed the war effort the concern of every man and woman, rich and poor across the four nations of the British Isles. The London-based diarist, Anna Larpent, recorded the intertwining of public affairs and personal life during these years as a social visit was suddenly interrupted by news of the crucial naval victory at Cape St. Vincent in February 1797. 'Thus', she reflected in her journal 'are the events of life public and private mingled'.[3] A year later, in a remote region of the West of Ireland, a country rector, quoted above, related his experience of French invasion to a more universal sense of upheaval and disruption. As George Steiner memorably wrote: 'It is the events of 1789 to 1815 that interpenetrate common, private existence with the perception of historical processes.... Wherever ordinary men and women looked across the garden hedge, they saw bayonets passing'.[4]

The interpenetration of historical process and private existence in Britain and Ireland is one of the central themes of this study, which draws upon the eyewitness accounts, letters and diaries of soldiers and civilians to explore how the Revolutionary and Napoleonic wars were experienced and narrated by contemporaries. Such sources have not yet achieved the status accorded to autobiographical writings from the First and Second World Wars. The vivid personal testimonies written by soldier poets and memoirists of 1914–1918 and the home-front diaries collected by the Mass Observation project between 1939 and 1945 have played a vital role in shaping our understanding of these conflicts, foregrounding their subjective and quotidian impact. By contrast, a recent anthology of war diaries includes only one brief extract from the Napoleonic period, whilst James Treadwell's study of autobiography in the Romantic period does not consider the numerous military memoirs produced in this period.[5] Yet one of the striking consequences of these wars is the emergence of the war memoir as a distinctive and hugely popular genre, a development that can be linked to a fundamental transformation in how war was experienced and interpreted.[6] While this study is largely based on contemporaneous accounts rather than retrospective memoirs, here too the soldiers and sailors of the French wars proved prolific writers, as the vast and surprisingly under-exploited collections of letters and diaries stored in archives across the British Isles attest.[7] For civilians as well, the ideological earthquake of the French Revolution and the wars that followed meant that national and international affairs and their parochial and personal ramifications became a pervasive presence in private correspondence and journals, where ordinary men and women reflected upon what many perceived to be historically unprecedented events.[8] Attending to the ways in which contemporaries wrote and interpreted their experiences of war in this era not only restores some sense of the human impact of these conflicts, but can also provide a fresh perspective on the historiography of warfare in this period and the intertwining of civilian and military experience.

Both historians and literary scholars have begun to recognize the centrality of warfare to our understanding of Georgian culture and society. The gradual displacement of the industrial 'revolution' as the dominant explanatory mechanism in narratives of eighteenth-century social and political formation has directed attention to other agents of change. As Clive Emsley observed, in one of the first scholarly studies of the domestic impact of the French wars, military service rather than employment in an urban textile factory was probably the single dominant collective experience for the labouring classes in the late eighteenth and early nineteenth century.[9] The pan-Britannic character of the armed forces from the mid eighteenth century onwards has also marked out warfare as obvious terrain for the so-called 'new British history', which seeks to bring the mutual relationships between the component nations of the British Isles into a single historical frame, an approach developed most influentially in Linda Colley's seminal work, *Britons: Forging the Nation, 1707–1837*.[10] Tracing the construction of British national identity from the Anglo-Scottish Act of Union in 1707, *Britons* identified the key elements out of which a collective sense of Britishness was constructed: a shared Protestantism positioned against a predominantly Catholic continental 'other' and a pronounced popular Francophobia reinforced through a series of wars against the French. Colley accords the period 1793–1815 a pivotal role as the experience of protracted warfare, threat of invasion and mass mobilization intensified the processes through which Britishness was constructed. Britain, she concluded, was 'an invention forged above all by war' and a culture 'that largely defined itself through fighting'.[11]

Since its publication, Colley's thesis has generated, and continues to generate, much debate. It has been criticized for understating the fractures within British Protestantism and the persistence of sub-British patriotisms, whilst overstating the extent of popular loyalism and the depth of anti-French feeling during this period.[12] The history of British Francophobia is certainly more complicated than a static binary model allows. As a political stance, anti-Gallicism, from the mid eighteenth-century onwards, was particularly associated with oppositional, reform movements and was, more often, deployed not in defence of the status quo, but against the oligarchical aristocratic elite and its perceived cosmopolitanism and Francophilia. It was as much a product of anxieties within concerning the erosion of national liberties or the enervation of the national character as a response to threats from outside.[13] While the conflation of anti-Gallicism and anti-Jacobinism during the 1790s would see this rhetoric employed to more conservative ends, the dramatic changes wrought by the Revolution also meant that France divested itself of many of the key features associated with this particular national stereotype as it supposedly broke free from the shackles of absolutist monarchy and Catholicism.[14] Over the course of the wars too, the stereotype of the emaciated, fanatical Jacobin soldier would give way to a more admiring view of Napoleon's disciplined and professional troops. As this study suggests, a residual Francophilia often coloured British perceptions of their opponent, especially amongst the elite, whilst the French were not always the dominant 'other' against whom national character was defined.

Colley's account focused, in the main, on consensus rather than conflict; it is possible, however, to present an equally persuasive narrative of this period which emphasizes the centrifugal forces unleashed by the French Revolution – the radical challenges of the 1790s, the United Irish rebellion of 1798, and, from 1811, the Luddite protests – as much as the centripetal tendencies fostered by the wars. The sweeping teleological thrust of *Britons* is in part nuanced by its insistence that local and national affiliations could be sustained and accommodated within a wider British framework, and indeed that Britishness, rather than being imposed from the English centre, was often enthusiastically championed by the peripheries. The argument falters, however, when extended to Ireland, which was excluded from Colley's study on the grounds that its predominantly Catholic population and historical alliances with France debarred it from the key elements of national bonding: Protestantism and Francophobia. Hence, although this period witnessed the formal incorporation of Ireland into the United Kingdom in 1801, its alienation and separation from the union a hundred and twenty years later is presented as a *fait accompli*.[15] Yet Ireland was a vital participant in the British 'armed nation' and hundreds of thousands of Irish men, both Protestant and Catholic, served in the army, the navy and the militia during the French wars.[16] If war and military service are viewed as central to the consolidation of an emerging sense of 'Britishness', then Irish sailors and soldiers must be understood as subject to the same integrative processes as their counterparts in Scotland, or Wales; their experiences are consequently included in this study. While this book does not deny Ireland's problematic relationship to the union, it will, it is hoped, illuminate some of the complexities of, and alternative possibilities contained within, that relationship.

The formative role attributed to the Revolutionary and Napoleonic wars in the shaping of national consciousness is not restricted to Britain, but has long been considered a pan-European phenomenon. The explanation for this intensification of national feeling is often related to a profound shift in the culture and mode of warfare during this era, from the 'limited' or 'cabinet' warfare of the eighteenth century, fought between professional soldiers with minimal civilian involvement, to a state of 'total war', in which all of a society's resources – its economy, culture and people – were mobilized. This interpretation has been championed most recently by David Bell. Bell identifies in these conflicts several features which mark them out as the precursor to the 'total' wars of the twentieth century: the abandonment of the code of civilized restraint that had previously regulated military engagements; the demonization and dehumanization of the enemy 'other'; and the emergence of a distinct cleavage between military and civilian society that ultimately resulted in the imposition of military values upon the civilian sphere.[17]

Bell's argument is largely based on the example of France, where there was a series of transformations in the structure, character and political role of the armed forces, as the elite-dominated armies of the *ancien régime* gave way to the citizen-soldiers of the revolutionary order and finally the military dictatorship of Napoleon Bonaparte. This particular model of 'total' war is more problematic when applied to Britain. Despite the expansion of the army and navy and the introduction of limited reforms, British military culture in these years was arguably marked more by continuity than change, although the proliferation of specially constructed barracks and the prolonged absence of the army on overseas campaigns may have contributed to a sharpening division between the military and the civilian population. By adopting an alternative view of 'total' war, one which emphasizes the blurring, rather than the polarization, of the military and civilian spheres, however, it is possible to identify a more wide-ranging militarization of society, as Britain, like many other European states, partly followed the French example by arming its civilian population. In either case, there are still significant questions to be asked about the shifting and evolving relationship between the military and civilian spheres during this period. Did soldiers, for instance, continue to understand themselves as belonging to a transnational military community, or did they fashion a new identity as heroic embodiments of the nation? Did the experience of combat and campaign result in a heightened consciousness of the military as a separate caste, increasingly segregated from and in tension with civil society? How did the nation's 'citizen-soldiers' who left their farms, workshops and trading houses to drill with muskets on the parade ground negotiate the transition between civilian and military identities?

During the Revolutionary and Napoleonic wars an estimated one in four men of military age bore arms in either the regular or auxiliary armed forces. Significant transformations in the gender order and the emergence of a newly virilized and martial model of national identity have been traced to this far-reaching militarization of national life. An ethos of 'heroic endeavour and aggressive maleness', according to Colley, fed into a conception of Britain as 'an essentially "masculine" culture ... caught up in an eternal rivalry with an essentially "effeminate" France'.[18] Yet, despite recent work on war and masculinity in this period, we still know relatively little about the military context and institutional cultures in which many men's masculinity was formed and performed.[19] Here, personal narratives can tell us a great deal about how masculinity was practised and understood by members of the armed forces, revealing some of the tensions and continuities between civilian and martial gendered identities, an issue which is explored in Chapters 2 and 3.

Identity, then, and in particular the 'master category' of national identity, has been a central concern in recent studies of the Revolutionary and Napoleonic wars. Scholars have tended to focus on how particular visions of the nation, and national masculinity and femininity, were elaborated and instantiated in the press, poetry and theatre, in public debate and civic and political ritual; it is the public expression of identity rather than its personal meaning that is consequently privileged. While it is possible to 'read-off' much about how identities were lived and experienced from such material, this may obscure the extent to which identity construction is an individual as well as a collective process, one which takes place in both the personal and the public imaginary. This is already implicit in many of the models of identity formation which have underpinned recent scholarship on this subject. The notion of 'othering', as Carolyn Steedman reminds us, describes the workings of a process through which 'experience shaped the sense of self and nationhood' and involves the use of 'a particular model of the human mind and a paradigm of psychological explanation'.[20] Yet this subjective, experiential dimension is often overlooked. Much has been written about the pamphlets, broadsides and caricatures which repeatedly contrasted British Protestant rectitude, constitutional liberty and the manliness of the national character with the superstition, slavishness and effeminacy of the Gallic foe, but we still know comparatively little about how ordinary Britons internalized and applied such rhetoric.

One approach that has rooted understandings of national self and foreign other more firmly in lived experience has been the history of travel and cross-cultural encounter.[21] Such an approach can also profitably be applied to the study of identity in wartime. One of the dominant features of all wars, including the Revolutionary and Napoleonic wars, is the mass movement of peoples: from the (mostly) voluntary travels of soldiers and seamen to the prolonged overseas internment of prisoners of war. In an era of mass soldiering this meant that travel and knowledge of foreign countries, previously the preserve of a small privileged group, became an experience shared by hundreds of thousands. As this book argues, the experience of dislocation and the ethnographic eye which Britons brought to bear on their wartime journeys can tell us much about how they constructed and interpreted their own gendered and national subjectivities. Though the contrast between 'self' and 'other' was frequently invoked in such encounters, the process of contact and comparison often operated in unexpected ways to reveal affinities across national boundaries, as well as fractures and differences within the nation.

If we turn to the other most commonly cited model of identity construction, Benedict Anderson's formulation of the nation as an 'imagined community', we can see how this too implies a subjective process that depends upon the ability of the individual to internalize and imagine the nation.[22] This process may work in tandem with concepts of 'othering' or 'bonding-by-exclusion', but it suggests, to cite Steedman once again, 'a quite different psychological model, of incorporation, appropriation, interiority and sameness'.[23] Anderson's contention that the modern national consciousness was made possible by the development of print capitalism, which allowed individuals to imagine an affinity, or relationship, with millions of others whom they would never meet, may be particularly salient when considering the British civilian experience of war in this period. Because the war, or at least the central activity of war – fighting and killing – took place far from the nation's shores, various forms of representation were required to bridge the gap between civilians and the forces fighting overseas, so that Britons could imagine themselves as 'a nation at war'. Indeed, it is this aspect of the wars – their heavily mediated character – that may truly mark them out as the first 'modern' wars.[24] Developments in postal communications not only connected together peoples from across the four nations, but also helped to narrow the gap between home and front. Though domestic reports on the progress of the war remained subject to a time lag, the rapid dissemination of news of the latest victory, or defeat, meant that such events were experienced with an unprecedented degree of simultaneity.

To return to the view of war as an arena for heightened human mobility, it is possible to see how these two modes of identity formation – one which assumes that such encounters result in the 'discovery' of difference and another which implies the 'discovery' of sameness – may be rather arbitrarily applied. Recent studies of war and identity have assumed that the expansion of the armed forces during eighteenth-century conflicts, which brought together hundreds and thousands of men from across the British Isles, necessarily had an integrative effect, as differences in religion, ethnicity or language were overlaid by a common sense of purpose and a new understanding of the ties that bound these disparate groups together. Similarly, it has been speculated that the militia regiments that criss-crossed the country during these years would have also helped to erode local particularities and engender wider loyalties.[25] This is not to say that these institutions and encounters did not, in certain instances, have such an effect, but nor should it be assumed that they resulted in the discovery of a shared Britishness, for to do so supposes that there was a pre-existing, shared Britishness waiting to be discovered.

The privileging of personal experience that informs much of this study might seem to go against the grain of recent historical scholarship. The linguistic 'turn' encouraged a degree of scepticism regarding the 'evidence of experience' to be found in personal narratives and the belief that they contained an experiential truth that lay outside of publicly circulated discourses.[26] Yet attending to the discourses through which both identity and experience are constructed, does not necessarily invalidate the use of personal testimony as a source, or the reconstruction of experience as an object of historical study. Awareness of the dynamic relationship between the narrated self and the broader cultural context can provide a fruitful perspective on the relationship between the individual subject and the broader narratives mobilized by war, as is explored in Chapter 1. Indeed, historians have increasingly called for a 'properly grounded notion of "identity" which includes autobiographical experience',[27] an approach that has been employed profitably in studies of twentieth-century wars to explore, for instance, how women constructed their experiences through available models of wartime femininity.[28]

If the relationship between experience and language or discourse is problematic, so too is our understanding of the relationship between individual and collective experience. It would seem impossible to speak of a single, shared experience of war. Besides the gulf that may exist between the combatant's and the civilian's war, even the recollection of the same battle by two soldiers of identical rank and regiment may differ widely. In that case, a study based on individual testimonies risks splintering into numerous micro-histories, a disconnected collection of variegated and personal experiences. Close attention to 'texts of experience', however, can illuminate the broader shared frameworks of interpretation and meaning production that are brought to bear on diverse encounters. As this study suggests, the apparent tensions between experience and discourse, personal and collective identities can be reconciled through an emphasis on narrative. Understood as an individual, as well as a collective mode of consciousness, identity, as Kathleen Wilson puts it, depends 'upon the ability of individuals to insert themselves into the weft of collective narratives'. Identification is, therefore, 'a psychic as well as a social production that certain kinds of sources, such as diaries and memoirs, may allow us to track with some care.'[29]

The fashioning of personal experience into coherent narrative is, of course, a process that is more readily traced in memoirs or autobiographies, where the individual has time to reflect on, arrange and interpret their experiences. This study draws mostly, though not exclusively, on unpublished and published accounts written in the period between 1793 and 1815, not because such sources necessarily provide a less mediated, or more 'authentic' account, but because autobiographies, often written much later, are more likely to reflect the cultural climate in which they were written. Despite revealing a great deal about the commemoration of the wars and the politics of military reform in the nineteenth century, the accretion of later historical perspectives renders such texts problematic when trying to reconstruct the frameworks of meaning production that prevailed during the wars.[30] It was only after the wars, however, that many ordinary soldiers and seamen began to write up their recollections and omitting these accounts means that the analysis risks being disproportionately weighted towards the literate and educated. These parameters have therefore been flexibly applied, with later memoirs and campaign narratives being used selectively where they can shed light on the culture and experiences of the other ranks.

Unlike other forms of historical documentation, such as newspapers, 'ego-documents' can vary widely according to the self-reflexivity and literary capabilities of the writer; narratives that are particularly thoughtful or evocative are invariably privileged. So, for example, having researched naval letters and journals held at the National Maritime Museum and elsewhere, my impression is that the surviving material is not as abundant, nor, for various reasons, as richly textured, as that produced by members of the army. Consequently, the navy, despite its significance to the British war experience, figures less prominently in the following chapters. Regrettably, such criteria also results in a disproportionate emphasis on the experiences of the middling and upper classes, although, wherever possible, I have tried to draw in additional voices and perspectives. Making meaningful comparisons between regions, or nations, has proven similarly challenging. This study is based on manuscript material held in national archives in Scotland, Ireland, Wales and England, with additional material drawn from local archives in Kent and Yorkshire, and from published diaries and sets of correspondence. Although it is pan-Britannic in scope and alert to regional and national diversity, it is not primarily concerned with delineating the differences between, say, the Scottish and Welsh experience of war, a comparative approach that would require a quite different source base.[31]

Narrative then provides one of the central themes of this study. Chapter 1 outlines some approaches to, and distinctive features of, the three main categories of war narrative: combatants' letters and journals; prisoner of war narratives; and accounts by civilians. This emphasis on narrative makes it possible to situate war experience, including the experience of combat and campaign, within a broader cultural and literary frame. In its essentials, the soldiers' experience of war has sometimes been represented as unchanging and universal.[32] While we now know much more about how transformations in technology and culture shape combat experiences, the narration of that experience is still sometimes subsumed into a transhistorical 'soldiers' tale'.[33] A detailed analysis of accounts of campaign and combat, however, reveals the extent to which these experiences and their narration drew upon historically specific forms of representation, from Romanticism and the Gothic novel to the picaresque adventure tale. Civilian testimonies too were variously informed by, or dissented from, dominant narratives of war, from the terrifying imagined invasion scenarios that circulated during the invasion crises of 1797–1798 and 1803–1805 to the emerging 'pleasure culture of war'. Perhaps the most powerful narrative that is said to have emerged in this period is the representation of these conflicts as national wars, fought between peoples rather than kings, and fuelled by a mass-based patriotism. Despite the newly ideological character of the contest between the British and French forces, however, I suggest that traditional understandings of warfare remained influential among both members of the military and civilians. Personal and regimental honour, rather than national glory, continued to be a guiding principle in combatants' assessment of their service and many contemporaries still viewed war as the product of the 'ambitions of kings and princes' rather than a conflict between mutually hostile peoples.

The second major theme of the book is encounters. In several respects, the experience of war in this period can be understood in terms of a series of encounters: between men from across the four nations of the British Isles who were drawn together in the armed forces; between militia regiments and the civilian populations amongst whom they were stationed; between prisoners of war and their French captors; and between British troops and the culture, landscape and peoples of those countries in which they campaigned. The book argues that these interactions provided a crucial context for the articulation of national and other identities, but it also underlines the unpredictable outcomes of such encounters and their capacity to dissolve or solidify perceived differences. As we shall see, British soldiers' victorious march into France was widely narrated as an entrance into a shared Anglo-French zone of civilization, whilst the experiences of militia regiments stationed in Ireland appeared to confirm the profound alterity of that nation.

The third and final theme of the book is the relationship between the military and civilian realms. This study is one of the first to integrate the military and civilian experience of these wars and it uses this distinctive focus to explore a number of themes: the tensions and continuities between civilian and military identities; the shared cultural and literary frames that allowed combatants to bridge the divide between home and front; and the ways in which war was brought home to Britons. Despite the long duration of the wars and the rising prestige of the military, this did not result in a pronounced cleavage between the armed forces and civilian society, or the imposition of martial values upon the domestic population. Nor did the armed forces act as a crucible for a new hegemonic model of masculinity. Instead the 'gentleman-amateur' ethos of the British officer corps continued to incorporate various modes of masculine behaviour, some of which were drawn from the civilian sphere with others relating more specifically to the culture of the army. On campaign, officers worked hard to maintain the connective tissue that bound them to their civilian selves. By narrating their sensitive responses to the sublimity and horror of war for a domestic audience, they were able to reassure those at home that they had not been brutalised by war.

Chapter 1, 'Narrating War', highlights the literary genres and conventions that influenced combatants and civilians' war writing and considers how these wars, in turn, may have promoted particular transformations in autobiographical writing. Chapter 2, 'Soldiers and Sailors', explores how the armed forces' new recruits negotiated the transition between civilian and military worlds. Chapter 3, 'Combat and Campaign', follows these British and Irish soldiers onto the battlefield and analyses both how they narrated the experience of combat and the ideals that sustained them through their campaigns. Chapter 4, 'Travellers in Uniform', turns to an often neglected dimension of the history of warfare – the soldier as traveller and ethnographer – to show how British troops in this period were engaged in mapping the boundaries of European civilization. Chapter 5, 'Prisoners of War', examines the experiences of British detainees in France and their efforts to construct communities in captivity. Chapter 6, 'Citizen-Soldiers', focuses on civilian–military mobilization and the indifference and resentment that often lay behind the image of a unified nation-in-arms. Chapter 7, 'Bringing the War Back Home', investigates the home front's mediated experience of war and the sometimes ambivalent response of the domestic public to an emergent 'pleasure culture of war'. The concluding chapter 'A Waterloo Panorama' endeavours to pull together these various strands, demonstrating, through a discussion of Waterloo narratives and post-war commemorations, how the narration and interpretation of these wars continued to be contested in the period after 1815.

1
Narrating War

I feel half ashamed to intrude on your agreeable Pursuits with my Letters, but you live in the Country enough to know & feel one's Avidity for News concerning the great Mart of Intelligence – London, whence I no longer expect to hear Talk of Impossible Descents of *French Imperialists*.

Hesther Piozzi, Brynbella to John Lloyd, London, 14 June 1804[1]

I will now give you some account of our late expedition. Though you must not expect a minute detail of the operations, as that would be totally out of my power and entirely foreign to my present purpose. I will briefly relate what happened within my own knowledge, and should there be an error in my Orthography, I shall trust to you to make an excuse, provided you show this Epistle to any of your friends, as I am fully aware of my own inability in writing for public perusal.

Lieutenant John Christopher Harrison, Colchester Barracks,
20 November 1807[2]

What does it mean to privilege personal writings as a source for the study of warfare? What do letters, diaries and other first-person narratives reveal that other official or public documents – institutional records, newspaper reports, literary and visual representations – may not? Most obviously, their value can be understood to lie in the subjective, personal viewpoint which they appear to afford and their proximity, whether physical or temporal, to the events they describe. Yet, Lieutenant Harrison's letter describing his recent involvement in the bombardment of Copenhagen, quoted above, suggests how even accounts of extreme experiences can be alert to style, audience and reception. Such texts can be viewed neither as repositories of raw, unmediated experience nor as the private outpourings of an authentic self. We therefore need to be attentive to the generic conventions that structured these documents, their envisaged audiences, the languages upon which they drew and the purposes for which they were written.

By the 1790s the post boy had been replaced by new high-speed mail coaches which connected together provincial and metropolitan cultures.[3] While London remained the epicentre of a network of news and correspondence, the 'great Mart of Intelligence' as Hesther Thrale Piozzi described it, private letters as well as the public press allowed rural residents like Piozzi to keep abreast of the latest reports from the capital. The introduction of a military postal service, meanwhile, ensured that the letters of serving soldiers and sailors filled columns of newsprint and provided a vital source of information on the fortunes and experiences of those fighting overseas. As developments in the postal system expanded the circulation of personal accounts of the wars, the unparalleled scale and intensity of these conflicts combined with new modes of literary expression to foster an enhanced appreciation of the subjective impact of warfare. The soldier's and sailor's tale of war, it has recently been argued, changed in this period as combatants began to write with greater sensitivity about the 'inner experience of war' and to stress the uniqueness of that experience.[4] According to Peter Fritzsche, the momentous events set in train by the French Revolution and the wars that followed meant that civilians too began to understand themselves 'as taking part in historical struggles and accordingly put value on their contributions and testimonies'. The result was a proliferation of vernacular, unauthoritative narratives of public events described in memoirs, letters and diaries.[5]

Although discussions concerning the value of personal testimony have moved on from questions of 'reliability', the representativeness of this category of sources, which, after all, only represent the thoughts and experiences of a fraction of the literate population and which, by definition, provide a particularized, subjective window onto historical processes, remains open to debate.[6] It may be impossible to construct a coherent picture of wartime subjectivity out of such 'kaleidoscopic fragments', but certain patterns can be traced.[7] This chapter considers some of the distinctive features and literary contexts of three main categories of war writing – combatants' letters and journals; prisoner of war narratives; and texts that record civilian experience – and suggests how the multiple influences that shape such texts add to rather than detract from their richness as a source for the study of wartime mentalities.

Writing and fighting

Since the publication of Paul Fussell's seminal study *The Great War and Modern Memory* (1975), both historians and literary scholars have paid increasing attention to the narrative construction of the 'soldiers' tale' in the twentieth century: the elisions and distortions resulting from censorship and the translation of combat experience into language, their indebtedness to prevailing literary and cultural conventions, and their relationship to processes of personal and collective remembrance.[8] Until recently, war narratives from earlier periods have not received the same degree of analysis.[9] Yet in several respects our understanding of military experience can profit from such an approach, particularly when it comes to debates around the 'communicability' of war experience and the gulf in understanding that can open up between military and civilian realms during wartime.

The letter is in many ways emblematic of the separations occasioned by war, between the soldier and his friends or family and between the military and civilian worlds. It is perhaps for this reason that the letter from a soldier at the front to a woman at home has been viewed as the 'classic wartext'.[10] This close relationship between the letter form and the experience of war can itself be traced to the eighteenth century, often described as the 'century of the letter'.[11] Throughout the period, the epistolary genre was the favoured form in novel writing. Works such as Samuel Richardson's *Pamela* (1741), Rousseau's *La Nouvelle Heloïse* (1761) and Goethe's *Sorrows of Young Werther* (1774) presented the letter as a mode of expression especially suited to personal effusions of sentiment and sensibility. While the epistolary novel portrayed the letter as vehicle for natural, spontaneous and private communication, eighteenth-century letter-writing practice was in fact a highly crafted, rhetorical act, a social performance that staged the self for a particular audience.[12] The proliferation of letter-writing manuals offering models of epistolary composition attests to the highly stylized nature of the eighteenth-century letter. These manuals provided templates appropriate to a vast range of social and professional circumstances including, by the end of the century, letters from military personnel. *The New Universal Letter Writer* (1795), for instance, contained model letters specifically for military correspondents, including one 'From a Young Officer in the Army to a Gentleman's Daughter, with whom he is in love' and another 'From a Young Officer ordered to his Regiment in Minorca to a young Lady whom he had courted'.[13] The latter offers a fairly typical example of the overwrought display of emotional anguish and suffering characteristic of the 'culture of sensibility', as the officer reflects upon the cruel separations caused by war:

> What unhappiness to us, and devastation among the human race has the ambition of princes & the perfidiousness of ministers occasioned! Husbands obliged to leave their beloved wives and dear little children; every relation is broken ... Did you know my dear what a struggle I have between my love and duty, you would consider me an object of compassion.[14]

Articulating a residual understanding of war as the instrument of ambitious princes and scheming ministers rather than the concern of the nation, this model letter foregrounds the tension between the soldier's civilian and military identities, between 'love and duty'. There seems to have been little expectation that the soldier correspondent should adopt the heroic language of a national war effort; rather it was the language of intimacy and affection that was deemed appropriate to such epistolary communication.

The cultivation of seemingly unforced intimacy and emotion advocated in such manuals was an important aspect of wartime correspondence.[15] Men serving with the military often had clear expectations of how contemporary letter-writing conventions should shape their own and their correspondents' letters. Frustrated by the brevity of his wife's letters, William Wilkson, master of a naval gunship, provided instructions on how to write more expressively. She might, he suggested, look to Samuel Richardson's Pamela, who excelled at intimate epistolarity, as a 'caracter [*sic*] highly worthy of imitation'.[16] 'I should imagine you would feel a pleasure in excelling in that art' he chided:

> of communicating our Ideas to each other on paper, which I think is the greatest blessing we can possess when absent from each other, why should we not converse as if we were immediately together, the intent of letter writing is that the person writing should conceive the person that he writes to, to be by the side of him, and to write as familiar as if he were talking to him alone.[17]

Soldiers and sailors were often conscious of the need to make their letters interesting and amusing for their recipients. Whilst letters to male correspondents tended to go into some detail about military strategy and tactics, or opportunities for promotion, letters to female relatives and friends adopted a lighter, more intimate style that blended expressions of affection with regimental gossip and anecdotal observations on the character and landscape of the countries through which they travelled.[18]

In recognition of the importance of epistolary communication to soldiers and their families, the British army established the first field post office during the Duke of York's expedition to the Helder in 1799. During the Peninsular campaign, a Sergeant Postmaster was appointed to manage army communications and intelligence. Soldiers and sailors understood the importance of letters home in assuring families and friends of their health and safety, particularly after a battle. If wounded, they were anxious to reassure their correspondents before the lists of casualties were publicly printed. During the siege of Toulon, Philip Hay wrote to his mother, 'in the greatest distress imaginable for fear you sho'd see the Public papers before you receive this Letter, true I am wounded but not at all dangerously'.[19]

Despite the concessionary rates for the rank and file, relatively few letters from ordinary soldiers have survived. Although regimental and garrison schools for ordinary soldiers had been in existence since the seventeenth century, with a more extensive system of regimental education introduced by the Duke of York in 1811, signature literacy for private soldiers has been estimated at around 41 per cent and many members of the other ranks would have lacked the writing skills necessary to correspond with their families.[20] Those who could write seem to have done so infrequently and their letters tended to be brief, functional and fragmentary. The correspondence of Private James Reid shows the effort some soldiers made to communicate with their families. His first letters home after joining the 92nd regiment were not in his own hand, but his writing gained in confidence as his military service progressed. In 1804 he informed his sister that 'I was practicing myself in reading and writing all times when I can get an opportunity of doying [sic] so and this is my own hand of writ [sic]'.[21] The practical as well as emotional functions of the ordinary soldier's letter home were underlined in Reid's instructions that 'when you do not recive [sic] letters from me you may know all is not well with me, if I should fall in the field & not return home you will keep this letter … and go to the Pay Master of the District … and collect my Copenhagen Prize money'.[22]

While the letter played an important role in maintaining the intimate and affective bonds between combatants and those at home, they cannot be read as purely private or personal documents. The eighteenth-century letter writer was acutely aware that even if he or she did not write for publication, their letter could be circulated amongst a much broader group than those to whom it was addressed and might also find its way into print.[23] Though soldiers regularly complained that the British newspaper reading public knew more about the progress of a campaign than members of the army, their letters could still be seen as a key source of information from the front line. Sometimes soldiers asked their correspondents not to show their letters outside the family.[24] Others clearly wrote for a broader audience and saw themselves as supplementing public reports on the war. Following the bombardment of Copenhagen in 1807, John Christopher Harrison sent his father a detailed account of the expedition which included transcriptions of official documents, general orders and the articles of capitulation, as well as his personal diary of the campaign.[25] Writing from Spain in 1812, Lieutenant George Hennell expressed his gratification on learning that his description of the storming of Badajoz had given a 'great deal of pleasure to many' and 'that many approved the style of writing'.[26]

Throughout the wars, personal letters from members of the army and navy were published in the press. In the 1790s *The Times* established the first foreign news offices commissioning letters from abroad in order to publish 'its own epistolary version of the war.'[27] While there was no official censorship in operation during this period, Wellington testily declared the British army 'the most indefatigable writers of letters and news that existed in the world' and issued a general order in 1810 urging his officers to be more discreet in their published correspondence. Eager to see how the war was represented to the British public, officers paid close attention to, and often commented critically on, these published accounts. Lt. John Aitchison explained to his father that the private communications from the army in Portugal printed in the *Courier* 'are to us … extremely amusing as compared to the *real truth*; they exceed the most ridiculous burlesque'.[28] Officers' letters were thus embedded within a broader print culture of war reportage and their accounts of war were shaped by and responsive to these published accounts. This may explain the form which many letters took, veering between an intimate conversational tone and more detached, impersonal accounts of military manoeuvres and the conduct of the campaign. Officers writing from the front often tailored their accounts to the sensibilities of an elite male audience for whom the consumption of martial intelligence was an important 'accoutrement of gentlemanly identity' as gazettes were intensively read and discussed in gentlemen's clubs and subscription libraries.[29]

Over the course of the war, numerous narratives of British expeditions and campaigns based on officers' diaries were published, serving as a stimulus and model for other officers. Those who kept journals, to be sure, rarely suggested that they did so with publication in mind. Most claimed that they were for their own, or their family's, amusement. William Paterson, a civilian volunteer who joined the British forces in the Peninsula in 1813, described how, before leaving for the continent, he determined to:

> write a little journal of the adventures which I might witness in that Country and particularly of my own various employments and marches with a description of the scenery and Towns through which I might pass; these united with my remarks on the customs and manners of the inhabitants of a climate so eminently different from that which I had left... I flattered myself would at some future period afford an hour of amusement to myself as well as to the amiable companion and sweet little children left behind me in Scotland.[30]

As Paterson's commitment to recording the scenery, customs and manners of Spain and Portugal suggests, campaign journals were also, in part, travelogues. Travel literature had, by the 1790s, become one of the best-selling genres in Britain, as the Grand Tour became an indispensable element of gentlemanly education, and imperial expansion and voyages of exploration brought intensified contact with new landscapes and peoples. The reading public's appetite for travel literature was further whetted in the period 1793 to 1815 as civilians' opportunities for continental travel were severely disrupted, at the same time as the army and navy were deployed across the globe.[31] Works such as Thomas Walsh's *Journal of the Late Campaign in Egypt* (1803) and Robert Ker Porter's *Letters from Portugal and Spain* (1809) were as much travel narratives as they were military accounts, and in their journals and letters home soldiers and sailors often adopted the persona of the ethnographic observer commenting upon the culture and character of the countries through which they travelled, an aspect that will be expanded on in Chapter 4.

Many diarists underlined the importance of recording immediate impressions of events whilst they remained uncorrupted by the distorting effects of memory. The opening page of Major Edwin Griffith's daily journal was inscribed with the motto: 'One line on the spot is worth half a page of recollections'.[32] The idea of immediacy or the capacity of such sources to capture the texture and subjective experience of being at war is, of course, a key problematic when using diaries and letters. Eyewitness accounts by those who have experienced combat present, perhaps, the most compelling challenge to notions of experience as a linguistic or discursive event. The soldier-narrator derives his authority from the fact that *he was there* and has witnessed events outside the normal range of human experience. At the same time, the experience of campaign and battle can be understood as intensely physical and visceral, variously composed of the sounds of cannons roaring, the smell of gunpowder, the sight of eviscerated comrades and the physiological effects of overwhelming fear and bodily deprivation. This is a central paradox of 'the soldiers' tale'. On the one hand it is marked by the desire to assert the authenticity of his account, whilst on the other the embodied nature of that experience may put it beyond linguistic expression. As Samuel Hynes puts it 'the man-who-was-there asserts his authority as the only true witness; but the truth that he claims to tell is compromised by the very nature of memory and language'.[33]

Soldiers' and sailors' desire to accurately convey the experience of war and to carry the reader with them on their journeys could thus be in tension with the need to reassure friends and families of their well-being and the difficulties involved in communicating the terror-laden intensity of battle. A letter from John Mills, written shortly after the battle of Fuentes de Oñoro in 1811, illustrates the strain which these conflicting objects could impose. Mills began by assuring his mother that he 'had never been better in my life', a commonplace phrase in military correspondence during the wars. He briefly noted that his regiment had suffered a severe cannonade and that he had been charged with burying the dead, but declined to go into further detail, observing that a full account would be provided by the newspapers. Despite Mills' circumspection, the letter's confused and repetitive structure betray signs of what might be described, anachronistically, as 'combat trauma'.[34] Mills declares once again that 'I never was better in my life' but also confesses that 'my head is so bewildered I hardly know what I am writing'. He concludes with an apology for the letter's rambling structure and depressing content: 'the news I have given you I am afraid is not cheering or entertaining but really I am quite puzzled'.[35]

If we understand trauma as a response to an overwhelming event which resists verbal expression and therefore remains locked within the body, then such experiences would indeed seem to be beyond language.[36] Yet trauma may also be registered in language, through its 'hesitations, indirections, pauses and silences', a process that is evident in Mill's letter.[37] Moreover, while soldiers sometimes pleaded their inability to describe what they had witnessed, even these silences can be understood as a rhetorical act, a deployment of the 'inexpressibility motif'. Though this seems to assert the incommensurability of language and reality, 'the insistence on unspeakability does not undermine, but rather adds to, description.'[38] Combatants' claims that they could not fully convey the horrors of war were often accompanied by a series of graphic vignettes. One account of the Battle of Talavera began by announcing that 'to enter into particular details would be shocking', but proceeded to describe, nonetheless, scenes of soldiers dying, of limbs lost to rottenness, and the derangement that had driven a young ensign to his death.[39]

The urge to describe war's brutalities, whilst insisting upon the 'inexpressibility' of combat experience has often been understood as an immutable feature of the soldiers' tale. Recent scholarship, however, has traced its origins to specific developments in the late eighteenth century. According to Bell, the Revolutionary and Napoleonic wars marked a transition from an eighteenth-century conceptualization of warfare as a recurring and ordinary facet of human existence to an understanding of war as an extraordinary aberration in the progress of human civilization. This view of war as an extreme state of affairs combined with Romantic modes of self-expression to shape new ideas about the impact of the war on the individual. A growing conviction that only those who had experienced combat could really know 'what it was like' in turn contributed to a sharpening division between the military and civilian realms, and a militarist belief in the moral superiority of the armed forces.[40] Arguing along slightly different lines, Yuval Noah Harari identifies a similar change in the expression and interpretation of warfare between 1740 and 1865, one closely associated with an evolving cultural landscape in which the discourses of sensibility, sensationalism and Romanticism emphasized the transformative impact of extreme experiences upon the individual. As an early-modern Cartesian model of military conduct that affirmed the mind's ascendancy over the body gave way to sensationalist psychological models, in which the body served as a source of knowledge, so 'war became a *Bildungsroman*, in which the body taught the mind through a process of experiential revelation'. Harari further connects this trend to developments within military discourse, in particular a newly found respect for the common soldier, who, he argues gradually came to be seen as an autonomous, thinking and feeling being rather than a docile automaton.[41] While Harari's argument is based primarily on military memoirs, the evidence of contemporary letters and diaries would seem to support the claim that a more introspective mode of war writing emerged in this period, although a different interpretation of what this meant for military identities and hierarchies is proposed in Chapter 3.

Historicizing the experience and narration of war focuses attention on the 'cultural baggage' that soldiers carried, along with their muskets and camp kettles, into the theatre of war. In his study of First World War writing, Paul Fussell illuminates the extent to which soldiers' accounts drew upon a shared literary repertoire. This he attributes to the 'unparalleled literariness' of the British army in the First World War. The reading culture of the Napoleonic army was, by comparison, much more restricted, but there is evidence of a relatively active literary community amongst the officer class. If we consider that dramatic staple of the soldiers' narrative – the bullet deflected by a book fortuitously tucked into their regimentals – we can find an eclectic range of works performing this talismanic role, from the letters of the seventeenth-century salonnière Ninon de Lenclos to the essays of Alexander Pope.[42] Such incidental references to polite literature underline the continued influence of a culture of gentility on the British officer. Requests for the latest 'fashionable' books or literary periodicals whilst on campaign can be seen as another means through which soldiers maintained the connection between their civilian and military selves.[43]

A bibliography compiled by a tutor on board the HMS Royal Sovereign for his young naval pupil in 1808 gives some sense of military reading tastes in this period. Noting that certain novels 'are read by almost everybody' and are therefore 'common subjects of conversation', he recommended the following works: Cervantes' *Don Quixote*, Alain-Renè Lesage's *Gil Blas*, Henry Fielding's *Tom Jones* and *Joseph Andrews* and Tobias Smollett's *Roderick Random* and *Humphrey Clinker*.[44] Smollett had served as a naval surgeon in the 1740s and his novels' colourful array of military scenes and characters formed a common reference point in war narratives. The Spanish settings of *Don Quixote* and *Gil Blas*, which Smollett translated into English in the 1750s, meant that both works also figured prominently in accounts of the Peninsular campaign. Written within the picaresque tradition, broadly defined, the comic adventures of Fielding and Smollett's peripatetic protagonists would have struck a particular chord with the experiences of campaigning soldiers and sailors. Collectively, such works presented a vision of war and militarism as grotesque, highlighting its brutal, outlandish and absurd aspects. In Smollet's *Roderick Random* the eponymous hero endures a succession of horrific experiences, including being lashed to a table during a naval battle while he is splattered with the blood, brains and guts of injured sailors. Yet after each episode Random rebounds quickly and shows little sign of trauma. The carnage of war was described in unflinching detail but its psychological impact was not explored in any depth. The theatre of war revealed the base, vicious elements of human nature; it did not bring forth hidden nobility or reveal deeper truths.[45]

Though the grim, sarcastic humour that characterized literary treatments of war for much of the eighteenth century can be found in soldiers' and sailors' narratives from the Revolutionary and Napoleonic period, their accounts reveal an evolving understanding of war as at once brutal and ennobling, terrifying and sublime. It is difficult to trace this mode of war writing to any single literary template or group of texts, but the Gothic novel appears to have provided combatants with a more psychologically introspective and complex language with which to describe the subjective experience of war. Strongly influenced by Edmund Burke's theorization of terror and sublimity, 'tales of terror' by authors such as Anne Radcliffe and Matthew Lewis were immensely popular during the period and the genre's themes of dislocation, violence and alienation may have been particularly resonant for soldiers separated from their homes and families and plunged into a sometimes nightmarish world of brutality and death.[46] The Gothic offered an imagery and aesthetics through which encounters with the horrors of warfare could be articulated and contextualized. During the 1807 expedition to Copenhagen, for instance, Captain Thomas Browne described how the British army established a battery in a graveyard:

> into such a spot, man's last abode, war found its way, and the earth which covered the dead, was raised into a battery, to pour death and destruction upon the living, who had deposited them there. There was in one corner of this burial ground a sort of Mausoleum, which covered a very large vault. Some of our soldiers broke open its door & descended into it. I followed them, and as the night was rainy, we struck a light there, and remained an hour or two, as the best shelter we could have. On the sides around us coffins were placed.[47]

It is a scene which is in many ways 'pure Gothic', evoking the genre's obsession with tombs and sepulchres, while also conveying the soldier's keen consciousness of his own mortality and proximity to death.

Often set in the distant past and in a Southern European location, the Gothic novel's pronounced anti-Catholicism and preoccupation with malicious abbesses and depraved monks further shaped soldiers interactions with the Catholic peoples of Spain and Portugal. In Captain Edward Hodge's account of a reconnaissance mission to the Bridge of Zamora in Spain he described his journey through a wild landscape infested by wolves and banditti. As night drew in and a fog descended he was forced to take shelter in an isolated monastery. 'Throughout all this', he confided in his diary, 'I could not help fancying myself a hero of one of Lewis' or Radcliffe's romances'.[48] Steeped in the imagery of the Gothic novel, Hodge's account and his self-imagining as a Gothic hero suggests how certain literary forms could shape not just the writing of war experience, but also the very texture of that experience.

While the rank and file's campaign narratives were often perfunctory and rudimentary, there are some examples that stand out for their vigorous literary style. Perhaps the most well known are the letters of Private William Wheeler. Wheeler was self-educated and unusually well read: in 1812 he plundered books from the Retiro in Madrid and distributed them to others who were, like himself 'fond of reading'.[49] His fondness for reading is confirmed by the breadth of literary references in his correspondence, ranging from

Shakespeare to *Robinson Crusoe* and *Tristram Shandy*. The narrative sophisti-
cation of Wheeler's letters was indebted to a variety of literary models, most
obviously the picaresque. It was a genre which Wheeler may have encountered through popular chap-book literature or the works of Fielding and
Smollett. Indeed, certain comic incidents described by Wheeler, including
his unwitting consumption of cat stew cooked by a well-meaning French
prisoner of war, consciously, or unconsciously, echoed similar episodes in
the adventures of *Gil Blas*.[50]

For the officer this genre offered a route back to a world of childhood fantasies and adventures. Yet the picaresque, which often focused on characters
of humble birth, spoke more directly to the plight of the ordinary soldier. As
several studies have shown, it provided an especially fruitful framework for
the narration of working-class experience and soldiers' experiences in particular.[51] Like the picaresque traveller, the ordinary soldier narrates his circular
journey away from home and back again conveying little sense of linear
development or personal evolution. In Wheeler's letters we can identify
several elements of the genre: an episodic and digressive structure, densely
packed with humorous anecdotes and hair's breadth escapes, interlaced with
the occasional grotesque incident. Most of all, his narrative captures the
dizzying sense of the picaresque protagonist caught up in a series of events
beyond his control, subject, as Wheeler put it, to the fickle whims of 'dame
fortune'.[52] In a similar vein, a corporal's account of the British army's retreat
to Bremen in April 1795 evoked the vicissitudes of his life on campaign and
the fantastical quality of the changing scenes through which the soldier
moved:

> It is something like a dream or fairy vision…we who had lately been so
> buffeted about by fortune and the French, driven like vagabonds through
> frost and snow, over all the wilds of Holland…Now to be seated in the
> most elegant apartments, servants attending ready to anticipate every
> wish; beds of the softest down to repose upon….it seemed like some
> sudden enchantment.[53]

The picaresque flourishes in Wheeler's letters were more than a stylistic
device. It was a narrative mode that conveyed the powerlessness of the
ordinary soldier's life on campaign. As a form of storytelling that eschewed
progressive narrative arcs, it could also capture the rank and file's experience of a service in which there were few opportunities for promotion and
advancement.[54] The choice of narrative mode, whether the picaresque or the
more psychologically introspective *bildungsroman*, then, could reveal much
about combatants' interpretation of their war experience and how these
related to broader identities of class and rank.

The richness of Wheeler's letters is in many ways unusual, if not unique.
The majority of personal narratives by members of the other ranks were much
more rudimentary: reconstructing the experiences of the ordinary soldier and

sailor from such laconic sources can be a difficult task. A literate sergeant might keep a journal of the army's marches that gave brief details of the distances travelled, the towns through which they passed, the quality of their quarters, but such accounts tended to include little personal reflection or comment.[55] Similarly, the naval logbook provided the dominant model for sailors' journals and they were, consequently, primarily concerned with recording weather patterns, the ship's manoeuvres, and the performance of daily duties and punishments.[56] It was only after the wars that many ordinary soldiers and seamen began to write up their recollections.[57] Used selectively and carefully, such accounts can provide some insight into the culture and experiences of the other ranks, as I will explore in Chapters 3 and 4. Many of the accounts composed during or shortly after the wars, it should be noted, were written by converts to Methodism and other evangelical religious communities; they constitute a distinct subgenre of the war narrative, one coloured by a particular religious perspective.[58] Often written for personal, spiritual development rather than publication, these texts presented the soldier's war experiences as a series of salutary tests and trials.[59] Surrounded by the vice and wickedness of the barracks, the religious soldier described his efforts to maintain his piety and faith in such a profane setting. The experience of war was presented as an intensely personal spiritual battle as the soldier struggled with his faith in the face of death. As with other forms of war writing, the choice of narrative mode and the explicitly spiritual framework through which war experiences were imbued with meaning, connected the personal experience to a broader narrative of communal identity: in this case that of the small but relatively active evangelical grouping within the armed forces.

Prisoner of war narratives

Prisoner of war narratives occupy an intermediate position between military and civilian war writings. Accounts of imprisonment at the hands of the French enemy often featured in soldiers' and sailors' campaign narratives but, as Napoleon's edict of March 1803 reclassified the category of prisoner of war to include non-combatants, and the war at sea saw private merchant seamen interned in French prison depots, the experience of captivity would be shared by military and civilians alike. Their accounts blend together several of the different genres and literary conventions that can be found in campaign narratives, as well as drawing on the tradition of the captivity narrative.[60] Particularly associated with tales of early American settlers' abduction and imprisonment by Native Americans as well as the wider European experience of captivity in North Africa, the Middle East and Asia, the captivity narrative was a popular, well-established and protean genre that encompassed both fictional and factual accounts.[61] While the most famous examples dealt with the experience of captivity in extra-European contexts, the characteristic mixture of spiritual autobiography, ethnography and adventure tale can also be found in the writings of British captives in France.[62]

Accounts by prisoners of war, both published and unpublished, often veered between highly personalized stories of isolation, oppression and hardship, and narratives which drew parallels between individual and collective struggles, dramatizing the encounter between captive and captor as a conflict between a national self and the enemy 'other'. Living with the enemy, these captives were uniquely positioned to observe the French at close quarters, though, as with earlier captivity narratives, this prolonged contact always raised the danger that the prisoner might 'go native'. Several former detainees published their narratives during the wars with the aim of presenting to the public the brutalities of the French regime and the contrast between British liberty and Gallic tyranny. As the author of one such account proclaimed, its purpose was:

> ... to point out the treatment of those British subjects; who, by the fortune of war, are, or have been placed in the *power* of French *mercy*. Britons! Who are born in a land of liberty, endowed with all the privileges of a free people, under a mild and happy government, you will shudder at the facts now proved against those who have boasted, and continue to boast, that they have opened the eyes of Europe.[63]

Published narratives often stressed the stoic endurance of the captive, furnished examples of the author's active or passive resistance and concluded with a thrilling yarn involving ingenious disguises and hair's breadth escapes.[64] Unpublished diaries, memoirs and letters, by contrast, might employ a rhetoric of suffering and lamentation to convey the dehumanizing and isolating effects of incarceration and the strain it placed on both personal and collective identities. Their authors drew upon a rich literature of confinement and exile in order to give expression and meaning to their own experiences. The diary of John Robertson, master of a merchant vessel imprisoned at the citadel in Arras, adopted a scriptural language of lamentation and resignation from the Books of Jeremiah and Job to articulate his distress at his unfortunate fate, apparently forsaken by God and his fellow man. Shortly after his capture, he wrote:

> I now began to be very disconsolate in my unfortunate, but unavoidable situation walking about the yard for days and ready to sink in the earth; under a pressure of grief and sorrow, and no one to reveal my mind to, that could give me any relief ... .Surely thinks I; I cannot survive long, in this Dilemma and made me cry out in a flood of tears (while by myself) O Lord is not my grief more than I can bear, yes, I was ready to say, it is better for me to die than live.[65]

The archetypal eighteenth-century figure of exile and isolation, Robinson Crusoe, also found an oblique echo in prisoner of war narratives. Like Crusoe in

Defoe's novel, Robertson found solace in the Bible, which provided consoling passages apposite to his situation.[66] Other narratives contained more explicit references to the tale of the shipwrecked sailor. Describing his astonishment at encountering another English prisoner during his captivity, Lord Blayney remarked that 'Robinson Crusoe could not have been much more surprised at hearing his parrot cry *"poor Robin!"* than I was at being addressed in an English voice'.[67] Some prisoners turned to poetry to convey the sufferings they endured in captivity, and these may have been consciously or unconsciously modelled on Laurence Sterne's sentimental vignette 'The Captive'. Traces of Sterne's rendering of the prisoner 'his body half wasted away with long expectation and confinement' can be read in 'An Evening's Contemplation in a French prison', a portrait of the solitary prisoner's misery at sundown:

> Now sable Night o'er all her mantle Throw
> And solemn silence reigns throughout the year
> ... Save that from yonder room in mournful strain
> With melancholy tone and plaintive air
> Some tender father to the night complains
> Of children left without a parent care.[68]

The poem transcribed in Robertson's journal belonged to a larger corpus of poetry produced by British prisoners detained in French citadels. Printed and pasted up in common areas and often copied into prisoners' personal diaries, these poems helped to create a textual community within the prisons' walls. The prison poets articulated an experience of painful isolation that clearly resonated with their fellow captives, while also fostering a community of suffering amongst those wrenched from the sustaining collectivities of family, friends and nation, ship and regiment. The tension between a rhetoric of exile and abandonment and one of communal and national solidarity that often marked prisoners' writings reproduced and reflected their own understanding of the experience of captivity as at once a profoundly personal experience, and one that was collective and shared, a conflict that is explored in Chapter 5.

Writing the war at home

The experience of British civilians who remained at home, confined in the 'island prison', has been described aptly as one of 'living through, but not in a war'.[69] War was a pervasive presence in Britons' lives. It impinged upon and shaped various facets of their everyday existence, but spared from invasion, occupation and conflict on their own soil, British civilians' experience of war remained heavily mediated. Their personal writings were not framed by the war, or committed to recording its progress to the same extent as those directly engaged in the conflict. An exception to this is the correspondence between soldiers, sailors and their families.[70] Regrettably, letters from families to those fighting abroad rarely survived the rigours of a campaign, although we know how highly these communications were valued. Such was the clamour of troops for letters from home, which were only distributed after official army communications had been processed, that in 1810 the commanding officer of the British forces in Lisbon had to be instructed to protect the unfortunate postmaster from 'the violence or impatience' of officers.[71] Soldiers and sailors regularly urged their correspondents not to exclude any family or local gossip, however trivial, the minutiae of everyday life acquiring an added significance and nostalgic interest in the context of wartime separation. The few sets of correspondence between civilians and relatives in the military that survive give some insight into the efforts they made to bridge the separations created by war. Martha Freer, for example, writing to her sons fighting in the Peninsula, continued to perform her maternal role from afar, expressing her solicitude for their welfare by sending them shirts, towels, pillow cases and table cloths, accompanied by, perhaps less welcome, advice on their conduct. 'I do hope my dear boy that you will be prudent and careful', she cautioned, 'do avoid that part of the regiment which is gay and giddy ... Be sure that you make yourself perfectly acquainted with the history of England and do not forget your grammer [*sic*].'[72]

For those with less immediate connections to the conflict overseas, the wars remained a recurring topic of epistolary discussion. Rumours about the outcome of battles or the threat of invasion were continuously circulated through networks of correspondence, along with expressions of joy at significant victories or despondency at defeat. Letter writers reported on military mobilization in their own regions to correspondents across the four nations, proudly noting local demonstrations of loyalty or the comings and goings of various militia regiments. As a shared conversational theme, the wars knitted together a community of letter writers who anxiously followed the progress of a contest in which they were all, to some degree, implicated. For the many men who became involved with the national defence corps, military business occupied an increasingly substantial portion of their time and correspondence. The minutiae of militia organization and the broader events of the war were thus interwoven with the more parochial, quotidian matters that comprised the standard content of the eighteenth-century letter: family and local gossip, health and illness, legal and business affairs.

The pervasiveness of war in Britons' everyday life can be measured by the ways in which the languages of war filtered into these more personal discussions. Commenting on her recent ill health only months after the outbreak of war in 1793, Ann Murray Keith, sister of the Scottish diplomat Sir Robert Murray Keith, assured her correspondent that like a true British patriot, 'I fight a bold Battle, & ... have an admirable Constitution & no radical evil has ever shaken it'.[73] During her father's tenure as Governor-General of Bengal, Harriet Elliot, daughter of Lord Minto, went so far as to write letters in the form of a mock newspaper entitled 'The Comet'. In a column headed

'Invasion' Elliot reported in the style of the military gazette on the family's domestic affairs:

> the garrison is uncommonly healthy, and well supplied with everything – and unanimously attached to their Commander ... Nevertheless they look forward with considerable solicitude to the more perfect protection that may be expected from their Eastern allies at no very distant period.[74]

While news and novelties were the staple currency of eighteenth-century epistolary exchange, the conventions of diary writing – its dailiness, the lack of a clear addressee and absence of hindsight – made it a form less well suited to registering novel historical processes or the changes wrought by war. Even if it is minimally defined as a text written in the first-person, in separate instalments, usually on a daily basis, a diary can assume a range of different forms and styles.[75] Many share the features of what Lynn Bloom has described as the truly private diary, those 'bare-bones works' written primarily to keep records of 'income, expenditures, the weather, correspondence, family events, visits, leaving everything largely uninterpreted except for brief comments such as "had a nice evening"'. They are often 'so terse that they seem coded', unintelligible to anyone outside the author's immediate family or community.[76] Furthermore, space for reflection or elaboration on events may be constrained by the printed pocket book format in which these diaries were often written. Even when they did not use a specific printed diary or memorandum book, diarists often imitated their form, ruling the page to construct evenly spaced boxes into which their entries could be written.

The relationship between these cursory entries and the broader wartime context, however, can be reconstructed by attending to diaries' extra-textual or printed apparatus. Commercially produced volumes with names such as the *Ladies British Diary* or *Imperial Pocket Book, and Albion's Ladies Companion* clearly encouraged the diarist to locate their personal experiences within a broader national and imperial framework. Images of war could also be used to market such volumes. In December 1793, for instance, an advertisement for ladies' pocket books in the *Bath Herald* was embellished with a representation of British troops preparing to join the army on the Continent.[77] Employing the traditional form of an almanac, the space for journal writing was often embedded within a collection of illustrations, poems, stories, calendars and puzzles.[78] Much of this printed material was ephemeral or trivial in nature, but it was also responsive to the events of the war. The lists of fashionable country dances that appeared at the beginning of women's printed journals often referred directly to British military endeavours and included dances such as 'Old England's Heroes', 'The Tars of the Victory' and 'The Vittoria Waltz'. Copies of popular songs such as the 'Maid of Tagus' from the theatrical afterpiece 'Ciudad Rodrigo', which celebrated British successes in the Iberian peninsula, further established the patriotic tone of such volumes.[79]

The printed text in such diaries can be understood as prescribing particular gender-specific modes of wartime behaviour. The interweaving of fashion, sociability and militarism evident in the patriotic titles of country dances, for example, promoted British women's engagement with a 'pleasure culture of war'.[80] The pocketbook diaries of Fanny Knight, Jane Austen's niece, illustrate how national militarization became an element of social life, which she incorporated into the usual round of engagements and tea parties. From 1805, she noted her regular attendance at Volunteer reviews and panoramas depicting British victories, as well as a party on board a man-of-war. Her pocket diary for 1806 included two ballads, 'The Soldier's Daughter' and the 'Disbanded Soldier' focusing on the plight of distressed soldiers' and their families. Pleading for compassion towards those who fought 'that ye might be free', these pieces drew upon understandings of women's particular sympathy with the sufferings occasioned by war, and an expectation that their contribution to the war effort was best expressed through charity. It was an expectation that Fanny Knight fulfilled as she recorded in her diaries several donations to 'poor sailors'.[81]

Pocketbooks designed for men, by contrast, tended to include more practical information. These often asserted the owner's social position and provincial identity with titles such as *Kearsley's Gentleman and Tradesman's Pocket Ledger* or *The Yorkshire Memorandum Book*.[82] These titles reflected the regional character of many men's involvement in the war, which was expressed through membership of local militia or Volunteer regiments. The printed paraphernalia appended to these locally produced volumes traditionally listed useful details on county administration such as the names of deputy sheriffs or magistrates. During the war years these were joined by military lists naming the Officers of the Militia, Yeomanry and Volunteers of the county towns. The inclusion of chronicles of county history further situated the diary within the context of war and local militarism. A pocketbook printed in Canterbury in 1802, for instance, contained the 'Kentish Chronologist', a detailed list of events in the county's recent military history, which recorded the establishment of the Royal Cavalry Barracks in Canterbury in 1794, the Royal Review of the Volunteers and Yeomanry of Kent in 1799 and the encampment of 30,000 men on Barnham Downs for the expedition to Holland the same year.[83] The covers of diaries and notebooks sometimes carried illustrations of drill positions designed to help the novice officer learn his manual exercises.[84] Again, there is an evident relationship between the diary entries and the printed text, perfunctory details of militia drills and parades reproducing the expectations of masculine military service inscribed in the diaries' printed apparatus.

There was a revival in this period of the commonplace book, in which material from printed and manuscript works, as well as conversations and sermons were transcribed and glossed. Although lacking the self-reflection and personal detail associated with the private journal, commonplace books can provide important insights into the history of reading and reception. This is especially pertinent when considering the British experience of war, which was heavily filtered through textual and literary representations. In his study of the romantic-era reading public, William St Clair, notes the frequency with which verses from patriotic war poetry were excerpted into manuscript miscellanies.[85] In diaries from this period, the most commonly transcribed commentaries on the war were taken from sermons preached on Fast days and at Thanksgiving services and could range from brief notes of the biblical passages upon which the sermon was based to more extensive accounts of its arguments.[86]

One of the most influential forms of diaristic practice in this period remained the spiritual journal, which, from its emergence in the late sixteenth century had encouraged self-examination as a key element of religious practice and godly self-fashioning.[87] In her diary Mary Cobb (neé Blackburn), a member of a Baptist congregation in Margate, responded to the outbreak of war in 1793 with a series of spiritual meditations on the fate of Britain, in which she reflected upon the link between individual and national salvation. 'The times are very dark' she wrote:

> The Lord only knows what will be the issue of this heavy cloud that hangs over our guilty heads as a nation...It matters not who is against us if He be for us...May He in great Mercy appear for his British Israel & in all this confusion may each one seriously ask himself what have I done – How much have I done to accumulate the Sin of the Nation.[88]

Blackburn's diary continued in this heavily introspective vein, the war acting as a backdrop and prompt to her religious reflections and personal monitoring. The inwardly-oriented nature of the journal meant that the events of the war and her personal experience of military mobilization remained largely unrecorded, despite the fact that her husband, the prosperous brewer and banker Francis Cobb, whom she married in December 1794, was captain of the Margate Volunteers.[89] The military context however, manifested itself indirectly in the volumes in which she wrote. The cover of one of the many notebooks she used bore the image of an officer of the London Association of Volunteers in full uniform brandishing his musket, making the volume a striking combination of martial patriotism and spiritual introspection.[90]

A residual conception of the diary as an act of spiritual accounting may explain the frequency with which Britons employed religious or providentialist interpretations of war in their journals: it was a mode of interpretation which the diary form privileged and possibly encouraged. The early modern idea of the diary as a balance sheet recording duties fulfilled and neglected and the receipt of blessings and misfortunes, also continued to shape journals in the later period. To a certain extent, the recording of war within a diary could be easily assimilated to its original function as a financial, emotional and spiritual account book. In the same way diarists, drawing upon newspapers reports, often kept tally of the progress of the war by making detailed records of the numbers of dead, wounded and captive, enumerating cannons seized and lost, or, in naval engagements, the quantity and size of gunships captured. In his diary entry for August 1810, William Vavasour reported 'accounts of a dreadful battle between our troops & the French near Toledo the English in killed wounded reckon 5000 – the French are said to have lost 10000 and & have retreated leaving behind 20 pieces of cannon.'[91] This can be understood as a form of 'war accounting' which involved totting up or 'reckoning' French losses and British gains.

It is possible, however, to identify a move towards a more secular and historically self-conscious mode of diary writing in this period. This impulse towards self-historicization can be linked to the perceived acceleration of historical time around 1800 which, as Reinhart Koselleck has argued, dramatically widened the gap between the 'horizon of expectation' and the 'space of experience'.[92] According to this interpretation, the momentous events set in train by the French Revolution and the wars that followed saw a move from a conception of history as relatively static towards a new conception of temporality in which the present was understood as a state of transition to an uncertain future.[93] The move between historical epochs, formerly understood as a process of slow-moving change occurring over many generations, could now be experienced within a single individual's lifetime. Moreover, the collective experience of the Revolutionary and Napoleonic wars made it increasingly likely that contemporaries would come to understand themselves as subjects and agents of historical change. This new conception of historical process was reflected in an outpouring of personal narratives shaped by an understanding that 'the story of private people pertained to the general unsettlement of society'.[94]

British civilians, admittedly, did not experience the chaotic sequence of revolution, invasion, occupation and exile that made many continental Europeans so acutely aware of the rupture between remembered experience and an uncertain future. Yet a similar consciousness of the unparalleled nature of events in this era and their capacity to infiltrate the personal and the domestic can be traced. The journals of Anna Margaretta Larpent provide a compelling example. Larpent's seventeen volumes of diaries, written between 1773 and 1830, have already been extensively mined by scholars of Georgian society and culture. As the wife of John Larpent, examiner of plays in the office of the lord chamberlain from 1778 to 1824, whom she often accompanied to the theatre and assisted in his work, her journals provide an invaluable window onto the theatrical and cultural life of eighteenth-century London. A voracious and highly methodical reader who kept detailed notes and commentaries on her reading, her journals have also been used to reconstruct female reading and intellectual self-fashioning.[95] Larpent's journals can also be read as a war diary, one which is particularly

well-attuned to the ambivalence of the British experience of war, the unsettling awareness of a conflict that was both present and absent, hovering on
the edges of everyday life.

The intermingling of the everyday and the extraordinary, domestic affairs
and international events, was carefully recorded in Larpent's wartime journal:
the sewing of flannel waistcoats for British soldiers added to the routine
needlework and mending that she did for her family; an evening assembly
suddenly broken up by the arrival of orders instructing military officers to
embark for Dunkirk.[96] Larpent's daily reflections suggest that she was both
conscious of and troubled by the mediated experience of war, in which the
spectacle and heroics of battle were so often foregrounded whilst its human
costs were forgotten. As will be explored in greater detail in Chapter 7, her
responses to theatrical and artistic representations of warfare were suffused
with unease regarding the emerging 'pleasure culture of war' and the ethical
implications of consuming war at a distance.

Like many women at this time, Larpent questioned whether the restricted
compass of her life furnished sufficient material for a diary. Yet, in using her
journals to chronicle the experience of everyday war in Britain and to record
her personal responses to public events, she was also validating her own status
as a witness to history. Despite her devout Anglicanism, Larpent tended to
situate contemporary events within secular-historical narratives rather than
religious-providentialist frameworks. She was an avid reader of historical works
because they allowed her to 'trace changes in civilization to their cause & to
mark the operation of external circumstances on morals, manners, government & society'.[97] Larpent articulated an Enlightenment understanding of
history in which the quotidian world of 'morals and manners' was equally
weighted with and inseparable from the political and military spheres. As
well as appreciating the domestic impact of historical events on past societies, Larpent's reading of contemporary history encouraged her perception
of the wars as a distinctive rupture, characterized by unprecedented change.
Reviewing the German essayist Friedrich Gentz's *On the State of Europe before
and after the French Revolution*, a work which encapsulated this conception of
the present as a radical disjuncture from the past, Larpent was struck by 'the
magnitude of what has passed in ye last 150 years, the rise of Russia, Prussia
and America seemed great events till all was darkened by the vast explo-
sion of the French Revolutions'.[98] The sharpened sense of the incongruous
co-existence of peaceful pursuits and military mobilization that distinguishes
Larpent's diaries can, in part, be traced to this consciousness of how momentous historical currents also flowed through the everyday.

Conclusion

The use of diaries and letters as a source for war experience promises neither
pure empirical accuracy nor access to unmediated subjective authenticity.

War narratives, like all forms of autobiographical writing, must be understood less as a malleable receptacle for the author's experiences and more as a mould that shapes what is recorded and how it is understood and expressed. Yet recognizing the generic conventions and literary templates that shape such writings does not put 'lived experience' beyond the reach of historical inquiry. Rather it allows us to explore how experiences are lived, constructed and interpreted through language. Indeed, it is by excavating some of these frameworks that we can tentatively connect together the personal and the collective and suggest how individuals' narratives of war reflected wider class, gender, religious and occupational identities. The comic, episodic structure of the ordinary soldier's story of war, for instance, and the more psychologically introspective accounts produced by some officers could reflect different understandings of their place within the military hierarchy and of the meaning and impact of war upon the self.

Although personal narratives were often shaped by inherited conventions such as the spiritual journal or the captivity narrative, the form and language of such documents were by no means static or stable. A gradual shift from the depiction of war as grotesque, to an understanding of war as horrific but also sublime, was registered in combatants' accounts. Accounts by prisoners of war alternated between those which adopted a biblical language of lamentation and told stories of solitary suffering, and those which struck a more patriotic tone and situated their personal struggle within the broader context of a conflict between nations. The exceptional and unexpected sequence of events that followed the French Revolution prompted and was interpreted through an evolving conception of the diary as both a personal and historical chronicle and a deepening sense of the interpenetration of the quotidian and the historical.

2
Becoming Soldiers and Sailors

In November 1808, seventeen-year-old William Thornton Keep left his family in London to begin a career in the army. His departure had been marked by 'tears' and 'tender embraces' as he set off 'to encounter the world and scenes so entirely new to me'. Keep had never travelled further than Windsor and during the coach journey to Winchester, where he was to join his regiment, he sat in silent reflection, anxiously clutching a bag of treats prepared by his mother. His route into the garrison-town took him through the medieval entrance gate and he imagined the warriors that had passed under the same arch in the age of chivalry, an age which, he observed, 'could not have excelled...what is going on here in our present war with Bonaparte'. Once inside the gates he was immediately struck by the military figures that filled the streets, the Band 'in their fanciful apparel' and the officers and soldiers saluting each other as they passed.[1]

This was a strange and unfamiliar scene of martial activity, nonetheless, having donned his regimental dress, Keep began to feel more at home with his new soldierly character as 'their uniforms corresponding with my own made me feel as if I already belonged to them'. Entering the barracks that were to be his new home, he was awed by the 'soldierlike aspect of every-thing around me...the display of the implements of war and the discipline prevailing among those to be engaged in it'. The forbidding appearance of his new residence was somewhat softened by the warm welcome of its inhabitants. Joining the regimental mess, he was pleased with the character of his fellow subalterns, a diverse but 'gentlemanlike group' drawn from across Britain and its empire. They included the son of the Lieut. Governor of the Isle of Man, a Quaker, a poor but kind-hearted Scottish Ensign and a 'well-connected and rich' Lieutenant who, Keep suspected, 'derives his parentage...on the maternal side from a Hindoo'. In the transition from son to soldier, Keep had exchanged the familial home for a new fraternal community of 'brother officers'.[2] Keep's experiences: the separation from home and family; the introduction to an unfamiliar military world; and assimilation into a new martial family drawn from across the British Isles, would be replicated by hundreds of thousands of men during the Revolutionary and Napoleonic wars. While this experience was not in itself new, it would become an increasingly common rite of passage for British and Irish men during this period. By the end of the wars, the initiation of these 'Johnny Newcomes' into the world of the army and navy would be satirized in a set of comic poems with accompanying sketches by Thomas Rowlandson, which charted the travails and indignities endured by the military novice.[3]

This chapter examines how these new recruits narrated the experience of becoming a soldier or sailor, and the identities and modes of belonging that were formed in the process. William Keep may have lent an elevated tone to his martial aspirations by invoking the chivalric warriors of a bygone era, but the majority of entrants into the armed forces explained their decision to enlist in more pragmatic terms. One of the achievements of the British military in this period is that it was able to expand significantly without recourse to compulsory conscription (although the suspected Irish rebel offered the choice of the red coat or death, or the fisherman plucked from his coastal community to man the nation's warships may have viewed matters differently). Rather than being motivated by a patriotic desire to serve the nation, military service was more commonly viewed as an avenue to manhood, a decisive break with parental authority and dependence. These aspirations were often confounded by the reality of life in the armed forces and the painful adjustment to military mores would be a dominant theme in soldiers' and sailors' narratives. Both the army and, perhaps to an even greater extent, the navy, had at their disposal a complex assemblage of rituals, symbols and rules designed to mould and reconfigure their members' identities – from the intensely physical drilling and disciplining of the other ranks to the more subtle, coercive pressures of the regimental peer group. Yet the transition from the civilian to the military world often remained incomplete as civilian mentalities and values were carried over into the army and navy. Nor did the military make much effort to impose a unitary pan-Britannic identity upon its multinational, multi-confessional recruits; rather it offered a reasonably tolerant environment in which a variety of identities could be expressed.

The British army and navy, 1793–1815

The unprecedented demands and sheer scale of the Revolutionary and Napoleonic wars inaugurated a dramatic reorganization of national military forces throughout Europe. In France, the decree of the *levée en masse* of August 1793, declaring all unmarried men of military age, regardless of birth or wealth, liable for service, vividly exemplified the conflation of the citizen and soldier that lay at the heart of republican ideology. The introduction of systematic annual conscription from 1799 ensured a regular flow of new recruits for the Napoleonic army. The revolutionaries' abolition of hereditary privilege introduced a degree of egalitarianism into the armed forces and the concept of the military as a career 'open to talents', in which a humble soldier's resourcefulness and bravery could propel him through the ranks continued under the more authoritarian Napoleonic regime.[4] Prussia's catastrophic defeat at the hands of Napoleon's forces similarly prompted a far-reaching reform of the army and the eventual introduction of mass universal conscription in 1813.[5] Military compulsion, in the form of conscription, was accompanied by inducements in the form of a potent military-patriotic rhetoric as 'the hero's death on the altar of the fatherland', previously reserved for officers of noble birth, 'was now open for the first time to ordinary men and deemed the highest form of patriotic sacrifice'.[6]

While many of the major powers of continental Europe came to see compulsory conscription as the only way to meet the insatiable manpower demands of the new era of mass warfare, it was a system of recruitment that remained unpalatable to the British. The proliferation of Volunteer units for home defence echoed in some ways the patriotic enthusiasm and democratic ethos imputed to the French revolutionary army, but traditional hostility to a standing army meant that compulsory conscription for the regular army was never officially introduced. Nevertheless, the size of the armed forces increased massively through voluntary enlistment: on the eve of the war the army's troop strength was at 50,000, by 1811 it had reached 219,000.[7] Similarly, there were 17,361 men registered on naval ships in 1792, but by 1810 this figure had risen to 146,312.[8] This augmentation of the armed forces was largely dependent on manpower drawn from Britain and Ireland. Whereas Britain had relied heavily on foreign mercenaries in previous conflicts, less than 20 per cent of the expanded army were of foreign extraction.[9] The need for manpower remained a pressing concern throughout the wars. While enlistment into the regular army continued to be on a voluntary basis, recruitment into the auxiliary territorial forces of the militia operated by a ballot system. As they offered a source of men already inculcated in the rudiments of military training, militia units were intensively targeted by recruiting parties for line regiments and between 1807 and 1812 an estimated 74,000 men migrated from the militia into the army.[10] In the early years of the war, the navy managed to expand its numbers through volunteering, with 62,800 men joining between 1793 and 1795. The much-despised system of naval impressment, however, remained in force throughout the period.[11] Though it is notoriously difficult to estimate, an Admiralty survey of 32 British ports between 1803 and 1805 indicated that as many as 48 per cent of the 11,600 men recruited into the navy during that period had been impressed.[12]

Admittance into the British officer ranks did not, as in some other eighteenth-century European armies, require proof of noble birth; the purchase system acted as a relatively effective social filter nonetheless.[13] Under this system, men entered the army by buying a commission as an ensign (second lieutenant) or cornet (the cavalry equivalent) and ascended the ranks by purchasing vacancies that appeared above them as officers retired, sold out, or transferred into another regiment.[14] The Duke of York's army reforms rectified some of the worst abuses of the purchase system. From 1795 it was stipulated that ascent through the ranks would be based on experience as well as purchase, which meant that schoolboys with money could no longer be installed as field officers. The sale of commissions, however, would not be abolished until the Cardwell reforms of 1871. Defenders of the purchase system saw it as a safeguard of constitutional liberty; it limited monarchical power by preventing the sovereign from removing officers at whim, for to do so would be tantamount to robbery.[15] According to the Victorian military historian Charles Clode, the Duke of Wellington preferred the purchase system because it helped bring into the army 'men of fortune and character – men who have some connection with the interests and fortunes of the country'.[16]

Though the army may have attracted men with wealthy connections, part of its appeal rested on the paid employment that it offered to the younger sons of the gentry, who could not expect to inherit land or titles.[17] However, members of the lesser gentry, who formed the largest group within the British officer class, often lacked sufficient money or interest to advance through the ranks. Their opportunities greatly increased on the outbreak of war. Rapid augmentation of the army led to an expansion of the officer corps, while the loss of officers in battle enabled advancement through the ranks without purchase. By 1810, in the bigger wartime army, as many as four-fifths of all commissions were held by non-purchase methods.[18] The large number of Scots and Irish who obtained commissions during the wars provides some evidence of the social dilution of the officer corps. Members of elite corps often looked with disdain upon the provincial officers of limited means who filled the ranks of less exalted regiments. Lt John Mills of the aristocratic Coldstream Guards wrote sarcastically of the Ulster smallholders, or 'Irish Gentlemen with great landed property in the north' who officered the 58th regiment.[19] The proliferation of regiments following the outbreak of war necessarily changed the social composition of the officer corps. The army increasingly recruited from the middling classes whilst a small proportion of ordinary soldiers managed to rise through the ranks. At the same time, the rising reputation of the army made it an increasingly attractive career for members of the British aristocracy, who entered into prestigious and socially exclusive regiments such as the Life Guards in increasing numbers after 1800.[20]

The technical skill required to command a ship meant that the eighteenth-century navy was perceived as a career more open to talents than the army. At Trafalgar, at least one of the commissioned officers had originally been pressed into service and Rear-Admiral Troubridge was the son of a pastry cook.[21] More typically, Admiral Nelson was the son of a clergyman and clerical families provided around 9 per cent of the officer entry between 1793 and 1815. An estimated 50 per cent of naval officers in the period came from professional families (medicine, law, the civil service), and nearly half of this group had fathers who had also been in the navy.[22] Although naval commissions were not subject to purchase and young officers had to pass a lieutenant's examination and provide proof of sea service, wealthy connections and access to patronage remained important if a sea officer wanted to rise in his profession. As with the army, opportunities for promotion increased during wartime, but there was also a trend towards greater social exclusivity as the navy attracted the English nobility's foremost families, thereby blocking advancement opportunities for other deserving candidates.[23]

The demands of mass warfare and the constant search for new recruits prompted efforts to enhance the conditions under which men served. In 1806 the army's requirement that men serve for life was abolished.[24] As Commander-in-Chief from 1795, the Duke of York introduced improvements in rations, health care and barrack accommodation, as well as some reform of the army's severe penal codes, earning him the soubriquet 'The Soldier's Friend'.[25] More innovative schemes were also developed to provide a rudimentary welfare system for soldiers' and sailors' families, including regimental schools for their children, disability and pension allowances.[26] Successive pay increases for soldiers were introduced in 1792, 1795 and 1797; though soldiers' pay remained significantly lower than the average plebeian wage.[27] These concessions were closely linked to fears that radical unrest would infiltrate the armed forces, the potentially devastating effects of which were demonstrated during the naval mutinies of 1797. Once quelled, the mutinies were followed by an increase in seamen's pay and a partial amelioration of the navy's notoriously harsh discipline.[28] For sailors in the Royal Navy, the lure of prize money, which could double or triple a seaman's pay, offered some compensation for the harshness of the conditions in which they served.[29]

During the wars, public perceptions of the armed forces and its members veered between hostility, pity and admiration as they had done for much of the eighteenth century. Popular patriotism may have trumpeted the valorous exploits of the ordinary soldier abroad and contrasted the unthinking impoverished automatons of the French army with their free, virile British opponents, but the soldier's life continued to be viewed as an 'exile from the ordinary world, bereft of the ties of social existence and deprived of the felicities and securities that these conferred'.[30] Far from being an exemplar of British liberty, the soldier was more commonly viewed as a slave, who had sold himself into bondage to suffer appalling conditions and a tyrannical disciplinary regime.[31] From the late eighteenth century, the 'poor soldier' or the 'broken soldier' was a familiar figure in sentimental novels, poetry and song.[32] While a more romanticized image of the British navy's 'Jolly Jack Tar' circulated in the cultural imaginary, the plight of the sailor torn from his family to spend years at sea at risk of shipwreck, disease and flogging also featured prominently in popular ballads.

The reputation of naval and army officers was marked by a similar ambivalence. Throughout the eighteenth century British society celebrated the heroism and patriotic sacrifice of its military men. As a maritime power, the nation's investment in the armed forces tended to focus on the navy which provided exemplars of masculine patriotism in the form of admiral heroes such as Howe and Nelson. The Royal Navy was perceived as a crucial agent of British commercial power and a bulwark of the nation's constitutional liberties.[33] The army's martial reputation, in contrast, had suffered in the wake of the American war and was further dented by their uninspiring performance during the continental campaigns of the 1790s, until the Egyptian expedition and subsequently the Peninsular campaign burnished the army's prestige and provided the nation with a set of soldier heroes to match their naval counterparts. This, according to Linda Colley, bolstered the military's image as a crucible of patriotic masculinity contributing to a 'cult of elite heroism'.[34] As Mary Crawford observes in Jane Austen's *Mansfield Park* (1814): 'The profession, either army or navy … has every thing in its favour; heroism, danger, bustle, fashion. Soldiers and sailors are always acceptable in society. Nobody can wonder that men are soldiers and sailors'.[35] Voiced by the frivolous and superficial Crawford, these remarks suggest some of the ambivalence towards the military that would emerge in Austen's depictions of vain, sexually dangerous militia officers. Moreover, while the bearing of arms has been viewed as the 'most authoritative fantasy of masculinity', during the Revolutionary and Napoleonic wars it was often the civilian national defence bodies that were understood to embody most fully Britain's independent and masculine character, and the manliness of the regular army was sometimes called into question.[36] Mary Wollstonecraft notably compared professional soldiers with women insofar as both were 'fond of dancing, crowded rooms, adventures, and ridicule' and she denounced the enervating effects of military subordination on the 'needy *gentleman*' who, anxious to advance, 'becomes a servile parasite or vile pander'.[37] Why, given these conflicting and often negative views of the profession of arms, did men join the armed forces during these years?

Serving the nation? The decision to enlist

For each recruit, the determination to join the navy or army depended upon a mixture of personal, social and economic factors, although individual narratives suggest that patriotism seldom played a deciding role. While there has been little systematic research into why individuals decided to 'go for a soldier' during this period, existing work has emphasised the powerful appeal which the colour and pageantry of military recruiting parties exerted upon prospective recruits to the rank and file.[38] Recruiting parties put a great deal of effort into creating military spectacles that would convince young men to enlist. Regimental posters in the style of theatrical playbills were pasted up in towns and villages advertising for men 'whose hearts beat high to tread the paths of glory' and underlining the many attractions of the regiment, not least its splendid accoutrements. This would be followed by a lavish and colourful parade of the regiment's finest recruits decked out in their best uniforms and accompanied by the regimental band.[39] Several soldiers' memoirs cite the allure of these martial displays in prompting them to enlist. As one observed:

> The roll of the spirit-stirring drum, the glittering file of bayonets, with the pomp and circumstance of military parade...passed in review before my imagination, in colours vividly charming: resistance was vain.[40]

Such references to the glamour of the military, however, were often followed by narratives, themselves conventional, which emphasized the gulf between this surface display and the realities of life in the army. These episodes served an important narrative function, setting up accounts of increasing disillusionment and salutary tales of feckless youth seduced into the military. The memoirs of evangelical soldiers, in particular, often presented the decision to enlist as a moment of moral weakness, as they succumbed to the 'worldly' temptations of the military. The autobiography of Joseph Mayett recounted how in 1803 'haveing [*sic*] the Spirit of Cain my own carnal nature soon Concurred with the temptation [*sic*] and Satan obtained his ends...I inlisted for a soldier'.[41] The experience of soldiering may have been 'the most common collective working-class experience' in the late eighteenth and early nineteenth centuries,[42] but the autobiographies of ordinary soldiers tended to depict it as a deviation from an expected life course, a particularly extreme example of the 'experience of life as counter-normative' that has been identified as a leitmotif of nineteenth-century working-class autobiographies.[43]

If the army and navy held few attractions for the British plebeian classes, there were powerful 'push factors' that motivated their enlistment. Even if the army became an increasingly popular vehicle for patriotic feeling during this period, this was not clearly reflected in recruiting figures. Although the yield of recruits was high in 1800–1801 and 1812–1813 when the army's reputation was enhanced by emphatic victories in the field, these were also years of famine and acute social distress.[44] For labourers facing penury and an inadequate system of poor relief the bounty of between £12 and £25 would, no doubt, have proved a compelling inducement to join up. Soldiers' memoirs suggest, however, that a significant social stigma continued to attach to those who enlisted. William Surtees, who joined the militia in 1798 and later volunteered into a line regiment, recalled that 'the life of a soldier was by no means considered in my village, at that time, at all creditable'. His decision to join the army and the disgrace which he had thus brought on himself was the cause of much grief to his parents.[45] A rupture with his parents or the broader community was not only the consequence of soldier's enlistment, but was often cited as the original cause of enlistment. One Edinburgh soldier narrated how he had squandered the superior education bestowed upon him by his 'poor but respectable' parents to pursue, against their wishes, a theatrical career. Estranged from his family and having failed as an actor he rashly joined a party of recruits to begin a bitter new life in the army.[46]

This narrative pattern, in which a familial estrangement precipitated entry into the armed forces, can also be found in sailors' memoirs. Following a quarrel with his father, Thomas Walsh determined that 'it was impossible for me to live a happy life at home' and resolved to join the navy 'as I wished to live in obscurity from all my friends or any that I ever knew'.[47] It is certainly likely that some recruits joined the army or navy in order to escape parental authority. There was no law preventing minors from enlisting against the wishes of their parents; a poster for the 14th Light Dragoons even appealed to potential recruits who suffered 'obstinate and unfeeling parents'.[48] At the same time, the recurring appearance of such episodes in soldiers' and sailors' narratives suggest that it also spoke to a deeper truth about the experience of life in the armed forces, one that involved an exile from home and a potentially painful rite of passage, as the parental family was exchanged for a new, perhaps more oppressive, military family.

For those entering as officers, the profession of arms offered a more respectable and less binding choice of career than was the case for the ordinary soldier or sailor. The decision to go to sea, or to join the army, however, could still arouse parental opposition. Robert Jones, a Montgomeryshire doctor, deliberated at length whether to allow his son to join the navy. Although he finally relented, he maintained his belief that life in the sea service was 'both irrational and unnatural' and feared that it would make his son 'a stranger to his family'.[49] As those who wished to make a career in the navy often enrolled at a young age, thirteen or younger, youthful impetuosity was often mentioned as driving the desire to go to sea. The commander of the *Minotaur* reported that one of his juvenile midshipmen had entered the navy against his parents' inclination, but 'his desire was so great that if they had not consented he would have gone before the mast, that is as a common sailor'.[50] Youthful enthusiasm for the military also figured in army officers' narratives of how they came to enter the profession. Harry Ross-Lewin, who joined the army in 1795, recalled his early 'predilection for the profession of arms':

...which began to manifest itself some time before the memorable event of the donning of my first jacket and trouser. Whenever I happened to be reported absent without leave... the domestics sent in search of me invariably directed their steps to the barracks, well knowing that they might be sure to find me there, watching with unwearied attention the progress of the drill, and endeavouring to imitate with my mimic gun the various motions of the manual and platoon exercise.[51]

The American war would have been ongoing through Ross-Lewin's early childhood and his boyhood play-fantasies suggest how this earlier conflict, despite its ignominious conclusion, may have fuelled imaginative identifications with the soldier as an idealized masculine figure.[52] His description of the day on which he left to join his regiment figured this moment as a significant threshold between boyhood and manhood. As he 'marched along exultingly' filled with military pride, he was overtaken by the family maid who had been dispatched by his mother in order to present him with a pair of forgotten stockings, an embarrassing reminder of the childish existence that he had only just left behind.[53]

Such accounts of youthful military enthusiasm seem to prefigure the narrative imagining of military heroism that Graham Dawson has identified as a powerful influence on masculine subjectivities from the late nineteenth century onwards. The majority of officers, however, described the appeal of the 'profession of arms' in terms of a less romantic, but equally influential, model of idealized masculinity: independence. The idealized figure of the independent man, as Matthew McCormack has shown, was held out as the epitome of manliness, citizenship and national character in Georgian Britain.[54] Defined in contrast to feminine 'dependency', masculine independence connoted self-mastery and financial autonomy. The purchase of an army commission, in itself a form of personal property, supposedly provided the conditions for the exercise of autonomy. In the navy a lieutenant's commission was considered 'an independency' entitling the holder to 'the rank of gentleman in every society'.[55] As one officer observed to his mother, who was anxious for him to leave the service, 'My profession alone renders me independent'.[56] For younger sons then, a career in the armed forces, in so far as it involved leaving the patriarchal home and becoming self-sufficient, provided a way of attaining this manly independence. The reality of life in service, however, meant that this much-cherished status frequently proved difficult to achieve.

Civilians into soldiers?

One consequence of the Revolutionary and Napoleonic wars that has been stressed in recent literature is the emergence of a pronounced cleavage between the military and civilian spheres.[57] According to this account, the armed forces evolved a distinctive sense of professional identity and an understanding of themselves as a separate caste. They increasingly came to resemble Erving Goffman's model of a 'total institution': a self-contained society that operates according to strict rules of subordination and in which all activity is collective and closely regimented. Such institutions have the capacity to become 'unique tools of socialisation' remoulding their members in accordance with their governing culture and values.[58] Perhaps the most striking symbol of the growing segregation of military from civilian life during this period was the intensive construction of army barracks throughout the British Isles. Whereas soldiers had previously been billeted upon civilian communities or accommodated in large summer encampments when not on active service, from the 1790s they were increasingly stationed in fortified barracks. In 1794 there was in Britain sufficient barrack accommodation for 18,000 men; by 1806 barrack capacity had risen dramatically to 125,000.[59] Throughout the wars there was continued opposition to the programme of barrack-building. Quartering the army in purpose-built structures, opponents argued, would further detach the military from the values and culture of civilian society, allowing it to be more easily used as an instrument of state repression. Supporters of the scheme, fearful of radical subversion within the army ranks, countered that it was precisely because soldiers would be thus insulated from political contagion that the programme of barrack-building was desirable.

For the majority of army recruits then, the passage from family and civilian life was marked by their entrance into the enclosed world of the military barrack. New officers often commented on this unfavourable introduction to army life. Having joined the 87th regiment at Colchester barracks, Ensign Wright Knox deplored the conditions in which he was now forced to live. 'I am afraid' he informed his brother,

> it will require a length of time and pleasant quarters to reconcile me to a Military life, at present I am in no great aspirations about it: coming from a healthy situation, a numerous and pleasant acquaintance, a house where you were your own Master: to a nasty bog, a set of strangers, and a Miserable wooden hut.[60]

In subsequent letters he expanded upon the 'miseries' of barrack life, 'we are 12 miles from any town no amusement whatever; I have not seen 5 men in coloured clothes since I came here'.[61] As Knox's reference to the absence of men in 'coloured clothes' or civilians suggests, not only were soldiers physically separated from civilian life, their uniforms also provided a powerful marker of this separation.

Of course, the opportunity to don the 'gold and scarlet' military uniform was often cited as one of the army's chief attractions. Regimentals flattered and enhanced the male physique and instantly signalled the manliness and 'respectability' of the wearer. Yet, as with other aspects of army life the uniform could act as a site of conflict bringing individual autonomy and military conformity into tension. Indeed, the ostentatious military uniform was not dissimilar to the traditional livery worn by servants of the nobility. 'The uniform's connotation of servility', as Scott Hughes Myerly notes, could therefore express visually 'the ideal of soldiers' total subservience to the will of those in command'.[62] The authority to dictate the design and pattern of military uniforms was one of the legal prerogatives of the British monarchy,

but colonels often asserted regimental independence by introducing devia-
tions in the standard design. For an officer of straitened means these frequent
alterations in dress could be both a financial burden and a trivial imposition.
As one disillusioned officer pointed out, a subaltern's pay was not sufficient
to cover 'the costly vain frippery ornamental dresses which our Lt Col. was
always loading us with'.[63]

Not all officers responded so negatively to the isolation and enforced
communality of the barracks. When he joined his regiment at their barracks
in Berry Head, Devon, William Keep was initially horrified at its desolate
location upon a remote cliff top surrounded by sea. Yet he soon reconciled
himself to this new situation and underlined the positive aspects of such a
sequestered society, in which the bonding between officers was necessarily
accelerated:

> Imagine so select a family inhabiting such a populous village, thus
> removed by a vast expanse of high ground from the main land...This
> is enough of itself to excite the beholder, but when turning attention
> to the inhabitants, all military heroes employed in such a war as this,
> and seeking a temporary repose here the mind is filled with curiosity and
> pleasure, for our pursuits are all the same, Guard mountings and Reviews
> with drums and trumpets, and banquets at the Mess tables where joyous
> festivity prevails.[64]

This peer-group bonding was a crucial element of military socialization,
fostering regimental cohesion and *esprit de corps* and sustaining the individual soldier in a new and strange environment. For Keep this was one of the
most attractive aspects of military life where 'the intimacies formed...keep
one in heart and cement an attachment to it'.[65] The Georgian army was not
an entirely homosocial space as ordinary soldiers' families often lived with
them, but for young commissioned officers the world of the barracks was a
world largely devoid of women of their own class. This did not necessarily
mean that an atmosphere of Spartan austerity prevailed within the barracks.
The home and the domestic realm were not simply the preserve of women,
but also served as an important source of authority for men.[66] In the transition from, as Lieutenant Wright Knox put it, 'a House in which you are your
own master' to the communal living of the barracks, officers sacrificed the
masculine status associated with being a householder. The bachelor existence of the soldier denied them the manly independence that came from
presiding over a household of dependents.[67] As a result, officers often tried
to reproduce domestic comforts and modes of sociability in the barracks.
Keep described his comrades' efforts to render their sparse accommodation
'snug' and to ensure that there was always 'a kettle simmering on the hob
prepared to welcome tea parties'.[68] As one of the regiment's mess committee
at Colchester Barracks, Thomas Browne was responsible for decorating the

communal living room and took evident pride in 'how comfortable it looked with its green walls and red curtains'.[69]

The regimental peer group could also, however, be perceived as a coercive and aggressive instrument of military indoctrination. Samuel Lumsden, a relatively new recruit, noted with a degree of unease the strict enforcement of codes of masculine honour and courage within his regiment which had a reputation as 'hard fighters' and a history of 'cutting' or shunning officers who did not do their duty:

> there is at present a Brevet, Lt. Col. & Captain of the 1st Battn. with us here and tho' he is fifty years of age & has a wife & two daughters yet do the officers treat him with the utmost contempt for his avoiding active Service, he has been extremely particular to me but I could not meet with an intimacy as it would be against the general sense of the Officers.[70]

A willingness to serve abroad, to share the rigours of campaign and to face the dangers of combat, was expected of an officer upon entering the profession of arms. Officers who shirked these duties were often dismissed as effeminate, lured by the glamour and spectacle of the military but unwilling to endure its hardships. 'I am sorry the army is disgraced by such beings' observed one lieutenant 'who study nothing but dress, foppery & debauchery'.[71]

Whereas officers generally shared private rooms within the barrack, the other ranks slept in crowded dormitories often sharing beds with another man. 'Many of the barrack rooms are uncomfortable', observed a private from Glasgow, 'on account of their size, containing sixty or more men. This greatly destroys social comfort: for one or two individuals can molest all the rest; so that select retired conversation cannot be enjoyed.'[72] Those ordinary soldiers who left accounts of their introductory experiences in the army generally stressed their revulsion at this enforced communality and their alienation from the other men's rough and profane habits. Their perceived aloofness often led to taunts from their fellow soldiers: if they refrained from swearing or drinking they were branded a Quaker or a Methodist; any display of learning drew forth calls of 'Dinna be gi'en us any of your grammar words' and if they tried to defend themselves verbally they were called a 'lawyer'.[73] However, many of these narratives were written by men who were, or would become, religiously devout, and by those whose literacy and education already placed them at a remove from the majority of the rank and file. One described how he was only able to gain the respect of his fellows once he had demonstrated physical courage by challenging a soldier to a fist fight.[74] In the crowded and brutal environment of the barracks, according to Joseph Donaldson, 'many men of ability and information...were forced from the intellectual height they had attained, down to the level of those with whom they were obliged to associate' sinking them to a point where 'they became best fitted for *tractable beasts of burden*'.[75]

Donaldson's view of the soldiers as 'tractable beasts', or 'docile bodies' that could be shaped in accordance with the demands of the military machine, reflects the intensely physical nature of the ordinary soldier's training.[76] At this time, the terms 'discipline' and military training were synonymous, discipline being defined as the 'instruction and government of soldiers'.[77] The regulation of the soldier's body was central to the practice of military discipline. As part of their uniform, ordinary soldiers often wore a leather neckstock, a painful collar which kept their head rigid and erect. Soldiers were drilled daily until the complex movements and manoeuvres became habitual. One private described this punishing regime: 'Forced from bed at five o'clock each morning, to get all things ready for drill; then drilled for three hours with the most unfeeling rigour'.[78] The dominant model of infantry tactics demanded a 'culture of forebearance' whereby soldiers refrained from firing until within very close range of the enemy. Only through repetition and habituation could such a counter-intuitive response be instilled. Eighteenth-century linear warfare, with its well-practised manoeuvres and densely packed lines was, in part, predicated on European officer corps' inherent distrust of the ordinary soldier: boxed in by sergeants and officers, the private could not turn tail and run.[79] As one soldier reflected, this training was designed to subsume the individual into the military body so that he became 'an atom of the army'.[80]

This approach to infantry tactics, based on the Prussian school of Frederick the Great, would be distilled into General Sir David Dundas' 'eighteen manoeuvres' which became the standard drill manual of all infantry battalions in 1792. Although Dundas's method of drill is often dismissed as promoting an overly conservative form of infantry tactics in an era when continental armies were moving towards more flexible and quick-moving formations, his manual has been credited with standardizing practices in the army, which had previously suffered from 'an incoherent diversity of manoeuvre'.[81] The development of light infantry tactics from the late eighteenth century, however, introduced a countervailing emphasis on skirmishing that required the ordinary soldier to be more than a cog in the military machine. General Sir John Moore was a prominent critic of Dundas' rigid 'eighteen manoeuvres' and as commander of Shorncliffe camp in Kent, the permanent base of the light infantry from 1803, he endeavoured to introduce more flexible and adaptive tactics that emphasized the individual soldier's skill and initiative. In the training of light infantry troops, psychological factors were as important as physical conditioning. As a manual for officers advised, instead of being held together by discipline and surveillance, the light infantry soldiers were sustained by fellowship and should 'if possible be allowed to choose their own comrades'. As they were liable to lose sight of their commanding officer during an engagement, much depended on the light infantry soldiers' 'unanimity' and 'their own judgment'.[82]

Yet while military theorists were beginning to stress the importance of morale, motivation and personal initiative to the combat effectiveness of the rank and file, a stringent system of military discipline and physical punishment continued to operate within the army. Flogging and the often capricious regime of martial justice that soldiers served under provided the most vivid example of the gulf between civil and military society.[83] These punishments were often highly theatrical and designed to inspire awe and terror in the troops: the offender was stripped and tied to the rack and his unit was gathered to witness the flogging, which was punctuated by ten drum beats between each lash. Many accounts from the other ranks record the shock and revulsion they felt upon first seeing a flogging. 'Terror' according to Joseph Donaldson 'seems to be the only engine of rule in the army'.[84] Accounts such as Donaldson's, written after they had left the army with a view to demonstrating the necessity of military reform, however, do not fully capture the moral economy which governed relations between officers and men. Ordinary soldiers, as Cookson observes, 'had a conception of their "rights" even if it often seemed to be nothing more than an elementary sense of justice and resistance to servility'.[85] The letters of William Wheeler illustrate both the rank and file's hostility to tyrannical commanders and their general acceptance of corporal punishment when it was administered fairly: while in the Surrey militia he rejoiced at the departure of the particularly cruel Major Hudson, nicknamed 'Bloody Bob', who 'delighted in torturing the men', but accepted the 'justness' of whipping a man for desertion.[86]

Although the Royal Military Academy had been founded at Woolwich in 1741 to train officers for the artillery and engineers, with a Royal Military College established in 1799 to educate officers in other branches, most commissioned officers' military education began when they joined their regiment.[87] An informal tutoring in the arts of war could be gleaned from the growing corpus of advice books and manuals aimed at young subalterns, such as the *Military Mentor* (1804) and David Dundas's *Principles of Military Movements* (1788).[88] As Ensign Samuel Lumsden confessed, 'I am well aware I am not "an Heaven born Soldier", and of course am a stranger by Nature to Dundas's nineteen [*sic*] movements, this I trust to remedy as far as I possibly can by an assiduous application'. Despite this determination to apply himself to the study of tactics, Lumsden's letters show him indulging in a round of pleasurable pursuits: 'reading, excursions in the Country and the usual routing of an officer's life'.[89]

David Bell has pointed to the increasing professionalization of the European officer corps during this period, whereby the traditional emphasis on the officer's gentlemanly bearing and cultured accomplishments gave way to a more scientific schooling in the arts of war.[90] While this may hold true for France, Prussia and other continental armies, in Britain the stress on personal comportment and gentility appears to have been maintained into the wars; a gentleman and an officer 'assumed his rightful position because of who he was, not what he had learned or achieved'.[91] At the same time, the expansion of the officer corps meant the entrance into the army of many men who were not by birth 'gentlemen'. For these individuals the process of becoming an officer involved more than learning drill and tactics, it also required attention to polite accomplishments and genteel manners, which ostensibly had little to do with the pursuit of war. The culture of politeness required men to display an ease and elegance in mixed company, to converse knowledgably about art and literature, and to charm and entertain ladies with their accomplished dancing or musicianship.[92] It is a culture that has been identified as breaking down in this period due to its negative associations with the French, a rugged British taciturnity replacing the polished elegance of the gentleman of manners.[93] Its residual influence, however, can still be discerned in the conduct of British officers. Before embarking for the Peninsula, Lt James Gardiner devoted himself to studying drawing and dancing 'for it will never do for an officer not to be able to dance'.[94] Others spent their leisure time practicing the flute or violin. Regimental messes established libraries and ordered the latest newspapers. Both at home and abroad, British officers produced and acted in amateur theatricals, a popular pastime amongst the eighteenth-century upper classes. These pursuits often had a military rationale. Dance and drill were closely aligned in eighteenth-century military theory: the elegance, dexterity and co-ordination imparted through dance supposedly contributed to the soldiers' strength and agility on the battlefield.[95] Dancing also had important social functions. By hosting balls, regiments were able to ease relations with the local societies amongst whom they were stationed. Such activities helped to maintain the army's 'amateur' ethos, ensuring that it did not become too detached from the civilian society whose interests it was defending.[96]

In other respects, military codes of masculine conduct were increasingly in tension with the norms of civil society. This was most evident in the culture of duelling. The armed forces had long been considered a bastion of the duel, as officers carried an aristocratic code of honour with them into service, but the army's attitudes towards such affairs remained ambivalent.[97] The duel could challenge the state's legal monopoly on violence and disrupt the internal unity of the officer corps; it was officially forbidden under the Articles of War. Yet it also demonstrated the qualities of physical courage, martial skill and honour that were central to constructions of military masculinity. Officers therefore had to negotiate between a powerful informal code of honour and official military law. The etiquette of the duel prescribed a specifically elite form of interpersonal violence. When two Irish officers came to blows over a woman at the Plymouth garrison in 1812 they were court-martialled. The perceived severity of their offence had been compounded by the fact that the brawl had taken place in full view of the private soldiers and without weapons. 'Had they fought with pistols or swords they would have been regarded as Gentlemen and caressed', a fellow officer remarked, 'but fighting with their hands has completely ruined their character.'[98] For soldiers from more modest backgrounds, the duel could be a means of affirming their claims to gentility, but it was also at odds with the British middling classes' growing distaste for such violent and excessive displays of aristocratic status.[99] Those used to this more moderate mode of manly conduct could find the army's honour code oppressive. William Thornton Keep, whose family was 'respectable' but not wealthy, described how due to such 'ridiculous punctilios' two of his comrades, formerly the best of friends, had been on the brink of duelling. Keep managed to orchestrate a reconciliation, but recognized that 'had it been found out…my conduct would have been considered highly dishonourable'.[100]

For subaltern officers the most difficult aspect of the transition from civilian to military life was the loss of independence it entailed. Independence, as already noted, was a central component of Georgian understandings of masculinity. While the army offered a potential route to achieving professional and financial independence, military discipline and subordination necessarily curtailed officers' individual autonomy. Subalterns complained bitterly and repeatedly about their subjection to the authority of superior officers. Lieutenant John Aitchison advised his brother against contemplating a career in the army, citing 'all *want of independence*' as the most challenging aspect of life as a subaltern.[101] In a series of letters to his family, Lieutenant William Coles recorded his increasingly fractious relationship with his commanding officer Colonel Kemmis, who, he believed, had singled him out for persecution. In his complaints against the colonel, Coles deployed the gendered vocabulary of 'virtue', 'corruption', 'luxury' and 'effeminacy' which was so central to eighteenth-century classical republican political discourse. Kemmis, he declared had 'become effeminate from comfort and indulgence' and was 'as much capable of commanding a Regt. in the Field as a Serjeant of Militia'.[102] Chief amongst his accusations was the claim that the colonel had become involved with the wife of a common soldier. The figure of the immoral and despotic ruler unduly governed by female influence was a common trope of classical republicanism. The recent scandal in which the Duke of York was revealed to have granted military promotions as favours to his mistress, Mary Anne Clarke, would have been an obvious reference point in this analysis of the relationship between sexual immorality and military corruption.[103] In such a situation it was impossible to practice the self-mastery and individual autonomy necessary to independent masculinity and Coles lamented that the 'pleasure of being one's own master' was a concept unknown in the army 'as a more slave like profession cannot exist'.[104] As he wrote to his brother: 'I wish professional profits would allow me to secure an Independence in some way and the Devil take me if I would not pitch the Red Coat to the Bottom of the Sea'.[105]

The 'wooden world'

If the army in certain respects became more detached from civil society during this period, the navy had long been perceived as a distinctive and separate community, a perception encapsulated in its informal title: 'the wooden world'. In Georgian Britain the sailor was both familiar and exotic; at sea he was lauded as the sturdy defender of the nation, on land deplored as disruptive and uncivilised; he was central to national identity, while existing simultaneously on the margins of the nation.[106] Sailors spoke a distinctive nautical argot, were identifiable by their short-waisted jackets and even, according to contemporaries, by their characteristic rolling gait, the product of long service on the high seas. Entrance into the navy then, involved not only the transition between civilian and military society, but also between life on land and life at sea. For new recruits it could be like moving to a foreign land. Accounts by those who joined the navy with little prior experience of this maritime community were often written in the style of an ethnographic survey, detailing the internal norms, law and language of another country. While narratives of naval life highlighted certain elements of military culture that were shared with the army – the culture of complaint amongst subaltern officers, the carefully choreographed displays of power and discipline – they depicted a world that was in many respects more profoundly alien.

The 'foreignness' and opacity of naval life is a dominant theme of the Reverend Edward Mangin's journal, in which he described the few months he spent as chaplain on board the HMS Gloucester in 1812. It manifested itself most obviously in linguistic difference and the rich lexicon of ship-board life that Mangin gradually mastered: 'I was now familiar with *comb-ings*, or *coamings*, and *shot-lockers*; the *splinter-netting*; the *throwing-out* and *answering* of signals; the *calling of the after-guard; up-hammocks* and *down hammocks; Parbowlings! and starbowlings.*'[107] The acquisition of 'sea talk' – both a technical vocabulary and a saltier slang – was an important part of the nautical novice's initiation. It demarcated sailors from landsmen, but also formed a common language for a community whose members were drawn from a diversity of regional and ethnic groups.[108]

If language provided one marker of the 'wooden world's' foreignness, the symbolic geography of the ship provided another. The shipboard theatre of power was often carefully delineated by visitors, in particular the emblem-atic space of the quarter deck. The eighteenth-century quarter-deck has been described by a modern anthropologist as 'sacred to the presence of sover-eign power in displays of etiquette and privilege. It was the captain's terri-tory – his to walk on alone, his to speak from but not be spoken to unless he wished it…It was the space of his sovereign's power, and all its trivial gestures and etiquette were its geography'.[109] Mangin was similarly struck by the complex naval etiquette which governed the quarter deck. Each man, he observed, upon ascending from the lower decks was obliged to doff his hat to the union jack, while no man could sit on the quarter deck or overtake the captain as he paraded there. Alert to the symbolically resonant intersection of space, gesture and power that inhered in these rules, Mangin advanced his own anthropological interpretation of what he acknowledged might be dismissed as 'frivolous' ceremonial. Such rituals, he maintained, were of 'the utmost importance to the well-being of Naval society' where the 'association of men full of passions and prejudices, huddled together in a floating prison' meant that 'even a momentary dereliction of forms might prove fatal to the general interest'.[110] For Mangin, however, the 'wooden world' ultimately proved to be too recondite, too self-enclosed. Unable to shake the conviction that 'I was out of my proper sphere' he resolved to leave the 'unnatural and perilous state of a mariner'.[111]

Mangin's awkward position within the shipboard hierarchy likely contributed to this sense of estrangement. The naval chaplain tended to be perceived as an 'inactive landman among busy seamen' and tensions between skilled seafarers and 'ignorant' landsmen formed one of the major fault lines in the shipboard community.[112] Robert Wilson, a merchant seaman impressed into the Royal Navy in 1805, recalled the scorn with which he was greeted by the crew of his new ship, who mistook him for a landsman on account of the 'long clothes' he wore.[113] Upon joining a new ship, whether as a volunteer or pressed man, all men were rated able seamen, ordinary seamen and landsmen according to their experience and abilities. Wilson's narrative describes this process and the subsequent allocation of duties upon the ship in some detail, noting how the ship's company was equally divided into two 'in a fair manner' so that the 'good men' were evenly distributed throughout both. Writing as a self-styled naval 'insider', he presented a rather different account of shipboard topography to that related by an 'outsider' like Mangin. For Wilson, the spatial organization of the ship was less about the enforcement of power and discipline, and more about the recognition of skill and expertise within the crew. The 'smartest' able seamen, those with more than two years experience, he noted, were generally stationed on the forecastle or in the tops. The less skilled seamen and landsmen formed the 'afterguard' and attended to the quarter-deck, while the waisters, the 'worst of landsmen' performed 'drudgery work' in the lowest part of this ship, the centre deck. Wilson summarized this hierarchy of skills in verse: ' ... the Topmen act the chief part/And boldly show the skilful seaman's art,/While others, less competent to their charge/On deck do haul upon the ropes at large'.[114] This understanding of the navy as a 'semi-meritocratic' structure in which the 'seamen's skilful art' was acknowledged and rewarded, appears to have reconciled some sailors to the asperities of shipboard life. Though Wilson had been pressed into the navy and wrote frankly about the dangers of shipboard life and the brutality of naval discipline he also took pride in the responsibilities and skill which his own position as a signalman required.[115]

Sailors' antagonism towards the maritime novice meant that the initiation of these 'greenhorns' into the enclosed community of the ship could be gruelling. It often took the form of pranks. Landsmen who joined the ship wearing long coats might have their tails cut off.[116] Upon joining his first ship as a naval surgeon, James Lowry was startled when, in the middle of the night, his hammock was suddenly lowered by mischievous members of the lower deck, a custom, he noted, which was intended to 'christen' new arrivals.[117] The most elaborate initiation ritual, however, was the 'crossing-the-line' ceremony that marked a ship's passage across the equator or, in voyages to the West Indies, across the Tropic of Cancer, and which drama-tized the division between experienced and novice sailors.[118] This raucous and highly theatricalized ritual was led and choreographed by those who had already crossed the line. Presiding over the ceremony was a sailor in the role of Neptune, dressed in a makeshift crown and trident, with a deck swab for a wig and a beard made out of roping. He was assisted by a 'Barber' armed with an iron hoop and a barrel full of slops to shave those who had yet to cross the equator. After shaving, novices were often ducked overboard, a humiliation that could be avoided by making an offering to Neptune.[119] The ritual and rhetoric of the ceremony made it an exemplary rite of passage, enacting a symbolic baptism, ritual birth and rebirth. It marked both the geographical passage from the familiarity of home to a new and unknown world, and the incorporation of the novice sailor into the nautical commu-nity. The offerings to, and obeisance before, the figure of Neptune also func-tioned as a ritual of propitiation to the natural elements that governed sailors' fates.[120] In addition, the ceremony adhered to the conventions of the carni-valesque, temporarily inverting the ship's hierarchy of power and authority. Both 'unbaptised' officers and those from the lower decks had to endure the ritual, meaning that, for a time, 'the true authority of the ship belonged to those who had already Crossed the Line, and not to any by right of their commissions or warrants or appointments.'[121] This subversive subtext was noted with disquiet by one officer, for whom the ceremony recalled 'the Roman Saturnalia, when the slaves were allowed to take all kinds of liberties with their masters, as the men here do with the officers who are not able by money or grog to bribe them into forbearance'.[122]

Nautical experience and knowledge could thus complicate and cut across hierarchies based upon rank. However, while all who joined a ship were 'rated' upon entry, social status still determined whether they were bound for the 'lower deck' or the 'quarter deck'. A small proportion, an estimated 2.5 per cent, of those destined to become officers entered the navy between 1793 and 1815 from the Royal Naval College at Portsmouth.[123] The majority of those with aspirations to become commissioned officers joined as 'First Class Volunteers'. Officially, they had to be at least thirteen years old and were required to spend two years in the navy before becoming a midshipman and a total of six years at sea before they could rise to Lieutenant.[124] Under the patronage of the ship's captain, these 'young gentlemen' began their professional training. The quality of this training was largely dependent on the disposition of the ship's captain. In a series of letters to his father, William Rennie, who joined HMS Ajax in 1809, detailed the anxieties and preoccupations of the aspiring officer. While there was no schoolmaster on board the Ajax, Rennie found some sympathetic officers who were able to assist him in 'Cyphering', 'Vulgar fractions' and 'Latin'. To his frustration, he found that his captain 'though undoubtedly a smart officer' provided limited opportunities to progress in his nautical education: 'he does not take any pains to learn you either Seamanship or Navigation...and few of Capt Otway's midshipmen are Sailors'.[125] Rennie seems to have reconciled to himself serving with Captain Otway. In a subsequent letter he acknowledged the benefit of 'cultivating the friendship of a man...who is possessed of much interest and might be the means of doing me many services'.[126] The patronage of a well-connected commander, as Rennie recognized, was vital to his advancement, but patronage alone was not enough; the aspiring officer also needed to demonstrate professional competence.[127]

While the importance of skill and experience in determining sailors' prospects helped to attenuate the sense of dependence that subaltern officers in the army so often bemoaned, the junior sea officer could also bristle at his subjection to the absolute authority of the ship's captain. The Reverend Mangin summarized the ambiguous role of a naval lieutenant as 'one half of their day slaves, and the other half slave-drivers' and the language of slavery was often used by officers to describe their situation: the navy was 'a house of bondage' wrote one, it was 'vastly worse than galley slavery' according to another.[128] An overbearing or unduly punctilious captain could challenge officers' cherished sense of manly independence and confound their expectations of the privileges which their status as 'gentleman' should confer. William Rennie, who by 1814 had exchanged into a new ship the HMS Malta, expressed his frustration with the culture of servility that his new captain encouraged. 'Nothing but the most abject submission can mollify him' he complained 'and an unembarrassed manner of addressing him is considered (from an inferior officer)...disrespect. He seems to forget that an Officer however below him in rank is still equal in birth and most probably his superior in education and manners'.[129]

An 'unembarrassed manner' was a hallmark of the culture of politeness, which encouraged ease and equality in conversation unencumbered by reference to social distinctions. For a young officer schooled in such values the abrasive experience of naval hierarchies brought into sharp relief the conflicts and tensions between his civilian and military identities. Like their counterparts in the army, naval officers found various ways to maintain the threads that bound them to their civilian selves: when in port they often hosted balls and dinners to help narrow the gap between the civilian community and the 'wooden' world. At the same time the recondite character of naval life, with its distinctive rites and rituals, made it a potent engine of acculturation. While social hierarchies mapped relatively easily onto naval hierarchies and connections and patronage remained important for advancement, the premium placed on professional skill and nautical experience provided a powerful inducement to identify with the values and culture of the navy. For the lower decks too, the value placed upon occupational skill provided some compensation for the severities and sacrifices of shipboard life.

A school of the nation?

In the wake of the 1798 Irish rebellion, the Anglo-Irish officer Harry Ross-Lewin recorded, hordes of 'wretched, misguided peasants' suspected of involvement in the rising were transported to the army depot in Chatham. Upon arrival all traces of their previous lives and appearance were obliterated as their 'sticks, clothes, and bundles were heaped together and burned' and the men were 'bathed in cisterns, put into the barber's hands to have their hair cut close, and provided with new undress clothing'. By the end of this process, they had become 'well-looking soldiers' who would soon prove 'second to none in gallantry in the field'.[130]

Ross-Lewin clearly had considerable faith in the army's ability to transform recalcitrant Irish peasants into loyal British soldiers. While the military establishment's principal concern during these years was the transformation of their civilian recruits into effective soldiers and sailors, an additional consequence of this channelling of manpower into the custodianship of the fiscal–military state, it has been suggested, was the integration of soldiers and seamen into a larger national community. While the administrative and political dimensions of the incorporation of Scottish and Irish manpower into the British army have been addressed, little attention has been paid to how service within this genuinely British force shaped soldiers personal understanding of their relationship to the United Kingdom.[131] Yet the power of the armed forces to act as 'schools of the nation' has long been a central element in accounts of nation building. These have tended to focus on two key mechanisms linking military service and the construction of cohesive national communities: firstly, the army's role as an agent of socialization and of national and ideological indoctrination; and secondly, its ability to draw together individuals of diverse religious, ethnic and national backgrounds in a common cause.[132] The idea of the army as an agent of socialization and a potential school of the nation is closely linked to its supposed evolution in this period into a 'total institution' whose members, separated from their families and civilian life, were particularly susceptible to military and potentially national indoctrination.[133]

The armed forces certainly would seem to have provided fertile ground for the germination of pan-British allegiances. By 1800 the military was the only profession whose members 'uniformly operated in an all-British context'.[134] According to Cookson's analysis of army returns, the army in 1813 was about one-half English and Welsh, one-sixth Scottish, and one-third Irish. Within the officer corps Scots and Irish were even more strongly represented, with an estimated 24.3 per cent being of Scottish origin and 35 per cent coming from Ireland.[135] Both Scottish and Irish troops had a long history of service in the armies of continental Europe, partly sustained in the first half of the eighteenth century by a continued attachment to the exiled Stuart dynasty. But enlistment in the French or foreign forces was not simply an index of allegiance to the Jacobite cause; it was as much a product of a broader pattern of labour migration from the European peripheries to the manpower hungry armies of the continental powers. Once the expanded British army was able to offer an alternative market for military labour from the Seven Years War (1756–1763), it soon established itself as the preferred destination for Irish and Scottish men seeking to earn their livelihood as a soldier.[136]

The army's potential to act as an instrument of national integration has been most fully explored in relation to Scotland. The incorporation of Highland soldiers into the army after the Jacobite rebellion of 1745 supposedly demonstrated how a 'disloyal' group could be assimilated into the British state through military service.[137] By the time of the Revolutionary and Napoleonic wars, Highland regiments had become 'proud symbols of Scotland's ancient nationhood and of her equal partnership with England in a British empire'.[138]

Recent scholarship has developed a more nuanced perspective on the relationship between Highland recruitment and British national identity, highlighting the intricate interplay of local, civilian and professional identities that shaped Scottish soldiers' engagement with the fiscal–military state. An understanding of the Highland soldier as a pragmatic actor with a well-developed understanding of his rights has replaced more romanticized images of the tartan-clad warrior loyally following his clan chieftain into the British army.[139]

From the outbreak of the Seven Years War (1756–63) the ever increasing manpower demands of the British military fiscal state would direct attention to Ireland as a potentially fertile recruiting ground. Despite official prohibitions forbidding Catholics from bearing arms, from the 1750s they would be enlisted surreptitiously into the rank and file and, more openly, into the marines. The British government, keen to exploit this untapped military resource would conciliate the Catholic community by offering incremental relief from the penal laws in exchange for Irish soldiers. Autobiographical evidence suggests that most Irish Catholics who enlisted into the rank and file of the British army did so for much the same reasons as their English and Scottish counterparts: a lack of alternative employment, a yearning after military adventure and foreign travel fuelled by the tales of veteran soldiers, and a desire to 'shake off the trammels of parental guidance'.[140] Added to these were more particular local factors. The areas which saw the most intensive recruitment were also those in which sectarian disturbances had been most concentrated during and after the violent upheavals of the 1790s – north Leinster, north Connaught and south Ulster – an environment, which, as Cookson notes, produced a climate of social instability and population movement conducive to military recruitment.[141] A reluctance to draw from the defensive reserve of Protestant manpower meant that recruitment was often focused on Catholic areas. As regiments raised in Ireland tended to be immediately posted abroad, this strategy could be presented to Protestant opinion as a means of ridding the country of its most turbulent elements. In the counter-revolutionary crackdown that preceded and followed the 1798 rebellion, the recruitment of suspected subversives assumed a more coercive form: convicted rebels, sentenced to transportation to New South Wales were often offered the option of enlisting in the 'condemned' regiments destined for the West Indies.[142]

While the army's rank and file would be opened up to Irish Catholics, both willing and unwilling, from the 1750s, it was not until the introduction of the relief act of 1793 that Catholics were allowed to hold military commissions. Before 1817 they were officially forbidden from holding these commissions outside of Ireland, resulting in an anomalous situation whereby Catholic officers technically had to resign their commissions whenever they travelled to England or Scotland. The entrance of Catholic émigrés into the British forces following the French Revolution seems to have softened attitudes on this question and there were Catholic officers in the army throughout this period, although their numbers were probably small.[143] Increasing toleration on the part of the British military establishment in combination with the aggressive purge of the French forces after the Revolution facilitated the transfer of Irish Catholic officers, who had continued to look abroad for a military career, into the British military service. Several leading figures from the Irish regiments of the French army fell victim to the guillotine. The more fortunate left the French army to join the royalist forces assembling beyond France's borders and then transferred into the British service upon the formation of the Loyal Irish Brigade in 1794. These regiments had a very brief existence: all had been disbanded by 1798 and the officers scattered through the British army.[144]

This was the path followed by Captain Peter R. Jennings. His fragmentary narrative – part memoir, part diary – is a rare example (indeed, the only one of which I am aware) of an autobiographical account by an Irish Catholic officer from this period. Born in Ballinrobe, Co. Mayo in 1770, Jennings described himself as the descendant of an ancient and distinguished family, whose property and fortune had been ruthlessly expropriated by the 'Lawless followers of the Lawless regicide "Cromwell"' – a characteristic expression of the ideology of dispossession that prevailed amongst the 'underground gentry' of eighteenth-century Ireland.[145] In 1788 he followed his two brothers into service with Berwick's Irish regiment in the French army. When, in 1791, the army introduced a new oath of allegiance to the 'Nation & Constitution' replacing the former pledge of 'fidelity to the King', Jennings, along with the rest of Berwick's regiment, defected to the royalist forces then assembled at Koblenz. He served with the allied forces until they were forced to retreat into northern Holland by the ascendant republican army and then sailed for Britain to join the Irish brigade in 1794. The brigade was disbanded in 1798 and Jennings was placed on half pay. Not wishing 'to remain an idle member of the community at a time when the dearest interests of the Country were at stake, & when the energies of the state were called forth in support of a just & lawful War', Jennings re-entered active service as an officer in the 28th

Foot.[146] Over the next ten years he would take part in several major British expeditions, including Minorca in 1800, Egypt in 1801 and South America in 1806.

For Peter Jennings there was little apparent tension between his former service for the Bourbons and his active contribution to the British war effort. Like his co-religionists who had enlisted in the rank and file from the 1750s onwards, the opening of the higher ranks provided a new alternative employment route for the career soldier. Professional motives could also be reconciled with more ideological considerations. He had a clear antipathy to all republican regicides, whether English or French; the transfer of allegiance from the Bourbon to the Hanoverian dynasty therefore reflected a broader commitment to the established political order of *ancien régime* Europe. Moreover, while Britain's role in previous eighteenth-century conflicts was often cast as a crusade in defence of the European Protestant interest, the French revolutionaries' aggressive drive for dechristianization meant that the war against republican and even Napoleonic France could now be presented as a struggle between the European Christian order and an imperialist atheist state, a position with which Jennings, a devout Catholic, would, no doubt, have been sympathetic.[147] From this perspective, there was no paradox in an Irishman, even one who recalled with bitterness the Cromwellian dispossession of his ancestors, accepting a commission in the British army.

Jennings' career indicates a pragmatic adjustment to shifts in the European military market and transformations in the religious and political order, but the fragmentary diary he kept during the wars suggests that he also came to develop a personal investment in the honour and reputation of the British army and that he actively supported and identified with two of the key elements of Britishness: the nation's commercial pre-eminence and its continued imperial expansion. Following the failed expedition to South America in 1806, for example, Jennings not only lamented this stain on the British army's military record, but also the loss of British territory in Montevideo, a conquest which, he believed, would have been of great benefit to commerce and manufactures especially, he noted, at a time when Napoleon's Continental System excluded British trade from European markets. If no substitute outlet could be found, Jennings feared, 'her opulence and grandeur in the Scale of Nations must naturally diminish, as, by her commerce she exists'. 'Still', he concluded, 'I trust she will exist long after the Nations around her shall have fallen into decay and that her Sons may never lose sight of those principles which brought their Country to the proud rank she at present holds'.[148]

Jennings' identification with British ambitions and triumphs appears to have been the product of extended military service, rather than the consequence of any purposeful patriotic or national indoctrination on the part of the military establishment. There is little evidence that the state tried to actively propagandize its captive audience of soldiers or to promote order and combat effectiveness through patriotic appeals. The substantial Irish presence within the army, as Cookson notes, may well have inhibited the development of a pronounced 'King and Country' ethos.[149] It is likely that developments across the channel strengthened the military's reluctance to act as a school of the nation. As the French army of the 1790s linked ideological and emotional commitment to the republic with its success in combat, the soldiers of the republic underwent an intensive exposure to revolutionary propaganda. Whilst a prisoner of war on board a French naval ship, the British marine officer Watkins Tench observed with curiosity the vessel's intensely ideological environment. The slogan *Liberté, Egalité, Fraternité, ou la Mort* prefaced every written order and republican iconography was omnipresent. Called to the quarter deck at eight o'clock, the crew 'with united voice':

> ... sang the Marseilles Hymn, with a fervour and enthusiasm of manner which astonished me... The sublime music of this fine lyric composition, the gaiety breathed by the *Carmagnole*, and by many other popular airs which are continually in their mouths, during their most ordinary occupations, must produce a prodigious effect on the pliant minds of Frenchmen, and highly contribute to invigorate that spirit of idolatry for a republic, and that hatred and contempt of monarchy, which it is so much the interest of their leaders to encourage.

Witnessing these scenes of republican spirit, Tench reflected on the marked contrast between the French and British armies:

> We fire, indeed, a few lazy guns on the anniversaries of the King's birth, accession, and other similar occasions; but we never stimulate the passions of our soldiery, by recalling them to their memories, in periodic exhibitions, the days on which their forefathers won the fields of Agincourt, Blenheim, and Minden; nor re-animate the ardent energy of our seamen, by public recitals of the victories of a Russel, a Hawke, a Rodney, and a Howe. And yet the histories of the greatest nations, both ancient and modern, sufficiently demonstrate the power of such exhibitions over the human mind.[150]

Tench may have overstated the lack of patriotic symbolism and ritual within the army. Upon enlisting each recruit swore an oath to 'be true to our Sovereign Lord King George, and serve him honestly and faithfully'.[151] Military uniforms bore the king's cypher and crown, a symbol of the soldier's personal allegiance to the monarch.[152] Patriotic songs such as 'Britons' strike home' and 'God save the King' were played at regimental reviews or before battle. The British army also borrowed some of the French republic's more stirring tunes: in 1793 the 14th Foot led an attack on a French battery during the campaign in Flanders while the band played 'Ca Ira!'.[153] As well as marking the birthdays of the British royal family, officers of the 7th Light

Dragoons wore black crepe to mourn the execution of Marie Antoinette.[154] Moreover, the anniversaries of famous victories, such as the battle of Minden, *were* commemorated by the army. On the 47th anniversary of the battle in August 1806, Thomas Browne wore a rose in his racoon hat to commemorate the British soldiers who, advancing through the rose gardens leading to the battlefield in 1759, had similarly decorated their hats with this symbol of England.[155] In this instance, however, Browne was commemorating his regiment's participation in the victory, an example of how regimental loyalty tended to supersede broader national or Britannic identifications. The use of royal symbols in army ritual and regalia, similarly, bespoke a traditional idea of the soldier's loyalty to the person of the sovereign, rather than a more emotional commitment to the defence of the nation.

The navy, by contrast, seems to have cultivated a more overtly patriotic environment. Soldiers, coming from the ideologically lukewarm environment of the army, were often struck by the ardent patriotism expressed by sailors. Whilst on board naval transports, Private William Wheeler recorded how the crew would spend their evenings 'immortalizing the heroes of gone by days by singing songs to the memory of Duncan, Howe, Vincent and the immortal Nelson'. He was particularly amused by the seamen's outrage at the mistreatment of the Union Jack by a French ship, which, in full view of the British fleet had 'placed the British Jack under their bows for the ship's company to evacuate on'. Wheeler could not help laughing at 'one of our honest Jacks' who felt a 'personal insult at such an unwarrantable dirty trick'.[156] Wheeler's account reproduced the stereotype of the Jack Tar as 'the unthinkingly loyal "son of Brittania"' which had been the predominant image of the sailor in the eighteenth century. This image was severely shaken by the 1797 mutinies, after which it was increasingly recognized that the sailor's loyalty could not be taken for granted but 'must be won by sophisticated and reasoned argument'.[157] In an effort to persuade seamen of their patriotic duties and attachment to the nation James Stanier Clarke the chaplain of *L'Impeteux* from 1796 preached a series of hortatory sermons to the ship's company. These included a discourse 'On the Love of our Country' in which he urged his audience to guard their innate loyalty against the wicked and insinuating forces of republicanism, highlighted the 'island nation's' historical role as a bulwark of liberty and concluded with a rousing exhortation that united the sailor's duties to their religion, families and nation:

> On that altar which our forefather's reared to Liberty, the flame of patriotism arises! Around it let every age and rank assemble...and take that oath which the Genius of Britain proffers: WE SWEAR, THAT WE WILL REMEMBER THE LORD! WE WILL FIGHT FOR OUR BRETHREN, OUR SONS, OUR DAUGHTERS OUR WIVES AND OUR HOUSES! AND WILL FIRMLY UNITE IN THE PRESERVATION OF HER, WHO DWELLETH, WITH SO MUCH TERRIBLENESS IN THE CLEFT OF THE ROCKS; WHOSE RAMPART, AND WHOSE WALL – IS FROM THE SEA![158]

It was not only ordinary sailors who were educated in such patriotic principles. Robert Deans, a naval schoolmaster, composed a series of instructive essays for his midshipmen pupils that included an essay 'On the love of one's country' in which patriotism was promoted as 'one of the noblest passions that can warm and animate the human breast'.[159]

It has been suggested that officers had a more permanent investment in the navy and the prestige of the service than ordinary sailors who often moved between merchant and naval vessels.[160] Yet seamen's journals suggest that many had an intense attachment to the navy and took pride in its successes. While this does not come through in the content of the journals themselves, which are generally laconic and logbook-like, their flyleaves often contained transcriptions of patriotic ballads celebrating the navy's most famous victories. Copied into the journal of Richard Johnson, for instance, are two tributes to Admiral Nelson 'The Hero of the Nile' and 'The Glorious 1st of August 1798' as well as verses commemorating Admiral Duncan's victory at Camperdown in 1797, with the lines: 'Inrol'd in our bright Annels [*sic*]/Lives full many a Gallant Name/But never a British heart conceived a prowder [*sic*] deed of fame/To shield our liberty and Laws/And Guard our Sovereign Crown/As Noble Dunkin [*sic*] Mighty army achieved at Camperdown'.[161] The painstaking effort with which Johnson transcribed these verses, which fill pages and pages of his journal, give some insight into their personal significance. Indeed the very act of transcription might be understood as a means through which the language of loyalism was internalized.

Overt expressions of patriotism in the writings of members of the British armed forces from this period are relatively rare. Officers might allude to the 'leading principle, the Amor patriae' but in general the mirror in which their honourable self-image was reflected was not that held up by the nation, but by their fellow officers.[162] Similarly, the ordinary soldier or seaman rarely expressed a commitment to a larger, national cause, nor was this necessarily expected of him. Service in the army or navy, however, may be expected to have contributed to a less overt form of British national consciousness. After all the armed forces were the only genuinely pan-British profession at this time, and in the case of the army, it was perhaps one of the few institutions to which the adjective 'British' was regularly attached.[163]

Certainly, the image of the army as a melting pot, bringing together individuals from the component nations and regions of the British Isles, appears quite often in soldiers' accounts. In 1812 William Thornton Keep was quartered in barracks with the 88th regiment, or Connaught rangers and a detachment of the 11th (North Devonshire) regiment. The officers' mess, he noted, contained a 'strange medley' of 'young men from the three Kingdoms', though this was 'not unconducive to the pleasures of the service in which we are engaged from the variety of characters it produces'.[164] Private Wheeler similarly recorded a speech from his regimental Colonel in which he celebrated the strength which the army drew from its diversity: 'Here is John Bull from England; Sawney from Scotland and Paddy from my own country.

By God we will not only beat the French but we will eat them afterwards!'[165] As these examples suggest, the image of Britain that the army's pan-national character made visible to its members, was of a nation composed of separate but equal kingdoms, not a transcendent or unified whole, nor one that could necessarily command an intense emotional attachment.

The extent to which soldiers developed shared attachments to comrades from the different regions and nations of the British Isles provides one way of gauging how military service extended soldiers' mental horizons. Such surveys are necessarily impressionistic. Cookson observes that soldiers tended to form their closest friendships with men from their own countries.[166] Yet counter examples can also be found. Isolated from the 'knowing boys' of his regiment, Joseph Donaldson, a Protestant Scot, developed a firm friendship with Dennis, an Irish Catholic, who 'was of a warm, generous-hearted disposition and never flinched from me in distress.'[167] Though the author of the *Journal of a Private in the Seventy-First's* closest companion was a fellow Scot, their friendship also transcended traditional parochial attachments: he was a Protestant lowlander, his comrade Donald MacDonald a Highland Catholic.[168] Soldiers' letters are peppered with fragments of regional and national dialect that they absorbed from the army's cultural and linguistic mélange. William Wheeler, for instance, would often preface a certain phrase with 'as the Irishman says' or 'as the Cornishman says'.[169]

Of course, the British army's linguistic diversity extended beyond dialect to encompass the distinctive languages of the Celtic nations (as well as those spoken by other foreign troops within the army). The Highland regiments, in particular, often specified that officers had Gaelic so that they could communicate with their men.[170] In his poem on the Battle of Holland, the Scottish Gaelic soldier-bard Corporal Alexander MacKinnon drew a distinction between the Highland troops and the 'English speakers' (*Luchd na Beurla*) alongside whom they fought.[171] Linguistic difference between soldiers would presumably have formed an insuperable barrier to meaningful interaction or exchange. One private recalled how on his first night in barracks he had been kept awake by a cacophony of different tongues which he likened to the 'confusion on the plains of Babel'. In this state of mutual incomprehension, the assembled Welsh, Irish, Scottish and English recruits were reduced to hurling evocative insults at one another.[172] On his first night in barracks, Joseph Donaldson similarly remarked the diversity of accents he encountered, ranging from 'the Irish brogue' to the 'distinguishing dialect' of the cockney.[173] It is possible that the army rather than eroding regional and linguistic particularisms, served to affirm the difference of its constituent members. Indeed, though the reproduction of regional dialects in soldiers' narratives was often relatively affectionate, they tended to reinforce national stereotypes such as the comic 'bulls' or blunders commonly attributed to the Irish. In this vein, an English officer in an Irish regiment referred to his men as 'wild Irishmen'.[174] Even admiring observations on national characteristics could underline the alterity of certain parts of the United Kingdom. Though William Keep was greatly impressed by his first view of the Highland regiments, his description underlined the exotic and 'picturesque' appearance of 'these warlike North Britons'.[175]

The closed community of the warship provided an environment that was perhaps even more conducive to the forging of a common identity.[176] The regional and national mixture within the navy was roughly comparable to that of the army. A sample of men from ships commissioning at Plymouth in 1804–1805 shows that 47 per cent were English, 29 per cent Irish, 8 per cent Scottish, 3 per cent Welsh, 1 per cent from the Isle of Man and the Channel Isles, with 11 per cent originating from outside the British Isles.[177] Seamen's narratives rarely allude to regional or national differences amongst the ship's crew, perhaps indicating the extent to which such distinctions were subsumed by their collective identity as sailors. As one seamen observed to his mother, the sailor's isolated and nomadic existence at sea meant that 'he is everywhere but belongs no place'.[178] Nevertheless, ordinary sailors clearly distinguished between their shipmates who were of British or Irish origin and the 'foreigners' who composed the remainder of the crew. William Hamilton complained that his ship, HMS Orquixo, was very badly manned as it had only '35 or 36 Englishmen, Scotchmen and Irishmen, among the whole, the rest being foreigners'.[179] Robert Mercer Wilson was similarly scathing in his assessment of the 'd_m__d scoundrels of foreigners that belonged to our ship'.[180] Within this crude xenophobia, there emerges a rudimentary image of Britishness defined against the foreign 'other'.

The army's capacity to engender a common sense of Britishness was threatened by the various religious constituencies that it encompassed. The Army Chaplains' Department, which was established in 1796, was an exclusively Anglican body. While the Church of Scotland was allowed to appoint chaplains to serve Presbyterian soldiers stationed in Scotland, they were not appointed to Scottish regiments, nor allowed to minister to their co-religionists serving outside of Scotland. Nor were other religious minorities, Catholics and non-conformists, represented by the Chaplains' Department.[181] The extent of the army's concern with the spiritual well-being of its troops has been recently re-evaluated by Michael Snape, who notes that both the Duke of York and the Duke of Wellington were patrons of the Naval and Military Bible Society, an organization established by William Wilberforce to provide bibles to soldiers and sailors.[182] Nevertheless, the army does not seem to have cultivated an overtly Protestant atmosphere. While attendance at church was compulsory for regiments in garrison, on campaign the severe shortage of army chaplains meant that divine service was but irregularly performed. As one officer noted during the Peninsula campaign 'the appearance once now and then of the Chaplain serves to remind us that we are Protestants, no more'.[183]

In response to the substantial Irish presence in the army, an estimated quarter of the entire strength, the military establishment adopted a more relaxed policy on Catholic worship, becoming, according to Snape 'a national model of confessional tolerance'. Catholic soldiers serving in Ireland were granted permission to attend Mass in 1793 and this was extended to the army as a whole in 1806.[184] Official army policy on Catholic freedom of worship, however, was often inconsistently applied at regimental level.[185] Charles O'Neil, a private in the 28th regiment, recalled how, as late as 1811, he had been court-martialled and flogged after refusing to attend a Church of England service while stationed in Gibraltar.[186] The example of O'Neil suggests that experiences in the British army could nurture a sense of grievance amongst its Catholic recruits, but his account was not necessarily representative. Rather than hindering Catholic worship, the army may well have been the first context in which many Irish soldiers encountered a formalized and regular form of devotion, as distinct from the more relaxed and domestic mode of religious practice that prevailed in Ireland prior to the post-famine 'devotional revolution'. Roman Catholic chapels flourished in the port and garrison towns of Southern England during the wars and it may not have been until they joined the British army that many Irish soldiers experienced regular mass attendance.[187]

Pockets of prejudice remained. Some Catholic officers may have had their promotions blocked, whilst General Picton's animadversions on the 'religion and country' of the Connaught Rangers famously drew forth the regiment's ire.[188] Often though, it was intra-Irish sectarianism that seems to have been imported into the army. Major General James Kemmis of the 40th regiment, an Anglo-Irish officer from Laois, was unabashed in declaring his 'deep-rooted antipathy to papist Irish' and displayed a marked hostility to Irish Catholic officers who managed to obtain commissions.[189] The surprise with which ordinary English soldiers viewed occasional outbreaks of sectarian violence between Irish soldiers, suggests that they understood it to be a peculiarly Irish affliction. 'There is not, in many cases, in Ireland, much love lost between the protestant and papist', observed one English private, recalling a violent dispute between a Catholic and a Protestant soldier in his regiment.[190] There is little evidence that British Protestant soldiers' interactions with their Catholic comrades were marked by any significant anti-Catholic sentiments.

The connection between Protestantism and British national identity, as critics of Linda Colley's thesis have pointed out, was also undermined by the internal fractures within British Protestantism.[191] In the army, this was most strongly manifested by the distinct Methodist sub-culture that existed within the other ranks. Methodism found a foothold in the army during the War of the Austrian succession (1739–48), and through the efforts of the leading revivalists, and a band of soldier-preachers soon flourished. Methodism tended to find a particularly receptive audience amongst marginal groups like soldiers, its providentialist message resonating with their habitual fatalism. The rapid expansion of evangelical religion in Britain during the period 1793 to 1815 was replicated in the ranks of the army. Regular prayer meetings were established in garrisons, on campaign and in prisoner of war camps. Such religious gatherings often provided a welcome release from the tedium of life in camp or barracks where there were few alternative recreational outlets. The spread of Methodism was viewed with some suspicion by the Duke of Wellington, who believed such associations provided a dangerous alternative focus for his soldiers' loyalty, but the army establishment did little to actively suppress it.[192] Accounts by Methodist soldiers suggest the intense bonding and personal attachments that developed within these communities. While stationed in Ireland, a private in the 38th began to attend a Methodist meeting and soon developed a 'Love and Affection for the people of God with whom I conversed...that far surpassed all that I had ever felt for my Nearest Relatives on earth'.[193] For these soldiers their primary affinity lay not with the nation, or the regiment, but with other members of their spiritual community.

Regimental and naval attachments

To be attached to the subdivision, to love the little platoon we belong to in society, is the first principle (the germ as it were) of public affection. It is the first link in the series by which we proceed towards a love to our country and to mankind.[194]

Edmund Burke, *Reflections on the Revolution in France* (1790)

Edmund Burke's choice of metaphor to describe how local and personal attachments evolve to encompass larger impersonal identifications seems particularly apt when considering the bonds and affinities fostered by the military. It articulates a distinctively British way of envisaging the nation, as an amalgamation of families, regions and component patriotisms, as opposed to the one and indivisible nation of the French republic. In a similar way, the ships and regiments into which the navy and army were subdivided provided not only a microcosm of the diverse regions, nations and religious denominations that comprised (after 1800) the United Kingdom of Great Britain and Ireland, but also a familial community where these affections could be practised. For sailors, the navy, arguably, provided a context in which several interlocking identities could be articulated: an occupational identity which differentiated seamen from landsmen; a naval identity expressed through their pride in the navy's victories and its admiral heroes; and a perhaps more muted sense of Britishness which drew on the distinctive maritime identity of the British Isles. Added to these, was the particular attachment that sailors developed for the vessels in which they sailed and the crews in which they worked. Crews would often follow a naval captain into a new ship and a degree of familial loyalty could develop between captain and his company. The men of *L'Impeteux* called their captain 'Father'.[195] When he was forced to take leave of his crew after his ship was wrecked, Captain Robert Barrie confessed his emotion at having to 'bid farewell to a set of men it will almost break my heart to part with & I believe their attachment to me is not less sincere'.[196] The personal pride and affection which sailors could develop for the vessels they manned is well illustrated by Robert Wilson's account of his ship *Unité* which, he boasted, 'had every good quality...we were counted the smartest ship in the sea'. Rejoining the *Unité* after a cruise on another vessel, he was delighted by its order and cleanliness and the smartness of the sailors: 'it was like coming into a palace yard to come on our ship's quarterdeck from that of the *Minstrel's*'.[197]

Within the army the regimental unit also promoted a degree of familial attachment in the form of the horizontal bonds between soldiers and the vertical hierarchies that regulated the relationships between officers and men. A benevolent paternalism, it has been suggested, increasingly shaped officers' interactions with the rank and file, as officers came to take a greater interest in their men's moral and spiritual welfare.[198] Subaltern officers were expected to attend to the interior economy of the regiment and to closely monitor the activities of their men: the cleanliness of their quarters, when they ate, when they slept. They were also supposed to protect their men against exploitation, ensuring that the clothing, equipment and food with which they were provided were of sufficient quality. 'Every subaltern officer' the *Regimental Companion* (1811) enjoined, 'ought, as soon as possible, to get acquainted with the names and characters of the troop he belongs to' (in the same sentence, he also advised them 'obtain a thorough knowledge of the different horse').[199] Certain commanding officers demonstrated an awareness that regimental cohesion depended on more than disciplinary threats alone and actively promoted positive relationships across ranks. William Wheeler wrote with enthusiasm of the two days a week set aside for regimental games, when all ranks of the 51st would play cricket, football, or box together, a tradition which, he claimed, produced an 'excellent feeling between officers and men'.[200]

Strict codes of deference, subordination and social segregation were, nonetheless, rigorously enforced. Officers could be charged with conduct 'unbecoming an officer and a gentleman' if they were found fraternizing with their subordinates.[201] NCOs who stood between the rank and file and the officer corps were discouraged from developing overly-familiar relationships with those under their command or their superiors. When, in 1809, the sergeants of 1/7th Fusiliers presented their Captain with a testimonial congratulating him on a promotion and expressing their high regard, they were severely reprimanded for presuming to comment on a superior officer's conduct.[202] Officers did not have that intense attachment and loyalty to their regiment that would characterize the British army from the late nineteenth century and they often moved rapidly through different regiments as commissions became available for purchase. Despite William Keep's avowed attachment to the 77th he left after only a year and would re-enter the army in a different unit.[203] Ordinary soldiers, on the other hand, were much more closely tied to their regiment: an estimated 80 per cent spent their military careers in a single regiment.[204] Consequently, the world of the regiment framed ordinary soldiers' experiences in the army to a much greater extent than their officers. Whilst the eccentric Colonel Mainwaring is a central character and source of humorous anecdotes in William Wheeler's letters, in officers' narratives the rank and file tend to be anonymous and marginal figures. Indeed, some officers could barely contain their revulsion at being brought into such close proximity with the labouring classes. Observing the conduct of his men and their wives, while confined together on a transport en route to Portugal, George Woodberry professed himself 'disgusted with Man and Woman (of the lower order)'.[205]

Relations between officers and men tended to be more affectionate in regiments with a strong local composition, where a more harmonious hierarchy based on the landlord–tenant relationship could be reproduced. Certainly, officers were more likely to take an active interest in men from their own localities. During the Peninsular campaign, Capt George Bingham sent his mother regular reports of the Dorsetshire men in his regiment so that she could satisfy inquiries at home.[206] In his letters home, Capt J. C. Harrison relayed news of the men who had followed him from the Worcestershire militia into the 23rd regiment and for whom he clearly expressed a personal solicitude:

> I gave Sergt. Carter the things his wife sent him, he is very well and being employed with our Quarter Master...I gave Boy Harper his things and have ordered him to write to his mother. Scott is made a Sergt. Mr Bowler as great a pickle as ever. I have desired him to write to his mother, and I have also made enquiry respecting John Price who died of a fever at Martinique.[207]

The regimental structure of the British army continued to support such regional and sub-national affiliations. While the French revolutionary regime had severed the links between individual regiments and particular provinces, fearing that such parochial attachments would inhibit the construction of a truly national army, the British army during the same period did the opposite, strengthening the links between counties and their regiments.[208] The connection often remained nominal, as recruitment for regiments took place far from the counties and regions with which they were supposedly associated: despite the number of Worcestershire men in Harrison's regiment, it was ostensibly a Welsh regiment.[209] There were, however, exceptions to this, most notably the Highland regiments, and several of the Irish regiments also maintained strong regional links: the 88th was particularly associated with Connaught, the 18th and 27th regiments, with Ulster.[210] Andrew MacKillop rightly cautions, however, against overstating the role of the regiment in shaping Scottish soldiers' identity. Many of the Highland regiments established between Culloden and Waterloo did not survive the particular conflicts which they had been established to fight and would therefore have had a limited purchase on their recruits' affections. Nonetheless, major Highland regiments such as the 42nd, 71st and 92nd survived the Napoleonic wars (even if they became increasingly less 'Highland' in composition as they absorbed both Lowland and Irish soldiers).[211]

All regiments of the British army cultivated distinctive identities through careful attention to the minute differences in uniform, the proud display of regimental colours, mascots and nicknames, but the 'national' regiments were understood as promoting a particularly intense *esprit de corps*.[212] As with the invention of national traditions, regiments of relatively recent creation quickly accumulated a collection of customs, ceremonials and symbols. The Royal Welch Fusiliers celebrated St David's day by compelling each member of the regimental mess to eat a leek, the size of which was determined by the length of their service.[213] On St Andrew's day the officers of the 95th regiment dined together.[214] On St Patrick's day in 1813 the English officers of the 18th Hussars treated the Irish officers to dinner whilst the men celebrated in a more raucous fashion. It also provided an opportunity to underline the link between regimental and national honour, as the Regimental Orders reminded the men that, 'Ireland looks to the 18th as peculiarly her own to uphold her name by their good conduct abroad.'[215] The regimental system provided a particularly appealing and flexible model for imagining the United Kingdom, in which political union did not preclude the expression of national distinctiveness. The intrinsic appeal of the national corps to their recruits, however, cannot be assumed. Prior to enlistment, local and parochial attachment, or *dúthcas* as it was known in Scottish and Irish Gaelic, may have been more significant than any broader national consciousness.[216] Indeed, the national regiments, with their panoply of symbols, songs and rituals, may well have been the most fully elaborated form of Irishness or Scottishness to which the rank and file had yet been exposed.

Elaborately choreographed rituals of inclusion and exclusion further enhanced the regiment's ability to mould and command its members' loyalties. Malefactors – thieves, deserters, or prostitutes – could be 'drummed out' of the regiment, a ritual which involved the offender processing up and down a regimental line to the 'Rogues March' before being banished from the camp or garrison.[217] As well as shaming rites, the regimental hierarchy could also offer rites of redemption. At Horsham barracks in 1810, a sergeant who had deserted was allowed to rejoin his regiment on condition that he pass twice under an arch formed from the regimental colours and be declared 'regenerated'.[218] Perhaps most significantly, in the absence of a system of rewards and distinctions to recognize acts of gallantry by soldiers or subal-tern officers, the regiment provided a vital mediator between the individual's honour and that of the nation. As we shall see in the next chapter, it was as part of a regimental unit that soldiers and junior officers conduct in battle was judged by the public. As Ensign Keep and Private Wheeler prepared to embark on their first campaign in 1809, the need to maintain regimental honour was uppermost in their thoughts. 'The 77th was ever a most gallant Regiment' wrote Keep, 'and I trust will maintain its character'.[219] Wheeler, meanwhile, attempted to convey to his correspondent the stirring effects of a speech by the regimental colonel prior to their departure.

> He shewed us the word *Minden* on our Colours, and reminded us it was inscribed on our breast plates…Our country expected much from us, the Regiment in its infant state had performed prodigies of valour…would it not be expected we should eclips [*sic*] them in glory.[220]

Conclusion

Writing of the armies of the European *ancien régime*, the historian of the age of democratic revolutions, Robert Roswell Palmer, described them as 'divided internally into classes, without common spirit, into officers whose incentive was honour, class-consciousness, glory or ambition, and soldiers enlisted for long terms…who were thought incapable of higher sentiments, and whose strongest attachment was usually a kind of naive pride in the regiment.'[221] This would begin to change with the French Revolution as dynastic wars gave way to people's wars and the soldier's personal honour became inextri-cably entwined with the honour of the nation and accessible to men of all ranks, who were (rhetorically, at least) bound together in a patriotic frater-nity. In the case of the British army, however, despite its rapid expansion, the introduction of a limited range of reforms and an evolving recognition that the private soldier could be granted a degree of personal autonomy, many of the characteristics of the *ancien régime* army, as described by Palmer, would survive up to and after 1815. For officers, personal reputation often remained as important as patriotic sacrifice in the service of the nation, their performance in the ballroom as significant as their performance on the battlefield. Rather than producing a hegemonic model of masculinity, in which national character, martial values and manly identity were seamlessly blended, the 'gentleman-amateur' ethos of the British officer corps incor-porated various modes of masculine behaviour, some of which were drawn from the civilian sphere with others relating more specifically to the culture of the army. The young subaltern had to steer a course through complex and sometimes competing codes of manly behaviour to assert his status as both an officer and a gentleman. For the other ranks, the tension between mili-tary and civilian identities may well have been less acute. Soldier narrators commonly described themselves as already estranged from civilian society (though in the case of the pious or learned soldier this sense of estrangement would be carried over into the army). A proportion of those pressed into the navy, meanwhile, would have had prior experience of shipboard life, experience that was recognized and rewarded by the navy.

The armed forces similarly operated to minimize potential conflicts between the rank and file's pre-existing identities and those instilled by the army. In the case of Irish Catholic soldiers, the army offered a relatively tolerant environment, or at least one in which overt expressions of Protestantism were discouraged, and may even have provided a welcome refuge from more rancorous sectarian tensions at home. Of course, it cannot be assumed that recruits' religious and national identities were very deeply engrained to begin with: the army may have been the first place where the Irish Catholic soldier had access to regular worship, or the recruit from Carnaervonshire encountered a Welshness expressed through leeks, dragons and the celebration of St David's day. In the navy, where there were no regional or national layers to mediate between the ship and the navy as a whole, an institutional Britishness seems to have been more widely embraced. The army, by contrast, did little to foster its members' attachment to the United Kingdom, or to recognize the service of all ranks through the distribution of awards, honours and memorials. Yet while this may have attenuated the identification between the soldier and the nation, it may also, as we shall see in the following chapter, have prevented the army from becoming estranged from civilian society, a society whose values the officer class at least continued to uphold.

3
Combat and Campaign

The morning on which his regiment departed for the Peninsula was one Lt Sullivan would never forget. The troops marched out of Hyde Barracks to crowds of spectators cheering and huzzaing, waving their handkerchiefs and hats in an effusion of patriotic enthusiasm. 'Every man', he wrote, 'seemed inspired to pluck a laurel for his rising country...the thunders of applause and the blessings of the multitude bestowed upon us – surpassed everything I ever witnessed'. Yet, he continued 'I can scarcely bring myself to write the last few lines – oh how differently did my hopes & thoughts turn out to what I had anticipated'.[1] In Sullivan's account written after two years campaigning, the jubilant scenes and buoyant expectations that preceded his first expedition acquire an air of unreality: the youthful soldier filled with optimism is barely recognizable to the Peninsular veteran, the two selves separated by the experience of war. In this narrative arc from innocence to experience we can find several seemingly familiar elements of the soldier's tale: the sense of estrangement from the pre-war self; the move from optimism to disillusionment; and the ironic clash between the expectation and the reality of war.

The narrative of disillusionment is, of course, particularly associated with the First World War, the exemplary 'ironic' war, in which the glorious illusion of battle was violently dislodged by the mechanized horror of trench warfare. The Revolutionary and Napoleonic wars did not produce a collective story of disillusionment, though the contrast between the glittering spectacle of war and its horrific and brutal reality featured often in soldiers' personal narratives.[2] As this chapter will suggest, however, the contrast between the exterior and interior of war, its sublimity and its horrors, was often held in balance by combatants, as they wrote as both participants in and spectators of war. If the realities of war did not quite match their expectations, neither did they profoundly shake their cultural assumptions.

This chapter explores how the experience of combat and campaign was narrated by soldiers and what these accounts reveal about relationships between officers and men, between the soldier, the nation and the French enemy, and between civilian and military society. Although campaigning soldiers increasingly insisted upon their compatriots' ignorance of the true horrors of war, this did not, in Britain at least, result in the development of a closed military world bound together by its shared experience of combat and estranged from civilian society. Rather the cultural and literary resources which soldiers drew upon to narrate their experiences of war can be understood as forming a bridge between the civilian and military worlds, keeping open the channels of communicable experience between home and front. Moreover, the narratives of inner development, the displays of sensitivity to the sublimity and horror of war which feature in officers' accounts, did not necessarily engender a sympathetic identification with the common soldier who shared their hardships, but were often the means through which they asserted their difference from the unfeeling mass. The strict hierarchies that governed the army were thus reproduced as hierarchies of sensibility, reinforcing rather than collapsing, the boundaries between officers and men.

The British military experience, 1793–1815

Between the first expedition to Holland in 1793, and the final contest against Napoleon at Waterloo, the British army engaged in a series of campaigns that took it across Europe and the Mediterranean and beyond the continent to South America, the West Indies and Southern Africa. This chapter does not attempt to give a detailed history of the various theatres of war, though it recognizes that the experience of war and combat was shaped by the particular circumstances of each campaign, which varied in length, intensity and mode of operation. On certain expeditions, such as that to North Holland in 1799, the British soldiers went into action almost immediately upon disembarking. In the Peninsula meanwhile, the major battles were punctuated by long intervals, winters spent in quarters and exhausting marches through Portugal and Spain. Besides the actual experience of combat, each campaign presented different dangers, hardships and horrors for those involved. In the pestilent marshes of the island of Walcheren, where a force of 40,000 soldiers was dispatched in 1809, the greatest threat was malaria or the 'Walcheren fever', which infected over a quarter of the troops and left nearly 4,000 dead.[3] Late in 1808, the retreat to Corunna led by Sir John Moore involved an arduous march in appalling winter conditions through the Cantabrian Mountains, which resulted in over 5,000 deaths. Marching through torrents of rain, the army was forced to abandon men, women and children to die by the roadside. It was, in the words of one officer 'one of the most dreadful and fatiguing campaigns that was ever heard of in the annals of British history'.[4] While such hardships were an important aspect of the soldiers' experience of campaign, the primary focus here will be on the experience of combat.

This chapter is also more concerned with the soldier's experience of war than with the sailor's. As well as the crucial victories which the British navy secured during the wars, its fleets were from 1793 almost constantly in action blockading the French and seizing their ships, providing escorts to convoys carrying supplies to Britain and transporting troops for overseas expeditions. For sailors, therefore, the line between campaign and ordinary service was much less sharply defined. Moreover, in their accounts of naval engagements sailors were even more likely than soldiers to adopt a detached and impersonal mode of narration, in which the ship, rather than the individual, was the central unit of description. They therefore lack the personal perspective and detail that enables a reconstruction of the experience of war and its interpretation.

The experience of war is inevitably shaped by soldiers' expectations, by what they know and what they think they know about war. The bewilderment and disillusionment associated with the First World War, it has often been argued, was compounded by the profound disjunction between soldiers' inherited imagery of cavalry charges and pitched battles, and the mass industrialized warfare they encountered at the front. In turn, an imagined construction of the First World War would shape combatants' experience of later conflicts: when he fought in the Spanish Civil War George Orwell was disconcerted to find that he was engaged in night-time ambushes rather than digging trenches.[5] Though all wars, as Fussell observes, are worse than expected, shifts in the mode and conduct of warfare can widen the gulf between expectation and reality, forcing the soldier to rewrite received 'war scripts'.[6]

In terms of the mass mobilization of human, material and economic resources, the Revolutionary and Napoleonic wars inaugurated a new era of warfare that was reflected in the scale and intensity of the conflict. Prior to 1790, very few battles had involved more than 100,000 combatants; in 1813 the battle of Leipzig engaged 500,000 troops. This marked a decisive shift from the more 'limited' attritional warfare of the eighteenth century, where a massive commitment of troops was, if possible, avoided, and where material and ideological restraints inhibited the escalation of conflict, towards modern 'total war'.[7] At the same time, despite certain innovations in military tactics, the technology and conduct of warfare remained in many respects the same. On land, the army's mobility was still constrained by human and horse power, whilst battles continued to be fought at close quarters with muskets, cannons and swords. For the uninitiated, the experience of war is always a journey into uncharted territory, but continuities in the technology and material experience of war meant that for the men who fought in these conflicts it was not an entirely unfamiliar landscape.

If the fundamental material conditions of warfare differed little from those of earlier conflicts, historians have begun to point to broader intellectual shifts in the understanding of warfare that shaped how it was conducted.[8] This has been described by John Lynn as a transition from the military Enlightenment, with its emphasis on the scientific principles and formulae that governed war, to military Romanticism, in which psychological factors, *morale, esprit* and appeals to the passions of the troops, were increasingly understood as vital to an army's success. These insights would be developed and applied most fully in the French army, with Napoleon embracing and embodying the ideal of the Romantic military genius. At a strategic and tactical level, military Romanticism would be adopted only partly by the British army. Despite the efforts of Sir John Moore, the military establishment continued to look back to the classic techniques of the eighteenth-century Frederickian Prussian army. While military Romanticism may have had a limited impact on the British army at a tactical and organizational level, the influence of Romantic culture can nonetheless be discerned in how its soldiers narrated and interpreted the experience of combat, as they became ever more concerned with describing the inner experience of battle and their emotional and psychological response to what they had witnessed. As the understanding and narration of warfare developed in this period it came to be understood not just as a set of 'events', but as a series of 'experiences'. Soldiers' accounts thus came to centre on key episodes which would become a commonplace of military memoirs: the eve of battle, the baptism of fire and the aftermath of combat.[9]

'Shells into my soul': the experience and narration of battle

The army command appears to have done little to prepare soldiers psychologically for combat. Patriotic exhortations to the troops before battle seem to have been rare, though regimental commanders may have spoken a few words to remind their men of the need to maintain the unit's reputation.[10] Nor were they necessarily given any spiritual direction. 'The people of England', lamented William Wheeler, 'little think how her soldiers are neglected respecting spiritual aid'. In winter quarters, the army chaplains might, weather permitting, perform divine service for the troops on a Sunday, but once the campaign season began, according to Wheeler, even this nugatory attention to soldiers' religious welfare evaporated.[11] Soldiers tended to fall back on a mixture of superstition and fatalism. Presentiments of death were commonly recorded in memoirs. As John Kincaid later observed, such premonitions were remembered only when proved accurate though he knew of 'as many instances of falsification as verification', which suggests that they were an accepted mechanism through which soldiers could articulate their fears and anxieties.[12] Most commonly, soldiers' fatalism was summarized in the oft-repeated observation that 'every bullet has its billet'. As already noted, evangelical Protestantism's appeals to providence tended to resonate with the soldier's engrained fatalism, but even those who were not of an evangelical persuasion often drew on a providentialist framework to regulate their anxieties prior to battle. The night before an anticipated engagement, Captain John Charleton of the Royal Artillery wrote to his wife that, 'If Providence ordains I fall tomorrow know my beloved wife this night is spent in prayer for thy health and prosperity as well as all our little ones'.[13]

Soldiers also found more oblique ways to express their fears and anxieties prior to battle. This often centred on descriptions of the elemental and natural surroundings of the battlefield. During the 1799 expedition to Holland, Lt John Hunt described the evening before an engagement, as a 'particularly gloomy night':

> a hollow sea roaring close by and excepting which, the greatest silence reigned throughout, you might have heard a whisper....between us and the water was a space that appeared darker than the other parts that surrounded you, this was produced by a body of Russian Infantry...these circumstances combined and to a Person who had never before witnessed any thing similar, produced scenes for reflection and crouded [*sic*] many Imaginations on the Mind.[14]

This passage exemplifies a particular Romantic aesthetic: nature provides a sentient echo of human thought and feeling, and a vehicle through which the soldier can articulate fear and apprehension prior to battle.[15] Nature could also be harnessed to express the jubilant anticipation and confidence that, according to Rory Muir, was vital to troops' success in combat.[16] Over the course of the Peninsular campaign the violent thunderstorms that often preceded Wellington's victories would come to be seen by his troops as an omen of success.[17] The diary entry of John Aitchison, written after the British victory at Salamanca in 1812, for instance, described the thunder storm that broke as the troops marched towards the battleground:

> it seemed as if the fire was sent by heaven to assist our righteous cause – here was a grand and imposing spectacle ever was witnessed – upwards of 20,000 men formed in line and close columns of brigades within musket shot only seen by the flashes of lightning. In such circumstances, it is surprising how the mind turns every appearance to our advantage. This night we were confident of victory.[18]

Aitchison had by this stage already fought in several battles and experienced the misery of retreat, yet his capacity to view war as a sublime spectacle remained. The spectacle presented by a massed army was often cited by eighteenth-century theorists of the aesthetic as a prime example of the 'sublime'. The 'sublimity' of such a scene derived partly from its scale and the mental energy required 'to comprehend the vastness of that which commands our attention', as well as the association of ideas which it set in train. 'A fleet, or army, makes us think of power, and courage, and danger and presents a variety of brilliant images', wrote the Scottish philosopher James Beattie. Yet in order to produce that pleasing astonishment and admiration indicative of the sublime, the spectacle 'must be either imaginary, or not entirely pernicious'.[19] The pleasurable terror of the sublime spectacle depended upon the viewer's secure distance from violence and destruction. For soldiers such a spectatorial distance was impossible, yet they often recorded their rapture at being both participants and spectators in such scenes. 'My eyes was ravished at the sight,' wrote one private of the troops massed to face the French at Salamanca, 'I never looked at any scene with such delight'.[20] Others, however, were more attuned to the contrast between the external spectacle of war and the brutal reality, a contrast frequently drawn by opponents of war such as the Friends of Peace. As the British army crossed the river Ebro in 1813, their brightly coloured uniforms and glittering bayonets illuminated by a setting sun, Thomas Brown conceded that such a scene would make 'War a vision of romance to passerby' but that 'all its horrors would have been lost sight of.'[21]

British officers' accounts of the eve of battle displayed their ability to register sublime impressions and to reflect in some degree on complex emotional states. Their accounts of the experience of battle were more laconic. Writing in 1811, Sir Walter Scott bemoaned the flatness of soldiers' narratives of combat and their inability to communicate the immediacy and emotional charge of battle:

> I don't know why it is I never found a soldier could give me an idea of battle. I believe their mind is too much upon the *tactique* to regard the picturesque ... The technical phrases of the military art, too, are unfavourable to convey a description of the concomitant terror and desolation that attends an engagement.[22]

Scott's chivalric fantasies of heroic individual combat here collided with the realities of modern artillery, mass armies and collective manoeuvres. This period saw some move toward granting soldiers' greater autonomy on the battlefield, a trend exemplified by the green-jacketed rifle brigade, who, not coincidentally, would furnish some of the most well-known memoirists of the Napoleonic wars. Nonetheless, the conservatively inclined David Dundas strongly opposed any effort to foster soldiers' independent initiative and his eighteen manoeuvres continued to dominate military training.[23] Despite the much vaunted independence of the national character, it was widely believed that the French soldier showed greater independence of thought and a deeper understanding of military tactics than his British counterpart.[24] In battle, it was British troops' coolness and steadiness under fire, their ability to remain motionless while under attack and to preserve order in the midst of chaos that was often championed and contrasted with the frenzied enthusiasm of the French.[25] Fighting in close formations that marched and fired on command, the individual soldier was submerged in the collective military body and the opportunity for individual agency or heroism was necessarily limited.[26] Following his first experience of combat at Flushing in 1809, William Wheeler rather than recording the physiological and emotional temper of battle, simply recalled a series of commands 'Wheel into line', 'Prime and Load' and the manoeuvres executed by his subdivision as it 'broke into column' and marched in 'double quick time'.[27]

The majority of battle narratives, as Scott observed, assumed the detached tone and bird's-eye perspective of the battle despatch. For any subaltern with ambitions to become a field officer this was an aspirational form of writing, a professional skill that they sought to master. Such accounts were generally compiled from information available after the battle and tended towards the euphemistic: a particularly heated engagement might be described as 'a smart skirmishing', or a 'brisk engagement' in which the troops were 'teased with shells'.[28] Soldiers were, nonetheless, keenly aware that the battle despatch was more than an objective account of the course of the battle. As one of the key vehicles through which the British public were informed of the army's successes or sufferings, it also required some narrative flair. Officers often criticized the terse style of Wellington's despatches. As one lieutenant exclaimed after reading Wellington's terse account of the Battle of Salamanca: 'His Lordship may fight, but damn me if he can write … and a story well told is, you know, half the battle'.[29]

Some officers left more revealing depictions of the emotional impact of battle. Promising to record for his brother 'those facts I witnessed and relate exactly my feelings' George Hennell attempted to recreate the sensations experienced during his first combat:

> When the balls began to whiz I expected every one would strike me. As they increased I minded them less. I viewed calmly the town & to the whizzing of the balls soon became accustomed … I assure you my reflections were very serious ones and at the moment when I expected instantly to be summoned before the Judge that knows every thought as well as deed. These reflections threw shells into my soul that were more formidable than all the balls that were fired from the French batteries that night.[30]

Hennell was a devout Unitarian, whose bible reading frequently drew derisory responses from his more 'profane' fellow officers. The account of his 'baptism of fire' drew upon both a spiritual strain of reflection and the sensationalist psychology associated with Rational Dissent that was deeply concerned with the impact of experience upon the individual consciousness. Hence, his narrative was more concerned with the psychological effects of battle, the shells thrown into his soul, than with its physical impact.

Both the detached mode of battle narration and the more introspective vein that focused on the 'inner experience' could relieve soldiers from the responsibility of writing about the central feature and purpose of war: reciprocal killing and injuring. Although war can be understood as 'the most radically embodying event in which human beings ever collectively participate',[31] soldiers' tendency to suppress descriptions of the physical impact of combat has often been noted.[32] The experience of pain, wounding and death made visible the vulnerable human bodies that were elided in the image the collective military body which formed the principal unit of description in battle despatches and soldiers' narratives. Of course, during this period soldiers were more likely to die from disease and privation than in combat. Between 1793 and 1815, the British army lost an estimated 240,000 men, of whom perhaps only 27,000 died in battle or from their wounds.[33] Yet it was on the field of battle that the qualities of martial skill, physical bravery and honour that were central to constructions of military masculinity were put to the test. It was, as one officer put it 'a true trial of a man's courage...if you are ordered to charge an enemy you will discover what quantity of that necessary ingredient you possess'.[34]

Wounding itself had ambivalent connotations. In a military context, in which physical prowess and the aesthetics of the male body adorned in gorgeous uniforms were highly valued, the maimed or injured soldier was deprived of the bodily attributes that underpinned his masculine identity. As one officer, whose physical debilitation forced him to retire from the army, lamented, no longer able to exercise 'the manly step in which I trod to duty's call', he was now reduced to 'a captive wretch in woe's dark dungeon bound'.[35] For the ordinary soldier, it was often a more instrumental view of the body as a source of work which shaped their response to injury. A Highland soldier left blind after the first campaign to the Peninsula bewailed the affliction that had ended his military career leaving him a 'blind beggar, a burden to my friends'.[36] Yet, at a time when the body of Britain's most celebrated hero, Admiral Nelson, was conspicuously marked by his amputated arm and missing right eye, the wounded body could also become an emblem of valour and a model of masculine desirability.[37] The aesthetic value of a well-placed amputation was drily considered by Lieutenant John Mills, who imagined having his arm 'cut off in the interesting part, neither too high to be a stump, or too low to look vulgar'.[38] Moreover, it was often officers' ability to receive wounds with fortitude and equanimity, rather than their ability to inflict wounds, which served as the principal arbiter of masculine honour during this period.[39] When the two Freer brothers were wounded during the storming of Badajoz, their parents were informed that William had borne the amputation of his arm with 'such courage and fortitude that words could not express'.[40] His brother meanwhile wrote that while he had been injured through the testicles, 'it has not done my parts any material damage', an assurance that despite his wound his manliness remained intact.

The inner experience of wounding or the figure of the body in pain, are notably elusive in representations of war from this period, so that while 'bodies *en masse* are pierced, maimed, dismembered and crushed...descriptions of individual suffering are blandly erased'.[41] Soldiers' accounts of battle display a similar reticence regarding their own experience of wounding, and the death and wounding of others. Of course, this did not mean that graphic instances of the damage inflicted by war on the human body are entirely absent, or that soldiers were unaffected by the loss of comrades but, for the most part, their narratives did little to challenge the conventional imagery of the noble, heroic battlefield death. Descriptions of officers' deaths often replicated the stylized battlefield tableau of eighteenth-century military painting, exemplified by Benjamin West's *Death of Wolfe* (1770), in which the dying soldier, surrounded by his comrades, is a model of self-control and heroic self-sacrifice. Relating the death of a lieutenant in his regiment after the battle of Alexandria, one captain wrote:

> He was perfectly collected in an instant, & being aware that his wound was mortal, expressed his happiness in having fallen in the defence of his country, & said to me 'If this is death I die happy, I feel no pain, Write to my Mother but break the news of my death as tenderly as possible. To my brother Edward send my sword.' & then taking leave of every man of the Light Company by shaking each by the hand, was taken from the field without once uttering a groan or for an instant losing the same firmness & serenity of mind.[42]

Accounts of the death of a brother officer were usually accompanied by eulogies on their character and military accomplishments. These private acts of commemoration which reproduced publicly sanctioned discourses of 'honour' and 'sacrifice' can be understood as a means through which officers imbued such losses with meaning, and as a protective mechanism that reassured them their own service was not entirely in vain. Paying tribute to a young cornet who had died at Vitoria, George Woodberry inscribed the following lines in his journal:

> No he shall rank with other heroes blest,
> Whose lengthened years had drawn their talents forth
> With Moore or Vassall warm each Briton's breast,
> And teach our Youth to emulate their worth.[43]

The death of an officer did not always inspire such lofty sentiments. As losses within the regiment enabled those below to advance through the ranks without purchase, officers listing their unit's casualties after a battle would often note the number of steps which now remained to their achieving a higher rank. In a subsequent diary entry, Woodberry recorded this more cynical response: 'Capt. Kennedy is dangerously ill – Smith in high spirits, because he is next for the Troop and thinks K. may die'.[44]

If officers' accounts of their fallen comrades tended to describe idealized death scenes in which the messy reality and visceral agony of the battlefield were obscured, the death of the ordinary soldier was rarely commemorated in such elevated style. The regiment's rank and file could die *en masse*, but the names and fates of individual soldiers were rarely mentioned by officers. The common soldier was even denied the nobility and dignity in death accorded to officers. Thomas Browne compared their death throes to those of wounded animals:

> I have observed a Soldier, mortally wounded, by a shot through the head or heart, instead of instantly falling down, elevate his Firelock with both hands above his head, & run round & round, describing circles before he fell, as one frequently sees a bird shot in the air, flying round in circles as it falls to the ground & in like manner, Men, when badly wounded seek for the shelter of a stone or a bush, to which they betake themselves, before they lie down, for support & security, just as birds, or hares do.[45]

Whilst the officer in death became an exemplar of national masculinity, a model of resignation and stoic fortitude, in the view of the officer class the ordinary soldier in his dying moments became less than human, a mere animal.

The common soldier was not insensible to this view of the rank and file as disposable components of the military machine. 'I have often been tickled in reading the General despatches of the Army', wrote William Wheeler:

> when some Lord or General or Colonel has been killed and wounded. Fame takes her trumpet and sounds it through the world...General B is severely wounded, with a long panegaric [*sic*] of his military virtues and services...But who shall record the glorious deeds of the soldier whose lot is numbered with the thousands in the ranks who live and fight and die in obscurity.[46]

In response to this public indifference, Wheeler took it upon himself to commemorate the ordinary soldier, writing his own tribute to a comrade who had been severely wounded, acknowledging that whilst his exploits and fate might pass unnoticed by 'the world', his letter would serve as a memorial.

Soldiers, of course, were not just victims of violence but also its agents. Joanna Bourke has made a provocative case that soldiers in the twentieth century, far from recoiling from the infliction of violence, often exulted in the opportunity to shed the blood of others.[47] The bloodthirsty, and sometimes fantastical, accounts cited by Bourke, in which soldiers wrote gleefully of enemy kills, are rarely to be found in battle narratives from this period. Where they do occur, they were often couched in the jocular, sporting language of the hunt, with soldiers writing of 'bleeding my sword' or of striking a French 'buck'.[48] The narrative of Private Wheeler, however, does reveal some urge to 'kill-and-tell'. At St Jean de Luz he described his joy at avenging himself upon a French 'rascal' who had picked his pockets earlier in the battle. In another letter he candidly described an attack on a stray party of French dragoons that left 'not one to return to tell the tale' and secured a 'rich booty' for Wheeler and his comrades.[49] These episodes have a strong flavour of campfire storytelling, in which the rank and file exchanged adventures and exploits, a form of soldierly bonding and camaraderie that Wheeler fondly describes in his letters.

The wider absence of accounts of face-to-face killing may be attributed to the fact that only an estimated one in four soldiers ever actually killed an enemy, and most of these deaths were probably the result of unaimed musketry, or artillery.[50] Amongst officers, the reluctance to describe their role in the killing or wounding of enemy soldiers derived in part from sensitivity to their correspondents and the lack of an appropriate language to describe such deeds, but also from a deeper conviction that the British (or at least the English) military character was neither bloodthirsty, nor zealous in battle, but marked by coolness under fire and humanity towards the enemy. While cavalry officers were the most likely to engage in hand-to-hand combat, direct physical encounters with the enemy amongst the unmounted were rare. The weapons carried by infantry officers had little lethal value and they were more likely to conceive of themselves as 'directors rather than agents of violence'.[51] Again, officers' reticence regarding their personal involvement in mass violence was framed by an understanding that such dignified restraint was not necessarily exercised by the rank and file. Lieutenant Woodberry wrote dismissively of his regiment's 'wild Irishmen' boasting of the men they had killed.[52]

Though soldiers' narratives of the experience of battle are often marked by omissions and occlusions, the aftermath of battle is often described in much more graphic terms. The more evocative quality of these descriptions can be partly explained by the space for reflection which the conclusion of a battle allowed, but also by the wide range of literary and artistic imagery upon which soldiers were able to draw. As noted in Chapter 1, the Gothic provided a particular potent language for describing such scenes. Just as the evocation of horror in the Gothic novel often centred upon a single grotesque object, so soldiers also tended to focus on particular instances of the macabre.[53] Following one of the battles of the 1799 Dutch campaign, Lieutenant John Hunt was struck by the sight of a French soldier's half-buried corpse 'his toes, hands and about half of the arms sticking out of the earth with the hands crossing each other'. 'It was', he wrote, 'an object of so singular a nature I feel compelled to relate it'.[54] Others drew upon shared artistic frames of reference to convey a more panoramic view of the aftermath of battle to their correspondents. Describing the battleground at Salamanca one officer wrote:

You have frequently seen paintings of a field of battle with a hussar and his horse lying just as they fell and weltering in their gore; another with his head cleft in two, many in all positions, some dead, some wounded. This was one of the scenes for a mile.[55]

Despite the undoubted horror of such scenes, officers often returned to the battlefield days and sometimes weeks later to engage in sombre contemplation. George Woodberry deliberately returned to the field at Pamplona a few days after the battle in order to reflect upon the 'horrors of war'.[56] In the wake of the battle of the Pyrenees, William Keep traversed the mountainside where the skeletons of fallen soldiers lay bleaching in the wind and reflected on the awful juxtaposition whereby the 'beauties of nature blended with objects terrible to contemplate.'[57] This image of the natural landscape gradually assimilating the carnage of war attests once again to the influence of Romantic aesthetics on officers' battle narratives. Romantic culture was fascinated by the aesthetic effect of loss, ruin and decay and the workings of the passage of time to which all living and material things were subject.[58] The reconfiguration of the battlefield as a picturesque landscape seems to have allowed officers to modulate the rawness of their combat experiences into something that could be contemplated with a degree of detachment. These carefully staged meditations on the battlefield also provided another opportunity to display their sensitivity to such scenes, reassuring both themselves and those to whom they wrote that they had not become inured to them.

This Romantic vision of war, in which the battlefield became a sublime spectacle and object of contemplation, was supplemented by the depiction of war as grotesque that drew upon earlier modes of representation. A recurring feature in descriptions of the aftermath of battle was the sight of soldiers' wives traversing the field in search of plunder. By 1813 when the British army was at its greatest strength at around 330,000 men, it is estimated that somewhere between 20,000 and 33,000 women were also on campaign.[59] In soldiers' accounts they were often figured as unfeeling harpies preying with 'merciless avarice' on the dead, stripping both 'friends and foes' to the skin.[60] Officers often referred to the wives of the common soldiers as 'Moll Fathoms', a reference to the eponymous camp follower of Tobias Smollet's novel, who stalks the fields of war, poignard in hand, stabbing wounded soldiers and collecting her booty.[61] Women's engagement in such battlefield looting was most likely an economic survival strategy for military couples; with soldiers' wives poorly provided for on campaign they had to find other sources of income. The officers who described such behaviour, however, did not perceive it as evidence of uxorial devotion; rather it symbolized of war's capacity to draw forth the worst aspects of human nature.

The contrast which officers drew between the camp followers' calloused attitude to the miseries of the battlefield and their own more sensitive responses to such scenes is emblematic of a perceived hierarchy of feeling in military narratives. Sarah Knott has observed a similar arrogation of sentiment by the officers of the American Revolutionary army, for whom sensibility provided 'an elitist tool of competition and peer display'.[62] Although British officers' responses to war were shaped more by the introspective language of Romanticism than the lachrymose culture of sensibility, these displays of sensitivity seem to have played a similar role in elite self-fashioning, distinguishing officers from the coarseness of the common soldiery. While officers' accounts of the eve of battle attested to their ability to register sublime impressions and reflect on complex emotional states, they tended to deny ordinary soldiers' capacity to feel and reflect on such occasions. George Hennell, a 'gentlemen volunteer' who joined the army in the Peninsula as a private in the hope of obtaining a commission without purchase, was shocked by what he perceived to be the rank and file's coarse indifference and empty bravado prior to battle. To Hennell they seemed entirely lacking in fear or feeling, as they raucously discussed 'what they will do with the fellow they lay their hands on. What they intend to get in plunder'. 'It is more like a fairtime', he concluded, 'than the beginning of a bloody action'.[63] Accounts of the aftermath of battle similarly differentiate between officers' ability to reflect upon the experience of battle and ordinary soldiers' indifference to such melancholic scenes, 'singing and swearing...while their comrades lay round them in heaps of dead'.[64] While war was increasingly understood by the elite male as a *bildung*, which strengthened and ennobled their inner character, such interior development was denied to the other ranks. Musing on the different impact which the sustained experience of campaign had on the characters of officers and men, one officer observed that the latter appeared 'to become daily more ferocious & less fit for return to the duties of citizens' whilst the officers seemed to become 'more thoughtful & humane, & more anxious to exert themselves in softening the misery with which they were surrounded.'[65]

Certainly, accounts by the rank and file suggest that the aftermath of battle was often suffused by an almost carnivalesque atmosphere as the tension and discipline of the battlefield gave way to more riotous behaviour. After the battle of Vitoria, in which there had been a general dissolution of order amongst the ranks, Wheeler described the scenes in the British cantonments as like 'an Arab camp after a successful attack on some rich caravan' a scene of 'hurly burly, frolic and fun'. A fair was established to sell the plunder which soldiers had seized from the retreating French forces where they traded wine, cognac and portraits of Napoleon. The 'market soon changed into a grand maskerade [*sic*]', as British soldiers wandered the camp dressed in French uniforms heavily weighted with military honours, and in women's dresses 'richly embroidered with gold and silver'. Yet such raucous behaviour can also be understood as a means of coping with the strains and sorrows of battle. As Wheeler observed, men drank, sang and danced after a heavy engagement in order to drive away 'the blue devils'.[66]

'To the honour and glory of the British nation': comrades, regiment and nation

While the aftermath of battle prompted officers to contemplate the 'horrors of war', these were also the moments at which both officers and soldiers reflected upon the personal bonds and attachments forged by campaign, and the wider import of the battles in which they fought. Unsurprisingly, the loss of comrades provided one of the dominant themes of these reflections. As one officer remarked to his sister after the death of the companion with whom he had 'messed, lived and fought' for nearly five years, 'Excuse my warmth, but I had rather have lost some relations'.[67] For a private in the 71st regiment the sight of mass graves filled with soldiers after battle was greeted with indifference, but the death of his companion and 'bed-fellow' Donald, whose body he had found heaped upon a cart by the back door of the military hospital at Flushing had a profound impact. 'There was a vacancy of thought and incoherence of ideas', he wrote, 'that remained with me for some time; and it was long before I could open a door without feeling an unpleasant sensation'.[68] Even without a medicalized discourse in which to situate such experiences, the intense emotional connection between the opening of a door and the death of his comrade displays signs of what would now be categorized as post-traumatic stress.

The importance of comradeship in sustaining men through campaign and combat is now a cliché of military scholarship, but its role in combat effectiveness and troop morale was only beginning to be theorized fully in this period.[69] Amongst the rank and file there was a rudimentary sense of the importance of 'small unit cohesion' to troops' confidence in battle. When a new draft of soldiers recently sent from England was distributed through Wheeler's regiment, separating him from a comrade 'who had stood next to me in many fights', he immediately objected and arranged to be positioned once again next to his old battle companion.[70] The bonds of trust and affection forged within a regimental unit were also gradually coming to be seen as vital in achieving military success. The expedition to north Holland in 1799 was notable for its use of militiamen, an act issued earlier that year having allowed militia volunteers to enrol in the regular army on unusually favourable terms.[71] Several accounts of the expedition attributed its failure to the introduction of these new volunteers into regiments where they 'were unknown to their officers and by them unknown.'[72] The concept of *morale* developed by French military theorists was just starting to filter into British military discourse.[73] After the failed first assault on the Castle at Burgos in 1812, Lieutenant John Aitchison wrote critically of the decision to splinter the British forces into separate detachments:

> in such operations prodigies are required of men and they are realized through confidence ... where much is required let every assistance, real or imaginary, be brought forward and on such occasions employ whole regiments or detachments from one corps – their honour then becomes pledged and from a reciprocity of confidence in the Officer and Soldier and Soldier and Officer, even seeming impossibilities are overcome.[74]

An understanding of the importance of 'reciprocity of confidence' between officers and men in enhancing combat effectiveness did not mean that divisions between leaders and led were submerged in a unifying rhetoric of 'brothers-in-arms'. Aitchison was relatively rare in the sympathy he displayed for the plight of the ordinary soldier; in most officers' accounts the welfare of the rank and file, their deaths and hardships, are marginal matters. That is not to say that officers were unconcerned with the well-being of their men – it was, after all, their duty to ensure their welfare and good conduct – but the development of a collective military fraternity based on the shared experience of campaign was not part of the narrative of war recorded in their diaries and letters.

If the experience of campaign often fostered close bonds between men and their comrades, overseas service could also augment corporate and collective identities within the army. The eight infantry divisions into which the army was divided all acquired nicknames during the wars many of which alluded to their roles and performance in the Peninsular campaign. The Second Division became known as 'The Surprisers' after taking the French by surprise at Arroyo, Molinos and Almaraz. The Fourth Division was known as the 'Enthusiastics' on account of their conduct at the Battle of the Pyrenees.[75] Active service similarly added to the array of customs, traditions and symbols around which regimental identities coalesced. When the Spanish mistook the figure of the Brittania on the regimental badge of the 9th Foot for the Virgin Mary, they were dubbed the 'Holy Boys'. To commemorate their involvement in the Battle of Corunna and the death of General Sir John Moore, a black braiding was incorporated into the uniform of the regiment's drummers. The 48th meanwhile would mark their distinguished performance at Talavera by celebrating an annual 'Talavera day'.[76]

The regiment, as noted in Chapter 2, provided a crucial mediator between the soldier's personal honour and the honour of the nation. It was as part of a regimental unit that junior officers' conduct in battle was judged by the public. Particular instances of collective gallantry were noted in the battle despatches and marked through the distribution of battle honours, which recognized a unit's battlefield accomplishments by incorporating the title of the campaign or battle into the regimental colours. In the weeks following a battle, subalterns anxiously scanned the military gazettes to see if their regiment's participation had been mentioned with approbation. A lieutenant in the 53rd Foot recalled that his father had declared it 'the happiest day of his life' when he read the account of the Battle of Talavera, in which his son's regiment had been praised for its gallantry and discipline.[77] Equally, if a regiment was judged to have behaved badly it could be considered a source of deep personal shame for its officers. This is well-illustrated by the case of Lieutenant George Woodberry of the 18th Hussars, a regiment whose reputation rapidly floundered towards the end of the Peninsular campaign.

When he embarked for active service in Spain at the beginning of 1813, Woodberry was eager to go into action and confident that the regiment would not 'disgrace themselves' but would 'return home...with Laurels'. This optimism was misplaced. The Battle of Vitoria in June 1813, though a significant victory for Wellington, was followed by excessive looting by British troops and both the men and officers of the 18th Hussars were heavily implicated. The Duke of Wellington singled out the officers for his particular disapprobation, banning all promotion within the regiment. The 18th was the only regiment engaged at Vitoria not to be awarded a battle honour. This was a source of intense anguish for Woodberry. 'I want language to express the grief I feel on the Occasion', he confided in his journal 'to think I should have come out with a Regiment who have contrary to all expectation acted so differently'. This profound sense of shame was compounded by the knowledge that reports of the regiment's disgrace had been carried to England. By September 1813, Woodberry recorded that: 'Every subaltern officer of the Regiment that is out here seems anxious to leave the service, all disappointed – I may say disgusted – having entered the Service in a Regiment that all Ireland [the 18th were nominally an Irish regiment] & England look'd to for something great.'[78]

How far soldiers understood their war experiences in terms of a collective national narrative, or saw their sacrifices and successes as contributing to the glory of a larger national cause is more difficult to evaluate. Soldiers often expressed an investment in the institutional reputation of the British army without subscribing to a broader understanding of themselves as agents of the nation. And victories on the battle field were hymned as testaments to the gallantry and worth of the British army. Following the Battle of Alexandria in 1801, Capt. Jennings proudly declared it a 'campaign that will forever resound with the highest honour and glory to the name of a British soldier...the British army this day proved itself worthy of its name, and manifested to the world what it is capable of performing.'[79] Significantly, Jennings, was an Irish Catholic officer, and his self-identification with the honour of the British army suggests how the experience of campaign could provide a context for the articulation of broader pan-British allegiances. As we have already seen, this did not necessarily mean that national particularisms were entirely subsumed. After the fiercely fought Battle of Talavera, an officer from Co. Sligo assured his brother that 'none but *true Brittons* and *Real Irish* could withstand so heavy a fire', pointing to the possibility of a complex and complementary relationship between Irish and British identities.[80]

Scottish troops seem to have similarly derived a degree of pride from the rising reputation of the Highland regiments during the wars. Private Alexander Gellen of the 92nd regiment recorded for his parents the plaudits paid by General Cathcart to the Highlanders' gallantry after the battle of Copenhagen, 'he said...my eyes could not believe to see you march up so camly [sic] so unconcirned [sic] before the guns and...then rush forwards like so many wild Lions.'[81] In repeating these laudatory speeches, the Scottish soldier absorbed and affirmed prevailing constructions of the Highlander as a warrior possessed of an almost primitive ferocity and physical courage, a construction that set these regiments apart from the dominant model of British military character which emphasized coolness and restraint.[82] In his verses on the Dutch expedition, The Gaelic soldier-poet Corporal Alexander MacKinnon would similarly invoke Abercromby's tribute to the 'proud and untreacherous' (*árdanach neo-fhoilleil*) Highland troops.[83] Yet Mackinnon's poetic accounts of the army's campaigns also referred to his involvement in a broader pan-British (*Breatannaich*) endeavour, suggesting how the military experience of the Highland soldier may have exposed him to the wider concepts of Britishness.[84] Indeed, invocations of 'Britishness' tend to occur more frequently in accounts by Irish and Scottish troops than in those by English officers. The London-born William Thornton Keep, for instance, celebrated the victory at Vitoria as a day 'that will be numbered in the brilliant annals of old England'.[85] The phrase 'old England' was relatively capacious and was regularly employed by Irish and Scottish troops to refer to their homelands.[86] Nevertheless, the tendency of non-English soldiers to locate their service within a broader British framework appears to support the argument that the idea of Britishness resonated most at the margins, rather than at the centre of the Union.[87]

If the euphoria and exaltation generated by a military victory could thicken the affective bonds that connected the individual soldier to his regiment, army or nation – bonds, which, as we have seen, could also be attenuated by the experience of shame or disgrace – any consideration of the relationship between combat experience and identity must also take into account the galvanizing influence of another equally powerful emotion: hatred towards the enemy. According to Bell, the aggressive dehumanization and demonization of the enemy partly explains the intensity and ferocity with which the Revolutionary and Napoleonic wars were fought. Abandoning the shared aristocratic code of military values and the battlefield *politesse* that gave eighteenth-century warfare its more restrained or 'limited' character, the French republic moved towards a conflict based on 'absolute enmity'.[88] However, as the case studies selected by Bell suggest, a deep-felt animosity between opponents was most evident in those conflicts, such as the Vendée, Calabria or the Iberian Peninsula, where the French forces faced a popular insurgency. The role which national antagonisms played in encounters with more conventional forces, like the British, is less clear.

As noted in Chapter 2, the British armed forces did not, on the whole, cultivate an overtly ideological environment or barrage their men with patriotic propaganda and it seems that the dehumanization of the enemy played little role in the military establishment's understanding of combat effectiveness.[89] British soldiers were unlikely to represent their French opponents as the cringing, undernourished fops of popular xenophobic discourse. In combatants' accounts from the 1790s, there is evidence of a negative and derogatory stereotype of the French republican soldier, the uncouth and squalid sans-culotte too ignorant to understand the ideals he was supposedly fighting for, and French troops were sometimes referred to as 'Carmagnoles' after the popular revolutionary ballad they sang on their way into battle. Whereas the soldier of the French republican army may have been viewed as a radically different, ideological opponent, the Napoleonic soldier, stripped of the overt Jacobinism of his predecessor and dressed in elaborate uniforms, seems to have been a more familiar and culturally intelligible figure. The splendid uniforms worn by the Napoleonic officers were often objects of intense admiration. Before the battle of Pyrenees, Thomas Browne described the dashing appearance of the French Grenadiers, who, ranged before the British lines 'in their Bear-skin Caps with red feathers, & blue frock coats appeared the most warlike body of Troops possible'.[90] Under Napoleon the French had proved themselves a formidable military power and the attitude of British soldiers was often more emulative than contemptuous. As one officer explained to his father: 'You have no idea how Superior they [the French] are in the art of war & the English even in endeavouring to copy them make but a poor resemblance'.[91]

A degree of mutual respect, then, often prevailed between the French and British forces and soldiers readily conceded the gallantry and skill of their opponents in battle. Fraternization between the opposing sides was relatively common. In 1810, the French cantoned at Santarem invited British officers stationed nearby to their amateur theatricals with the promise of absolute freedom of return. The outposts of both armies were often situated very close together and soldiers would cross the line to drink and share stories with their French counterparts. These friendly exchanges sometimes concluded with a promise of kind treatment were either side to be captured by the other.[92] Warm friendships could also develop between British soldiers and French prisoners of war. During his convalescence at a military hospital in Fontarabia, William Wheeler struck up a firm companionship with a young French corporal, who spent hours by his bedside relating anecdotes of his service and confiding his longing to return to home.[93] In such cases, a soldierly solidarity based on the shared experience of military service and its attendant hardships could transcend national antagonisms. According to John Westcott, the men were always happy to share their grog with a French prisoner of war, whom they looked upon 'only as a brother soldier in distress'.[94] Moreover, there seems to have been an understanding that the French and British participated in a shared code of military honour. The soldiers of both nations were horrified by the mode of warfare practiced in the Iberian Peninsula and perceived its forces, both regular and *guerilla*, as particularly savage and cruel.[95] French prisoners of war, according to one officer, lamented that 'the troops of the two first nations in the world should cut one another to pieces for such a parcel of brutes as the Spaniards'.[96] William Wheeler and the French corporal had initially bonded through their mutual contempt for the Spanish and Portuguese. The cordial relations that often existed between French and British soldiers, their regard for each other's military capabilities and their shared contempt for those who deviated from the rules of war suggest that vestiges of the transnational military community of the *ancien régime* survived into the era of national armies.

The theatre of war: actors and audience

The relationship between the military identity forged within the British army and a broader patriotic attachment to the wartime nation, can be more carefully tracked by analyzing soldiers' responses to domestic representations of the army and its campaigns. Soldiers often arranged for newspapers to be sent to them on campaign and showed a keen interest in how the war was presented to the British public. Amongst officers the most popular paper was the governmental *Courier*, a choice which suggests the generally conservative leanings of this group. As already noted, tributes to regimental gallantry or reports of regimental disgrace in the British press, were eagerly pored over and provided an important link between the soldier and the nation. At the same time, as the wars progressed, a gulf of incomprehension could open up between the army and the nation it supposedly served. Stationed in the pestilential marshes of the island of Walcheren where many soldiers had succumbed to disease, an officer observed how 'ill timed and cruel' it was to read parliamentary debates on the progress of the war and find '"much laughter" so frequently in Italics in the same column'.[97] This tension between public opinion and the views of the campaigning army risked becoming particularly acute during the Peninsular campaign. Officers were notably critical of what they saw as the British public's unfounded faith in, and enthusiasm for, the Spanish cause. When they found the Spaniards' patriotic mobilization to be far more lacklustre and shambolic than they had been led to believe, they increasingly questioned the nation's war aims. As John Aitchison remarked after the Battle of Talavera: 'John Bull will be kept in remembrance that he is superior to a Frenchman and this has been I believe all we ever got by our expeditions to the continent'.[98]

Aitchison's identification of John Bull with the civilian nation would be echoed by many other officers, only very rarely did they imaginatively identify with this supposed emblem of British national character. Indeed, although the figure of John Bull momentarily acquired more martial characteristic during the wars, he remained in essence an embodiment of British civilian society.[99] It was a model of national character that could seem remote from the experiences and military identities of campaigning soldiers.

The estrangement between the British soldier and the civilian population at home, embodied in the figure of John Bull, is well-illustrated in these verses transcribed by a subaltern officer in Spain in 1813:

> Oh plenteous England, comfort's dwelling place
> Blest be thy well fed glossy John Bull face!...
> Inoculated by wild Martial ardour
> Why did I ever leave thy well-stored larder?
> Why fired with scarlet-fever in ill time
> Came here to fight & starve in this cursed clime![100]

Embodying variously the commercial character of the small shopkeeper and the rustic stolidity of the yeoman farmer, John Bull furnished a figure around which officers' resentments with the civilian nation could coalesce. These resentments could be inflected by class hostility, as officers bemoaned the 'surly, discontented' dispositions of an imagined 'John Bull', begrudging the taxes that funded the army and inveighing 'against his sovereign, his minister, and everybody in the country who has the rank of gentleman'.[101] Most commonly, John Bull was figured as the audience towards whom their performances in the theatre of war were staged, so that a particular victory might be noted as 'one which must give pleasure to John Bull'.[102]

The metaphor of the theatre of war appears frequently in officers' accounts and illuminates some of the complexities of British military identity and its relationship to the British civilian nation. Amateur theatricals were a particular popular pastime amongst British officers on campaign, one of the practices through which they maintained their connection to the class whose interests they were defending, and their identity as 'gentlemen' as well as soldiers. With its colourful costumes, choreographed movement and regimental music, the army was in many ways a highly theatrical institution.[103] The roaming life of the soldier on campaign could be compared to that of a party of strolling players and their impromptu encampments likened, as one officer put it to 'a fête champêtre or vauxhall'.[104] The idea of war as an elaborate performance staged for the benefit of a domestic audience provided a particular framework through which soldiers understood their war experience and exertions.

While the distinction between soldier-actors and their audience suggests a growing gulf between military and civilian spheres, it was partly soldiers' ability to view and narrate war as both actors and spectators which prevented such polarization. As already noted, when viewing the instruments of war from a distance soldiers were able to retain their appreciation for war's pomp and pageantry. As they witnessed sieges, battles and bombardments they often had recourse to theatrical imagery; a well-executed engagement, for instance, could be described as 'stage-like skirmishing'.[105] This tendency is particularly evident in descriptions of night-time engagements and bombardments, where the drama and visual intensity of the scene was heightened by the spectacle of a ship or town burning against the night sky. The assault on Copenhagen in July 1807, during which the city was bombarded for three successive days and its wooden buildings set ablaze, prompted enthusiastic descriptions from officers who watched the city in flames from the safety of the British fleet. It was, according to John Christopher Harrison, 'the grandest sight I ever beheld...It would make an excellent thing for a panorama'.[106]

This reference to the relatively new technology of the panorama, which had been developed in the 1790s and was often used to depict naval engagements, suggests how far soldiers' experience and narration of war was filtered through a civilian optic. The introduction of the panorama has been linked to the 'detheatricalization' of warfare, the cylindrical canvas supposedly enabling viewers to position themselves in the midst of battle and to view the scene from the 'authentic' perspective of the soldier.[107] Yet, in continuing to use theatrical imagery in their accounts of military actions, officers seem to have eschewed the very immediacy that such representational techniques promised the public at home. By composing what they witnessed into a spectacle, they were able to maintain the connections that bound them to their civilian selves and to preserve some of their belief in the romance of war. Hence, a diary of the bombardment of Copenhagen began by asserting that this 'stands first in the list of grand, awful and beautiful sight I have yet beheld' one which 'would form an elegant subject for a Transparency' and then proceeded to describe the continued shelling of the city over three nights as if they were successive acts in a play, the third night/act being attended 'with improved Scenery & machinery'.[108]

Fussell has pointed to a similar tendency towards the dramaturgic in British soldiers' narratives of the First World War, a tendency which he attributes to 'the vividness of the sense of role enjoined by the British class system'.[109] In Georgian Britain the relationship between theatricality and social status was perhaps even stronger, as class and power rested upon elaborate performances of prestige within the 'theatre of greatness' and aristocratic dominance of the military ensured that this theatricality was carried over into the army.[110] Most of all, theatricality and the dual role of the soldier-actor/soldier-spectator allowed for the possibility that once they had played their part and shed their colourful uniforms soldiers would be able to return to their civilian selves and that 'just as a play must have an ending, so might the war'.[111]

For some the conclusion of the war was the point at which they could admit to the horror they had witness and the strain they had endured. William Keep, who had entered the service in 1808 filled with youthful enthusiasm and chivalric ideals, wrote to his mother 'Now that I am no longer exposed to such dangers I need not conceal from you that war is a heart sickening and most revolting scene of bloodshed, from which I am very happy to escape'.[112] Yet for many soldiers the conclusion of the war and the defeat of

Napoleon seem to have affirmed rather than challenged the righteousness of the cause in which they had fought. The British victory prompted an excited rush of superlatives: the 'annals of history' did not record a more 'glorious, active and eventful' campaign, wrote one officer.[113] They self-consciously exulted in their involvement in this epoch-making event. John Rous of the Coldstream Guards looked forward to marching into London:

> with a regiment that has assisted to drive the French from Lisbon into their own Country, with an army which has proved to the world the superiority of the British arms compared with those of the French, and which by their example have assisted in bringing matters to a crisis so glorious to England, and added to the future welfare of the world.[114]

In their letters and journals soldiers thus echoed and amplified the acclamatory and triumphalist rhetoric of the victorious nation. This personal investment in the prestige of the army and unquestioning acceptance of the rectitude of the war may be explained by the fact that, for officers at least, these campaigns played a vital role in securing their class interests: the defeat of French ensured the security of their property and prestige, whilst their sacrifices on behalf of 'John Bull' vindicated elite dominance at home and in the armed forces.[115] The response of the rank and file, who would receive little recognition for their sacrifices and who faced an uncertain future, was more muted. Wheeler looked forward to landing on his native shores with 'many a brave and gallant comrade, with whom I have braved the dangers of many a hard fought battle'.[116] It was this small group of comrades, the subject of Wheelers' tales and tributes in his campaign narrative, that endowed his personal war with purpose and meaning. Yet Wheeler's enthusiasm for military life remained undiminished; the end of the war was tinged with regret as it meant the loss of the structure that had shaped his daily existence for nearly five years and he hoped that it would not be long before he should hear 'the sound of the soul-stirring bugle again'.

Conclusion

In his analysis of the Revolutionary and Napoleonic wars, David Bell boldly links together the emergence of new understandings of the sublimity and horror of war and the authority endowed by combat experience with the ascendancy of militarism and the polarization of the military and civilian spheres. In this chapter we have seen how British soldiers often narrated their experiences of combat and campaign in a way that privileged their sensitive responses to the spectacle and tragedy of war, stressed the elevating influence of war on the individual character, and gloried in the success of the British army. Yet we know that these wars did not produce a mass narrative of disillusionment nor did they result in the aggressive imposition of military values upon civilian society which Bell, thinking primarily of the Prussian and French models, identifies as a consequence of the Napoleonic conflict. Instead, Britain was able to shrink the army and retreat from the militarized rhetoric of the wartime nation with relative ease.

The explanation for this is complex and various, but soldiers' narratives can afford some insight into how the relationship between wartime nation and its armed forces was negotiated during these years. Officers drew on a range of cultural and literary forms – romantic, picturesque, spectacular – to represent their experience of war. Instead of driving a wedge between civilian and military society, these shared languages acted more like a bridge. As we shall see in Chapter 7, the British home front also struggled with the tensions between the spectacle of war and the suffering it caused. For officers, the ability to reflect sensitively on what they saw and experienced was a way of maintaining the connective tissue that bound them to their civilian selves, an assurance that they had not been coarsened or calloused by military life. It thus affirmed the prevailing gentlemen-amateur ethos of the British army, the sense that their military persona was just one of a number performed roles and identities. In continuing to view the ordinary soldier as bereft of such refined sensibility, the officer class denied that the shared experience of suffering and hardship could form the foundations of a collective military ethos that transcended class and rank. Indeed, if an intensified attachment to the military and its values did emerge from the experience of combat and campaign it was more likely to be found within the rank and file, for whom the dislocation from civilian society was more profound and the closed world of the regiment more significant.

4
Travellers in Uniform

In a letter of 1810 Lady Harriet Elliot, daughter of Lord Minto, turned her thoughts to the campaign in the Iberian peninsula, in which many of her acquaintances were engaged. 'If the Spanish Business has been unprofitable in other respects', she observed:

> it has at least given an opportunity to many of our young men to leave Bond Street and Newmarket and see a little of the world, and I should think that traveling into a Country so new to everyone as the greater part of Spain at a time when their attention & interest is excited by the Scenes that have been passing there, would be more useful to a young man, than a winter at Paris or Vienna was formerly.[1]

Lady Harriet Elliot's comparison of the military campaign in the Peninsula to the Grand Tour may seem a little strained. Yet, at a time when access to the continent was severely limited and the majority of ordinary Britons were confined to the nation's 'island prison', soldiers and sailors were conspicuously mobile. One of the central but frequently overlooked aspects of the soldier's experience of campaign during this period is the opportunity it presented for travel and contact with unfamiliar cultures. British soldiers' and sailors' accounts of their journeys across and outside the European continent provide a unique record of a collective encounter with foreign cultures and landscapes. Soldiers were often forced to develop close links with the local communities amongst whom they lived and, in the case of the Peninsular campaign, with whom they fought. These relationships were by no means always amicable, but the experience of living in Spanish or Portuguese billets brought the army into close proximity with the inhabitants of the region. Military campaigns, as Elliot noted, also required them to travel to countries that were not on the standard tourist itinerary.

Recognizing the centrality of travel to the soldier's experience provides a different angle on the relationship between war and national identity. For it was these day-to-day encounters, as much as encounters on the battlefield, which brought to the surface the complex and sometimes inchoate understandings of national identity and national difference that combatants carried with them on campaign.[2] As British soldiers journeyed to the West Indies and Egypt, the Iberian Peninsula and France, the Low Countries and Denmark, they set about mapping the unstable boundaries of European civilization and surveying the intricate markers which they understood to define that civilization.

Soldiers as travellers

Research on the eighteenth- and nineteenth-century travel narrative has tended to focus on the grand tourist or intrepid explorer rather than the soldier traveller. Yet soldiers' accounts were as much travel narratives as they were narratives of war, as attested by the numerous works written by members of the army that catered to public interest in the customs and culture of those countries in which they fought. In his *Letters from Portugal, Spain & France* (1815) the army surgeon Samuel Broughton deliberately excluded any reference to military affairs, concentrating instead on the architecture, agriculture and peoples of the three countries.[3] Such publications fed into a broader appetite for travel literature amongst the British reading public. Works on foreign travel, voyages and exploration constituted one of the most popular genres in this period, and it is therefore unsurprising that many soldiers modelled their letters and journals on the travelogue.[4] Of course, the experience of travellers in uniform who come to a country to fight is very different from that of the tourist who comes in peacetime for pleasure, or the explorer. When George Robert Gleig published his account of the Peninsular campaign in 1825, he was at pains to distinguish his memoir from those of 'military tourists' who sought to enlighten their readers on the habits and character of the Iberian peninsula. 'No man who journeys through a country, in the train of an invading army', he maintained, 'ought to pretend to an intimate acquaintance with the manners of its inhabitants. Wherever foreign troops swarm, the aborigines necessarily appear in false colours'.[5]

British soldiers' experience of foreign countries was undoubtedly distorted by the wartime conditions under which they travelled. The Iberian Peninsula which these troops encountered was in the throes of a brutal and desperate guerrilla war against the occupying French forces, in which many of the restraints of conventional warfare had been entirely abandoned. Many features of Spanish and Portuguese life which, as we shall see, were read as evidence of the inhabitant's regressive practices were themselves products of resistance to French influence on the Peninsula: the traditional dress that Britons took as an emblem of Spain's backwardness had been adopted as a patriotic gesture against French fashions; the resurgence of bullfighting, which was seen as proof of the barbaric inclinations of the Spaniards, was a reaction to the 'enlightened' reforms introduced by the pro-French regime from the 1790s.[6] Though British officers made some effort to learn the languages of the Peninsula, for the most part linguistic difference remained an insuperable barrier to meaningful contact. As one officer commented, without a shared language, the culture of the region was scarcely legible 'you merely look over it as a picture' and 'try to guess what it is intended for'.[7]

For officers, playing the tourist provided an important means through which to maintain their civilian identity whilst on campaign. Service overseas allowed them to display the taste and connoisseurship associated with polite masculinity, as they picked their way through the rubble of war-torn European cities to visit museums and art galleries, wrote detailed notes on Spanish palaces and cathedrals, and applied their classical learning to Egyptian antiquities. For the rank and file, service abroad presented an unprecedented opportunity to extend the limited compass of their lives, and the lure of travel and adventure in distant lands was often cited as a motivation for enlisting. Between 1793 and 1815, British forces served in Holland, Spain, Portugal and France, as well as in extra-European campaigns in the West Indies, Egypt, South American and South Africa.[8] The naval theatre of war was even more global in scope with operations extending across the Mediterranean, and the Atlantic and Indian oceans. While sailors' global voyages undoubtedly yielded many opportunities to see distant and 'exotic' lands, this aspect of the naval experience does not appear to feature so prominently in surviving personal narratives. It was the army's land-based campaigns that produced the richest and fullest accounts of cross-cultural encounter and which are consequently disproportionately represented in the following discussion. The long conflict in the Iberian Peninsula, in particular, created an extended 'contact zone' between British soldiers and the peoples and cultures of Southern Europe.[9]

In soldiers' letters and journals the moment of departure for overseas service was often narrated as the point at which a sense of national belonging began to crystallize. For many, the voyage out marked the first time they had been at sea, a novel experience that was often fraught with anxiety as they faced the prospect of sea-sickness, shipwreck and an induction into the strange and unfamiliar 'wooden world' of the British navy. Unlike the majority of continental European soldiers, for whom the passage from the 'homeland' into 'foreign' territory was registered through gradual shifts in language, costume and architecture, or the crossing of geographical boundaries, such as the Pyrenees and the river Memel, the sea provided a clear demarcation between 'home' and 'other' for all British soldiers, whether they voyaged for a day to Holland, several weeks to Lisbon or several months to the West Indies. As the transport ships sailed out of port and along the coast, the voyage also generated a sharpened awareness of Britain's identity as an island nation. Lt G. J. Sullivan described the emotional impact as he left Britain's 'fertile and romantic shores' to set sail for Portugal, 'everyone seemed to gaze around with a wistful eye that clearly spoke – "ah Britain when shall we see thee again?"'[10] Britain's natural border and the bridge that allowed it to exert a global reach, the sea acquired a particular affective charge for those serving abroad. As one officer wrote upon seeing the Bay of Biscay, invoking the panegyric to England in Shakespeare's *Richard II*, 'what sensations did the view of the sea excite in us as we stood looking "toward that land, that dear dear land, that England"!!'[11] Upon reaching the Portuguese coast following the disastrous retreat to Corunna in 1809, a private soldier of the 71st regiment gazed out upon the expanse of water and similarly reflected on the indelible connection between 'Britain and the Sea', two words, he wrote, 'which cannot be disunited. The sea and home appeared one and the same'.[12]

The departure from Britain, then, partly created the context in which soldiers and sailors understanding of the nation and of 'home' could take shape in a process of nostalgic reconstruction. Indeed, up until the twentieth century the most widely diagnosed psychological affliction in the military was 'nostalgia' or 'homesickness'. The condition had been diagnosed as early as the Thirty Years War, when the soldiers of the Spanish army of Flanders dispatched to the Netherlands with little hope of leave were identified as suffering from *mal de corazón*. One of the earliest accounts of the illness listed among its symptoms constant expressions of praise for one's native land, combined with disparagement of other regions, and described it as a disease which particularly affected soldiers. For much of the eighteenth century, medical interest in nostalgia had been largely confined to the German-speaking areas of Europe. From the 1790s onwards there would also be an intensified interest on the part of French physicians. The conscript soldiers of the French revolutionary army, drawn from remote villages, were understood as peculiarly susceptible to nostalgia. Known in France as *maladie du pays*, two epidemics supposedly swept though the French army in 1793–1794 and again in 1799, manifesting themselves in a listlessness, lack of appetite and depression amongst the troops.[13] Nostalgia was also a recognized term in British medical discourse; in 1781 the regimental surgeon Robert Hamilton diagnosed the illness in a Welsh soldier stationed in Ipswich, who, denied furlough, had succumbed to a severe depression.[14] The wars of 1793 to 1815 saw no mass outbreaks of nostalgia amongst British troops, nor did the term filter into soldiers' narratives, which often declared their zest for the 'gypsy life' of a soldier. Nonetheless, at times soldiers could express an overwhelming homesickness. During the expedition to Egypt, Thomas Peacoke described his depression of spirits and longing to be 'under the shade of some friendly tree in England', concluding dejectedly 'I sigh after Old England most amazingly'.[15]

The receipt of letters often set in train a series of nostalgic recollections and soldiers on active service frequently begged their correspondents not to omit any detail of family life or local gossip, however trivial. The letter functioned as a material token of home and an imaginative bond between soldiers and those they had left behind; it could narrow the distance between home and front, but could also serve as painful reminder of that distance. Writing from the malarial marshes of the island of Walcheren, William Keep reflected on the contrast between his present situation and 'the happy spot from which your letter was directed...it set my fancy at work in picturing you seated at the cheerful window, with the balsams, and the balmy breezes you was literally inhaling, compared with the vapours that hang over this unfortunate island'.[16] Images of the familial hearth, perhaps the most resonant symbol of home, recurred frequently in soldiers' correspondence, the reunion around the 'cheerful fire' acting as the focal point for their nostalgic yearnings.[17]

The nostalgia for home could also be triggered by particular dates in the national calendar. For the hunting and gaming officers, the commencement of the shooting season could carry their thoughts back to friends and family, whilst an Irish soldier might be seized by an overwhelming desire to return home on St Patrick's Day.[18] For nearly all troops, Christmas was a particular period for nostalgic reflection and they often went to great lengths to procure plum-pudding or other national foods to mark the day which, as one officer observed, 'involuntarily makes an Englishman think of roast beef and mince pies'.[19]

The Iberian Peninsula

It has been estimated that the British Army made as many as 211,000 soldier deployments to the Iberian Peninsula between 1808 and 1814. Although the actual number of soldiers who served in the Peninsular campaign would have been slightly lower (the deployment figures include those who had two 'tours of duty'), these figures nonetheless give some sense of the scale of the militarized encounter that took place between British troops and the peoples and culture of Spain and Portugal.[20] The Spanish revolt against their Napoleonic occupiers and British military intervention in the Peninsula in 1808 had seen the centuries old enmity between Britain and Spain replaced by a new enthusiasm for, and interest in, Iberian culture and politics. At the time, Spain and Portugal were two of the least visited of the Southern European countries. Spain's inaccessibility and the lack of an established infrastructure for tourists meant that the area was rarely included on the eighteenth-century Grand Tour.[21] British knowledge of the Iberian Peninsula was largely drawn from Cervantes' chivalric romance and the picaresque writings of Alain de Lesage. As Walter Scott observed in June 1808, 'to have all the places mentioned in Don Quixote and Gil Blas now the scenes of real and important events...sounds like history in the land of romance'.[22] Like Scott, British officer's often expressed their astonishment at suddenly finding themselves embarked for 'the land of romance'.[23] *Don Quixote* and *Gil Blas*, books that many would have read in their youth, were the most commonly referenced works in their accounts of the campaign. With their

Spanish settings, both works provided a convenient map onto which journeys across Spain could be plotted, and a means of anchoring new experiences in familiar fictional worlds. Upon arriving in a new town or village soldiers often commented that this was the place where Gil Blas had been imprisoned, or where Sancho Panza had been tossed in a blanket.[24]

The romance of the Iberian Peninsula, however, quickly gave way to disillusionment. One of the most frequently narrated passages in soldiers' letters and journals from the Napoleonic wars is the voyage into Lisbon. In 1812 Lt Sullivan described the impressive prospect that unfolded before him as he sailed into Lisbon harbour 'everything tells you that you are approaching a magnificent city'. Yet upon disembarking he found 'nothing but filth & dirt of every description'. The Portuguese capital, he concluded, was like 'a fine woman with a beautiful face – but filled with duplicity & every vice'.[25] This ironic contrast, between Lisbon's glittering white exterior and the squalor and vice within, featured repeatedly in soldiers' narratives and set the tone for much of their writing on the Peninsula.

Before disembarking, British soldiers were enjoined to treat the inhabitants, their allies, with respect, and warned that any failure to do so would exact a severe punishment.[26] The British command was particularly anxious to avert any possible religious conflict between their troops and the Catholic peoples of the Iberian Peninsula. General orders were issued instructing British soldiers to pay full and proper respect to Catholic processions. This had unintentionally comic consequences. Unable to distinguish between communion rituals and the public acts of penance enforced upon local malefactors, British troops would ostentatiously doff their hats and present their arms to the offending criminal, believing that he was 'the Host'.[27] The practice of extending regimental hospitality to the local population, which officers used to ease military–civilian relations when stationed in British garrisons, was continued on overseas service. In 1813, for example, the officers of the Coldstream Guards encamped at Puebla, improvised a ball for the local elite to celebrate George III's birthday where they served a lavish supper consisting of all their rations and punch served in camp kettles.[28] Officers, nonetheless, often commented that they had little meaningful contact with the Spanish and Portuguese and that it was the rank and file who adapted more easily to the manners of the country and showed a greater facility in acquiring the language.[29] As one officer noted, the men of his regiment 'never stay anywhere long without becoming associates with its inhabitants; our train of washer women is nearly triple what it was'.[30]

Despite such instances of friendly relations between the British forces and their Iberian allies, soldiers' complaints against the country which they had been sent to defend began almost immediately upon landing. The filth of Lisbon, where pedestrians were liable to have chamber pots emptied upon their heads, the squalid appearance of its inhabitants, and the swarms of monks that filled the streets were constant themes in their correspondence and diaries. 'What an ignorant superstitious, priest-ridden, dirty, lousy set of poor devils are the Portuguese', exclaimed William Wheeler shortly after his arrival, 'Without seeing them it is impossible to conceive there exists a people in Europe so debased. The filthiest pig sty is a palace to the filthy houses in this dirty, stinking City'.[31] Wheeler's comments point to the close association between dirt, disorder, superstition and Catholicism that coloured soldiers' encounters with the inhabitants of the Iberian peninsula, one which drew on long-standing connection between pollution, real or imagined, and alterity.[32] These perceptions of difference in turn, shaped and reinforced the soldier-traveller's imaginings of home. Comparing the Portuguese peasantry to the 'polished and enlightened inhabitants of my own Happy Country', William Paterson, a Volunteer soldier from East Lothian, concluded that they were 'worse than Barbarians' and looked back on the 'cold & bleak Hills of my native Country as an Elysium when contrasted with the sultry suns, the ruined villages, the slothful & indolent natives and the immense uncultivated plains of this Southern clime'.[33]

The process of contact and comparison through which soldiers constructed their understanding of 'home' and 'other' drew upon and reinforced a series of binary oppositions – cleanliness/filth, enlightenment/superstition, and industry/indolence – that can be understood as subsidiaries of a single master binary: Protestantism/Catholicism. As noted in Chapter 2, the British army was neither a repository of Protestant values nor a bastion of anti-Popery. Any nominal Protestant identity within the armed forces was further diluted once it went overseas. The number of chaplains who accompanied the army was small; they were generally perceived as inattentive in their duties, and had little contact with the soldiers. Yet British troops' sudden immersion in Catholic culture seems to have affirmed a residual Protestant identity, more cultural than theological in character, as they mobilized the full range of stereotypes and suspicions associated with British anti-Catholicism. British troops treated Catholic ritual and iconography with a mixture of fascination and horror. Given the highly theatrical nature of the British military, it is unsurprising that officers were attracted to the glitter and pageantry of Catholic ceremonies, which, as one lieutenant observed, were 'very imposing'.[34] However, for the majority, exposure to Catholic rites triggered a residual Protestant sensibility, which valued simplicity and plainness over display and decoration: the mass was therefore dismissed as mere 'mummery', the profusion of statues and icons as 'idolatry' and the rich ornamentation as 'gee-gaws'.[35] While soldiers were often quartered in monasteries and convents, they continued to view Catholic orders with suspicion, accusing their members of fattening themselves on the misery of the population and remaining indolent whilst their nation strove to repel the French foe.

The anti-Catholic rhetoric which suffuses British soldiers' accounts of the Iberian Peninsula was supplemented by an understanding of Spanish Catholicism as particularly cruel and sinister, an association nourished by tales of the Holy Inquisition's fanaticism. Although William Wheeler befriended an Irish friar during his stay in Madrid, he found that he could not overcome his prejudice against the Catholic priesthood. Having read the history of the Inquisition he remained convinced that 'the priests only want the power to establish the infernal court again.'[36] The Gothic novel was a key medium through which such images of Mediterranean Catholicism were transmitted. Matthew Lewis' best-seller *The Monk* (1796) presented a disturbing picture of Spanish religious life populated by depraved monks and malicious abbesses. The combination of a prurient fascination with Catholicism's arcane ritual, and horror at its perceived irrationality, that characterized the Gothic is also evident in officers' narratives.[37] This is particularly evident in accounts of Spanish nuns, visits to convents being one of the favoured pastimes of British officers during the Peninsular campaign. While narratives sometimes recorded charming scenes of youthful nuns serenading their authors with Spanish airs from behind their grille, these encounters were shadowed by a conviction that beneath this beguiling surface there lurked dark and malign powers. Attending the investment ceremony of a young novitiate, one lieutenant expressed his pity for this 'poor miserable creature' and speculated that she had been 'compell'd to that life by a cruel father or mother to enrich some more favourite child'. The same officer also readily believed that an inmate of the convent had been immured and starved within its walls after eloping with a French soldier.[38] Both episodes could have been lifted straight out of a Gothic novel.

British troops' Protestant sensitivities were no doubt further aroused by the experience of living amongst peoples who, they believed, deemed all non-Catholics 'heretics'. This produced an unsettling reversal of positions as the travellers became the objects of religious prejudice. Writing resentfully of the Portuguese tendency to dub all Englishmen heretics, Private William Wheeler observed that if an English soldier wanted to befriend the natives they had to pass for an Irishman, only then would they be 'considered one of themselves, a good Christian'.[39] As Wheeler recognized, in the Iberian Peninsula, Irish was considered synonymous with Catholic, consequently his Irish comrades often enjoyed a very different, much less fractious, relationship with their Iberian hosts. Rifleman Benjamin Harris recalled the surly reception he and his comrades received upon entering a Lisbon shoemakers shop 'the only words I could at all comprehend being "Bonos Irelandos, Brutu Englisa [sic]"'.[40] The locals' sense of affinity with their Irish co-religionists could also express itself through a more tolerant attitude towards soldierly excesses. After illegally commandeering a bullock from a Portuguese local, a crime which could be punishable by death, one Irish sergeant recalled that the charges had been dropped once his comrades had assured the animal's owner that the offender was an Irishman and a 'good Catholic', arguments which, the sergeant noted, proved 'irresistible'.[41]

Whereas the experience of overseas campaign, particularly during the Peninsular war, could reaffirm for Protestant soldiers a rudimentary sense of a religiously grounded national identity, for Catholics in the British army these encounters must have had a quite different resonance, illuminating the transnational bonds which they shared with a larger religious community. During the expedition to South America, Captain Peter Jennings had his newborn son baptized in a Benedictine monastery in Brazil, one of the fathers of the order acting as godfather.[42] The head of a Lisbon monastery, where the Connaught Rangers had been quartered upon their arrival, called the 88th 'his own regiment'.[43] One of the most significant expressions of the continued connections between Irish and continental Catholicism was the network of Irish colleges spread throughout Spain, France and Italy, which were, in a sense, the religious counterpart to the Irish brigades of European armies. In the eighteenth century these seminaries functioned as 'lifeboats that preserved the Irish priesthood' in the face of the penal laws.[44] These colleges, and the broader network of émigré Catholics in the Iberian Peninsula, took a particular interest in the religious welfare of the Irish soldiery, with chaplains from the Irish college ministering to Catholic troops stationed in Lisbon.[45] These shared affinities necessarily complicated any sense of national difference based on religious antagonism, though Catholic soldiers could also experience the Iberian Peninsula as radically strange and 'other'. Looking back on his time in the Peninsula, the Catholic private Charles O'Neil stressed the fundamental tensions between the Spanish and the British 'so unlike in their customs and manners, so different in language, religion and education'.[46]

In many soldiers' accounts the oppositional model of national difference was supplemented by a more complex understanding of a hierarchy of nations calibrated according to differing stages of civilization. This stadial model of national development, particularly associated with the Scottish Enlightenment, provided a crucial taxonomy for classifying societies in terms of their levels of political, social and economic advancement, from primitive nomadic 'savages' to progressive commercial economies. According to this schema, Britain's commercial pre-eminence, urbanized landscape and culture of improvement positioned it at the apex of civilization and functioned as a point of comparison by which to survey and assess other cultures. The encounter with the Iberian Peninsula was therefore narrated as a temporal transition from British modernity to an earlier stage of historical development. The primitive state of Portugal, according to one officer 'carried the mind back to centuries past', while another observed that Spain was 'at least a century behind England in everything'.[47] For soldiers, the foundations upon which British modernity rested became clearer as they noted their absence from Iberian culture and society. They were surprised by the lack of a middle class and provincial elites, and by the relative scarcity of 'gentleman's seats'.[48] Coming from a country in which an increasingly sophisticated postal network and established press culture had helped to connect together geographically diverse regions, British officers reported critically on the low levels of national integration and national consciousness they discerned in the Iberian Peninsula. The inhabitants, according to one officer, had little idea whether 'Spain and Portugal is a Continent, an island or a peninsula'.[49] 'The Galicians', observed another, 'are as perfectly ignorant of what their neighbours the Asturians are about as the moors can be; and the arrival of a common courier in a Spanish town creates a greater sensation there than the arrival of an ambassador extraordinary would do in England'.[50]

At the same time, narratives of civilization allowed for differentiation between Portugal and Spain, usually to the advantage of the latter, whose inhabitants were described as 'much cleaner, better dressed, and altogether neater and more industrious' and as exhibiting 'greater tokens of civilization in their domestic concerns'.[51] As Mary Louise Pratt observes, such civilizational narratives and attendant discourses of progress and improvement encouraged eighteenth-century traveller's to interpret the landscapes they encountered as 'unimproved' and to evaluate what they saw in terms of commercial potential.[52] Whilst this way of seeing is conventionally attributed to European's colonial encounters with non-European landscapes and cultures, it also shaped soldiers' accounts of Spain and Portugal. As they marched across the Peninsula, troops frequently commented on the region's levels of cultivation and agricultural development. This attention to the agricultural potential of the land arose in part from the campaigning army's need to provision its soldiers from local resources. Responding to his father's surprise on hearing of the lack of supplies and rations which the British forces endured in the Peninsula, John Aitchison, an officer from East Lothian explained that:

> There is such an inconceivable difference between the state of cultivation in the Peninsula and Great Britain that in calculating on the operations of an *auxiliary* army in Spain you must divest yourself of every recollection of the *improved condition* of Scotland…. So much indeed is Spain behind the improvement that I have doubts whether the strongest language I could make use of in a letter would be sufficient to convey to you an idea of the extreme barbarity of the inhabitants and the consequent impoverished state of the soil.[53]

These instrumental assessments of the Iberian landscape also reveal traces of the appropriative or expansionist impulse associated with colonial discourses. Soldiers frequently admired the fertility of the land and its potential for development; some even dreamed about settling in the country and purchasing a small estate.[54] Underpinning these fantasies was a belief that the Peninsula only required the civilizing and improving influence of the British to release its full potential. As one officer commented, 'What would an Englishman make of this country – They would be able to supply half the continent with corn and fruit'.[55]

In appraising the culture and landscape of the Iberian Peninsula these military travellers were engaging with a long-standing debate regarding Spain and Portugal's uncertain position within European civilization.[56] According to the so-called 'Black Legend', Spain had been consistently represented from the early modern period as cruel, fanatical and lacking those qualities commonly regarded by other Europeans as civilized.[57] From the Spanish passion for bullfighting to the brutal tactics employed by the *guerrillas* against the French, British soldiers drew ample evidence to support their claim that the peoples of the Peninsula were characterized by a 'savagery' and 'barbarity', which, according to one soldier, 'can scarcely be credited to Europeans'.[58] Placing Portugal firmly outside the boundaries of European civilization, the military chaplain Samuel Briscoe dismissed it as 'a Hottentot country'.[59] Ironically perhaps, many viewed war as an instrument through which the Peninsula could be raised to meet these standards of civilization. British troops noted approvingly the civilizing effects of the French occupation of Spain, which had led to the abolition of the Inquisition and the introduction of more 'enlightened' government.[60] Even the destruction wrought by war could be viewed as having positive consequences. Noting the recent introduction of the harrow plough amongst Portuguese farmers, John Aitchison reflected that the devastation caused by marauding armies had 'been of benefit to the country in exciting the natives to exertion which left to themselves they would never have made'.[61] Though many British officers remained sceptical as to whether the Spanish bid for independence would establish a new era of constitutional liberty, others were more hopeful, believing that the Peninsula campaign would lay the seeds for Spanish regeneration and that 'renewed & engrafted with British valour & liberty' Spain could recover 'her ancient fame & renown'.[62]

This narrative of Spain's decline from its former proud position as a bulwark of Christendom tapped into a further eighteenth-century discourse: classical republicanism. According to this cyclical view of history, empires, such as the Spanish and Portuguese, were subject to decay and degeneration as they lost their martial character under the corrupting influence of luxury and despotic government.[63] While cyclical accounts of national history were gradually being supplanted by more linear, civilizational narratives, they continued to provide a powerful and highly gendered language for understanding national difference. British soldiers were notably critical of the Portuguese and Spanish troops they fought alongside. After the Battle of Talavera in 1809 the Spaniards were widely accused of cowardice, of having thrown down their arms and abandoned the field.[64] This confirmed the perception that the Spanish were fatally lacking in the qualities of masculine, martial independence, that combination of 'valour and liberty', which distinguished the British. In the words of one officer they had 'plenty of powder but no balls'.[65] The *guerrilleros'* efforts to expel the French from their country inspired British soldiers to adopt a more admiring view of the nation's peasantry, in whom they discerned traces of a 'manly independence' not dissimilar to that of their own countrymen. In contrast to 'freeborn Britons', however, this national manliness had become enervated and effeminized under a corrupt and despotic regime, consequently, as one officer commented 'the Spanish character so individually independent, is nationally dependent'.[66]

As noted in Chapter 2, soldiers' subjection to a strict system of military discipline and subordination often problematized their performance of a national masculinity that accorded central importance to personal autonomy and independence. Moreover, as the rigours of campaign reduced their scarlet regimentals to faded tatters and the anxiety of combat quelled their martial ardour, the gulf between soldiers' fantasies of military heroism and the realities of military life, no doubt, widened further. Contact with and differentiation from national 'others' provided one mechanism by which the tensions that threatened the coherence of British military masculinity could be resolved. It was impossible to esteem these foreigners, one officer explained, because 'they are deficient in manly principles which particularly elevate Englishmen above the Inhabitants of any other Country'.[67] At its most basic, the contrast between the virile, masculine British forces and their effeminized allies was articulated through a comparison of their respective physical attributes. Describing the entrance of the Royal Horse Guards into Salamanca in 1812, an observer emphasized the effect of this imposing spectacle of British manhood upon the Spanish: 'so different did they appear to the astonished Inhabitants from their own diminutive Horses and their degenerate Soldiers that they seemed to look upon these noble Troops as more than mortal'.[68]

Soldiers' observations on the customs and manners of the Spanish and Portuguese also led them to pay close attention to their domestic relations. A key aspect of the construction of national difference during this period involved the observation and comparison of the relationship between the sexes that prevailed in different countries. Enlightenment sociological and ethnographic discourses stressed the multiplicity of gender relations exhibited by different societies and judged nations' claims to civilization according to the relative status and treatment of women.[69] Britain prided itself on the elevated condition of its countrywomen, and this perceptual frame was clearly employed by British soldiers who wrote critically of the jealousy of the Spanish men and the narrow confinement in which 'these ruthless modern vandals' held their women folk.[70] As Lt William Coles observed of the Portuguese:

> by custom great restrictions are placed on the women, in fact you never see a Female who has any pretensions to respectability on the outside of the Door of the house ... Altho' the men have little courage or conduct to boast of in the field, where real courage is requir'd, they are the greatest Tyrants in the World over the female part of their family.[71]

Through these various observations on national difference a more unified image of British military and national masculinity could emerge, obscuring the tensions that threatened the individual officer's male identity and bolstering his sense of British masculine superiority. In comparison to the diminutive and cowardly Spanish and Portuguese, the British soldier was physically impressive and courageous. As a 'freeborn Briton' whose liberties were ensured under the British constitution, he exemplified a manly independence that contrasted with the enervated and dependent state of the Iberian Peninsula. And unlike men in less civilized nations, he did not abuse his position of manly superiority by tyrannizing over women, but treated them with humanity.

Mapping European civilization

As we have seen, soldiers' accounts of Southern Europe, though partly concerned with the particular differences between Britain and the Iberian Peninsula, were also engaged in a wider process of surveying and defining the boundaries of European civilization, and delineating Spain's and Portugal's problematic relationship to European modernity. The distinctions between Europe and its 'others' were further elaborated by those involved in campaigns beyond the continent's borders. If the sea marked the definitive boundary between 'home' and 'away' for British soldiers and sailors voyaging to Europe, the trans-Atlantic passage to the West Indies involved an additional line of demarcation as ships crossed the Tropic of Cancer. The crossing-the-line ceremony, discussed in Chapter 2, not only functioned as a carnivalesque reversal of the shipboard hierarchy, but also dramatized the transition from a broadly defined 'European space' into the 'torrid zone' of the tropics.

The West Indies was the destination which British soldiers and sailors most dreaded. The struggle for control of the Caribbean colonies and the lucrative trade in sugar, spices and slaves constituted the deadliest campaign of the wars. Between 1794 and 1796, nearly 40,000 men died on West Indian service.[72] Whole regiments were decimated by the yellow fever. This high mortality rate tended to dominate soldiers' accounts of their Caribbean service. In Jonathan Leach's recollections his experiences in Antigua and Barbados were presented as an unrelenting catalogue of disease, suffering and death, summarized in the chapter contents as:

Death of the Commander in Chief...The Regiment suffers dreadfully from yellow fever; Hurricane; Officer's funeral; The military governor & his brigade major die...Death of Sir William Myres, the new Commander in Chief in West Indies; Terrible mortality in his family; Death of the new Governor of Antigua; Great mortality in the 96th regiment in Antigua...Sudden death of several soldiers from extensive heat; The

68th regiment is sent to Antigua; Its immense losses by climate; More funerals... My health begins to suffer.[73]

The West Indies largely figured in such accounts as a zone of pestilence which consumed and destroyed British soldiers. While both the French- and British-occupied islands on which the army was stationed supported complex and highly intricate Creole societies, soldiers did not devote the same degree of attention to the culture of the Caribbean as they did to that of the Iberian Peninsula. Perhaps the cultural hybridity of West Indian Creole society, its status as both 'foreign' and 'colonial', problematized the act of comparison and differentiation, though more probably the pressing issue of survival in a hostile climate checked any interest in ethnographic observation.[74] One feature of Caribbean society, which was difficult to ignore, however, was slavery. Jonathan Leach recalled his horror at seeing both men and women forced to labour in the plantations under the blistering noonday sun and registered his contempt for the system by taking potshots at the slave driver.[75] A more strident critique of slavery can be found in the narrative of Andrew Bryson, a Belfast United Irishman impressed into West Indian service after the 1798 rebellion, who described in some detail the miserable condition of the enslaved population and the brutal character of the planters.[76] Of course, the British army was actively involved in suppressing the slave rebellions which had erupted in the Caribbean and many British soldiers appear to have accepted the necessity of defending the plantocracy against the 'cruel' and 'savage' insurgents.[77] The colonial gaze through which such travellers viewed the West Indies focused primarily on the racial 'otherness' of the black population and the fertile abundance of the islands. Arriving in Barbados from the British garrison in Halifax, Thomas Henry Browne remarked on the sudden transition from 'the rugged and leafless shores of North America, and its fair inhabitants' to 'the luxuriance of the Plaintain and the Coca-nut trees, and the squalid darkness of the negro'.[78]

Physical and racial markers of difference became more important as soldiers and sailors travelled outside the areas they identified as European. Narratives of campaigns in Europe tended to describe in great detail the customary dress of the countries through which they travelled, seeing, for example, in the antiquated costume of Southern Europe proof of the region's inferior civilization. By contrast, when James Lowry a naval surgeon landed on the coast of North Africa in 1798, his first voyage, as he put it 'out of Europe', he was thrown into 'a state of consternation' by the sight of the inhabitants, 'their manners and complexion so different from our own'. Such a response did not necessarily involve the privileging of physical difference over differences in culture and custom. 'Complexion' in the eighteenth century did not merely denote skin colour, but could also be used to identify a variety of traits and dispositions derived from the particular climatic conditions in which a people lived, a meaning suggested by Lowry's coupling of 'manners and complexion'.

It was only towards the end of the century that differences in skin colour came to be seen as a primary signifier of difference; for much of the period racial characteristics were understood as malleable and susceptible to different influences.[79] These continuing indeterminacies in constructions of racial difference are evident in Lowry's account of his participation in the Egyptian expedition of 1801. Catching sight of his face in a mirror, deeply tanned by the scorching Mediterranean sun and swollen from insect bites, he saw a surprising and unfamiliar figure and was suddenly convinced that 'I was transformed into an Arabian; but as my rational ideas got the better of my ocular speculations, I was soon convinced that I was still an Irishman'.[80] Like the soldier who feared that immersion in the Catholic culture of the Peninsula might erode his native Protestantism, exposure to the North African climate could complicate the distinction between the self and foreign 'others'. In both instances the meaning and importance of religious and physical markers of identity was brought into question and simultaneously affirmed.

The team of 170 French *savants* that accompanied Napoleon's invasion of Egypt in 1798 with orders to research every aspect of Egyptian culture, topography and antiquity provides one of the most striking examples of the conjunction of war, ethnography and travel in this period. Although the British expedition to Egypt had no such official exploratory aims, accounts of the expedition such as Captain Thomas Walsh's *Journal of the Late Campaign in Egypt* (1803) tapped into the popular fascination with the 'antique' land of Egypt, providing a detailed and lavishly illustrated description of the region and its Turkish rulers. British officers' classical interests were clearly stimulated by their encounters with the monuments of ancient Egyptian civilization as they visited the Pyramids, temples and other sites of antiquity. Capt. Dundas of the Royal Staff Corps and Lieut. Desade of the Queen's German Regiment managed, after repeated visits, to decipher the inscription on the base of Pompey's Pillar, a feat which, Walsh proudly noted, 'none of the French Savants or Literati appear even to have attempted during their long stay in the country'.[81] British military engagement in Egypt and the Middle East during the wars fuelled public and scholarly interest in the region: the British seizure of the Rosetta Stone from the French in 1801 would spark a century of Anglo-French Egyptological rivalry.[82]

If the officer's experience of Egypt was shaped by his knowledge of classical history, for the ordinary soldier and sailor the voyage to the Middle East involved an encounter with a culture and country largely known from their reading of the Bible. British military involvement in the eastern Mediterranean at this time prompted an intensified engagement with the 'Holy Land' and utopian visions of the 'New Jerusalem' amongst plebeian millenarian movements at home.[83] In turn, the campaign in the Middle East acquired a particular significance for the more devout soldier as it opened up the prospect of actually seeing the lands described in the Old Testament. As one private wrote: 'I felt more than usual interest in looking at those places, from what I had read of them in the Scriptures. Little did I think, in reading of them when a boy, that I should one day see them.' The expedition therefore became a means of testing the authority of the scriptural account. As his ship sailed towards Alexandria, under a heavy fall of rain, his fellow soldiers 'who were of a deistical turn', began to question the accuracy of the biblical prophecy that no rain would fall on Egypt as punishment for its infidelity. It was, the soldier confessed, an 'apparent contradiction' which he found deeply unsettling. Yet, upon landing 'on Scripture ground' his faith was reaffirmed. Passing the ruins that marked the former 'glory of ancient Egypt' and observing the 'wretchedness' into which the Egyptians had sunk, he saw this as a 'fulfilment of Jehovah's threatenings' and 'evidence to the truth of the Scriptures'.[84]

James Lowry, the brother of an Ulster Presbyterian minister, similarly interpreted the Egyptian campaign through a biblical lens, relating what he saw to particular passages of scripture. When the British convoy arrived in Marmorice Bay he declared his pleasure at being:

In that quarter of the globe where, according to the sacred records, the Divine Being planted the Garden of Eden ... and likewise that this quarter became the nursery of the world after the Deluge whence the descendants of Noah dispersed different colonies into other parts of the Globe.[85]

Lowry's reference to the 'descendants of Noah' points to the continued influence of a theological view of ethnicity, which posited the monogenic origins of the human race from Noah's sons: Ham, Shem and Japhet.[86] When Lowry's ship anchored close to Rhodes, for instance, he described it as the place 'peopled by the grandsons of Japhet'. This interpretation, rather than maintaining a rigid binary between the European 'self' and non-European 'other', allowed for degrees of consanguinity between the peoples of the earth. Although by the late eighteenth century such interpretations were being gradually supplemented by polygenic theories that stressed the distinctiveness of human races, Lowry's observations suggest that they remained an important element in the diverse vocabulary with which differences in ethnicity were described and explained.

While Egypt's centrality to both classical history and the history of the Judaeo-Christian world made it an object of fascination for military travellers, their appraisals of modern Egyptian culture and society emphasized the degeneration and stagnation of Egyptian civilization, rehearsing a vision of the country languishing under Oriental despotism familiar to readers of the French *philosophe* the Comte de Volney's *Travels through Syria and Egypt in the years 1783, 1784 and 1785* (1788).[87] Although the traditional early modern distinction between Christendom and the Islamic world would surface in soldiers' remarks on the Mohammedan 'infidel', for the most part they paid little attention to the religious cultures of the Middle East, focusing instead on secular markers of difference and well-worn stereotypes of Eastern indolence and barbarity.[88] Once more, the seclusion of women 'kept in close confinement by those savages' was read as evidence of the despotic and regressive practices of the East.[89] The veiled woman was the object of intense curiosity. When a group of British sailors armed with swords tried to force some of the local women to reveal their faces, it almost resulted in a serious diplomatic rift between the British and their Ottoman allies.[90] One soldier reflected on the strangeness of this practice to, as he put it, 'European eyes'. The assumption of a European gaze, as distinct from a British or Protestant perspective, characterized accounts of Egypt expeditions, indicating how intra-European differences could be dissolved by extra-European encounters as soldiers charted the boundaries of European civilization.

Making connections

Surveying the customs of the Egyptian peasantry, a Glasgow-born soldier on the 1801 expedition remarked upon the similarity between the plaid-wearing 'Arab shepherds' and their counterparts in the Highlands. The huts in which they lived, he noted, were 'mere hovels, in comparison to which the worst cabins in Ireland are palaces'.[91] The identification of affinities between foreign cultures and landscapes and the 'Celtic' peripheries of the British Isles points to the complex relationship between 'home' and 'abroad' that often emerges in soldiers' narratives from this period. As observers mapped what they saw back on to the United Kingdom it often exposed fault lines within the nation.

The filtering of unfamiliar landscapes through the imagined geographies of the British Isles featured most frequently in soldiers' observations on the Spanish and Portuguese countryside. As he marched out of Lisbon through the rolling Portuguese countryside and into Spain, the Dorsetshire officer George Bingham repeatedly noted the similarities between the Welsh and Iberian landscapes. Porto de Moz was 'most romantically situated' and 'very like the Vale of Llangollen', whilst the more mountainous regions of the Spanish Extremadura, he observed, were 'as fine as the wildest parts of Wales'.[92] Though couched in the appreciative language of the picturesque, by making connections between the scenery of Wales and that of the Iberian Peninsula, Bingham was also drawing an implicit contrast between the gentle, domesticated and cultivated English landscape and the more rugged and barren terrain of the Celtic fringes.[93] It was not until he came to Burgos with its 'well-cultivated valleys, trees alongside the side of brooks and frequent villages', which he judged to be the 'pleasantest' spot he had visited, that he was reminded of his native Dorset. The Scottish highlands played a similar role in English soldiers' topographical imagination. As one officer wrote from San Ramon, 'our situation here is most romantic and I suppose nearly as destitute of cultivation as the Highlands of Scotland'.[94] Given British soldiers' tendency to position the Iberian Peninsula outside the norms of European civilization, the similarities which they discerned between this region and the British peripheries seemed to underline the divergent levels of progress within Britain itself.

The connections between the 'other within' and the 'other without', however, were most emphatically expressed in reference to Ireland. As one of the British army's major garrisons, a large proportion of soldiers would have been stationed there at some point in their military career, and it provided a recurring reference point in their travels through the Peninsula. Ireland functioned as a synonym for squalor, poverty and backwardness. The miserable huts of the Portuguese peasantry were frequently compared to the proverbial Irish cabin,[95] whilst a visit to a market fair in Coimbra, wrote one officer, 'immediately brought Ireland to my recollection ... the throng, the blue cloaks of the women, and the dirt and filthiness of it all'.[96]

Campaigns in Northern Europe could reveal more positive affinities between 'home' and 'abroad'. During the Walcheren expedition, William Keep noted approvingly the industry and cleanliness of his Dutch co-religionists.[97] Just as Catholic soldiers' experiences in the Iberian Peninsula revealed their connection to a larger culture of European Catholicism, so too Protestant soldiers' travels in Northern Europe reaffirmed their membership of a transnational religious community. During the liberation of the Low Countries in 1813–1814, John Stevenson, a Methodist army preacher, found his prayer meetings well attended by Dutch Calvinists and reflected positively on the ties that bound Protestants together despite denominational and national differences.[98] On the Danish expedition in 1807 many officers commented on the close similarities between the culture, countryside and architecture of Denmark and that of England. Entering a house on the Danish seashore in order to view the battle, Thomas Henry Browne was surprised to find it 'completely decorated in the "English fashion"' and hung with pictures of English views, with a garden laid out in the English 'style'.[99] Visiting Copenhagen's coffee shops, museums and galleries, the soldiers seemed to recognize a commercial modernity and a shared Northern European civilization that connected the two nations. It was perhaps for this reason that the British troops expressed such an intense sympathy for the Danes whom they had been sent to fight. This sympathy derived in part from the widely held belief that Denmark was an innocent victim of the conflict with Napoleonic France. Yet it is also probable that in viewing the 'fair faces and curling locks' of the fallen Danish student soldiers and observing the destruction which the British bombardment had wrought on what they considered a centre of 'polite' and 'modern' culture, the troops were able to imagine more vividly the 'dreadful effects of war in your own country'.[100] It should be noted, however, that not all soldiers felt such sympathy for the Danish. An Aberdeenshire private, clearly able to nurture a grievance, believed that the assault on Denmark was a justifiable retaliation for 'former times...when they invaded our North Country and raveshed [*sic*] and plundered all before them'.[101] It is a reminder that the very different historical memories of the national groups that composed the British army could produce quite different readings of national affinity and enmity.

British soldiers' accounts of campaigns in Denmark and Holland point to a view of Europe divided by shared culture and religion into Northern Protestant and Southern Catholic zones of civilization.[102] France (traditionally Catholic, but not Southern European) necessarily occupied an ambivalent position in relation to this civilizational axis. Yet, as the British army crossed the Pyrenees into southern France in late 1813 it was widely narrated as a passage from Southern European barbarism into a shared Anglo-French zone of civilization. 'I hope never to see Spain or Portugal again' wrote John Rous, as he crossed the border, 'we are now in a civilized country'.[103] Indeed, the entry into France was described as something akin to a homecoming. The fertility of the countryside, the well-ordered towns, elegant public buildings and the civility of the inhabitants all drew forth the admiration of the British troops and they repeatedly commented upon the resemblance between France and their home country. As one officer wrote, 'were it not for the language I could fancy myself in England'.[104]

The British army had been braced to face a popular armed resistance; instead they found to their surprise that they were warmly received by the French and 'much better treated than in Spain and Portugal'.[105] Wellington ordered his troops to remember that it was Napoleon and not the French nation that they were fighting and, for the most part, relations between the British and French civilians remained amicable as they travelled north towards Paris. Following the abdication of Napoleon, troops' travels in France began to assume more of the character of a leisurely holiday than a military occupation. Writing from Toulouse in April 1814, Edwin Griffiths observed that 'I consider myself more as a young gentleman making a tour in the south of France than an officer on service'.[106] Indeed, officers readily reverted to the role of the pre-war grand tourist and proved particularly keen to practice and improve their French: Griffiths was immensely flattered to be taken for a native speaker.[107] As they enjoyed comfortable quarters and a pleasurable round of balls, visits to the theatre and other amusements, officers confessed their reluctance to leave the country. 'I never felt such regret at the thought of quitting a place in my life', reflected Lt James Gardiner after receiving instructions to embark for England: 'I quitted England and my family with delight when I set off to join the army in the Peninsula but the thought of leaving Castell Sarazin perhaps never to see it more gives me greater pain than I could have thought possible.'[108]

The sense of being 'at home', or at least 'at ease' in France, which is so pronounced in officers' accounts of the occupation, may be attributed to several factors. The elites who made up the majority of the officer corps had traditionally been characterized by their Francophilia and cosmopolitanism and, despite pressure from the middling and plebeian classes to demonstrate a greater commitment to anti-Gallic patriotism, an affinity with the French may still have been the default setting for many officers.[109] Moreover, as we saw in the previous chapter, British soldiers' attitudes towards the Napoleonic forces were rarely coloured by any Francophobic animus and the fact that Britain had not been invaded meant that they did not carry a more personalized sense of grievance against the French. Most of all, these positive appraisals of France and the French point to the limits of the antagonistic, binary model of national difference and national enmity in this period. Though the opposition between Catholic superstition, indolence and despotism and Protestant enlightenment, industry and freedom, undoubtedly provided an important structuring principle in soldiers' accounts of the Iberian Peninsula, these differences were largely filtered through a civilizational model of nationality. Whilst this tended to be underpinned by a belief in British (or at least English) superiority, in elaborating a supposedly universal set of criteria for judging and ranking nations (commerce, cultivation, the status of women) rather than a more particularistic vision of nationality based on culture, language and character, it allowed for the identification of affinities between nations as well as differences.[110]

Coming home

The dispassionate language of hierarchies of civilization, of course, carried little of the affective resonance conventionally associated with ideas of 'home' or 'homeland'. While British soldiers may have signalled their reluctance to leave France, the voyage home completed the sequence of separation, exile and return that has been central to the soldiers' tale from Homer's *Ulysses* onwards. The home, whether conceived of as the family, their region or the nation, was the object of nostalgic yearning and the touchstone for soldiers' observations on national difference. In narrating the return home the trope of the 'island nation' again figured prominently. John Charleton wrote affectionately of landing once more on 'this Happy little island' and of embracing his family 'a happiness that cannot be described and can only be conceived by those who have experienced a separation such as this'.[111] The Clare-born officer Harry Ross-Lewin similarly described his joy at reaching 'the happy shore of old England, the land of liberty and sterling worthy'.[112] Indeed, many Irish officers narrated their arrival in England as a homecoming, suggesting an affective attachment to the British Isles as well as a narrower identification with their natal country. Disembarking at Deal, James Lowry demonstrated his 'joy at embracing England' in a very literal fashion by falling to the ground and running the pebbles through his hands. It was only several weeks later that he was able to sail home to Ireland, when the first view of the 'mountains of Wicklow and the gentle rising hills of Clantorf [*sic*]' he wrote 'excited gentle rising emotions in my breast'.[113]

The homecoming could also be fraught with anxiety. As he approached his native village Lowry was in the 'greatest suspense', not knowing whether he would find his relations alive or dead.[114] And it could be narrated as a moment of dislocation, when the soldiers' remembered image of home was challenged by the changed landscape that they encountered upon their return. One private soldier's 'hope and joy' at returning to Edinburgh seeped away as he looked upon a strange and unfamiliar city where 'so many alterations had taken place'.[115] This sense of estrangement from the country which he had left may have been more acute for the ordinary soldier, whose prospects on returning were uncertain, and who perhaps faced a greater challenge reintegrating into a civilian society: for a number of years after the French wars disbanded sailors were identified as the largest group of beggars in London.[116] More commonly, the strangeness of home was narrated positively, as the everyday sights and sounds of British life assumed an agreeable novelty for those who had grown unused to them.[117] Accounts of the 'shock of the familiar' in soldiers' narratives usually segued into a reflection on the striking contrast between 'home' and 'abroad' and the recognition of national superiority which the experience of separation, travel and return had affirmed. In this vein Edwin Griffiths wrote:

> no transported convict, no dungeon'd captive ever hailed their restoration to liberty & to light with greater satisfaction or glee than I have experienced since I touched on my native shore; not from any dislike to foreign service, but from my detestation of every thing Spanish when I think of their uncultivated country, their stone walls, their ill contrived houses, their filthy towns, their wretched food & their disgusting manners, & compare them to our fields, our hedges, our woods, our clean wide streets, our comfortable houses, & the hospitality of the inhabitants...I can leap from the earth for joy, and in an ecstasy thank the gods that I was born an Englishman.[118]

Conclusion

Travel and cultural encounter do not necessarily reveal any new insights on the part of the traveller; soldiers' campaign narratives tend to recapitulate well-established prejudices and affirm comfortable conceptions of national superiority. Nevertheless, the role of this mass experience of travel and campaign in giving shape and substance to understandings of national difference should not be underestimated. Its influence would have been intensified as soldiers and sailors communicated these experiences to their friends and families, and subsequently published accounts of their travels for the general public. For particular regions, like the Iberian Peninsula and

Egypt, military narratives would remain the definitive travelogue well into the nineteenth century.

At the same time, we must be cautious in identifying a single, stable model of British identity in these sources, or a single interpretation of national difference. The meanings of 'home' and 'nation' were clearly very different for the Irish soldier who embraced the shores of 'Old England' and the English soldier who found echoes of Ireland in the Iberian Peninsula. Equally, these narratives reveal the diverse range of frameworks through which other cultures were viewed and appraised, from the scriptural to the secular, from accounts of the rise and fall of empires to linear and hierarchical models of civilization. The oppositional model of national identity was clearly important in military travellers' interpretations of the Iberian Peninsula, but was often articulated through a more calibrated language of civilization, a language which could be used to identify affinities as well as differences. Indeed, perhaps the most striking aspect of these campaign narratives is the strong sense of affinity that British soldiers expressed for France and the French. Though the contest between Britain and France was the most sustained of the Revolutionary and Napoleonic wars, for both nations it may have been cultural encounters across and beyond Europe, more so than their violent encounters with each other on the battlefield, that had the most lasting impact.

5
Prisoners of War

Galled was my neck by strong Iron chains
I suffered much, tho' vain it was to complain
Vainly I thought my suffering could not last
E'e this mortal thread of life was past
Torn were my feet by the stones for want of shoes
Poverty and misery before me were my views
Recalled was often my Nation & my home
I bore with patience the sequel of my Doom
Sometimes I wanted even Bread to eat
O then I knew that Liberty was sweet
Never more I thought to see my home again...

Lines written in the notebook of Sergeant
Samuel Oakes, Royal Marines[1]

These verses written by Samuel Oakes, a Royal Marine imprisoned in France, provide a moving depiction of the prisoner of war's plight. The intensification of conflict in this period and the consequent transformation in the conventions governing the exchange of prisoners of war meant that Oakes, alongside thousands of British soldiers, sailors and civilians, endured a captivity of much greater duration than had been the norm in previous European wars. Many did, as Oakes feared, die before they saw their home again. Oakes' lament is an example of a text intimately shaped by the context in which it was produced. An acrostic, the first letter of each line spells out the site of the unfortunate prisoner's captivity: Givet Prison. It is part of a corpus of accounts structured by the experience of imprisonment in the period 1793 and 1815. While the number of British prisoners in France was comparatively small – an estimated sixteen thousand – many wrote poetry, kept journals or published retrospective memoirs of their experiences. Relatively little recent attention has been paid to these texts: the last major study was published over fifty years ago.[2] Yet prisoner of war narratives foreground several issues critical to our understanding of the ambivalence of wartime identities. Imprisonment undermined detainees' personal identity as they lost many of the status signifiers they enjoyed at home or in their professional life; it also involved the imposition of a collective identity as military and civilians alike were classified as agents of the British armed nation. The experience of captivity provided a vivid dramatization of the encounter between defiant, freedom-loving Britons and the tyrannical French enemy, but also created bonds of interdependence and sympathy between captor and captive. Within the walls of French fortress towns and citadels, the prisoners reconstructed various aspects of British society and culture to forge a community in exile; yet, in this 'little Britain' overseas, as in the nation itself, religious, ethnic and social fissures would be readily apparent.

Prisoners of war, 1793–1815

The Revolutionary and Napoleonic wars witnessed a decisive shift in the conventions that governed the detention, exchange and classification of prisoners of war. For much of the eighteenth century an informal international consensus regulated the treatment of prisoners of war helping to reduce the number of prisoners and the duration of their internment. The establishment of cartels – named after the ships that carried captured prisoners – allowed for the regular exchange and repatriation of prisoners and spared warring states the expense of keeping and clothing these captives. Officers typically spent only a short period in captivity. The prevailing system of *parole d'honneur* allowed captured officers to return to their homeland on the proviso that they would not to take up arms either for the duration of the conflict or for an agreed period of time. Official regulations on the treatment of prisoners of war were, to be sure, frequently flouted. The rank and file, along with those officers who broke their parole or refused to accept the terms of *parole*, often endured appalling, overcrowded conditions.[3] Nonetheless, a degree of restraint tended to characterize the classification and treatment of prisoners by both the British and French and neither nation regarded non-combatants as potential prisoners of war.[4] This informal code of honour meant that despite certain constraints Britons continued to travel to the continent throughout the Seven Years War (1756–1763) and American war (1775–1783).[5] As an English minister at Berlin who had travelled through France during the American war explained to the German court, he never once feared for his safety because 'il y a long temps que les Anglais et les Francais sont des peuples civilizés'.[6]

Between 1793 and 1815, this shared code of 'civilized' conduct would come under severe pressure. In June 1794, during the radical Jacobin phase of the French Revolution, the republican regime decreed that no British or Hanoverian troops were to be taken alive. Though largely ignored by French commanders in the field, who realized that it would put their own men at risk, the decree set the tone for a new mode of warfare in which the civilities of the old regime were progressively undermined.[7] In 1793 the French National Convention officially rejected the custom of *parole d'honneur*. French officers who had been released on condition that they would not take up arms again were ordered to disregard this obligation and immediately return to active service.[8] The Napoleonic regime saw a softening of the more extreme rhetoric regarding prisoners of war; the traditional system for the exchange of prisoners, however, would not be resumed for the remainder of the conflict. France and Britain entered into cartel negotiations at various points between 1802 and 1813, but these discussions never reached agreement, in part due to Napoleon's blunt appraisal that the French could afford to lose more of their men to imprisonment than the British. Consequently a general exchange of French and British prisoners of war was never established, though repatriations of small groups of prisoners would take place throughout the wars.[9] Moreover, under Napoleon there was a radical reclassification of the category of prisoner of war. In 1803, after the break down of the Peace of Amiens, Napoleon issued an edict ordering the detention of every British male between 18 and 60 then on French soil.[10] Many of those detained in 1803 did not return to Britain for several years. The confinement of British non-combatants was justified on the grounds that these *détenus* would, if they returned to Britain, be liable for service in the militia. It reflected a vision of the Franco-British conflict as a 'total war' in which the distinction between combatants and non-combatants could no longer be sustained.

The British state never introduced any equivalent detention of French civilians, though the numbers of French prisoners of war interned in Britain – an estimated eighty thousand officers and men – was much higher than the figure for Britons held in France.[11] Of these British prisoners, around six to seven hundred were civilian *détenus*, the remainder were primarily members of the Royal and merchant navy, who had been captured by French vessels, or shipwrecked on the French coast.[12] From 1803, the distribution centre for British prisoners in France was the fortress town of Verdun and it was here that the majority of *détenus* and officers were held for the duration of their captivity. Outside of Verdun, a series of depots was established in frontier fortresses along France's north-eastern border to detain those prisoners who were not commissioned officers, or eligible for parole. As well as the main non-penal depots in Arras, Auxonne, Besançon and Givet and elsewhere, there were also penal depots at Bitche and Sarrelibre for escapees or those convicted of a crime.

As the distinction between the prisoners held at Verdun and those interned elsewhere suggests, the experience of internment was crucially shaped by an individual's rank and status. As with POWs in World War I, officers and men inhabited 'strikingly different worlds of captivity'.[13] They lived, for the most part, in separate depots, enjoyed fundamentally different rights and were subject to different restrictions. Civilians based at Verdun were generally lodged in private houses in the town. Though locked up in the fortress at night, detainees at Verdun could acquire a passport from the depot's commandant to leave the town and for those with money most privileges and freedoms could be secured. The daily *appel*, or roll-call, for example, could be avoided by paying a fee to the French magistrate.[14] The prisoners even received an allowance from the French, although this was carefully calibrated according to rank: colonels and naval post-captains received a monthly allowance of £4, majors and commanders £3, with those at the bottom of the scale, midshipmen, warrant officers and masters of merchant vessels receiving a more modest £1 and 5 shillings.[15]

Prisoners who were not eligible for parole and who lived in depots outside Verdun endured much more severe terms of captivity. The majority were lodged and boarded inside the walls of the frontier fortresses, either in barracks formerly occupied by the departed garrisons, or in specially built hutments. Here they lived in overcrowded dormitories or cells, sometimes below ground, and had little freedom of movement. They were moved frequently between depots and forced to undergo marches of hundreds of miles on foot. Their allowance from the French government amounted to a daily ration of one pound of bread and a portion of vegetables, and 1s 10 ½ d per month. In comparison to prisoners from other countries held in France this provision was relatively generous. All British captives were rated 'first class' and given the same pay and food ration as soldiers in the French army. The rest of the nearly half a million prisoners in Napoleonic France received half this amount.[16] Yet these allowances were still undeniably meagre and were periodically supplemented by donations from Lloyds' patriotic fund and charitable subscriptions from the more well-off members of the British captive community in France.

Becoming a prisoner of war: capture, captivity and escape

Prisoner of war narratives tended to veer between emphasizing the solitary helplessness of the individual prisoner and rehearsing the ways in which the personal experience of captivity exemplified collective struggles and values, between a rhetoric of suffering and lamentation and narratives of heroism and stoic resignation. Differences of emphasis typically emerge in prisoners of war narration of key moments or 'event-scenarios' which include the moment of capture, captivity, resistance/collusion, escape and liberation.[17] In narrating these episodes, prisoners of war not only dramatized particular notions of personal honour and national identity, but also articulated various understandings of the nature of warfare and the relationship between the individual and the wartime nation.

The moment of capture, as Alon Rachamimov observes, is a crucial pivot of the captivity narrative: the point at which the narrator assumes the new identity of prisoner. For the prisoner, these episodes often serve an exculpatory function, as they try to refute or pre-empt accusations of personal failure or cowardice.[18] Army or naval officers were often at pains to vindicate their conduct in the events leading to capture. The naval midshipman,

Edward Boys, began his memoir of captivity with a thrilling rendition of an engagement with the French off the coast of Toulon in 1803. By his own account, Boys had gallantly sacrificed his own liberty to provide a diversion that allowed his ship, the HMS Phoebe, to escape.[19]

Once captured the prisoner had further opportunities to demonstrate his manful resistance to the enemy. Quizzed on the strength and position of Nelson's fleet, Boys refused to divulge any information, despite being abused by his French captor.[20] Joseph Bull, an army captain who was captured off the coast of Connaught during the French expedition to Ireland, similarly stressed his principled refusal to give any assistance to the French. Exhorted by the French Commodore to reveal the state of the Killala defences in exchange for a guarantee of safe return, Bull insisted that 'his threats would by no means intimidate me or for a moment make me forget the duty I owed my country'. Like Boys he managed to reconcile the ignominy of capture with his personal sense of military honour, maintaining, somewhat tendentiously, that the delay his imprisonment caused the French had 'saved the lives of hundreds, nay thousands'.[21] These brief gestures of resistance provided an important counterbalance to the inevitable compromises and uncomfortable dependency upon the enemy that would mark the remainder of the men's captivity.

For civilian *détenus* the transition from liberty to captivity was less dramatic but equally shocking. The majority of Britons detained in 1803 had joined the deluge of tourists that descended on France following the Peace of Amiens. The *détenus* vigorously denied Napoleon's imputation that these travellers were potential foot soldiers of the British armed nation. Indeed, they maintained that it was precisely their unsuitability for military service that made their detention so unjust. As one of these *détenus* pointed out, the collection of gouty and consumptive invalids seeking the benefits of a southern climate, families hoping to economize, and artists, grand tourists and others wishing to see the sights of France, hardly constituted a threat to the French:

> The grand nation are desirous of detaining five hundred individuals between the age of eighteen and sixteen, under the pretext that they were bound to serve in the militia. Should he have passed these five hundred in review, he perhaps would not have found fifty capable of bearing arms.[22]

Though anxious to stress their remoteness from the British war effort, civilian detainees' narratives of their arrest were carefully figured so as to illustrate national qualities of spirit and resistance to tyranny. Maria Cope was one of the many travellers who had come to France with her family in order to economize. When French soldiers arrived at her lodgings bearing Napoleon's edict, Cope defiantly informed them that she was 'an Englishwoman & not afraid'. Captivity in France posed a fundamental challenge to the national attributes most closely identified with Britishness: independence and liberty. *Détenus* railed against the indignity of 'free-born Britons' forced to travel 'like culprits under the order of a constable'.[23] Upon arriving at the prison depot in Verdun, all the men were examined by the Commandant of the Citadel and required to give various personal details, including the names of their parents and grandparents. According to Cope, several refused to co-operate with this 'un-British' inquisition 'saying John Bull like, what is it to them, who my Grandfather was, I won't tell'. 'Threats of greater severity', however, soon overcame this gesture of defiance, the first of many concessions the British prisoners were compelled to make to the French captors upon whom they were dependent.[24]

As well as the challenge that it presented to detainees' sense of identity, whether professional or national, imprisonment also meant a dramatic rupture in their anticipated life course. Contemplating his fate shortly after being taken captive, Edward Boys was particularly frustrated that this unforeseen event had occurred on the eve of a possible promotion.[25] Peter Bussell, master of a merchant vessel captured in 1807, similarly reflected that:

> Only but a few days back I was looking forward with a pleasing view of future things, and partly arrived to the summit of my wishes, but where are they now?...I am a captive in the enemy's country and the Almighty alone knows how long my state of captivity may be. May He support me under every misfortune, and bless me with patience and resignation.[26]

Powerless to determine their own fate and future, prisoners of war, particularly those ineligible for parole, often presented themselves as the hapless 'sports of war'.[27] While they sometimes blamed the British government for failing to secure their release and the French for holding them captive, more often than not they cited the vagaries of 'cruel war' and the ambitions of 'princes and statesmen' as the source of their misfortune. This was a recurring theme in POW poetry. As one captive wrote:

> Statesmen with craft so keen their minds employ
> Thinking how first each other to annoy
> Each Nation still 'gainst each other's Plotting
> Carnage and Desolation lotting
> To Thousands who Innocent of the Cause
> Are suffering in France thro' wars cruel laws.[28]

By thus representing themselves as 'Innocent of the Cause', victims rather than agents of war, many prisoners contested the concept that these were 'national' conflicts, in which whole populations, military and civilian, were necessarily implicated.

There were some who tried to bring their fate to the attention of the British government by linking it more directly to the war effort. In April 1809, prisoners at the depot in Arras presented a petition to King George III in which they pleaded for further assistance from the British state 'to alleviate the calamities of captivity' and urged the adoption of measures which 'may tend to a speedy release'. In making their case they claimed they had 'patiently submitted to our fate, though contributing to the general good, with the greatest sacrifice – that of our liberty'.[29] Designed to persuade the government to press more vigorously for an exchange of prisoners with France, the petition was vague as to how exactly British captives were 'contributing to the general good'. Nonetheless, a sense that their suffering and detention had a broader meaning or patriotic purpose may have helped to reconcile some prisoners to their situation.

The most obvious means of asserting individual agency in the face of captivity was to try and escape. Yet, besides the practical difficulties involved in planning and executing an escape, the decision to flee also involved fraught questions of honour. Those on parole had given their word that they would not abscond and, while the tradition of parole had been weakened in the 1790s, it was a convention of war to which British prisoners and the majority of their French counterparts in Britain continued to adhere. Between 1803 and 1811 only twenty-three British officers violated their parole in France and they faced serious consequences upon their return to Britain. They could be reprimanded and demoted, sent back to France or discharged from the armed forces. Parole violators also risked the opprobrium of their peers. One midshipman who escaped from Verdun in 1806 without cancelling his parole was, on his return to England, shunned by his friends, evicted from his club, and expelled from the navy.[30] Parole thus linked together the individual's honour and the honour and prestige of the nation. Boys recorded his pride on being informed by a French general that the value of British officer's word of honour rendered a formal signature of parole unnecessary, noting the 'patriotic importance' of this 'compliment to our national character'.[31] Despite having several opportunities to escape from captivity, Boys maintained he could not do so until the French had withdrawn the terms of parole by refusing him freedom of movement. At this point, according to Boys, escape became a duty. Moreover it was a means of impressing upon the French 'the inefficacy of vigilance and severity, to enchaining a British officer, when compared with that milder and more certain mode of securing his person – confiding in his honour'.[32]

For those prisoners not bound by parole, the question of whether to escape was less closely tied to issues of morality and honour. Nevertheless, there were powerful disincentives for potential escapees. Some died trying to escape from the fortified prison depots. If recaptured they were incarcerated in the dungeons of the penal depots under much more severe conditions. In order to deter such attempts, the French routinely circulated declarations from recaptured prisoners, in which they described the sufferings which they had incurred through their rashness, and urged their countrymen to avoid a similar fate.[33] Furthermore, those who absconded jeopardized the privileges of prisoners who remained in captivity. Escape could therefore prove a divisive issue within the prisoner community. While some detainees assisted their fellow prisoners to escape, many others colluded with their French captors to prevent such attempts. Following a spate of escapes from the depot at Arras, the inmates presented a statement to the commandant promising, in return for an immediate restoration of their privileges, not to desert and to inform the authorities of any attempts to escape.[34]

Without the hope of escape, or release, the experience of captivity became one of passive endurance and resignation. As their fate was determined by the progress of the war and cartel negotiations between the British and French, prisoners tried to closely follow the course of the conflict. For those outside Verdun, without access to English newspapers, gathering accurate news on the war could prove difficult. While the *Moniteur* and the Parisian English-language newspaper the *Argus* were available in the depots, detainees treated these French reports, in which 'everything is in favour of themselves' with caution.[35] New arrivals in the depot, in particular British soldiers captured in Spain, were besieged with requests for news of the war. Reports and rumours were avidly pored over and discussed. As an inmate at Arras observed, 'I suppose not more politics is talked over in any coffee house...as is here upon the Rock'.[36] Mistrust of the available sources of news combined with a sense of powerlessness to create an environment in which rumours and superstition flourished.[37] Prisoners often searched the skies for portents, finding in celestial phenomena, eclipses and comets, indeterminate signs of their fate. In 1807 John Robertson recorded in his diary the various conjectures which the prisoners made after seeing a star blazing in the middle afternoon:

> some said it was an emblem of Peace; and some said one thing and some another, as for my part; I recollected the last time that ever I see such a thing, was the very day I heard the joyful tideings [*sic*] of last peace; Still it may not be so now. O Blessed day of peace; come when it will, will be a day of the greatest joy.[38]

The prisoners' anxious interpretations of these phenomena give some indication of the powerlessness and enforced passivity of their existence. Yet prisoners also found ways of reconciling themselves to their captivity, building communities in exile that gave some purpose to their confinement.

'A world in miniature': prisoner communities

In the account of his time as *détenu*, *A Picture of Verdun* (1810), the Jamaican-born author James Henry Lawrence provided a vivid description of the fortress town. It had been transformed by the confinement of British travellers, he wrote, into a 'little London', in which all the variety and diversity of British life could be viewed in 'small focus'. According to Lawrence, the prisoners comprised 'persons of every rank of life', who nevertheless found solidarity in the shared experience of captivity:

> All national distinctions between Irish, Scot and English had ceased, and their only contest was to do the honours of their respective countries on their particular Saints' days. All the clubs and messes were indiscriminately composed of the army, navy and civilians. Here sat the grand tourist, there a country squire, a manufacturer … Here sat a knowing one, who had the racing calendar by heart; and there a Cantab.[39]

This account perhaps exaggerates the social heterogeneity of, and intermingling between, prisoners at Verdun: members of the lower classes, for instance, were only allowed to remain there as servants to the 'gentle'. Nonetheless, it illuminates the extent to which the captive community was thought to function as a microcosm of the British nation. Despite the *détenus'* protests that they were innocent travellers rather than active members of the British wartime nation, it was their Britishness that defined them as captives. In Verdun, as in the other depots, Britons were segregated from prisoners of other nationalities held by the French. Thrown together by the vagaries of war and with little idea how long their captivity would last, the detainees developed a community in exile that could give some structure and purpose to their confinement, a community which attempted to reflect and reproduce the broader values, practices and identities of the British nation.

Studies of prisoners of war have often commented on the accelerated process of community-building which occurs in such contexts, as prisoners organize themselves to create, as far as possible, 'a home from home'.[40] As the description of Verdun as a 'little London' suggests, the community there mirrored, in many ways, the pursuits and lifestyle of the metropolitan elite, including its extravagance. Many of the *détenus* were able to draw on their personal fortunes whilst in captivity in France, and high-ranking officers, in addition to receiving an allowance from the French, were kept on half pay by the British state. In an effort to alleviate the tedium of imprisonment they spent liberally. As one observer commented, the *détenus* 'vied with each other in expence … without reflecting, that the more money they spent in France the less willing the French would be to release them'.[41] Indeed, realizing the prosperity which the prisoners had brought to the small fortress town of Verdun, other French towns regularly applied to Napoleon to have the British settled amongst them.[42] The captives held balls, assemblies, concerts, and hare hunts. They set up a 'tally ho' club, racing club and gambling club.[43] If these clubs reproduced the conviviality and dissipation associated with elite fashionability, others reflected the more sober values of British associational culture. Carron's coffee club house, for instance, provided its members with books, maps, gazettes and pamphlets and a forum for discussion and debate, and was considered 'most like the clubs in England'.[44]

By reconstructing various elements of the British public sphere on French soil, the prisoners were projecting a particular version of British national identity to a French audience. As several *détenus* noted with concern, the frivolity and dissipation of British society at Verdun was more likely to make the French doubt 'the *solide* qualities which they had considered the ingredients of the British character'.[45] These anxieties were partly assuaged through the prisoners' philanthropic activity. In 1805 a committee was established to attend to the education of the many children held captive in France, in particular the large numbers of boys in the merchant and royal navies who had been captured at sea. Funded by subscriptions from France and Britain, the committee began by founding a school for the British colony in Verdun and soon established further schools for prisoners at Valenciennes, Givet and Saarlibre.[46] These charitable exertions not only demonstrated the benevolence of British Prisoners, but also, they claimed, contributed to the maintenance of Britain's maritime prowess, as boys were instructed in reading, writing and the principles of navigation. According to the Revd Wolfe, one of the founders of the Schools Committee, the training which the young mariners received in France 'bore comparison with the best naval seminaries at home', and was of long-term consequence to the nation as both 'they themselves and the service are now reaping the benefit.'[47]

As well as organizing schools, the wealthy inhabitants of Verdun also raised subscriptions for less fortunate British prisoners. Such philanthropic activity allowed the *détenus* to invest their pleasurable recreations with patriotic purpose and to stress the bonds that united Britons in captivity, despite the distinctions of rank and fortune that separated them. The prologue to a farce performed at Verdun for the benefit of distressed Prisoners made these dual aims explicit:

> Our humble task, if you but grant the power
> Is but to soothe the poor man's cheerless hour
> It is the duty which we owe each other,
> For every British captive is our brother
> Laugh at us or *with* us then, is still meet
> That while we laugh our fellow captives eat.[48]

While the wealthy detainees may have vaunted the fraternal bonds that connected them to their captive brothers, charity, as historians of philanthropy have shown, is often a potent means of asserting social distinctions, simultaneously bridging divisions between rich and poor, whilst maintaining the boundaries between patron and benefactor.[49] Like the conspicuous consumption and fashionable display of the Verdun detainees, charity could be a way of combating the levelling effects of confinement and exile. One of the most active figures in prisoner of war philanthropy, Edward Reilly Cope, a member of the Schools Committee and one of the distributors of the patriotic fund, was painfully aware of the fragility of social distinctions in the face of common captivity. As he observed to his father, it was a constant struggle to support his family on the half pay he received as a Lieutenant-Colonel in an Irish fencible regiment without 'descending very far beneath your situation and my own and reducing my method of life to that of the inferior classes'.[50] Cope's active participation in prisoner of war charity may have been motivated as much by a desire to assert his authority over these fellow captives and to avert the social descent which he so dreaded, as by more benevolent impulses.

The less fortunate prisoners, confined to depots outside Verdun, were not just passive beneficiaries of their elite counterparts' largesse. Despite the harsher conditions of their incarceration, they too strove to construct some sort of organized community within the citadel prisons. In contrast to the elite pursuits of the Verdun community, British inmates of depots such as Arras were more likely to reproduce patterns of plebeian associational culture. During the early years of their confinement, in particular, there was a high death toll at the depot in Arras: in 1807 Peter Bussell recorded the deaths of 173 inmates.[51] As a consequence, Thomas Dixon noted that several clubs had been set up to purchase coffins and pay for the funerals of those who died, 'as before the french used to put them into carts and throw them into a hole which grieves the hearts of Englishmen'.[52] The importance attached to a 'proper' burial within British plebeian culture was perhaps intensified by rumours that the corpses of British prisoners were appropriated by French medical men for dissection. These informal associations replicated the activities of the friendly societies and burial clubs that flourished in Georgian Britain.[53] In other, more positive, ways the rhythms and rituals of the life cycle continued within the walls of the citadel. A small proportion of British women were held in the prison depots and in 1808 five children were born at Arras. Inevitably matches and marriages were formed between the captives, often uniting men and women from different regions of the United Kingdom: in July 1809, John Robertson recorded the marriage of a 'Wm Stention of St. Clears, Cornwall, to Susanna McKinney of Ireland ... the third wedding that we have had since the church was fitted up'.[54]

The church was an important focal point for the prison community at Arras. As Robertson observed, the citadel was like 'a little Town excluded from the rest of the world' or rather 'the world in Miniature':

We have a market 7 times a week, viz, every day, from the first of the morning till 10 o'clock; with commoditys [sic] of every kind of eatables; three cantines or public houses, where there is all manner of drinkables, a place of Divine worship, viz church of England (tho' in France) a desenting [*sic*] meeting, and a Roman Catholic Chapple [*sic*]; this latter have French Clargy [*sic*] perform the office of Mass every day, but few frequent this place except a few Irish; and some French that reside in the Citadel – here we have a prison within a prison... Here is two schools for the Instruction of youths... news papers is to be had at these before mentioned cantines... these are the chief amusements and pastimes in arras Citadel.[55]

Just as the *détenus* at Verdun strove to reconstruct forms of elite sociability during their captivity, so too the prisoners at Arras reproduced key sites of British popular culture – the market, the public house, the church and meeting house – within the citadel walls. The religious fault lines amongst the British captives were highlighted by the special provision made for different denominations. Methodists, in particular, formed an active and visible sub-culture in the prison depots and fellow captives often bristled at their pros-elytizing zeal.[56] The Rev. Robert Wolfe, an Anglican clergyman dispatched to Givet in 1805 to superintend the prisoners' spiritual welfare was, however, impressed by the Methodists' piety. In a spirit of ecumenicalism Wolfe estab-lished joint services for Methodist and Anglican prisoners, as well as organ-izing various activities – a choir, an orchestra, a school– designed to divert the prisoners from less respectable pursuits.[57]

These initiatives at Givet derived in part from a fear that ordinary seamen, once separated from their officers and the hierarchy and discipline of the ship, would degenerate into a disorderly mob. Yet, despite being removed from the organized patriotic ritual of the armed forces, sailors and soldiers at citadels such as Arras continued to mark and celebrate significant British anniversa-ries. On the 29th of May, or Royal Oak day, the date on which the escape and restoration of King Charles II was traditionally commemorated, the prisoners at Arras stripped the single small oak tree in the citadel completely bare in order to dress their clothes with its leaves.[58] At the citadel in Valenciennes, the British inmates celebrated the anniversary of Trafalgar by illuminating their windows and exhibiting patriotic transparencies 'in honour of that glorious victory'.[59] Such patriotic festivities clearly provided a release from the tedium of everyday prison life and an excuse for heavy drinking and riotous behaviour: Peter Bussell noted wryly that in celebrating King George III's birthday on the 4th of June, 'many took in more brandy and wine than they could well carry, being what I call very drunk'.[60] The ritualistic celebra-tion of patriotic anniversaries involved once again a self-conscious staging of Britishness towards a French audience, whose responses were carefully noted. When a group of British prisoners *en route* to Verdun celebrated the 4 June with several bottles of wine and multiple toasts, they were gratified to note that the French onlookers 'expressed satisfaction at our loyalty'.[61]

Whether they described the relatively free atmosphere of Verdun or the more confined conditions of the citadels, the writers of prison narratives were clearly fascinated by the microcosmic qualities of these spaces and the ways in which they functioned as 'little Londons' or 'worlds in miniature'. An obvious reference point was the immensely popular microcosm genre: illustrated encyclopaedias depicting scenes of fashionable society and low life, domestic trades and British regional costumes such as W.H. Pyne's *Microcosm, A Picturesque Delineation of the Arts, Agriculture, Manufacture, &c, of Great Britain* (1803, 1806, 1808) and Rudolph Ackermann's *Microcosm of London, or: London in Miniature* (1808). There were echoes too of the microcosmic island 'society' developed by the industrious Robinson Crusoe in Farrell Mulvey's tribute to the resourceful seamen of the fortress at Longwy, whose versatility of talents ensured that 'every trade, whether of convenience or use, was to be found in the depot'.[62] Captivity allowed the heterogeneous and impersonal nation to be experienced on a personal and tangible scale. If nations, in Benedict Anderson's formulation, are necessarily *imagined communities* by virtue of the fact that 'the members of even the smallest nation will never know most of their fellow-members, meet them, or even hear of them', in the prison depots the imagined community acquired a more concrete form.[63]

While the size of the prisoner of war communities allowed their members to experience the nation in small-scale form, the experiences of the prisoners were still mediated through an informal press and textual community. One of the most striking features of the British community at Arras was the large amount of poetry produced by inmates: all three of the surviving journals from Arras contain lengthy transcriptions of assorted verses. The poems were often pasted up in the communal areas of the prison depot. They reported and commented on prison life, articulating the frustrations, anxieties and hopes of the prisoners and rigorously policing and exposing any conduct that was seen to threaten the solidarity of the prison community. While their French captors were often the target of these verses, the prisoners' country was not immune from criticism. A poem entitled 'An Evening's Contemplation in a French Prison' sketched a mournful portrait of the British who languished in confinement, and of sailors who might have equalled the deeds of Admiral Howard or Nelson, but whose vigour had been withered by incarceration. In a pointed stanza, the poet indicted the British state for neglecting these 'brave sons of Neptune':

> Say after toils of war and battle gain'd
> With Trophies rais'd by them to Britain's fame
> Can you to steer the helm of state disdain
> Stamp on neglect like this a generous name.[64]

Although prisoners feared that they had been forgotten by their government, family and friends, the charitable subscriptions raised by Lloyds' Patriotic Fund provided some consolation. Moreover, the ties between prisoners and their home communities were maintained in captivity, as the sea ports, which had lost many sailors to imprisonment, sent donations to local men in France. Peter Bussell was a beneficiary of money sent from Weymouth 'for those belonging to any vessel of that port, who are prisoners here', while John Robertson similarly received donations from a subscription in his home port of Lynn, Norfolk.[65] The distribution of money and privileges amongst the prisoners, however, was a constant source of tension. At the beginning of their internment, prisoners destined for depots outside Verdun were classified into three different groups: ordinary soldiers and seamen; masters of merchant vessels under eighty tons; and masters of vessels over eighty tons. As masters of smaller ships, both Bussell and Robertson were ranked as masters 'under-tonnage' and were therefore allocated a smaller allowance and confined to the depot while the masters 'above-tonnage' were allowed to reside in the town. This affront to their status within the prisoner hierarchy was keenly felt by both men, Robertson bitterly noting 'what a privilege to live in town and be counted as gentleman, while we were on a level with the smallest boy in the Citadel'.[66] The masters made periodic efforts to have their precedence recognized by the French. In 1809, having been moved from Arras to the citadel at Besancon, they presented a petition to the prison commandant requesting that their treatment more closely reflect their status as men, who, while in Britain, had 'enjoy'd a superior Comfort to the general rank of individuals'.[67] The prisoner of war poetic press heaped ridicule on the masters' special pleading, circulating a poem which declared: 'my opinion of the matter/poor men that lives on bread and water/has more occasion for advance/ than any master that's in France'.[68]

The solidarity of the British prisoners was thus frequently threatened by the social hierarchies and differential treatment that shaped their captivity. While masters like Bussell and Robertson occasionally received liberty to leave the citadel, they looked with jealousy upon those masters allowed to permanently reside in town and the naval officers who occasionally left the comforts of Verdun and deigned to visit those held at Arras. 'The English nobbs', as Robertston described them, with their 'Coaches and footmen behind in Gold lace; such as these know little of captivity'.[69] Bitterness at the privileges enjoyed by the more fortunate detainees was compounded by a perception that those eligible for parole had developed an overly close relationship with their French captors. When Monsieur Duhamel, the commandant of the Arras citadel, left in 1808, the 'English dons in town' treated him to a farewell dinner at which they presented a gold snuffbox with an inscription expressing 'the esteem and gratitude' of the English prisoners to 'this friend of suffering distress'. The flattering address provoked outrage amongst those detained in the Citadel. Bussell reflected in his diary that the commandant might have 'behaved very well to those Navy officers, Bankers, and others who would very often give him a good dinner, but let us turn our eyes inward to the Citadel, to our unfortunate countrymen, and see if we can trace out any of his humanity'.[70]

British prisoners, then, had to strike a delicate balance between co-operating with their French captors, in order to improve the conditions of their captivity, and being seen to collude with them. These relations of interdependence complicated the antagonistic divisions between captive and captor. Nonetheless, those who were perceived to have crossed the line between the prisoners of war and the French authorities could be ostracized by their fellow Britons. A Mr Hinds, who served as a clerk and interpreter to the commandant at Arras, was widely vilified within the prison community as a traitor to his country. Again, prisoner poetry registered the prevailing attitude towards this 'young puppy', whose collaboration threatened British unity and solidarity:

> Since hard fate it doth decree
> That prisoners in this Land we be
> With hand and heart we shou'd agree
> To assist each other in calamity
> And thus united let all frenchmen know
> That we're a noble generous foe
> But alas not so it's quite contrary
> Without prudence I speak sincerely
> That a prisoner in the yard of Late
> Of consequential self conceit
> A swaggering youth as any in the Depot
> Its from an antient Briton sprung this beau
> The name of Briton might a generous heart inspire
> But not him he is a Traitor & a Liar.[71]

The gravest act of treachery which a British prisoner could commit was to join the French service. From the summer of 1804, officers from Napoleon's Irish Legion, which had been formed the previous year by Irish émigrés, regularly visited the depots in an effort to enlist soldiers.[72] Prison diaries from Arras routinely recorded these visits and the various enticements which the Irish officers used to lure men into the service; cards were circulated amongst the prisoners promising immediate liberty, good pay, food and clothing, as well as rapid promotion.[73] With these inducements and a liberal provision of free grog, the legion managed to persuade a number of inmates to join the French service, though rumours that 1,000 of the 1,200 prisoners at Auxonne had decided to enlist were likely erroneous.[74] Disdain for these deserters was forcefully expressed by the prison poetasters:

> Irish inlisting with the French
> Traitors to their country and rebles [sic] to their friends...

> But if they go to serve great Bonaparte
> I hope they never will from the field depart
> Till they have found what traitors ought to find
> That would desert their kindered [*sic*] and their friends
> May it be far from sons of Britons name
> To aid those Gallics or assist the same
> Altho' confind and bitter is our lot
> We'll brave it out, or perish on the spot.[75]

Prisoners' attitudes towards those Irish who enlisted in Napoleon's army illustrate the ambivalent position which this group occupied within the 'little Britain' of the prison depot. On the one hand, their desertion to the French was represented as a betrayal of a common British identity. At the same time, their Irishness already marked them out as an internal 'other' with potentially suspect loyalties. The separateness of the Irish within the prison community was made visible by their attendance at the citadel's Roman Catholic chapel where French clergy officiated. And while there is no reference to the celebration of distinctive Scottish, or Welsh festivities within the depot, the raucous and drunken behaviour of Irish prisoners on St Patrick's Day was regularly commented upon. In March 1809, John Robertson remarked that three of these 'Whiteboys' (a derogatory reference to Irish agrarian agitators) had been confined to the dungeon for drunkenness.[76] Though this hint at a lingering suspicion of the unruly Irish within the ranks of the prison communities, on the whole, there seems to have been little anti-Irish feeling. Even in the matter of desertion, it was recognized that English and Scottish prisoners had also joined the French service and diarists impartially recorded several instances where Irishmen had refused the blandishments of the French recruiting parties.

Captor and captive: British–French encounters

In order to endure a captivity of uncertain duration, British prisoners had to, in varying degrees, co-exist and co-operate with the French authorities and communities upon whom they were dependent. The nature of the relationship between the French and their captives was shaped by the terms of confinement for different classes of prisoners. Nonetheless, the enmity which could be sustained on opposing sides of the Channel, or of the battlefield, was more difficult to maintain after extended contact and interaction. According to James Lowry, a naval surgeon who was captured in 1803:

> Although we fight desperately against each other, after surrendering we act more like brothers...why should individuals remain any longer enemies (after the fulfilment of duty) for the ambitions of kings & princes.[77]

Lowry's comments provide another example of how remote concepts of 'total' or 'national wars' could be from the personal experiences of the men and women caught up in these conflicts. The relationships between British officers and their French captors continued to display the residual influence of a shared European military ethos and code of honour.[78] Most prisoner of war narratives written by army and navy officers stressed the civil and respectful treatment which they received from their French counterparts. 'No men on earth' wrote Joseph Bull of the French officers who had captured him off Killala bay, 'could behave with more generosity towards a prisoner than they did to me'.[79] Bull and his captors convivially shared toasts to the 'French Republic' and 'King George'.[80] Major-General Lord Blayney, one of the most high-ranking officers captured by the French, similarly remarked upon the liberal treatment he received at the hands of the French. Upon learning that Blayney had lost his sword after his capture, General Milhaud immediately presented him with his own, an affirmation of mutual respect which the British general gratefully accepted. While Blayney contrasted the generosity and civility of the French with his treatment at the hands of German and Spanish officers, his accounts of Napoleon's officers also tended to distinguish between those who were connected to the 'ancient French noblessese' and revolutionary *parvenus*.[81] Such distinctions were frequently drawn in prisoners' narratives. Edward Boys observed that when he met with an officer of the *ancien régime* he was generally treated 'like a gentleman' whilst from those 'sprung up from the revolutionary *canaille* we met with insolence and severity'.[82] It is difficult to tell how far these appraisals of French military character reflected British anti-revolutionary prejudice: Jeffrey Prendergast who was captured by the French in 1794, when French republican fervour was at its highest pitch, recorded civil treatment from his captors.[83] At the same time, it is possible that British prisoners enjoyed a more positive relationship with French officers who shared the traditional values of a hereditary military class. Captivity could reveal further bonds between the officers of the French and British armies. Bull discovered that two of his captors were 'brother Masons'. During his detention in France, Lt Robert Melville joined a Masonic lodge which counted several French officers amongst its members.[84]

The humanity with which the French treated British prisoners was underpinned by a recognition that according to the *fortunes de guerre* their roles might easily be reversed. Hence, there was a degree of reciprocity built into the captor-captive relationship. When Joseph Bull was finally permitted to return to England, he wrote to the French general from whom he had experienced such generous treatment promising that if he or any of his men were ever imprisoned in Britain he would do his utmost to return the favour.[85] The relationship between the French and those at the lower end of the prisoner hierarchy was clearly more asymmetrical. Bonds could, nonetheless, form between prisoners and their guards. When the gendarmes at Arras were ordered to join the French army in Spain, the British captives presented to the most humane amongst them certificates recommending them, in the eventuality of their capture, to their 'countrymen's benevolence'.[86]

Prisoners also developed positive relationships with the French communities outside the prison depots. When severe fires destroyed part of the town of Arras, the British not only helped douse the flames, but also organized a subscription for the victims.[87] These acts of charity were reciprocated by the French: on several occasions, the residents of French towns through which British prisoners marched organized collections to help those whose tattered clothes and bare feet betrayed their distressed state.[88] As military conscription rendered male labour increasingly scarce, detainees were given leave to ply their trades in the fortress towns and, presumably, such day-to-day interactions further helped to erode national barriers. In December 1812, for instance, Peter Bussell recorded the marriage of a British prisoner to a local Frenchwoman.[89] The fact that the work prisoners were commissioned to undertake often contributed to the French war effort – making clothes for French troops and saddles for the cavalry – does not seem to have troubled them.[90] Many prisoners occupied their time studying French.[91] Farrell Mulvey, an Irish surgeon and civilian *détenu*, went so far as to draw a parallel between the cultural education received by seamen in the depot at Longwy and that usually reserved for gentlemen on the Grand Tour. The sailors learnt French in the depot's charitable schools and practiced the 'contredanse Française' while courting local women. 'The rough diamond', Mulvey concluded, 'was polished in France'.[92]

Like the campaign journals discussed in Chapter 4, prisoner of war narratives were also, in part, travelogues. As many British prisoners acknowledged, their captivity gave them a unique opportunity to observe the culture and character of post-revolutionary France at first hand. For Watkins Tench, a royal marine captured in 1794, his first landing on French soil was accompanied by intense anticipation. 'There are moments when I am almost tempted not to regret a captivity', he wrote, 'which opens an inlet into this extraordinary country at such a period as the present'.[93] Tench published the letters he had written as a prisoner in France in 1796, contributing to a small but widely read set of English eyewitness accounts of the French Revolution that included Helen Maria Williams' best-selling *Letters Written in France* (1792–1796). Like many Britons, Tench implicitly contrasted British civility and honourable masculinity with the degradation of manners and masculinity in revolutionary France and the Jacobin 'reptiles' who addressed women of 'rank and delicacy' with roughness and impudence. 'The most effeminate and essenced *marquis* that ever consulted a looking glass', he opined, were surely preferable to such 'republican *coxcombs*'.[94] Such contrasts between French manners under the *ancien régime* and those of the new republican order, reveal one of the key problems that commentators like Tench faced when trying to elaborate a fixed French 'other' against whom British national character could be constructed. The rapidly shifting nature of French political and national identity in this period made it difficult to sustain traditional dichotomies between French and British national character.[95] The French revolutionaries' attempts at 'de-Christianization', for instance, unsettled the habitual opposition between British Protestantism and French Catholicism. Tench's letters suggest how this could destabilize the religious foundations upon which British identity was based. Visiting a cathedral at Quimper, he registered a degree of sympathy with the persecuted French Catholics, reflecting that 'the basis of their persuasion and mine was the same however we might differ in external forms of adoration'.[96]

The difficulty of identifying a stable French national character meant that most prisoner of war narratives from the 1790s focused on the gulf between republican rhetoric and practice. In his journal Joseph Bull cited several examples of such inconsistencies. Despite the French revolutionaries' 'boasted renunciation of all religion', when the sailors who held him captive were threatened with shipwreck they all began to pray. The fate of those who deserted or refused to join the French army and were condemned to hard labour proved the speciousness of French 'Liberty and Equality'.[97] Bull's captivity narrative drew upon a counter-revolutionary discourse that aimed to show those sympathetic to revolutionary radicalism the chimerical nature of French liberty and the superiority of the British constitution. He concluded his narrative with the hope that 'every subject of his present Majesty, who is secretly wishing for a French invasion, may find as liberal a specimen of "Liberty and Equality" as we have experienced'.[98]

The contrast between British freedom and French tyranny continued to be drawn in prisoner of war narratives from the Napoleonic wars, which drew attention to the harshness of French laws and the ubiquitous presence of French police. 'To see a fellow creature chained by the neck in this country is not uncommon' observed Peter Bussell in 1813, 'France swarms with gendarmerie, England has none, and her laws are mild. Her inhabitants are free, and she is an asylum for the distressed'.[99] Yet these reflections on national difference did not stem from a marked Francophobia. As the 'hapless victims' of war, detainees were more likely to sympathize with the wartime sufferings of the French and to stress the bonds of shared humanity that connected the two nations. During their marches through the French countryside, many prisoners noted with compassion the women forced to labour in the fields whilst their husbands were in the army. When Bussell read in the *Moniteur* of the sufferings of the French army in Russia, he did not exalt in this blow to the invincible Napoleonic forces, but expressed his pity for the French soldiers and his sympathy for the local inhabitants who had lost many of their relatives. Such expressions of sympathy did not necessarily preclude a patriotic identification with the British war effort. Reading an account of the British–American war in the same issue, which described America's confidence of success, Bussell rejoined that they should never underestimate the bravery of the troops in whose 'veins flow the blood of Englishmen'.[100] Nevertheless such patriotic pronouncements were tempered by his conviction that it was war and the 'malice and revenge' of 'a few ambitious individuals' that was the true enemy.[101]

Similar sentiments of benevolent universalism can be found in many other prisoner of war narratives. At the conclusion of his captivity, Watkins Tench stressed his own cosmopolitan patriotism and antipathy for 'national prejudices'.[102] While Lord Blayney's narrative contained bursts of national chauvinism and French stereotyping, he also claimed to deplore national prejudice and disdain those English resident in France who pretended to despise 'whatever is not English'. He did, however, believe that British national chauvinism could, in certain contexts, serve a beneficial purpose. Relating an encounter with a 'jolly Jack Tar' who was overwhelmed with joy at meeting 'a real countryman', Blayney acknowledged that:

> The cosmopolite philanthropist will here doubtless pity that ignorance, which thus creates national partiality and perpetuates national jealousy. But though we may desire to see this narrow prejudice swept from the minds of person in the higher classes, God forbid that ever the genuine John Bull should be so far enlightened. While every English soldier and sailor is intimately convinced that he is equal to two Frenchmen in any kind of fight, there is little danger of his not supporting that superiority; but let him once begin to doubt if a Frenchman is not as good as an Englishman and the odds are entirely done away.[103]

Officers' condescending indulgence of the rank and file's crude xenophobia and unsophisticated loyalty can be found in other accounts from this period. Joseph Bull, for example, described how a party of British sailors upon their release from a French prison marched out singing 'God save the King' and 'Rule Britannia', stopping at the end of every street to shout 'vive le Roi d'Angleterre'.[104] In such narratives, modes of patriotic and national identification were situated on a sliding scale from the narrow jingoism of the lower orders to the supposed cosmopolitan philanthropy of the British elite. In refusing to demonize the French, the literate and educated authors who produced accounts of their captivity may have been consciously distancing themselves from the perceived xenophobia of the British plebeian classes, although the experience of co-existence and contact with the French may have genuinely diluted national enmities. The impact of captivity on ordinary soldiers and sailors is more difficult to gauge, but it is not implausible that their sense of national identity was also complicated by interactions with the French, amongst whom they worked and even married. At the very least, as Bull's anecdote suggests, they had, by the end of their imprisonment, acquired sufficient French to proclaim their devotion to the British monarchy in the language of the enemy.

Conclusion

British prisoners of war were unfortunate casualties of the intensification of national conflicts in this period, which meant that long-term imprisonment became the norm and that civilians were viewed as potential combatants. We should not, however, overstate the ruptures occasioned by the transition from 'limited' to 'total' war. The significance which British prisoners attached to *parole d'honneur* and the civil treatment which they often received from their French captors suggests the continued influence of a shared transnational code of 'civilized' conduct. The strict segregation of captives according to whether or not they were deemed 'gentle' was similarly a relic of the *ancien régime*. The narratives of Napoleon's British prisoners point to the bonds of collective solidarity that were forged in captivity, as they sought to construct a 'little Britain' in exile. Yet these detainees still refused to frame their experiences within patriotic conceptions of warring peoples, and expressed a distinct sense that they were as much the victims of 'cruel war' as the victims of French tyranny. Despite the asymmetrical relationship between captor and captive, interaction and interdependence served in some measure to dilute national antagonisms and prisoners' hostility to their jailers often sat alongside sympathy for the larger French communities amongst whom they were based.

It is not implausible to think of the prisoner of war depots as sites of cultural exchange rather than conflict. In towns like Verdun, the clubs, race courses, and fashions introduced by the wealthy British may well have served as evocative reminders of this cross-cultural interaction long after the detainees had departed; the prisoners, in turn, were exposed to French culture and cuisine, learned the language and in certain instances married and settled there. As James Lawrence playfully suggested in a poem addressed to his countrymen at Verdun, the exchange of French Revolutionary émigrés and British prisoners of war could be understood as having a mutually beneficial effect on both nations: 'The French now behold you with admiration/And cry "Is this the humdrum jogtrot nation?"/The émigrés have much improved John Bull/The animal we find is not so dull...We'll teach him dancing, he'll teach us drinking/And we've the same antipathy to thinking'.[105]

6
Citizen-Soldiers

In 1795, John Marsh, a gentleman composer of some repute, whose interests included astronomy, accounting and scientific instrument-making, and who, in addition to acting as an overseer of the poor, was a founding member of the Chichester book society, a share holder in the town theatre, and leader of the local orchestra, added a new military pursuit to his already extensive list of pastimes. Invited to enrol in the second company of the Chichester Volunteers, Marsh initially signalled his reluctance: his son had already joined the first company and he felt 'one of a family wo'd be enough'. With some pressing, he eventually relented and attended the first meeting of the Volunteer company where he and the other new recruits 'practis'd standing at ease & at attention, facing to the right & left'. They agreed to meet four times a week thereafter to practice their drill. Whilst the first company of Volunteers, he recorded, had been primarily formed from young men and dressed in the short jacketed uniform of the light infantry, the 'elderly' inhabitants of Chichester, deeming such light dress inappropriate, had 'proposed forming themselves into a battalion company with coats, hats etc. proper for middle aged people'.[1]

Marsh's journals are narrated in a mock-heroic style that is alive to the foibles and comedy of Chichester life and he brought this comic touch to bear on the town's martial endeavours.[2] His humorous portrait of the aged denizens of Chichester, their patriotic zeal contingent upon the provision of appropriately flattering uniforms, provides a telling counterpoint to more heroic images of loyal citizens spontaneously stepping forth in defence of king and country. Marsh's personal mobilization was far from spontaneous. Yet it is possible to see how for many Britons during the war, involvement in military associations could be perceived as a natural extension of their involvement in the nation's flourishing associational culture.[3] The press, much of which was filled with lavish descriptions of Volunteer parades and loyal addresses from Volunteer units, actively sought to promote an impression of wartime unity and patriotic unanimity, but the letters and journals of individuals such as Marsh indicate that behind this excited rhetoric the experience of civilian mobilization was often deeply mundane. The family papers of local elites from this period contain numerous letter books detailing the minutiae of militia business, personal correspondence and journals are often filled with dry and business-like accounts of military service that do little to convey what would, for many civilians, have been a novel encounter with the military world. This did not mean that the encounter was without friction. For members of the middling classes, there was often a degree of consternation at finding themselves suddenly subject to compulsory rolls and registers, exercises and drill.[4] Many corps employed sergeants from the regular army as instructors; John Marsh described with amusement the novelty of the situation as the respectable members of the Chichester Volunteers were forced to take orders from a peremptory 'illiterate serjeant'. It was, he observed, like 'going to school again or being lectur'd like so many children'.[5]

Women were also called upon to contribute to the war effort. This too could be framed as an extension of peacetime charitable roles and responsibilities. However, tensions between the philanthropic and the military meant that this re-orientation of female associational life was not entirely seamless. For the wives of militia officers, particularly those who travelled with their husbands to Ireland, it could be a struggle to reconcile the imperatives of 'genteel' femininity with their proximity to military violence. Mass mobilization involved encounters not only between the civilian and military worlds, but also, for those who travelled with their regiments across the country, between different regions of the British Isles. The nature of these encounters ranged, as we shall see, from easy sociability to, in the case of Ireland, a more abrasive clash of cultures. Those sent to Ireland were no longer merely 'playing' at soldiers.

National defence bodies, 1793–1815

The Volunteers were one of a range of auxiliary bodies for national defence mobilized over the course of the wars to contribute the vital 'addition of mass' to the British war effort.[6] Distinct from the professional army, these armed bodies, while sanctioned and often coordinated by the state, remained embedded to varying degrees in the civilian societies from whence they sprang. The English militia had its roots in the seventeenth-century civil wars, when it had emerged as a republican counterpoise to the standing army of the crown. The militia forces that were embodied during the Revolutionary and Napoleonic wars were more immediately descended from the 'new' militia established in 1757 to defend against a threatened French invasion. The revived militia continued to draw on some of the oppositional independent ethos of its seventeenth-century predecessor, styling itself as a constitutional force opposed to the professional military. It was organized at a local level by the Lord Lieutenants, officered by the landed elite, and adopted measures to ensure that the appointment of officers would not be subject to government patronage and interference.[7] Yet it was also commanded by the king, funded by parliament and supervised by the army.[8] The militia was maintained into peacetime, but would not be fully embodied again until the American war. In 1792, with war imminent, the militia was mobilized once again. A voluntary subscription was introduced in 1794 to provide funds for the augmentation of the militia, which raised 5,000 militiamen and 6,000 Fencible cavalry. At the end of 1796, with the government anxious to release regular troops for service overseas, a supplementary militia of 60,000 men raised by ballot was proposed.[9] Initially, this supplementary force was to be given military training but not fully embodied, yet by 1798 it too had been mobilized. By 1799 the militia forces stood at 82,000, a figure which fell short of the projected strength of 106,000 but which was, nonetheless, treble the numbers at the start of the war.[10]

While conscription was never introduced in Britain, recruitment for militia regiments involved a degree of compulsion as able-bodied men between 18 and 45 were liable to be balloted for service. Under the militia acts, certain categories of persons were deemed exempt, including poor men under 5 ft 4 in. tall (lowered to 5 ft 2 in. in 1796), clergy, apprentices, sailors, workers in the royal dockyards and former militia officers. A balloted man could avoid service by paying a £10 fine to provide a substitute, although he would still be eligible for subsequent ballots. As the laws relating to the militia developed, the 'principle of obligatory personal service receded' as various strategies were developed to allow men to escape the ballot. In Scotland, subscriptions were raised to help hire substitutes for the poor, and elsewhere substitute clubs were formed to provide an insurance for those drawn for the militia.[11] These exemptions point to the broad distaste for militia service amongst the British population. In several respects, militia service during wartime differed little from service in the regular army. Once embodied a militiaman was required to serve for the duration of the war plus one month, and militia soldiers were also subject to the harsh system of military discipline. Though regiments could not be ordered overseas, they were often stationed far away from their home counties and many units served in Ireland during and after the 1798 rebellion. Over the course of the Revolutionary and Napoleonic wars, the militia would increasingly come to be seen as a training ground for the regular army and militia men were encouraged to enlist in line regiments: Private William Wheeler, for instance, joined the 51st regiment from the Royal Surrey militia.[12] The complicated relationship between the local militia, the state and the regular forces remained a contentious issue throughout the wars as local elites jealously defended the militia's status as a constitutional body for home defence rather than an adjunct to the standing army.

In Ireland and Scotland, the militia developed along rather different lines. While an Irish militia act had been introduced in 1715 it had lapsed by the outbreak of the war. The militia issue was particularly fraught in Ireland where the question of whether Catholics should be permitted to serve was vigorously contested. The 1793 Catholic relief act allowed for Irish Catholics to hold commissions in the army and was shortly followed by the Irish militia act. Although sectarian distinctions were not supposed to apply in militia recruitment, the rank and file was largely Catholic and it was mostly officered by Protestants. Initial attempts to ballot for the militia in the spring and summer of 1793 were greeted in several counties with violent protests. Opponents claimed that the militia would 'draw fathers from their families', leaving wives and dependents destitute. Resistance to the militia quickly tapped into a range of other deeply-felt Catholic grievances against the Irish administration. These anti-militia riots, which resulted in an estimated 230 deaths within the space of a few weeks, have been identified as a crucial prelude to the insurrection of 1798.[13] Nevertheless, as the ballot was tacitly dropped and measures introduced to reassure those eligible for the militia that there would be no overseas service and that provision for their families would be improved, resistance to the militia abated. Anxieties regarding the loyalty of the Catholic rank and file, however, persisted. By 1797, there was evidence that militiamen in various Irish garrisons had been suborned by the two main radical revolutionary groups, the Defenders and the United Irishmen. In May of that year, four members of the Monaghan militia which had been stationed in Belfast were tried and executed as United Irishmen.[14] The United Irish leadership had assured the French that in the event of an invasion the Catholic militia would quickly rally to the republican cause. Yet, when the rebellion broke, the Irish militia regiments showed that they were prepared to defend the state against the insurgents and from 1799 many regiments volunteered for service in England claiming that they wished to display their gratitude to the English militia for their assistance in 1798.[15]

The Scottish equivalents of the militia in the eighteenth century were the fencible regiments. Unlike the English militia, enlistment into the fencibles was entirely voluntary and soldiers could not be sent outside Scotland except in the case of an invasion of Great Britain, or with their consent. Several units, however, served in Ireland in 1798 and others were used to reinforce overseas garrisons.[16] In 1797, the militia was extended to Scotland. Whilst the recruitment quota in both Ireland and England had fallen relatively lightly on the population with a service ratio of one man in fifty, in Scotland the ballot was confined to a much smaller age group (19–23 year olds). Consequently each man on the lists had a one in four chance of being called to serve.[17] The ballots for the militia during the summer of 1797 provoked fierce opposition, particularly in the farming regions of the Lowlands which could ill afford to lose male agricultural labour. The perceived threat which the militia act posed to the family economy of these areas was reflected in the large number of women who joined the protests against the ballot. According to the Marquess of Yester, the Lord Lieutenant of East Lothian, the deputy lieutenants and magistrates responsible for implementing the ballot were, upon arrival at the balloting station, surrounded by crowds of people, 'chiefly Women, who were extremely clamourous...it was said we would not leave the Town alive and that they would have our hearts' blood before the hour was over'.[18] An address from the Lord and deputy lieutenants of Roxburgh responded to the unrest by clarifying the terms of the militia act (downplaying the chances of selection) and invoking Scotland's masculine and martial identity:

> we are unwilling to think that our Young Men are become so effeminate and spiritless and so unlike their Fathers, as to get the help of Women to raise mobs and clamours, in order to save them from ONE chance in a HUNDRED of bearing Arms for the King and Country, EVEN AT THEIR OWN DOORS.[19]

Despite these disturbances the militia was effectively established in Scotland after 1798–9. This was partly achieved through the development of a market in substitutes and the organization of subscriptions to help those who were balloted defray the costs of finding someone to take their place. Nevertheless, the proportion of principals (balloted men serving in person) within the British Isles was highest in northern Scotland, where soldiering remained a crucial source of employment for much of the population.[20] At its peak in 1805 the strength of the militia in England, Scotland and Ireland would be 89,000.

The organization of the militia was dependent upon a high degree of co-ordination and negotiation between the state and local authorities and was closely integrated with the broader strategic needs of the War Office. In contrast, the Volunteer forces were initiated by civilians at a local level though they increasingly came under the supervision of the state as the wars progressed. Enrolment in a volunteer corps required far less of a military commitment than membership of the militia. Unlike the militia, Volunteers were not liable for full-time service away from home, were subject to martial law only in the event of invasion, and were free to resign at any moment. As drilling and exercises were comparatively light, Volunteering could, in theory, be combined with a full-time occupation allowing members to maintain their civilian identities. The first efflorescence of Volunteering occurred between 1793 and 1794. While these forces have been seen as offshoots of the English and Welsh loyalist associations established between 1792 and 1793 to defend the British constitution against the threat of French-inspired radicalism, more recent scholarship has called into question the link between this counter-revolutionary movement and Volunteering. Rather than seeing the Volunteers as the ideological successors of the loyalist association, Austin Gee and John Cookson have stressed the fundamentally military, as opposed to political, character of these forces. Though the Volunteers in their 'law and order' role may have helped to curb the activities of British radical agitators, as they developed and became a genuine mass movement in 1797–1798 their role as a bulwark of national defence against the external threat of French invasion increasingly predominated.[21] By the time of the invasion scare in 1803 and 1805 the Volunteers had become the most numerous military body in the British Isles, comprising nearly 400,000 or around 18 per cent of all men of military age at its peak in 1804.[22]

The sheer scale of this mass civilian mobilization has placed the Volunteers centre stage in recent analyses of British armed nationalism during the Revolutionary and Napoleonic wars. The willingness of ordinary Britons to take up arms to defend the country is key to Linda Colley's argument for the depth of popular attachment to the British nation in this period. Yet, as Colley and other historians have noted, Volunteering was a complex and diverse phenomenon, one which cannot simply be read as a spontaneous demonstration of loyalty and wartime unity. In the first instance, the popularity of Volunteering varied widely across the regions of the British Isles. Inhabitants of those areas most vulnerable to French invasion, such as the southern and western coasts of England, showed the greatest willingness to enlist, with an average of 50 per cent of all men aged between seventeen and fifty-five volunteering to bear arms in 1803.[23] Scotland had one of the highest rates of Volunteering with roughly one in three adult males joining volunteer corps in Edinburgh, Midlothian and Peebles.[24] Volunteering was also a predominantly urban activity: an estimated three quarters of the corps in the earlier part of the revolutionary war, and over half in the latter part, were town corps.[25] The inward-looking and isolated rural areas of the country were much less likely to respond to a threat that appeared remote from their inhabitants' everyday concerns.[26]

In Ireland, Volunteering had more problematic connotations. The Irish Volunteer movement which had been raised during the American war in the 1770s had played a key role in the campaign for Irish legislative independence and the constitutional settlement of 1782. After the French Revolution, Irish radicals, inspired by the French National Guard, had briefly revived the Volunteers, but these bodies were quickly suppressed on the outbreak of war in 1793. The closest Irish equivalents to the Volunteer movement during this period were the Yeomanry corps. Overwhelmingly Protestant in composition, this body was often viewed as the armed defender of the Protestant Ascendancy and a counterpoint to the largely Catholic militia. Indeed, in the Irish context, rather than unifying the population, civilian–military mobilization arguably helped to entrench sectarian divisions, the yeomanry and the militia serving as 'the military expression of two rival "nations" that emerged in Ireland in the years after 1800'.[27]

Citizens as soldiers

> Vanguard of liberty, ye men of Kent,
> Ye children of a soil that doth advance
> Her haughty brow against the coast of France,
> Now is the time to prove your hardiment!
> To France be words of invitation sent!

> ...Left single, in bold parley, ye of yore,
> Did from the Norman win a gallant wreath;
> confirmed the charters that were yours before; -
> No parleying now! In Britain is one breath
> We all are with you now from shore to shore:
> Ye men of Kent, 'tis victory or death!
>   William Wordsworth, 'To the Men of Kent.
>   October 1803'[28]

Wordsworth's patriotic exhortation to the men of Kent illuminates several aspects of mass volunteering in this period. The valorous mobilization of citizen soldiers in these verses assumes a distinctly regional character, one that harks back to the heroic deeds of Kentish ancestors, while, at the same time, situating it within a unified British war effort stretching from 'shore to shore'. It is also a decidedly masculine effort, in which the nation's men will prove 'their hardiment' against the French foe. Wordsworth's rousing sentiments would be echoed by less accomplished writers in the flood of patriotic propaganda that poured forth during the invasion scares of 1797–1798 and 1803–1805. Ballads and popular verses urged Britons to step forward to defend their property, families and liberties and depicted enlistment in volunteer or militia regiments as a vital index of national loyalty and wartime unanimity. Such patriotic literature, however, cannot be read as a simple reflection of the motivations and allegiances of those who actually served in national defence bodies, not least because it was often targeted at groups whose loyalties were seen as uncertain.[29] The crudeness of patriotic propaganda made it an object of derision for many. When a series of 'Volunteer songs' appeared in the *York Herald* during the invasion scare of 1803, an amused reader caustically commented on this effort to rouse 'the patriotic fire "which slumbers in the peasant breast"', observing that the composition 'tears an allusion to tatters, to very rags & splits the ears'.[30] Even those charged with producing such rousing addresses could be cynical about their content. The chaplain of the Derwent Volunteers admitted that a loyal sermon he had preached to the men was 'a Rhapsody, deliver'd with a violence as suiting the ignorance and blunted perceptions of my auditors'.[31]

Though British men and women may have greeted the bombastic rhetoric that accompanied national militarization with scepticism, the epistolary networks that criss-crossed the country reporting on levels of military mobilization pulsed with competitive claims to shows of loyalty. Writing from Edinburgh to a friend in Bristol in 1798, Anne Murray Keith expressed her 'wish to send an account of our Volunteers and of the predominancy of loyalty here':

we have many a viper in our bosoms but thank God they are much crushed – in times like ours it is good policy tho' no foreign enemy threatened – to make as many hearts and hands our own as possible, a good infection spreads as well as a bad, & ev'ry Volunteer that enlists brings a little host at his back – the spirit is very general in our Country.[32]

Though Keith downplayed the threat of an invasion, during the 1790s Edinburgh and the south-east coast of Scotland were perceived as vulnerable to French attack, particularly after France took possession of the Low Countries in 1795. By emphasizing instead the internal threat from Scottish subversives, she echoed broader anxieties amongst the Scottish elite regarding the region's reputation for political radicalism. During the 1790s, the vigorous construction of an image of united loyalty and patriotism in Edinburgh was often achieved through intense social pressure, as those perceived to be insufficiently patriotic were coerced into more explicit displays of loyalty.[33] In 1797, it was reported in the *Caledonian Mercury* that an association of Edinburgh ladies had agreed to boycott the services of any of the sedan chairmen who had not enrolled in the Edinburgh Royal Highland Volunteers.[34] In such contexts, loyalty could not be assumed but had to be actively and publicly demonstrated. As Jessie Harden wrote after her brother and husband had joined the local Edinburgh Volunteer corps, 'In this time of general alarm there is a great bustle among all the Young Men as they think it quite necessary *to show* their Loyalty'.[35] While Scottish citizens may have been particularly keen to dispel doubts regarding their willingness to support the war effort, this did not necessarily mean that national attachments were dissolved within a wider British patriotism. Proudly reporting on the enthusiasm and discipline of the Edinburgh Volunteers 'composed of the most respectable young and midle [*sic*] aged men in town', George Home reflected on the broader influence of this martial resurgence upon the Scottish national character:

> for this Century past the Pedlar Spirit of money making and the vain Idle spirit of money spending has divided society, so that the bulk of the People are not now Capable of thinking of anything else, whether it is now or half a century hence we must recover in some degree to the ancient military spirit, or we must cease to be an Independent Kingdom.[36]

Home drew upon a long-standing discourse of martial civic republicanism closely associated with Scottish anti-unionist rhetoric, in which Volunteering formed part of a distinguished and distinctive Scottish military heritage, one which combined loyalty and national independence.

Outside Scotland, Volunteering could similarly be understood as a vehicle for the expression of sub-national patriotisms and identities. In 1803 Anne Cholmeley wrote an account of the preparations for national defence in North Yorkshire to her brother, then at Minto in Scotland:

> Mr Wynn Bellasyse is raising both cavalry and infantry. Mr Langley and Sir George Cayley are each raising 500 men. Mr Harland and Mr Fairfax

are raising Volunteers too so you see Yorkshire men are as much a nation of warriors as the Scotch.[37]

The chaplain of the Leeds Volunteers was equally keen to convey to his correspondent in London the loyalty and unanimity that prevailed in the region, assuring him that 'we are as busy here, as you are in London'.[38] As in Edinburgh, Yorkshire during the 1790s had been a centre of radical activity, a fact which may have lent an added urgency to such displays of competitive loyalty amongst local elites.

If a desire to prove their patriotic zeal and attachment to the state was a leading factor in many contemporary accounts of civilian mobilization, for others the question of whether or not to take up arms against the French depended upon a more restricted concept of national defence.[39] For such individuals, it was only the direct and immediate threat of invasion which could impel them to assume a military role. Christopher Bellew, an Irish Catholic whose brother had raised a militia regiment in Galway, outlined his minimal commitment to the patriotic war effort, writing in the aftermath of the failed French landing at Bantry Bay that:

> If I went into any corps in the Country, I should give a preference to that in which you were, but as my intention was founded on the presumption of *actual existing* danger as that is now removed in my mind it ceases to be a duty, and I feel no inclination, either to make a merit with Government or to compromise with public opinion.[40]

A willingness to defend their property and families marked the baseline from which individuals' commitment to the national war effort could be measured. As John Marsh wryly noted, once the immediate threat of invasion in 1797 had passed, the martial ardour of Sussex Volunteers soon cooled, and many resigned.[41]

Questions of national defence or patriotism apart, there could be multiple motivations and reasons for serving in these auxiliary military bodies. The fact that Volunteers were exempt from the militia ballot undoubtedly acted as an important incentive in prompting men to enlist in these corps.[42] Anna Maria Elliot observed with a degree of cynicism the local men's rush to join the Minto Volunteers. 'They are grown so Loyall [*sic*] since they find they are to be saved from the Militia', she reported 'that it is quite *affecting* to see how they *crowd* to our standard'.[43] As British trade suffered and the demand for agricultural labour shrank under the impact of a series of poor harvests, the militia often served as an alternative source of employment for both the labouring poor and the higher ranks. In 1798 Sir Christopher Courtney obtained a commission in the local militia for his dissolute son because 'there was no Prospect of his doing anything in the mercantile line till there was a Peace'.[44] While Joseph Mayett of Buckinghamshire was able to take advantage of temporarily high wartime wages for agricultural labourers, when this work fell off the only option available to him was to enlist in the Royal Bucks militia.[45]

There could also be intense social and familial pressures to enlist. During a tour of Scotland in the summer of 1803, Francis Cholmeley received strongly worded letters from both his mother and sister urging him to return to Yorkshire and do his duty as a member of the local elite by assuming command of the Brandsby Volunteeers. 'You are enjoying yourself amazingly just now' his sister Catherine scolded 'but as soon as you return home I assure you, you will not be quite so much at large, as you must volunteer yourself for the defence of your country'.[46] Such coercive pressures could take a more sinister form. Having declined to subscribe to the Wharfedale Volunteers in September 1803, William Vavasour received an anonymous letter criticizing his failure to show 'a proper spirit & liberality especially as regards the present times of danger'. During the earlier invasion scare, Vavasour had himself proved ready to deploy similar intimidating tactics. When one of his tenant's reneged on a promise to send his son into the corps he threatened them with eviction.[47]

The militia and Volunteers also held more positive attractions for those who enlisted. Membership enabled men of various ranks to achieve a degree of status and respectability within their communities. As Mark Philp observes, irrespective of class, all members of the Volunteers were treated by convention as gentlemen, allowed to wear uniforms, to carry arms and to parade.[48] For the agricultural labourer, the militia could provide an escape from backbreaking field work, as described in the Scottish Gaelic poet Duncan Ban MacIntyre's lament on the disbanding of the Breadalbane Fencibles:

> If we go to farm labour,
> Our shoulders will be bent with delving.
> Much better to be gentlemen,
> Lining up in the battalion.[49]

According to Western, lieutenants and ensigns in the militia tended to be 'needy individuals in search of a living and youths of impecunious family who wanted a military career on the cheap'.[50] Concerns regarding the instant respectability conferred by a militia commission are well-illustrated by the character of Mr Wickham in Austen's *Pride and Prejudice* (1813), who obscures his disreputable past by reinventing himself as a militia officer.[51] Volunteering raised similar concerns about social intermixing. Reginald Heber, nominal commander of the Hodnet Company of Volunteers in Shropshire, wrote warmly of the sociability that accompanied the collective gathering of county elites as regimental and battalion musters, a conviviality he compared to that of his Oxford College, Brasenose, the most popular college for the hard-drinking, fox-hunting country gentry. The limits of Volunteer sociability in bridging social divisions, however, was also highlighted in Heber's dismissive reference to the 'raffs' amongst the Volunteer officer corps, who, he complained in a letter to his brother, 'are all sober and leave as soon as they have finished their pint'.[52] Many Volunteer corps were based on professional affiliations and within these too, concerns were manifested regarding the need to preserve status distinctions. When the Royal Academy proposed establishing a Corps of Artists, a dispute arose over who might justifiably claim to be an artist, one member objecting that everyone enrolled would be classed as such 'however miserable his attempts' and 'that wd. Not be for the Honor of the Profession'.[53]

A further attraction of the Volunteers and militia was the forum they provided for masculine conviviality. Contemporary accounts of the Volunteers describe an intensive round of drinking and socializing that followed drills, parades and committee meetings. Although he was too old to serve himself, as deputy lieutenant of the East Riding, Christopher Courtney was actively involved with the organization of the county's defences. His diary regularly described long evenings dining and drinking with the militia officers. Bumper toasts were drunk, loyal songs sung and as Courtney repeatedly reported 'we were all very unanimous & sociable'.[54] Such conviviality was of central importance to wartime patriotism. In both its rituals and expression, Georgian loyalty was replete with the language of affection and attachment: to the king, to the established order, and to the companions with whom one associated in defence of the country. The culture of drinking and toasting established a context in which social and political differences could be set aside.[55] Personal narratives often made close connections between masculine sociability and loyalty. As Robert Elliot observed of his Volunteer corps 'we are all most perfectly Loyal, but also most perfectly drunken'.[56] This sociability could extend beyond the membership of particular Volunteer or militia corps to include regiments from other regions who were stationed in the locality. As they dined, drank and toasted, together loyalty and its practices could assume a less parochial character, with Cornish militia officers, for example, joining Yorkshire volunteers in expressions of mutual attachment.

Membership of the Volunteers and, to a lesser extent, the militia, also enabled British and Irish men to identify themselves as soldiers without requiring the same degree of commitment as enlistment in the regular forces. Neil Ramsey's study of John Clare's militia service notes the labouring poet's childhood fascination with soldiering, which functioned as a 'romantic idea of escape and transformation'. Clare's imaginative attraction to the transformative possibilities of the military, however, was coupled with a deep-seated fear and horror at the estrangements and hardships experienced by the regular soldier.[57] Indeed, though many ordinary soldiers who fought in line regiments had originally enlisted in the militia, other militiamen, such as Joseph Mayett, strongly resisted official inducements to volunteer for service abroad.[58] The Volunteers provided a less demanding arena in which fantasies of martial masculinity could be played out. Walter Scott's desire for a military life had been thwarted by a disability resulting from a child-hood bout of polio, but as a founding member of the Edinburgh Volunteer Dragoons he was able to satisfy his yearnings for soldierly adventure. Scott's Volunteer activity provided a crucial context and inspiration for his celebra-tory war poetry and he often composed verses in the intervals between drill-ing.[59] As he wrote from encampments in 1803 'to one who has like myself, *la tête un peu exaltée*, the "pomp and circumstance of war" gives, for a time, a very poignant and pleasing sensation.'[60] Scott's attraction to the glamour and thrill of military service was, nonetheless, balanced by more pragmatic concerns. Membership of the cavalry corps, he recognized, allowed him to associate with members of the Scottish elite who might act as future patrons for the struggling man of letters.[61]

A desire to prove one's manhood against the French may have inspired some to volunteer. As a pupil at Harrow, Thomas Law Hodges, who would later serve with the militia in Ireland, eagerly awaited a French invasion, hoping only that the French might land during the school holidays, so that he could enlist 'to stem the torrent of these atheists'.[62] For the young, a mili-tary uniform could confer instant manly maturity; Sir Christopher Courtney noted, for example, that his son 'looked older I thought in his Regimentals'.[63] For those of more advanced years an involvement in auxiliary corps could allow them to recapture a youthful virility: the commander of the Herford and Derwent Dale Volunteers observing that due to his military exertions 'I feel myself young again'.[64]

Nonetheless, the imagined attractions of military life were often under-mined by the day-to-day tedium of part-time soldiering. It is the fatigue and boredom of drill, exercise and regimental administration, rather than the patriotic thrill of military service, which tends to predominate in letters and journals. William Vavasour's diary recorded the irksome duties which his position as a Volunteer officer entailed, forcing him out in all weathers to attend military exercises and requiring him to spend long periods away from home doing duty in neighbouring regions. Stationed in Tynemouth, he reflected on the loneliness of 'an officer in out quarter without a single acquaintance in the neighbourhood'.[65] A recurring complaint of militia officers and civilian Volunteers was the time-consuming nature of their mili-tary duties which often drew them away from their civilian occupations. Requesting to be relieved from attendance at the Roxburghshire Yeomanry's field days, one officer stressed the strain which two years spent 'attending to the Drills and other meetings of a publick nature' had placed on his personal concerns and private business.[66] Although militia service often required indi-viduals to travel the length and breadth of the British Isles, many members of the Volunteer force were unwilling to make such a commitment. The Chichester Volunteers, for example, signalled the limited compass of their patriotism by refusing to serve outside of the city.[67] The Marquess of Yester,

Lord Lieutenant of East Lothian, insisted that, as the bulk of the county yeomanry was composed of substantial farmers who were actively engaged in supporting industry and good order in their regions, 'their Families and also the state would suffer more Loss by their being called from Home for any Length of Time than their Service could possibly compensate'.[68]

The tension between civilian and military imperatives was a characteristic feature of mass mobilization. Amongst the Volunteer rank and file a series of disputes concerning pay and conditions served to assert their status as citizens as well as soldiers. On occasion, Volunteer corps refused to act as a supplementary police force when called upon to do so by local magistrates.[69] While the militia increasingly came under the control of the regular army during the wars, its independence continued to be jealously guarded by local elites. As militia regiments were encouraged to volunteer for active service abroad Christopher Courtney expressed his unease at a measure, he believed, would make the force 'only a drill for the army'.[70] In many Volunteer corps the members' right to select their own officers was also a central component of the group's identity. When the Chichester Volunteers were first established, their selected lieutenants were vetoed by the county magnate and lord-lieutenant, the Duke of Richmond, who, John Marsh reported, did not approve 'of our having chosen our own officers.' Richmond, who, like many members of the patrician elite, had reservations about the formation of volunteer units, clearly saw dangerous seeds of democratic organization sprouting within the corps. The company agreed to suspend all meetings until the issue was resolved and it was only once they conceded that the exclusive choice of their own officers would not be a *sine qua non* that the Duke agreed to appoint the men originally elected.[71] In 1814 all the officers of the Belfast Yeomanry resigned when the Marquis of Donegall was appointed to the supreme command over their preferred candidate.[72] Such episodes point to the sectional interests and conflicts that lay beneath the surface image of cross-class patriotic unanimity. As Cookson argues, Volunteering was often a means of asserting the prestige and autonomy of urban communities, allowing urban elites to act independently of the largely aristocratic county authorities who were responsible for militia organization.[73]

The frustrations and challenges of assuming responsibility for a military body with little previous experience or training emerge clearly in the letters of Reginald Heber, the nominal commander of the Hodnet company of Volunteers in Shropshire. A well-established gentry family, the Hebers owned estates in both Yorkshire and Marton. Though Reginald's brother, Richard, was the official commander of the Hodnet Volunteers, his appointment as Colonel of the Craven Legion in Yorkshire meant that his duties in Shropshire were delegated to his younger brother. Only twenty-one and still a student at Oxford, Reginald evidently struggled with his new role. He complained of thin musters, the grumbling of the men, and the ridicule that the disorderly and often drunken force attracted from other companies and the local children. The importance of a corps' performance to personal, familial and local reputations encouraged competition: Heber reported with some relief that at the regimental muster in Shrewsbury in October 1804 the Hodnet company had improved sufficiently to be singled out as a model for others.[74]

Though Volunteering required British civilians to temporarily exchange their 'coloured clothes' for uniforms and to spend their leisure time learning military exercises, the fact that they retained a degree of autonomy and enjoyed a conviviality not dissimilar to other forms of Georgian clubbability meant that it could be woven relatively easily into the fabric of wartime Britons' everyday lives. This may explain the rather matter-of-fact treatment which amateur soldiering was accorded in contemporary letters and diaries. Militia service was more demanding and required a more intensive absorption into the values and discipline of the military than the Volunteers. As the militia riots of the 1790s indicate, for those upon whom the ballot fell most heavily it could be experienced as an unwelcome and excessive imposition by the fiscal–military state. Yet for the literate and propertied classes who organized and officered the militia, it was largely understood as a natural extension of their local leadership roles, roles which, as with the Volunteers, they were prompted to perform through a subtle combination of social and familial pressures rather than through a more abrasive demonstration of state power.

Linking Mars and Venus: women and the war effort

If fantasies of martial heroism were soon buried in the day-to-day tedium of amateur soldiering, civilian defence bodies can still be understood as marking out a masculine terrain of patriotic ritual, homosocial conviviality and martial endeavour. The exertions of Britain's 'citizen-soldiers' did not translate into a wider claim for political rights, but they did, arguably, serve to distinguish between the nation's active, masculine citizenry and its passive, feminine dependents. As their menfolk armed to repel the threatened invasion, some women expressed a degree of unease about their own relative passivity. 'I never felt such a coward before' reflected Jessie Harden, as she watched her male relatives busying themselves with preparations for the defence of Edinburgh.[75] At the same time, women contributed to the civilian war effort in a variety of ways, a patriotic contribution, which may have allowed them to 'carve out for themselves a real if precarious place in the public sphere'.[76] A full consideration of the extent to which war expanded or constricted the boundaries of women's activity is beyond the scope of the present study.[77] A fruitful alternative line of analysis, however, is suggested by Kathleen Wilson, who has directed attention to the ways in which warfare created opportunities for women's 'complicity with and resistance to the nation-state's injunction to militarism'.[78] Mass civilian mobilization

necessarily relied on the support of women, whether as enthusiastic spectators, dispensers of charity, or military wives. Yet their exclusion from the
defining activity of the British armed nation – the bearing of arms – and
their rhetorical positioning as repositories of wartime compassion and sentiment could at the same time induce a more questioning attitude towards the
process of militarization.

A brief survey of middling and elite women's diaries from this period reveals
the extent to which attendance at Volunteer parades and reviews became
incorporated into the usual calendar of tea-parties, engagements and assemblies. In the opening months of 1804, Christian Dalrymple of Newhailes,
East Lothian, recorded no less than nine trips to military field days.[79] Women
were very much integrated into these spectacles, demonstrating the comprehensive and unified character of the war effort by providing an admiring
audience towards whom manoeuvres and exercises could be performed. 'It
is pretty evident that the Poets who link Mars and Venus in lasting bands of
attachment' an observer of a Dublin military review wrote in 1803:

> were not bad judges of human nature...Sensible of these important
> truths, and of the vast influence of the fair sex, whenever they chuse to
> exert their authority in favour of the public welfare, it was therefore with
> delight that I beheld the last general review of the numerous yeomanry of
> this city and county, illuminated by the beauty of Dublin.[80]

The playfulness that characterized elite British women's engagement
with the 'extravagant spectacles of a glamorous and benign fiscal-military
complex' in previous conflicts, gave way, under the pressure of protracted
warfare and the ominous threat of invasion, to more sober and serious patriotic pursuits.[81] Women's contribution to the civilian war effort was most
commonly expressed through charitable activity; a contribution which
could be viewed as the feminine complement of male military service.
Whereas female philanthropy had traditionally focused on women and
children, during the wars it expanded in scope to include new objects of
benevolent interest, such as wounded servicemen and the Volunteer rank
and file. Women were responsible for an estimated twenty per cent of all
donations to the Voluntary Contribution, the fund introduced in 1798 to
help finance the war effort.[82] They were also active in providing clothing
to both the regular troops and the Volunteers, as satirized in Gillray's 1793
satirical print *Flannel-Armour* which depicts 'female patriots' taking a great
deal of pleasure dressing British soldiers in flannel undergarments of their
own manufacture.

Such appropriately 'feminine' tasks served in some degree to underline women's role as domestic auxiliaries to the military and complacent
supporters of the war effort. Yet a closer analysis of women's charitable
exertions during this period reveals a more complicated and conflicted

relationship between women and the British armed nation. In October 1803, a ladies committee for the distribution of flannel clothing was established in York. Its members included the Unitarian Catherine Cappe, who was responsible for several philanthropic initiatives in the city, and a broad coalition of women from the city's middling and upper classes, including Jane Ewbank, the daughter of an Anglican clergyman, whose diary recorded the progress of the association. As was the case for their male counterparts in the militia and Volunteers, York women's engagement with the war effort could be understood as an extension of their roles in the associational life of the city: Ewbank was a member of the Ladies Committee for the Gray Coat School and supported the Female Friendly Society that provided assistance to domestic servants.[83] The association drew together those upon whom the burdens of war fell most heavily and their genteel sisters in a common patriotic cause. Those who could not afford to contribute financially to the endeavour were enlisted to help in sewing flannel garments.[84] The initiative, however, proved controversial. Several of the local Volunteer corps rejected the committee's offer to provide flannel clothing to those most in need. When the committee's offer was read before one company, it was remarked that 'no man would chuse to accept a gift which was considered by the Ladies as a charity' a pronouncement that was quickly followed by cries of 'no-no-no' from the assembled auditors. The hostility which the proposal provoked was partly due to the use of the term 'objects of pity' to describe the intended recipients of the committee's charity. It was, Ewbank conceded, an unfortunate choice of words. Those men who accepted clothing from the association were jeered by the other Volunteer companies as 'objects of pity'. The Lady Mayoress was pursued through the streets by enraged Volunteers crying 'objects of pity'.

The evident resentment which the female committee aroused suggests some of the limits of wartime unanimity and its potential to fracture under the pressure of both gender and class conflict. Though wartime patriotism may have encouraged women to extend the scope of their philanthropic activity, their endeavours were by no means uncontested. By refusing to act as 'objects of charity' the Volunteer rank and file not only registered their hostility to the expanded scope of female philanthropy, but also their anxiety to assert and maintain the status achieved through Volunteering: they were masculine defenders of women, not passive beneficiaries of female largesse. The interference of female 'do-gooders' threatened the ideal of patriotic, cross-class, homosocial bonding upon which the Volunteers partly rested. For those women involved in the failed scheme, this unexpected hostility seems to have contributed to a lingering disillusionment with civilian militarism. Some months after the committee had been dissolved, Ewbank led a procession to the Minster cathedral to hear a sermon for the benefit of the Female Friendly Society. The previous day the Volunteer corps had also paraded to the Minster and in her diary Ewbank reflected on the contrast between the two processions:

the common observer may find less to dazzle; but to those who think & feel how unmixed the pleasure; how far more satisfactory to the reflection this assemblage, of the affluent who contribute their money & their time & pains for the succour of the indigent, of young and blooming girls... how much more satisfactory to the feelings I say is such an assemblage, than that of men glittering in arms & trained in the work of slaughter (tho' true the cause in the present case is just as glorious) & as such its defenders will claim our approbation and thanks; but our esteem & gratitude must still be deeply tinged with sorrow, whenever we reflect on the direful chances of war, or even the 'Price of a Victory'.[85]

Rather than acting as complement to masculine militarism, female charity, in Ewbank's reflections, is set in opposition to the martial posturing of amateur soldiers. In contrast to the pomp and splendour of the Volunteers which barely obscured their function as a vehicle for organized violence, the disinterested benevolence of the ladies could be viewed with 'unmixed pleasure'. Forcibly excluded from contributing to the civilian war effort, Ewbank seems to have assumed a more critical attitude towards the 'cult of militarism'.

Although the move from camps into barracks during this period signalled the increasing masculinization of military space, within auxiliary defence bodies the gendered boundaries between military and civilian society remained less sharply defined, and officers' wives often accompanied their husbands on militia service.[86] Rebecca Leslie, wife of the colonel of the Loyal Tay fencibles and Anna Walker, who was married to the colonel of the 50th regiment, both followed their husbands to garrisons in Ireland as part of the 80,000 strong force sent to pacify the rebellion. Subject, as Anna Walker put it, to all the 'uncertainty & discomfort of a Military life', they dutifully travelled across the length and breadth of the country, lodging in squalid country inns and draughty barracks, uprooting at a moment's notice whenever the regiment received new marching orders.[87] Despite these inconveniencies, both women closely identified with the military world that shaped their everyday existence; in a letter of July 1798, Leslie described herself as 'an old campaigner'.[88]

As colonels' wives, Leslie and Walker were expected to play a leading role in regimental life. They hosted and attended balls and suppers with local dignitaries, helping to smooth relations between the regiment and the communities amongst whom they were stationed. These relations could be fraught: in August 1803 Anne Walker received a visit from a furious Lady Donegall, venting her displeasure at the restrictions imposed on the citizens of Belfast following the 1803 rising.[89] Yet the presence of 'genteel' women appears to have lent the military garrison a more humane face, presenting their husbands as genial family men, rather than the commanders of a potentially oppressive armed force. The need to maintain warm relations with the locals meant that sociability was often more of a duty than a pleasure and Leslie received strict instructions from her husband to accept every invitation she received. Both women performed the role of the 'incorporated wife', their informal activities supporting and complementing their husbands' professional duties.[90] Walker frequently acted as her husband's secretary, transcribing fair copies of official documents and letters, whilst Leslie assisted her husband by preparing digests of all his correspondence.[91] They were also expected to take a particular interest in the women of the regiment. The conduct of officers' wives was closely scrutinized to determine whether they would enhance the regiment's reputation.[92] Acutely aware of military hierarchies, Leslie adopted a rather aloof attitude towards the 'Loyal-Tay-ladies' with whom she was forced to associate, bemoaning their vulgarity and their unwelcome insistence on keeping her company during her husband's absences.[93] Although the shared experience of garrison life did not necessarily generate an *esprit de corps* amongst the 'ladies of the regiment', the paternalism that shaped relations between officers and men was replicated in the patrician solicitude which Walker and Leslie expressed towards the wives of ordinary soldiers. When Walker learned that the 'poor Men's wives' had been evicted from the barracks in Longford she begged her husband to intervene on their behalf.[94]

By acting as agents of sociability, dutiful help-meets, and dispensers of benevolence, both women achieved a partial reconciliation between their participation in the masculinized world of the military and accepted codes of feminine behaviour. In their letters and Walker's journal they were at pains to emphasize the ordinary domesticity they sustained despite the unconventional and uncertain circumstances in which they lived: reading sentimental novels with their husbands, dispatching great coats to keep them warm whilst on duty. Their regiments' posting to Ireland was part of a larger 'Britannicizing' of the permanent forces in Ireland after 1798 and, as was the case for the women of the nineteenth-century Anglo-Indian community, Leslie and Walker's experience of garrison life was partly shaped by a sense of their own detachment from the British military project.[95] Yet the vulnerability of their position, and the blurred boundary between 'home' service and the front line, became vividly evident during the 1798 rebellion and the short-lived rising of 1803, as both women were forced to confront the violence and destruction wrought by civil war and a brutal policy of pacification. In June 1798, Leslie was left alone at the Carrickfergus garrison whilst her husband led a detachment of fencibles to meet the rebel forces at Larne. As reports reached the barracks that the rebels were massing nearby, she described the terror and confusion that rippled through the barracks as the alarm drum sounded and the regiment was ordered out: 'the screams of their wives and the cries of their children', she wrote, 'yet rings in my ears'. In a display of uxorial devotion Leslie determined not to return to Scotland.[96] At the garrison in Belfast in 1803, Anne Walker also recorded the fear and consternation generated by the rebel threat. 'Never', she wrote in her diary, 'can I forget the horror of that Moment – the Bugles were Sounded – the

Drums beat to Arms…Walker scampering like a Mad Man round all the Avenues of the Town. The Agony in which I passed the Night Never can be forgotten.'[97]

As the rebel insurgency was quickly and violently suppressed by the combined British and Irish forces, Leslie's investment in British militarism was increasingly set in tension with the compassionate sensibility which constituted the acceptable outlet for women's engagement with the wartime nation. Leslie was deeply unsettled by the cries of 'kill them' directed at the defeated rebels as they were marched into the garrison. 'You who know my heart & that I wd. Not willingly kill a fly', she confided to a friend, 'can judge how horrible this sounds in my ears'. She later wrote of the disturbed dreams caused by the sight of rebel heads atop the gates of Ballymena town.[98] Leslie was clearly troubled by her own complicity in the counter-insurgency campaign that had spread fear and devastation across Ulster. During a day trip to the Isle of Magee she observed the destruction which the Loyal Tays had left in their wake, the burnt-out houses and cowering demeanour of the inhabitants, and expressed her anxiety that the locals 'would find out & *hate* me'.[99] Reluctant to identify with the work of military violence, the feminine sympathy and compassion traditionally reserved for the suffering British soldier was now extended to their victims and those convicted of rebellion: Leslie intervened to secure a reprieve for a young rebel who had been sentenced to be flogged and successfully pleaded with her husband to release a Presbyterian clergyman with a large family from Carrickfergus jail.[100] Leslie's benevolent intercessions were combined with a belief that her husband was a model of leniency. In this way, she was able to reconfigure the British military garrison as a benign and merciful presence, rather than a coercive power. Anne Walker, in contrast, seems to have found her alignment with the garrison state less troubling. On viewing the newly erected barracks that dominated the bleak and desolate landscape of the Bog of Allen, she readily accepted the necessity of such fortifications which 'civilize and keep the Country quiet' whilst also drawing on her own experience of military life to express her sympathy with 'those who are doomed to inhabit them'.[101]

Despite the close, if unharmonious, relations between the two countries, prior to the Act of Union in 1801 it was widely accepted that 'the English public, knew little about Ireland, and cared less'.[102] Leslie and Walker's travels through Ireland thus provided an opportunity to acquaint themselves with this unfamiliar country at the moment it was incorporated into the United Kingdom, and their accounts can be situated within a broader corpus of travelogues produced in the wake of the Act of Union which sought to explain Ireland to a British audience. Their contrasting perceptions of the purpose and rectitude of the British military mission in Ireland would also be reflected in their differing accounts of the culture and character of the country. Shaped by a garrison mentality which posited a clear divide between the military and the hostile nation which it had been sent to civilize, Walker's narrative from the outset focused on the profound strangeness and otherness of the 'sister kingdom'. Upon first disembarking at Cork in 1802, she observed that the inhabitants 'looked extremely foreign', the 'dirty ragged appearance of the Common People' reminding of her Italy.[103] As she travelled up the country, she continuously reflected on the dirt, poverty and misery of the Irish, although she was quick to note instances of Irish hospitality, a cliché of English travel writing. For Walker, the Irish landscape was indelibly haunted by the legacy of the 1798 rising and in each of the towns where the regiment halted en route to Belfast she gathered anecdotes of the depredations committed by the rebels, thereby confirming her view of Ireland as violent, disorderly, and in need of pacification.

Whilst Walker's experiences of Ireland reinforced a sense of the island as fundamentally alien, Leslie's residence there seems to have engendered an enduring attachment to the country. Her letters' oft-repeated declarations of enthusiasm for 'everything Irish' were partly staged for the benefit of her correspondents, the Stewarts of Killymoon, Co. Cookstown, whom she had befriended shortly after the Loyal Tays' arrival. When she returned to Scotland in 1801 she proudly reported on how thoroughly 'Hibernicized' she and her husband had become: both had acquired an Irish brogue and on St Patrick's Day they planted a pot of shamrocks in remembrance of their Irish friends.[104] These affectionate bonds were, no doubt, strengthened by the cultural and religious affinities that already existed between the Scots and the Ulster Presbyterian community. Yet Leslie's celebration of the Irish–Scottish connection did not translate into support for a pan-British union. Indeed, as the preparations for union began during Leslie's stay in Ireland she emerged as a firm opponent, going so far as to attend a party wearing a turban emblazoned with the motto 'No Union'. Drawing parallels with the Anglo-Scottish union of 1707, she declared her belief that the measure would 'lose all the consequence of Ireland & sink her as poor Scotland has been sunk, into a paltry despised corner of Britain'.[105]

Encountering the British Isles

'Did the Warwickshire militia...teach the Irish to drink beer? Or did they learn from the Irish to drink whiskey?'[106]

Maria Edgeworth, Castle Rackrent (1800)

The cross-cultural encounter that formed a key element of Leslie and Walker's experience of military service produced different readings of Ireland's 'otherness', but in neither case does it appear to have fostered an intensified identification with the newly forged United Kingdom of Great Britain and Ireland. It was, however, widely believed that the militia could act as a vehicle for national integration. When a bill to authorize the service of the Irish militia in England was introduced in parliament in 1811, its proponents stressed the beneficial moral and political effects of such an exchange:

'new connections and friendships would be formed, not confined to one class or degree but extending generally through both nations'.[107] Even the more limited opportunities for travel available to Irish militiamen stationed at home, it was argued, could serve to remove parochial and sectarian prejudices.[108] As the militiaman criss-crossed the country, Colley speculates, he would have introduced and absorbed local customs, games and dialects, helping to extend his geographical and cultural horizons.[109] The cultural transfers which resulted from such encounters, however, are difficult to trace and their integrative impact uncertain.[110] Indeed, the most well-known cultural transfer to have resulted from the militia exchanges between Britain and Ireland is the introduction of the Orange Order to Scotland and Lancashire after the 1798 rebellion.[111] Moreover, it cannot be assumed that the civilian communities amongst whom county militias were stationed viewed their guests as cultural ambassadors for their particular *pays*. In many instances, the civilian–military divide may have been more salient than any inter-regional difference.

Though many militia officers expressed their reluctance to serve away from home, the opportunity to travel was welcomed by some of its members. In 1805, John Marshall, a captain in the Aberdeenshire militia, eagerly anticipated an exchange of Scottish and English regiments that would allow him to journey to England. It was several years before his wish was fulfilled, but when his regiment was eventually ordered south he was delighted to discover 'a very Beautiful Country such as I have often fancied England to be'.[112] James Radford, a lieutenant in the Royal Lancashire militia, reported in some detail on the areas through which he journeyed and the leisurely excursions he made to country houses and picturesque abbeys.[113] On his travels through the south of England he showed little consciousness of the north-south divide which is supposed to have emerged during this period.[114] The provincial towns of southern England were depicted as little different from their northern counterparts, the cathedral at Salisbury he likened to York Minster, Dover castle to the castle at Scarborough. For the relatively well-travelled militia officer there was perhaps little novelty in such journeys, whereas for the rank and file transported from the remoter regions of the British Isles to bustling ports and garrison towns, it would, no doubt, have opened up new vistas. Yet the impact of this wartime mobility can only be guessed at. Joseph Mayett, one of the few ordinary militia men to have left a detailed record of his service, displayed surprisingly little curiosity about the different regions to which he travelled, though his marches took him right across the south of England from Essex to Devon and north to Manchester and Berwick-upon-Tweed. The most significant aspect of the Methodist soldier's journeys lay in the active network of non-conformity which it revealed and upon which he was able to draw as he moved from place to place armed with letters of introduction from local ministers.[115] His militia service thus confirmed his membership of a broader national religious community.

While the system of quartering had been a source of tension between the militia and civilian populations in previous conflicts, the provision of barrack accommodation allowed for more cordial relations to develop between troops and townspeople. Visiting militia officers were quickly incorporated into the social life of provincial towns and often lavishly entertained by local elites. As contemporary diaries attest, the brightly clothed officer was a regular and highly visible attendee at balls, assemblies and the theatre. In 1798, a play performed at the request of the military associations stationed at Bury St Edmunds attracted the largest audience the house had ever seen.[116] The diary of Mary Anne Ffolliot of Boyle, Co. Roscommon, suggests the excitement and variety that the presence of different regiments from across the British Isles brought to the social life of a quiet, provincial town. The regiments were an endless source of gossip and scandal, and stories of duels and elopements were eagerly discussed amongst her female acquaintances, a 'militia mania' which Ffoliot gently satirized in her journal:

> Miss Elwood talking nonsense for an hour she says she quite dotes on the English officers and that they never had so pleasant a Regiment in Boyle, the present is always best with her, for I have heard her say the same of 5 Regiments...she said nothing could be gayer than Boyle at present. Balls at the Barracks for ever.[117]

As well as 'balls at the barracks' the militia brought other forms of entertainment to the districts in which they were quartered. Concerts were given by the regimental bands, horse races organized by the 'high-flying' gentry of the officer corps and inter-regimental cricket matches held between Volunteer and militia companies. Sociable relations between militia regiments and their host communities were governed by an implicit rule of reciprocity. When, for instance, the Romney Fencibles held a ball and supper for the inhabitants of Bury St Edmunds the invitation was only extended 'to all who had notic'd the Corps' since it had been quartered there.[118]

The easy sociability which militia corps generally enjoyed as they travelled across Britain and the lack of inter-regional friction or 'culture shock' that they seem to have experienced, points to the relatively high levels of integration which prevailed in Britain at the time of the wars. Militia regiments did not tend to travel to regions such as the Scottish Highlands, the romantic fringes of the island that British tourists were 'discovering' in this period, where the nation's cultural and geographical diversity may have been more apparent. The reverse flow of military traffic from these areas into more urbanized English settings could, however, generate unsettling encounters. Anna Larpent recorded her alarm at witnessing a company of drunken, brawling Highlanders during a visit to Portsmouth. Reflecting a lingering perception of the Highland soldier as a marauding Jacobite, rather than his more recent incarnation as a loyal tartan-clad warrior, she observed that 'There cannot be a more ferocious set of men than these unintelligent Scotsmen. They really are not human'.[119] However, such instances of national prejudice were rare. Where tensions did arise they tended to stem from civilian resentment of military impositions, rather than a particular hostility to the Scottishness or Welshness of a regiment.

Whilst the militia serving in Britain braced themselves for a French invasion that never materialized, in the 1790s their military effectiveness was put to the test in Ireland, where regiments such as the Welsh Ancient Britons would earn a fearsome reputation. In contrast to the conventional campaign narrative which was markedly reticent on the excesses committed by British troops abroad, militiamen's accounts of the campaign in Ireland often recorded the atrocities inflicted upon the civilian population with a frankness reminiscent of French soldiers' accounts of the Vendée, or the Peninsula.[120] Confronted with a popular insurgency, in which the lines between friend and foe, civilian and combatant, were dangerously blurred, the restraints of conventional warfare were abandoned as the militia forces participated in a merciless campaign against the rebellious population. As one soldier recalled, the Irish conflict was the scene of 'barbarities, not now practiced in the national wars of Europe'.[121] Archibald McLaren, a sergeant in the Dumbartonshire Fencibles, described in unflinching detail the brutality with which the campaign was fought, as the troops razed rebel villages to the ground, shot prisoners and unarmed civilians and, in one particularly horrific episode, gang-raped the wife of a suspected rebel.[122]

Though the bulk of the British forces arrived after the 1798 rebellion had been quashed, they came to a country where the embers of civil conflict still smouldered and the memory of military brutality remained fresh. Despite Maria Edgeworth's doubtful hope that the English militia might act as a channel through which English customs and manners could be engrafted onto Irish culture, and whisky-induced Irish disorder be exchanged for the more wholesome consumption of English beer, the fraught landscape of post-rebellion Ireland seemed an unlikely setting for such cross-cultural exchange. There is, nevertheless, evidence of relatively friendly relations between the British military and the native population. Gorey, Co. Wexford had been one of the areas which suffered most during the rebellion. Yet, according to one soldier, the locals flocked to the military camp to drink and dance with the troops, encouraged there by the Catholic priest.[123] When the Loyal Tay Fencibles returned to Scotland from Ulster, they were accompanied by a sizeable contingent of 'female Paddies'.[124] Outside of the garrison, militiamen stationed in Ireland discovered shared Irish–British religious and associational networks. The wavering faith of some of the non-conformist rank and file was revivified through contact with the active Methodist community in Ireland. Officers, meanwhile, extended the pan-British network of loyalism by joining local Masonic lodges. Whilst in Cork with the West Kent Militia Thomas Law Hodges was elected a friendly brother of the Youghal

Knot and celebrated St Patrick's day by wearing a green ribbon in his collar and marching with his new 'brothers' to the parish church.[125] Though the disturbed condition of the country did not make it a particularly restful station, militia officers duly acknowledged the proverbial Irish hospitality and the warm reception that, one English officer recalled, 'makes me always feel an interest for that part of the Empire'.[126]

This did not mean, however, that members of the militia came to see the Irish as West Britons, or that the 'internal frontiers' which demarcated their personal understanding of 'home' and 'away', 'self' and 'other' were brought into alignment with the newly expanded external frontiers of the British state.[127] If the militiaman's service in Britain revealed a landscape and society too familiar to merit extended reflection, his ethnographic reflex was jolted into action once he crossed the Irish Sea: Ireland remained effectively 'foreign', an unknown territory to be discovered and a problem to be explicated. Military narratives repeatedly stressed Ireland's 'otherness'. 'I was surprised even tho' I expected it in some measure', wrote Francis Wood of the West Yorkshire militia 'to see so total a Dissimilarity from the English in Dress, Manners, Cultivation & Mode of Thinking, acting and reasoning'.[128] The Irish gentry were described as feckless, grasping and largely absentee, the Catholic peasantry as indolent, superstitious and in thrall to their priests. Though the island's poverty and backwardness was a commonplace of British rhetoric about Ireland, according to officers' accounts the realities far exceeded anything they had previously imagined. 'If a person has never been to Ireland' reflected Thomas Law Hodges:

> He can have no conception of the deplorable condition of the lower orders – their wretchedness and misery is only equalled by their extreme Ignorance and brutal savageness – Good God! When I reflect on the situation of the meanest English Cottager, and then cast my Eyes on the uncivilized inhabitant of an Irish cabin...the comparison is too much in favour of my happy countryman not to exclaim – 'Can these two mortals own the same king, the same constitution, live under the Influence of the same Laws, and be as it were almost within sight of each other'.[129]

Although Hodges hoped that through the ameliorating effects of the union Ireland might be raised to meet British standards of civilization, the largely negative impressions of the country and its inhabitants which English officers absorbed from service on the Irish garrison seemed to foreclose the possibility that a shared British identity could be constructed between the two peoples. Indeed, the influence of military service in Ireland in shaping British perceptions of, and policy towards, the country should not be underestimated. The many thousands of officers and ordinary soldiers who carried back to their civilian lives an enduring image of Irish backwardness and Catholic superstition would, no doubt, have acted as important informal source of 'knowledge' on the country.

Conclusion

The mobilization of the civilian population on an unprecedented scale is one of the most remarkable features of the Revolutionary and Napoleonic wars. The men who turned their thoughts to the parade ground and the women who turned their needles to regimental colours, however, did not always see their newly martial avocations as worthy of extended remark; or, to put it another way, the extraordinary demands made by the armed nation were often rendered ordinary, even mundane. This is not to diminish the excitement that attended the arrival of a new militia regiment in a provincial town, the enthusiasm with which some greeted the opportunity to play at being soldiers, or the clash between military and civilian mentalities. Yet because it could be framed as an extension of peacetime civic engagements and as a consequence of familial or local pressure rather than state coercion, the process of transforming British subjects into part-time citizen soldiers was perhaps less fraught than it might have been.

This normalization of militarization, though, rested on fragile foundations. Militia service in Ireland blurred the boundaries between 'home' service and the front line, between 'civilized' and unrestrained warfare. The emollient sociability that eased relations between civilian communities and militia regiments in Britain served, in Ireland, as a flimsy veil covering the harsh realities of the garrison state. The hope that the militia exchange might result in positive cross-cultural contacts between Britain and Ireland was similarly based on an unduly optimistic perception of the militia as a vehicle for cultural exchange rather than violence. In Britain too, the normalization of militarization and the reconfiguration of military violence as pleasurable spectacle would, as we shall see in the next chapter, be a persistent source of unease.

7
Bringing the War Back Home

> Secure from actual warfare, we have lov'd
> To swell the war-whoop, passionate for war!
> Alas! For ages ignorant of all
> Its ghastlier workings...
> We, this whole people, have been clamorous
> For war and bloodshed; animating sports,
> The which we pay for as a thing to talk of,
> Spectators and not combatants!...
> ...Boys and girls,
> And women, that would groan to see a child
> Pull off an insect's leg, all read of war,
> The best amusement for our morning meal!
>> Samuel Taylor Coleridge, 'Fears in Solitude:
>> Written in April 1798, during
>> the Alarm of an Invasion'[1]

While the French army drove across Europe bringing war and revolutionary upheaval to millions, the British and Irish civilian experience of war and invasion, with the exception of the short-lived French invasion of the west of Ireland and a brief landing in Wales, was largely confined to the personal and public imaginary. The war was brought home to Britons in other ways – by the militarization of everyday life; through the letters of friends and relatives fighting abroad; and in press reports, literature and drama – but the central activities of war (killing, wounding, requisitioning and occupation) tended to remain beyond their immediate experience. Distanced from the brutality of war, British civilians were able to enjoy its vicarious excitements, an abdication of moral responsibility sharply exposed in Samuel Taylor Coleridge's 'Fears in Solitude'. Yet while Coleridge's poem appears, at first glance, to promote anti-war sentiments, it is in fact a warning against national complacency at a time of crisis, when a French invasion appeared terrifyingly imminent. According to Coleridge, Britons needed to exert their imaginations to apprehend the terrible fate that would befall them if war genuinely came home, so that they could prepare to 'repel the impious foe!'

Coleridge's verses point to some key tensions in the civilian experience of war. During the invasion crises of 1797–1798 and 1803–1804, the British public were encouraged to imagine the horrors of war and the terrible consequences of a French invasion. As we shall see, despite concerns about the politics of 'alarmism', personal writings from this period show that the prospect of invasion was experienced as a genuine threat. At the same time, the fact that most of the nation's fighting was conducted overseas meant that war was experienced in a highly mediated fashion. An emerging 'pleasure culture of war', the sanitized language of gazette reports, and a communal 'victory culture' arguably helped to shield ordinary Britons from the destructive reality of war.

The crystallization of national consciousness in continental Europe has often been traced to the 'concrete experience' of foreign occupation during this period.[2] While recent scholarship has stressed the more complex reality of co-operation and collaboration in the occupied territories,[3] these studies rely on an implied gap between the 'concrete' experience of war and the rhetoric of patriotic national mobilization. In Britain, by contrast, a clear dichotomy between wartime rhetoric and wartime experience is much more difficult to sustain. Without denying the material impact of the wars, it is important to recognize that the conflict was, in many ways, experienced through the imagination – whether that entailed raising the spectre of invading French hordes, or revelling in chivalric fantasies. This central aspect of the British civilian experience of war directs attention to the role of collective imagining in the construction of a national community. In Britain, national communal identification depended upon an integrated communications network through which representations of war could be disseminated and public opinion shaped.[4] The relative freedom of the British press, though increasingly circumscribed from the 1790s, meant that the meanings of the war were variously interpreted and understood. Nonetheless, loyalist propaganda, military gazettes and Thanksgiving sermons were crucial in establishing a sense of war as a 'national' experience. These texts were also concerned with prescribing a particular emotional response to the events of the war – fear and hatred of the French invader; pride in Britain's military prowess; joy at British victories – and, to a degree, they were successful. Yet, as this chapter suggests, the actual experience of invasion could challenge hostile depictions of the French 'other', whilst the injunction to imagine war as romantic spectacle or as a divinely sanctioned endeavour could be undermined by a countervailing insistence on its brutal realities.

French invasions

By the end of the 1790s, when the conflict was perceived to have become a defensive rather than offensive war, loyalist propaganda became ever more concerned with spelling out to the public the nightmarish consequences of a cross-channel assault and dispelling any illusion that the French came as liberators rather than rapacious conquerors. Loyalist atrocity literature and imaginary invasion scenarios thus sought to encourage 'large fractions of the population to simultaneously imagine the horrors of war and to direct those imaginings to the production of assent to military conduct'.[5] Imagined invasion scenarios were supplemented by supposedly 'authentic' reports of the French occupation of continental Europe. One of the most widely circulated pieces of atrocity literature from this period *A Warning to Britons against French perfidy and cruelty* (1798) was a graphic, and at times pornographic, account of the French forces' incursions into Swabia in 1796. It catalogued in lurid detail the horrors which a French invasion would entail: the desecration of religious sites; outrages against ecclesiastics of every persuasion; merciless plundering by the 'privileged locusts' of the republican army and the complete destruction of domestic and familial security. Playing on the well-established theme of the threat which the French posed to the safety of British women, it paraded a seemingly endless scene of ravishings. According to the author, no woman, young, old, sick or pregnant was spared from the 'brutal lust' of these 'depraved wretches'.[6] Such reports sketched a portrait of a 'new' ideologically motivated and unrestrained form of warfare, in which no distinction was drawn between combatants and non-combatants, with devastating implications for civilians and their property.

At a time when the loyalty of the populace remained uncertain, pamphlets like *A Warning to Britons* sought to impress on their readers the catastrophic consequences of a foreign invasion. While the threat posed by internal enemies and those sympathetic to the French Revolution dominated the propaganda of the 1790s, by the time of the second invasion scare in 1803–1805, when the political differences of the previous decade had supposedly been set aside in an upsurge of patriotic unanimity, the threat to the nation had come to be embodied by a single figure: Napoleon Bonaparte.[7] As Bonaparte's 'army of England' encamped at Boulogne, cartoons, songs, and broadsides depicted his forces descending upon the English coast in floating batteries, hot air balloons and other ingenious invasion machines. The whimsical quality of these invasion scenarios suggest how the very real threat of a French landing acquired a degree of fantastic unreality as it was represented to the British public. The theatricality of such representations emerges clearly in the many invasion broadsides that appeared in the form of mock playbills. A typical example advertised Bonaparte's forthcoming appearance in a 'Pantomimic Farce' entitled 'Harlequin's Invasion' to be performed in the 'Theatre Royal of the United Kingdoms', which would conclude with an uproarious staging of The Repulse; or, Britons Triumphant'.[8]

Such representations reveal an underlying uncertainty in the invasion literature: should the invasion threat be represented as apocalyptic tragedy or comic farce, as terrifyingly real and immediate, or an imaginative spectacle? The anticipated consequences of a French landing were marked by a similar ambivalence. Invasion literature prophesied the complete destruction of British customs, culture and character, the exchange of British liberty for French slavery, British roast beef for French *soupe maigre*, whilst confidently maintaining that any landing would be swiftly and emphatically repulsed by the nation's loyal armed citizenry.[9] This atmosphere of uncertainty was deftly satirized in an 1803 cartoon 'John Bull in a Dream or the Effects of Uncertainty!', in which a sleeping John Bull faces a confusing array of politicians and commentators. Some warn of an imminent invasion, whilst others reassure him that 'they'll never attempt it'.[10]

As studies of this vast quantity of invasion-related print material have noted, visual satires, broadsides and handbills cannot be taken as an unproblematic reflection of contemporary popular opinion, and it remains difficult to gauge precisely how they were read, or intended to be read. Consequently, as Mark Philp observes, we still know very little about 'the precise tenor of people's feelings at the height of the invasion threat'.[11] Loyalist and state-sponsored propaganda can be understood as intent on stimulating a collective atmosphere of fear, yoking together personal and national security to ensure patriotic unanimity and continued support for the war effort. Yet, as the mixed messages embedded within invasion literature suggest, there was also substantial doubt that such a shared emotional response could be relied upon, and a pronounced anxiety that certain sections of the population might view the prospect of a French landing with indifference, or even enthusiasm. Moreover, the manipulation of public fears was itself viewed with suspicion, with many commentators arguing that it could become a dangerous mechanism of social control and state repression. The term 'alarmist' first entered into common currency during this period and the figure of John Bull bothered by alarms and counter alarms would feature in satires by both Gillray and Cruickshank.[12]

Despite the prevailing atmosphere of uncertainty, anxieties about the possibility of a French landing form a recurring theme in letters and diaries between 1797–1798 and 1803–1805. While imagined invasion scenarios tended to focus on the south-east coast of England as the most likely point for a landing, none of the four nations of the British Isles was immune to the threat. Writing from Edinburgh in November 1803, Jessie Harden noted that 'There is now little else talked of than the French Invasion & everyone seems to think they will attempt to land at Leith...I have heard much of the same subject all summer but never took alarm till now, however I must say I feel extremely anxious about it'.[13] These anxieties were echoed by correspondents across the country. In this respect, invasion alarms succeeded in bringing individuals into a shared conversational and emotional community bound together by a common dread that they would be transformed from spectators into actors in the theatre of war. These epistolary outpourings of fear and apprehension could themselves become unwitting weapons of war. In 1804 the French captured a mailbag of 84 letters on board an East India Company ship bound for Madras, which were later published in the *Moniteur*. The all-absorbing topic of the intercepted letters was invasion, and they provided a vivid insight into the public mood, as it oscillated between confident declarations of British military preparedness and doubtful assessments of the loyalty of the lower orders.[14] For the purposes of Napoleonic propaganda, however, their main value lay in the extent to which they depicted a nation gripped by fear at the prospect of a French landing.

In this mood of watchful suspense, invasion alarms occurred frequently. These alarms were often triggered by the transmission of confused intelligence, or the breakdown of the systems set in place to alert the local population in the event of a landing. In 1797 a resident of Conway recorded a false alarm triggered by a naval patrol's mistaken sighting of French sloops off the north Welsh coast.[15] Fire beacons formed from stacks of furze set at intervals of two to three miles along the coast were used to signal the approach of a French flotilla, a defensive system that conjured up evocative memories of the Spanish Armada. The accidental lighting of one of these beacons at Castle Hume in Berwickshire on 31 January 1804 set in motion the sequence of signals through the region and resulted in the mustering of Volunteers and local militia corps as far away as the valley Liddesdale in Scotland, the most remote point reached by the alarm.[16] In the same month, Northumberland farmer George Culley reported another invasion panic caused by a mail coach guard, one of the principal sources of news in provincial communities, drunkenly declaring that 40,000 French had landed on the north-east coast. As the captain of the Cheviot Volunteers sounded the alarm in the village of Wooler at two o'clock in the morning, Culley described the ensuing panic:

> The drums beat *to arms*, the trumpets *sounded*, the old women *fainted*, the young women *wept and howled* for the loss of their *sweethearts, husbands* &c &c, the dogs *barked*, and in short poor Wooler was never in such a state before![17]

The prospect of a foreign invasion was undoubtedly a source of terror for ordinary Britons yet despite the lurid depictions of the French in loyalist propaganda, their mental image of the Gallic enemy seems to have remained nebulous. Some wrote of their fear of republican 'demons' or 'hell-hounds' or of waiting to meet the 'little Corsican', but for the most part it was the prospect of war on their home shores, rather than a specific image of the 'monstrous' French which seems to have been uppermost in Britons' thoughts. Indeed, hyperbolic accounts of French 'atrocities' were greeted with caution by some. When a conservative acquaintance presented the Belfast radical

Martha McTier with a copy of *A Warning to Britons*, she remained unmoved by its accounts of the depredations committed in Swabia, commenting drily 'what a scene of ravishings the good lady has sent me ... If it must be so God send us gentlemen'.[18] For those with personal knowledge and experience of France, sensationalized portraits of the enemy's savagery and barbarity could not entirely erase a deep-rooted belief in the essential humanity of the French. In July 1803 the artist Joseph Farington recorded 'the most distinct dream of Invasion that could possess the fancy':

> Of seeing the French boats approach in the utmost order, and myself surrounded by them after their landing. I thought they preserved great forbearance not offering to plunder, & that I was in the midst of them some conversing in broken English ... The knowledge I had of the French, while traveling amongst them, had enabled my imagination to represent them in their true Character, so that it seemed a perfect reality to me.[19]

Though Farington's imagined encounter with the French may have been sketched in less nightmarish colours than those commonly found in invasion literature, the fear that a landing would be accompanied by excessive plundering and severe economic dislocation was widespread. Perhaps unsurprisingly, it was not the threat the French posed to national culture or constitutional liberties so vigorously flagged in loyalist propaganda that most preoccupied contemporaries, but the security of their families and property. This was a dominant concern of the propertied classes and during the invasion crises many made preparations to secure their wealth and possessions. In 1797 Jane Osbaldeston instructed the agent of her estate in Scarborough to put all her most important legal documents into safekeeping in preparation for an invasion, whilst in Edinburgh in 1803 it was reported that many people 'go to the length to have their valuables, silver plate, Title deeds &c ready for removal'.[20] In August 1803 George Culley advised the steward of the family estate in Durham to sell all their fattened livestock, lest it fall into the hands of the invading French.[21] On the English south coast, where the threat seemed most acute, the response was even more dramatic and there were mass evacuations from the garrison town of Colchester in the summer and autumn of 1803. In a scene reminiscent of civilian refugees fleeing the war-torn regions of continental Europe, Jane Taylor described how she and her family squeezed into an overcrowded wagon which carried them to the relative safety of Lavenham in Suffolk. Their arrival, Taylor noted, 'excited much surprise and more alarm', with their sudden flight leading some in the village to believe that the family were in possession of some secret intelligence and had been 'admitted to Bonaparte's privy council'.[22]

The chain reaction of 'alarm' triggered by the spectacle of civilians in flight, points to the dangers of mass panic associated with such a pervasive climate of fear. The concept of civilian 'morale' would not, of course, be fully elaborated until the Second World War, but in trying to navigate between the extremes of popular panic and false complacency, invasion propaganda betrayed an underlying anxiety that agitation of public fear could lead to social breakdown and defeatism instead of acting as a spur to national unity. The British 'home front' was therefore encouraged to draw confidence from three main sources: the protecting power of Divine Providence; the military capabilities of Britain's untested citizen soldiers; and finally the nation's impregnable 'wooden walls'.

It was the last of these, the defensive strength of the British navy, in which the greatest trust was confided. Consequently, it was the naval mutinies of 1797, which revealed a devastating vulnerability in the islands' marine defences, that marked the lowest point in the wartime national mood. The naval mutinies at Spithead and the Nore in the spring of 1797 were widely narrated as an event of cataclysmic proportions. Across Britain and Ireland correspondents and diarists wrote of the 'horrid', 'dreadful' and 'shocking' reports of the convulsions in the Channel Fleet. In the diaries of Joseph Farington, the naval mutinies were recorded as a subject of conversation no less than sixteen times between May and June.[23] In Dublin, the Catholic campaigner Christopher Bellew declared the accounts to be 'beyond everything *bad* tis dreadful to think of having the Power of the Country directed against itself'.[24] So inextricably linked was the navy with British national identity and security that the crumbling of the wooden walls seemed to presage a complete breakdown of the social and political structure. If, as was widely believed, Jack Tar, the emblem of British loyalty, had been infected with Jacobin principles, the mutiny might, as one diarist feared, mark the 'Commencement of a Revolution in this Kingdom'.[25] For some the spasm of panic and anxiety that accompanied news of the mutinies was itself a source of irritation. Recording a visit to an acquaintance during which the mutinies had formed the principal topic of conversation, Anna Larpent expressed impatience with her host's exaggerated display of distress and the 'nonsense, tremor and affectation of feeling on the times'. 'True feeling' she concluded 'is very quiet in its effects, active not turbulent'.[26] Instead of superficial displays of feeling, the threat of national destruction, according to Larpent, required a quieter, more inward and stoical response. Indeed, the traumatizing impact of the naval mutinies can perhaps be measured by the speed at which Britons moved to forget the crisis once it had been quelled. According to one London diarist, by the time the mutineers were executed in July 1797, the mutinies had become subject to an enforced collective amnesia 'as if the Revolt had never existed' and were 'never mentioned in conversation'.[27]

As a national crisis, the mutinies appear to have provoked even greater anxiety than the French landing in Wales, where the imagined horrors of a mass French invasion materialized in the less terrifying form of a small-scale expedition which landed in Fishguard on 22 February 1797. Originally intending to land at Bristol, the detachment of just over a thousand troops was forced by bad weather to reset their course for the Pembrokeshire coast. The area was poorly populated and poorly defended; nonetheless, the French forces were famously deceived by local women dressed in the traditional red flannel and black peaked hats ranged atop the cliffs into believing that the coast was swarming with red coats.[28] Although the French outnumbered local troops by two to one, the expedition, assisted by the discovery of large quantities of Portuguese wine that had been shipwrecked off the coast a month previously, soon descended into chaos and disorder. Within less than three days, they had surrendered to Baron Cawdor, the commander of the local militia, and were taken prisoner.

Described by Gwyn Williams as a 'comic-opera landing', the French invasion of Wales is often viewed as more akin to farce than the tragedy prophesied in loyalist propaganda.[29] Yet despite its brevity and chaotic execution, contemporary and retrospective narratives of the landing tended to echo and reproduce many elements of the imaginary and authentic invasion scenarios published during the 1790s. In this way, events in Pembrokeshire appeared to enact on a miniature scale the more apocalyptic vision of a French invasion which Britons had been roused to expect. The republican soldiery's notorious hostility to religion was supposedly borne out in reports of the desecration and looting of St Gwyndaf's church in the remote village of Llanwnda near to where they landed. The image of the French soldiery as rapacious locusts stripping the countryside bare with their insatiable appetite for plunder also figured in several narratives. According to one account, they 'gave loose to every brutal excess that pampered and inflamed appetites could prompt them to'.[30] Following this narrative pattern, many accounts turned to the ill-treatment of women at the hands of the French. At least one told how the soldiers had shot and then raped a woman and included the telling detail that she was pregnant and that the violation had occurred in the presence of her husband, an echo of the gruesome scenes of female violation described in a *Warning to Britons*.[31] Finally, the response to invasion seemed to demonstrate the patriotic zeal and unanimity that animated the civilian population, even in this remote corner of the kingdom. On disembarking the French were reportedly greeted by an 'old loyal Taffy' crying out 'church, king and constitution', while the local populace clamoured to strip the cathedral of its lead to be cast into bullets.[32] This is not to suggest that there was no foundation to reports of French atrocities and Welsh phlegm, but the aspects and details which narrators tended to focus on were those which reinforced and conformed to well-established 'invasion scripts'.

The bitter aftermath of the Fishguard landing, however, suggests a more complicated chain of events, as the invasion brought to the surface underlying tensions and antagonisms within Pembrokeshire society. In the 'recriminatory mood' that, according to a recent account, was a leading characteristic of Pembrokeshire life after the invasion, Thomas Knox, Lieutenant-Colonel of the Fishguard Volunteers, was accused of cowardly conduct during the landing and in 1800 felt compelled to publish a vindication of his actions.[33] The allegations against Knox appear to have been driven by resentments on the part of the Pembrokeshire gentry prompted by the rising influence of Knox and his family, who were widely viewed as *arrivistes*.[34] Moreover, following the surrender, several local inhabitants were brought to trial charged with having been in collusion with the French. The accused were acquitted, but their arrest and the suspicion that fell upon many other members of the community at the time, testify to the deep-seated divisions that lay behind the apparent show of patriotic unanimity. Recent research on Welsh radicalism in the 1790s has revealed the extensive circulation of republican and oppositional literature in both Welsh and English at the time, raising the possibility that there may well have been sections of Pembrokeshire society who were sympathetic to the French invaders.[35] Even if the charges were groundless, the fact that the suspicions fell primarily upon prominent nonconformists illuminates the abrasive relationships that existed between the largely Anglican landed classes and local Methodist and Baptist communities. In his diary of a tour through Pembrokeshire, conducted shortly after the invasion, the Duke of Rutland, drawing on the opinions of the region's gentry, expressed doubts that the country people would have remained loyal had the French been successful. 'Fishguard' he concluded 'is one of the most disloyal places in Wales.'[36] Rather than uniting local inhabitants in the face of external threat, the French landing seems to have exacerbated underlying frictions and animosities.

The French invasion of Connaught the following year would expose in even more dramatic fashion the acute sectarian, ethnic and political tensions that wracked what had been considered a relatively tranquil province of Ireland. In certain respects, the landing in August 1798 did not differ dramatically from the previous year's expedition to Wales. The French force was roughly the same size, consisting of around a thousand soldiers, and the landing occurred in a similarly remote and isolated region of the country. There were, however, crucial differences. Whilst there may have been some in Pembrokeshire willing to rally to the republican cause, in Ireland the revolutionary army was joined by a local insurgency involving thousands (despite the fact that Connaught was an area in which United Irish organization had been relatively weak). Under the command of General Humbert, the French troops that landed in Ireland were of a superior quality to the troops that had been dispatched to Wales and were much more effectively disciplined and organized. With the support of Irish auxiliaries, they were able to make sustained progress through the country. Within five days of the landing they had secured a victory over a much larger force at Castlebar. A 'Republic of Connaught' was declared and the French army and its Irish recruits marched through Mayo and into the adjoining counties. On 8 September their progress was halted by a decisive defeat at the hands of state forces at Ballinamuck, and two weeks later the French and rebel insurgents remaining at Killala were overwhelmed. The French surrendered and were recognized as prisoners of war, whilst their Irish allies were massacred.

Although the invasion lasted little over a month, it would be remembered in vernacular historiography as 'The Year of the French' (Bliain na BhFrancach) or the 'Time of the French' (Aimsir na bhFrancach),[37] a temporal marker which connected this moment to the much longer experience of French invasion and occupation in continental Europe, referred to in Germany as *die Französenzeit* (Time of the French). The fact that the conflict in Ireland was also a civil war did not render such parallels redundant, a point which was emphasized in Rev. James Little, an Anglican clergyman, who kept a record of his ordeals during the invasion in which he noted that 'in all the countries in Europe into which the French have carried their invading arms...they have excited a civil war'.[38]

Like other invasion narratives, Little's diary of the French landing sought to convey to those who had not experienced conflict on their own territory, 'what the scourge of war is' and, more precisely, to illuminate the vicious character of the French forces.[39] He described in detail how the countryside assumed 'the deformed & dreadful aspect of war' as livestock trampled through corn fields while stacks of flax, abandoned mid-harvest, lay scorching in the sun. In Killala town, the scarcity of money led to the establishment of a barter system. The streets, meanwhile, were filled with the putrefying remains of cattle slaughtered to supply the French troops. This rotting flesh, 'too great for the dogs & hogs to consume', gave rise to a severe bout of dysentery amongst the townspeople. The scenes of devastation, dislocation and disease which Little described were those which could have been found in Flanders, Swabia, Italy, or any of the other war-torn regions of Europe, and Little was adamant that the 'system of destruction' had the same source, having been 'imported completely fabricated in all its parts by the French'.[40]

Though he expressed a pronounced hatred for the French and was certain that it was these 'machines, inanimate and inflexible to every human sentiment', and not the Irish peasantry, who were responsible for the worst excesses during the invasion, Little's personal encounter with the republican troops was relatively brief. Shortly after the landing a requisitioning party appeared at his door searching for horses. Unable to speak French, Little conversed with them in his stilted school-boy Latin. The encounter was awkward but not violent. Nevertheless, his inability to communicate with the French soldiers ensured that they remained a fundamentally alien presence.

This linguistic barrier may partly explain the sharply contrasting experience and perception of the French recounted in another narrative of the invasion by Joseph Stock, Bishop of Killala, and head of Little's diocese.[41] Stock's encounter with the French began the day after the landing when Killala Castle, the Episcopal Palace, was commandeered by the invading army. Crucial to Stock's experience of the invasion was the fact that he spoke fluent French, which allowed him to act as an interpreter for and mediator between the soldiers and local inhabitants. Though the Bishop's residence was soon filled with nearly 300 soldiers and their baggage, and Stock and his family effectively held captive, he readily conceded the excellent discipline and order which prevailed amongst the French troops, a discipline which he contrasted with the disorder of their Irish recruits. Indeed, the sympathetic account of the French in Stock's narrative seems to consciously challenge the lurid depictions of the Gallic foe in loyalist propaganda. Whilst contemporary invasion literature portrayed the revolutionary soldiery as gluttonous hordes with extravagant appetites, Stock stressed their modest tastes and simple requirements, noting that they seemed perfectly content to live on bread or potatoes. According to Stock, the troops quartered in the castle showed the utmost respect for his property, despite many temptations to plunder. One conscientious soldier even removed the Bishop's valuable dining set to the safety of the pantry away from the prying hands of his less honourable comrades. Instead of the aggressive hostility to religion imputed to the soldiers of the revolution, they showed the utmost respect for their captives' devotions, taking pains to ensure that the Castle was protected from any noise or disturbance on Sundays. And, finally, the Bishop emphasized the 'scrupulous delicacy' with which the women of the household were treated.[42]

Representations of the violation of the domestic sphere and the spectre of the French invader bringing war, destruction and desolation to the cottage, or, in this case, the castle door, was a key conceit through which loyalist propaganda sought to yoke together personal, familial and national security.[43] Yet in Stock's narrative the relationship between external threats and domestic security becomes increasingly complex. At the centre of his narrative is an account of three weeks following the departure of General Humbert, during which he and his family were confined to Killala Castle with a guard of three French officers. Thrown together by the vagaries of war, a strange intimacy seems to have developed between the Bishop's family and the French. Rather than disrupting familial bonds and domestic order, the French, in Stock's account, are incorporated into an expanded domesticity becoming, for the duration of the invasion, part of what he called the 'castle family'. They dined, drank and spent long evenings conversing together, the bishop's wife even playing cards with the commandant. The affectionate portraits and personal histories of the three French officers which Stock included in his narrative clearly showed the bonds which this daily intimacy produced. When the time came for the French to surrender, the Bishop recorded how 'we parted not without tears, with our friends and protectors'.[44]

The bonds that developed between the Bishop and the French were partly forged in opposition to the Irish Catholic rebels, who in Stock's narrative, lurk menacingly at the threshold of the Castle asylum kept at bay only by the family's French delivers and protectors. In this respect, Stock's account of the French was not so different from that of other Irish loyalist commentators. The comparison between the discipline of the French troops and the disorderly Irish rabble that had joined their standard was a common theme in loyalist histories of the Connaught rebellion and many were quick to note the contempt in which the Irish rebel forces were held by their supposed French allies. When, in the aftermath of the invasion, their French protectors were replaced by the officers of the Prince of Wales' fencibles who were quartered in Killala castle, the bishop expressed much more irritation at this imposition than he had ever directed at the French, and he was bitterly critical of the brutal and disorderly conduct of the loyalist forces who had been charged with pacifying the region. Stock was not alone in viewing the British and Irish forces as potentially more destructive than the French. When the Connaught gentleman farmer, Robert Ffrench of Monviea, heard reports in September 1797 that 30,000 soldiers under General Abercrombie were to be sent to Ireland to defend them from the French he noted in his diary 'Querie, which will do us most mischief?'[45] By refusing to reproduce a straightforward dichotomy between friend and foe, Bishop Stock's narrative complicated contemporary imaginings and depictions of a French invasion. His experiences during the landing provide an insight into the compromises and co-operation that might well have been necessary had the French succeeded in their invasion plans. In different ways, the landings in Wales and Ireland illustrated the unpredictable consequences of such an invasion, exposing, in the former case, communal tensions within the region, and, in the case of Killala, producing unexpected axes of amity and enmity.

A pleasure culture of war?

Invasion alarms, and the mass mobilization that accompanied them, ensured that war and its instruments became 'part of the natural ether for a substantial proportion of the British Isles'.[46] In the longer term, the experience of living in a country at war also meant experiencing the progressive militarization of landscape, culture and everyday life. Martello towers, army barracks, bustling arsenals, and dockyards transformed the landscape, whilst soldiers and sailors became increasingly familiar figures on streets and quays, as well as on the stage, in art and in literature. George Cruickshank's recollections of this period are frequently cited to give a sense of how this militarization of daily life was experienced: 'Every town was…a sort of garrison – in one place you might hear the "tattoo" of some youth learning to beat the drum, at another place some march or national air being practised upon the fife…and then you heard the pop, pop, pop, of the single musket, or the heavy sound of the volley, or the distant thunder of artillery'.[47] With its vivid evocation of the warlike sounds that resounded through the nation's towns, Cruickshank's description is usually taken as evidence of the thrill of this

folding of the martial into the everyday. Yet these reminders of the transformations wrought by war could provoke quite a different response. During a
visit to Portsmouth in the early stages of the war, Anna Larpent, focusing on
the visual rather than the aural, described the view of the 'first fortifications,
the first appearance of the military' which 'struck without pleasing me, the
forms of military discipline, the severity of making men into mere puppets,
the horrors of war, all present unpleasant ideas, however they were new to
me & I stared at all I saw'.[48]

Despite the threat of invasion that hung over the nation, and the devastating human and material costs of protracted warfare, it was, according to
a recent analysis, during this period that a 'pleasure culture of war' developed in Britain. Distanced from the brutal reality of war, civilians were able
to enjoy its vicarious excitements. The recreation of war as exciting and
romantic spectacle was central in overcoming concerns about the ethics of
war, providing a forum through which 'moral uncertainties over the use of
violence could be partly resolved'.[49] Yet the 'unpleasant ideas' suggested to
Larpent by the warlike aspect of the English coast indicate that this was not
a straightforward process. For much of the eighteenth century, depictions
of war had focused on its grotesque aspects, whilst the military had been
viewed with hostility as a source of tyranny and inhumanity. The 'pleasure
culture of war' required these long-standing associations to be overridden.

Letters and diaries from this period testify to an increasing disposition
on the part of civilians to engage in the pleasurable consumption of war.
Military tourism, the inspection of military fortifications, the viewing of
naval fleets, and the aesthetic appreciation of these expressions of British
defensive and offensive strength, became ever more popular. A *Journal of a
Tour round the English coast in 1795* gave a detailed account of a journey from
Ramsgate to Plymouth which was, in effect, a pilgrimage through notable
sites of military activity. During a two-month journey, the author enjoyed
guided tours of several naval dockyards; observed the Dover Volunteers
fire cannonballs at a dummy ship in the harbour; watched a review of the
Prince's Light Dragoons at Brighton; dined aboard a man-of-war anchored at
Spithead; and compiled detailed lists of the ships at every port or anchorage
through which he passed.[50] A journal of a tour through Kent undertaken
in 1809 similarly recorded in minute detail the defensive fortifications and
military encampments encountered along the way. At Chatham the writer
described with admiration a recently erected bomb-proof Fort, at the centre
of which stood a Martello Tower. Disappointed at not being able to inspect
the docks, he enjoyed, nonetheless, a tour of the Artillery barracks, which he
pronounced 'beautiful'.[51]

'Naval gazing' and trips to view the launch of a new warships or the departure of a military expedition were particularly popular. In 1800, Thomas
Pattenden, a keen amateur artist, drew on the conventions of maritime art to

describe the aesthetic effect of two men-of-war anchored in the Dover roads. 'The ships', he wrote, 'looked very grand as they laid with the sun shining full on their side and the sky behind was in dark cloud shadow, which made the ships make a splendid strong object from the effect of contrast which was beautifull [*sic*] indeed'.[52] For those with less artistic sensibilities, military tourism afforded the opportunity to survey and exult in these visible statements of Britain's military power. In 1809, the Kentish grocer, John Sills, and his wife, undertook an arduous journey to Dover by post-chaise, cart and foot, to see the grand fleet's departure for Walcheren. Noting that this was 'the one of the largest expeditions that ever sailed at once from English shores', Sills proudly recorded the size and strength of the expedition: '31 Sail of the Line, 95 Frigates, Bombs &c.-220 Gunboats' and 'a number of Transports to carry the Troops about 45 or 50,000 Troops on Board.'[53] A standard moment in accounts of tours of the English coast was the first view of the naval fleet on the approach to Portsmouth or Dover. Writers drew on the associational techniques integral to picturesque modes of viewing, as the sight of the assembled fleet set in motion a train of ideas, which led the observer to reflect on Britain's illustrious naval history, the unparalleled achievements of her naval heroes, and the pleasing sense of security which such views inspired. 'I had heard talk of the glorious deeds of our admirals and sailors, of the defeat of the Spanish Armada,' observed William Cobbett, recollecting the first time he saw the grand fleet anchored at Spithead, 'The sight of the fleet brought all these into my mind in confused order; it is true, but with irresistible force.'[54] In these instances naval gazing and the 'chain of emotions' elicited by such acts of contemplations were represented as thickening the bonds between self and nation. Rather than being seen as unwelcome obstacles in the picturesque traveller's quest for captivating vistas and crumbling antiquities, these expressions of the nation's defensive and offensive strength became objects of contemplation and pilgrimage in their own right.

Excursions to naval war ships also became an increasingly popular pastime for the British elite. During a holiday to Cornwall in 1800, Richard Heber was delighted when, armed with a letter of introduction to Admiral Lord St Vincent, he was invited to promenade 'one of the proudest terraces that can be trode [*sic*] by an Englishman, the Quarter deck of a 110 gunship'. His account stressed the civility of his naval hosts and the unexpected comforts of the upper decks: the captain's dressing room which held 'all the conveniences of a man of fashion', the well-stocked wine cellar, and the lavishly appointed dining table.[55] The vogue for naval tourism may have been a response to continued anxieties regarding the soundness of the nation's 'wooden walls' after 1797. For elite travellers, the opportunity to visit warships and to observe the navy at close quarter was one way of bringing the institution more firmly under the scrutiny of the civilian public. Such nautical day tripping helped to narrow the gulf between British civilians and the armed forces, and to enhance the navy's public image, proving, through displays of politeness and hospitality, that these sea-faring warriors were also worthy exemplars of British civility.

Britain's relative insulation from the destructive violence of war undoubtedly played a part in enabling civilians to derive pleasure from military spectacle. The recreational consumption of war can also be located within an evolving literary landscape. Poetry, in particular, was instrumental in mediating and representing war to the British public. For much of the eighteenth century, the imaginative powers associated with poetry, which allowed both poet and reader to transport themselves to the carnage and bloodshed of the battlefield, meant that war poetry often focused on the horrors rather than the glories of conflict. However, as Simon Bainbridge has shown, during the Napoleonic wars the sentimentalized and horrific depiction of conflict, which was the conventional theme of such verses, was gradually replaced by a more celebratory vision of warfare. The central figure in this reimagining of war as heroic spectacle was Walter Scott. In his hugely popular tales of chivalry in the Scottish borders, the realities of Napoleonic warfare, of mass armies and modern artillery were imaginatively translated into a world of heroic individual combat and broadswords.[56] In this way, modern war could be rendered palatable, even aesthetically pleasing for the British reading public. Together, *The Lay of the Last Minstrel* (1805), *Marmion* (1808), *The Lady of the Lake* (1810) and *Rokeby* (1813) sold tens of thousands of copies, making Scott by far the most popular writer in this period; their popularity, as William St Clair notes, is also evidenced in the frequency with which his verses on war and patriotism were transcribed in contemporary commonplace books.[57]

Chivalry, as popularized by Scott and others, provided an important vehicle through which conflicting responses to war could be reconciled. It distanced the representation of war from the immediate realities of modern warfare, whilst simultaneously providing a cultural script that allowed complex emotional responses to war to be simplified in the form of exaggerated gendered poses: weakness and vulnerability in women, heroism and protectiveness in men. The playing out of chivalric fantasies could thus be a vital element in the 'pleasure culture of war'. The diaries of elite and middling women suggest how their trips to the ships of war could become an occasion for re-enacting chivalric positions and fantasies. One memoirist recalled how the ladies hoisted on board by their blue-coated beaux 'used to affect more timidity than naturally belonged to them'.[58] And, as noted in Chapter 6, military volunteering in this period could also be understood as a form of chivalric play-acting.

There is, however, ample evidence of others who refused to view war through a chivalric lens and for whom the failure to be moved by military romance registered a self-conscious rejection of the imagined unanimity of the wartime state. More critical explorers of the British navy found disturbing evidence of a brutality that could not be kept at a distance or contained through aestheticizing strategies. In a 1798 tour of the English coast, John Housman described his descent from the elevated prospects above Portsmouth, where he surveyed the grandeur of the fleet, down into the port itself to inspect the battle-worn ships lying under repair in the dry dock. Up close, the British gunship the Royal George bore the scars of its most recent engagement, whilst the French prize it had captured exhibited even more vividly the 'dismal marks of the tragical slaughter'. Though the decks had been cleaned, still he found traces of human gore, even brains, tangible vestiges of a distant engagement brought shockingly home. It was a 'dreadful spectacle' that, he wrote, left him 'overwhelmed with horror at the folly and brutality of misled fellow-beings'.[59] A similar contrast between the sublime exterior and brutal interior of a naval fleet was drawn by the Lancashire radical, Samuel Bamford. On viewing a fleet of warship stationed at Yarmouth roads he observed that:

> the sight of those huge floating masses, instead of inspiring me with chiv-
> alrous feelings, called forth those of a quite different description. I looked
> upon them as so many prisons where men were hopelessly confined ... The
> fleet, as a whole, was certainly a noble spectacle to behold ... But its details
> I could not contemplate without a shudder.[60]

Though Bamford acknowledged the grandeur of the assembled fleet, the established sequence of emotional and imaginative response was short-circuited by his knowledge of the brutal naval discipline that reigned within. For those, like Bamford, who were liable to be impressed war could not remain distant, or romanticized. Bamford thus exposed the class politics of the chivalric martial ideal, one which bolstered the authority of the patrician elite, whilst inflicting horrendous hardship and suffering upon the poor.

To a certain extent, the ideological conflicts of the Revolutionary and Napoleonic wars can be conceived of as a battle over the public imagining of conflict. Wartime unanimity and national mobilization depended upon particular kinds of representation and fantasy, a fantasy of military power, glamour and heroism with which civilians could imaginatively engage through the 'pleasure culture of war'. At the same time, for opponents of the war, the evocations of war's horrors also required the public to exert their imagination to envision scenes that were beyond their immediate visual experience. In his study of the British liberal peace movement during the French wars, John Cookson argues that pacifists' ethical critique of war's intrinsic horrors was largely abandoned in favour of a more pragmatic emphasis on its economic and material consequences. The public's inability to grasp the full ghastliness of war was, he notes, a failure of the imagination which the self-styled Friends of Peace never forgave.[61] Yet outside the formal political activities of groups like the Friends of Peace, the ethical implications of the conflict seem to have remained a persistent source of anxiety. Take for instance, the Belfast naturalist, John Templeton's admonitory response upon hearing of a friend's attendance at a military review in Dublin's Phoenix Park. 'I really think it extraordinary' he wrote:

> that a Man possessing some portion of compassion for the Misfortunes of his fellow creatures should take pleasure in seeing preparation made for their destruction…Amidst all the pomp and glorious display you beheld today did you perceive no blood, did not the smoke of burning towns arise to your view, was your ears not filled with the cries of the Widows, the fatherless, and of the wounded soldiers, if none of all these things found a place in your imagination, you may have enjoyed the day and are fit to take your place among heroes.[62]

Such critiques of the moral corruption of military spectacle were particularly common amongst Rational Dissenters like Templeton, who drew on an epistemological framework associated with sensational psychology. According to this perspective, the glittering instruments of war could not be disconnected from the work of slaughter: the viewing of military spectacle invariably led through an association of ideas to the blood-drenched battlefield.

Betty Bennett's extensive anthology of the war poetry published in English, Irish and Scottish periodicals during the wars reveals that alongside the more straightforwardly patriotic effusions on British military victories there was a constant stream of verses which focused attention on the plight of war's victims.[63] Many of the verses directly attacked the calloused sensibility that could find beauty, pride and pleasure in military spectacle. The roots of the modern pacifist movement may be partly located in reactions against this putative 'pleasure culture of war'.[64] However, many of the key tropes and themes deployed by opponents of the war were also employed in more explicitly patriotic or loyalist compositions. Enlisted to the pro-war cause, the depiction of battlefield horrors could underline the sacrifices made by Britain's martial heroes on behalf of the civilian population. Moreover, the literature of invasion was equally concerned with bringing war in all its ghastly horrors home to the British public. War imagined could thus enable 'both bellicose and ethical thinking'.[65] As with the campaigning soldiers discussed in Chapter 3, it may have been entirely possible for civilians to hold in balance both the horrors and beauties of war.

While the imagining of war played a central role in civilians' experience and perception of the Revolutionary and Napoleonic conflict, this period also saw the proliferation of forms of representation designed to recreate a more immediate or 'authentic' sensory experience of the battlefield. Theatrical 'afterpieces' staged spectacular versions of military engagements, in which scenic devices, music, machinery and lighting were combined to create a virtual experience of the noise and action of warfare. This repackaging of war as spectacular entertainment often veered towards the kitsch. In 1793, a concert held in Edinburgh provided a musical re-enactment of the Battle of Verdun. The composition concluded with the band recreating the battle with kettledrums and trumpets, which, the *Caledonian Mercury* noted caused 'no small degree of alarm among the ladies'.[66] A similar 'battle piece' was performed in Chichester in 1800. Its disappointed composer, John Marsh, recorded in his diary that the recitative 'Make ready, present fire' had 'rather a ridiculous effect & set the people laughing', including the principal violin-cello who 'was ready to burst out' throughout the performance.[67] The jarring effects of theatrical re-enactments were similarly noted by Anna Larpent. Following a performance of 'The Siege of Valenciennes' at Sadlers Wells, she reflected that 'it was wrong to show the sorrows of the besieged on a stage and make a Joke of them'.[68]

While Larpent may have found the idea of 'war-as-entertainment' to be in bad taste, her diaries from this period demonstrate a more appreciative response to military art which sought to convey the experience of war with greater verisimilitude. Upon viewing Philippe de Loutherbourg's hugely popular *Lord Howe's Victory on the Glorious First of June* she was deeply affected, noting in her diary how it captured 'scenes of horror and generosity that agitate'.[69] Departing from the traditional conventions of naval art, de Loutherbourg's depiction of this crucial naval victory focused on the human drama that occupied the forefront of the painting as the ragged sails and broken topmasts of the British man-of-war loomed in the background giving 'a sense of desperate motion that is almost completely lacking in earlier battle paintings'.[70] For Larpent, the painting's appeal clearly rested in its capacity to 'agitate' and engage the sympathies, allowing a more complex and meditative response to scenes of war than did extravagant theatrical spectacles. The panorama's circular canvas promised an even greater proximity to the battlefield, allowing viewers to participate vicariously in the experience of war. In 1799, Larpent visited Robert Barker's panorama of Nelson's victory at the Nile in Leicester square, which she pronounced 'terrific'. The simulation of the 'terror' of war may have helped to bridge the gulf between spectators and combatants and to reassure viewers such as Larpent that they had not, as Coleridge charged, become inured to the violence and horror of conflict.

The panorama could also inspire a less reflective, more unproblematically patriotic response. In 1814 Lady Charlotte Bury attended a panorama of the Battle of Vitoria, which, a veteran of the battle assured her, was a most accurate representation. For Bury, maid of honour to Queen Caroline and a prominent member of the patrician elite, there was no question as to where her sympathies lay as she surveyed the scene. Dismissing the bravery of the ordinary soldier as merely 'mechanical', she identified instead with the elevated perspective of the victorious Wellington and his generals '*coolly gazing*' across the battlefield and 'reconnoitering the evolutions of thousands'. 'The dead and dying were lying strewn about' she recorded in her diary 'and yet, even in gazing at the representation, I sympathized with the enthusiasm of the living and the glory of the conquerors, more than with the sufferings of the fallen'.[71]

National rejoicings

In his paean to the English mail coach, Thomas de Quincey famously celebrated the coach's vital role as 'the national organ' carrying and diffusing the latest despatches from the Napoleonic battlefield, and described the electrifying impact of a laurel-decked coach as it thundered through the nation's towns to announce a victory:

> what a thundering of wheels! – what a trampling of hoofs! ... what redoubling peals of brotherly congratulation, connecting the name of the particular mail—"Liverpool for ever!" – with the name of the particular victory – "Badajoz for ever!" or "Salamanca for ever!" The half-slumbering consciousness that all night long, and all the next day – perhaps for even a longer period – many of these mails, like fire racing along a train of gunpowder, will be kindling at every instant new successions of burning joy, has an obscure effect of multiplying the victory itself, by multiplying to the imagination into infinity the stages of its progressive diffusion. A fiery arrow seems to be let loose, which from that moment is destined to travel, without intermission, westwards for three hundred, northwards for six hundred.[72]

Introduced in the 1780s, the British mail-coach service was the first attempt to connect different localities within one and the same communication network and to bring communities, which would have previously occupied separate time zones regulated by the church bell or village time piece, into a shared temporal framework. The mail-coach ran according to particular schedules and time co-ordination between different post offices en route became possible as each mail coach carried a time device set according to Greenwich Mean Time.[73] As the first British conflict to follow the establishment of this national communication network, the mail coach during the Revolutionary and Napoleonic wars, as de Quincey's essay suggests, also contributed to national synchronization in a different way: the coaches that brought news from the battlefield drew the various parts of the nation together as the mails radiated across the country, triggering explosions of collective euphoria.[74]

These accounts, fresh from the battlefield, could also work to collapse the temporal and spatial distance between home and front. The despatches written by Admiral or General following an engagement were sent via courier to officials at Whitehall and the Admiralty, and then reprinted in the official news bulletin of the British government, the *London Gazette*. Reprinted in the London and provincial press and made available in cheap editions, the 'Gazette Extraordinary' would thus potentially be read by hundreds of thousands of British civilians.[75] For de Quincey, the sequence of horse-powered motion and human emotion formed a powerful chain linking the civilian population to the 'field of mars' as the 'earthquake of battle' vibrated through the nation. Yet he also recognized that this rejoicing would not be universal. Recollecting a journey on a mail-coach carrying news of the British army's triumph at Talavera, he described a poignant encounter with the mother of a soldier whose regiment had been decimated in the battle. Rather than telling her of the probable death of her son, de Quincey instead extolled the bravery and heroism of his regiment 'how these dear children of England, officers and privates, had leaped their horses over all obstacles as gaily as hunters to the morning's chase' until the mother's fear was 'swallowed up in joy'.[76]

De Quincey's essay made several claims about the role of battle reports in shaping civilians' relationship to the wartime nation. British triumphs could submerge internal dissensions in a collective euphoria, but to achieve such transcendence the human costs of particular victories needed to be suppressed. Where de Quincey saw the chain of communication linking battlefield and home front as a bridge, this mediated consumption of conflict, according to Mary Favret, functioned more like a 'paper shield' protecting the British public from the destructive violence of war.[77] As contemporary commentators noted, because gazette intelligence was scrutinized by state officials before circulating more widely in the national press, it allowed the government to present a particular version of the war to the reading public. Critical commentaries on *Gazette* texts featured regularly in William Cobbett's *Political Register*, accusing the government of exaggerating British successes and underestimating casualties. In 1794 the *Morning Post* defined 'Gazette Extraordinary' as, 'A marvellous account, disseminated by persons in power, to *amuse* the public'.[78]

Gazette bulletins and a wider print culture of military intelligence played a key role in moulding civilians' perceptions of the war, though readers were not necessarily passive consumers of this state-sponsored literature. When the gazette for the Battle of Talavera reached Leeds, the woollen miller, Joseph Rogerson registered some doubt at the massive casualties reported on the French side, noting '*If this account be true* they have had 12 Men and upwards for our one slain'.[79] Responding to a friend's request for her thoughts on the navy's triumph at Trafalgar, Jane Taylor wrote, 'I thought that it was a very "famous victory"; did not you? And besides this, and much more, I though a great many things that the newspapers had very obligingly thought ready for me'.[80] Taylor demonstrated a self-conscious appreciation of the vocabulary through which Britons, instructed by the press, were supposed to understand and respond to military triumphs. Yet such dissenting voices are relatively rare. Private responses to the war usually coincided with those expressed in the public print media. Even opponents of the war, such as the Lewis-born London alderman, George Macaulay, who railed against the 'Kings, potentates, and ministers who are the authors of War' could celebrate Admiral Jervis' victory over the Spanish Fleet as 'a glorious achievement' exhibiting 'a splendour and importance beyond anything in Modern Times'.[81] Recording the latest news from the battlefield, diarists often echoed the breathless tones of the battle gazette. Sometimes underlined or marked by the heading 'GLORIOUS NEWS', these entries frequently concluded with a series of excited exclamation marks.[82] Civilians' appetite for detailed reports of the most recent victories can also be seen in the lengthy excerpts or cuttings from the press which were transcribed or pasted into their journals. Following the battle of Salamanca in July 1812, Joseph Farington made extensive notes on the victory, recording the key events of the engagement, the names of all the officers who had been killed or wounded, and various encomiums to British valour taken from newspaper reports.[83]

For many civilians then, the human destruction of war was filtered through the sanitized language of the battlefield despatch. Journal entries on recent battles often tallied up the number of British losses relative to the French, without reflecting on the painful losses that lay behind these impersonal statistics, though a personal or local dimension might be added through particular reference to men from the area killed in the engagement.[84] The total death toll for the entire conflict has been estimated at around 210,000 for the navy and army, including deaths from disease, battle and shipwreck, an excess wartime mortality comparable to that in the First World War, and few localities would have remained untouched by this loss of life.[85] The bulk of those who died in any given engagement remained unnamed in battle despatches. In the army, the number of officers who died in action or from disease during the conflicts has been calculated at 2,770, whilst estimated deaths amongst the rank and file and non-commissioned officers may have been as high as 141,000.[86] Thus, amongst the literate and educated classes most would have remained comparatively untouched by wartime bereavement, so that contemporaries were unlikely to think in terms of a 'lost generation'. Within their circle of acquaintances they may have known some who had lost loved ones, and memorials in parish churches across the country served as reminders of those who had fallen, but unlike the First World War, grief was not the crucial experience through which the propertied classes, at least, 'lived the meaning' of the French wars.[87]

For the plebeian families who provided the bulk of the nation's manpower, and who bore disproportionately the devastating human cost of the conflict, wartime bereavement was a much more common experience, but one which is difficult to reconstruct from available autobiographical sources. The plebeian experience of loss was ventriloquized by numerous writers during this period and the figure of the war widow, left bereft and destitute by the death of her sailor or soldier husband overseas, is ubiquitous in popular poetry and balladry. A sympathetic engagement with such images may have reassured the middling and upper ranks that the experience of loss was collective and national, rather than one which was disproportionately borne by the poor: they too could experience grief, albeit in a distant and safely sentimentalized form.[88] The sentimental responses elicited by these works were channelled into the funds for the relief of war widows established after major battles and naval engagements and these pecuniary gestures, combined with voluntary contributions for national defence and the much grumbled about wartime taxes, may have been understood as a financial counterpart to the sacrifice of life and liberty made by the poor.

Similarly, whilst the war was brought home to the lower orders in the form of long-term separation, personal loss and economic hardship, for the wealthier the progress of the war was largely measured in terms of its economic impact, particularly after Napoleon's introduction of the continental blockade in 1806.[89] Reports of overseas campaigns and treaties were eagerly scanned to determine their probable effect on markets. The Bramley mill-owner Joseph Rogerson closely followed events overseas and their impact on the wool trade. The Napoleonic occupation of Spain in 1808, for example, was only noted in connection with the positive effects it had on the cloth market, Rogerson noting in his diary that 'Fine Cloth has gone pretty well off today owing to Bonoparte [*sic*] having got possession of Spain again; Spanish wool [it] is supposed will be 2/ or 3/ per lb. higher'.[90] The Northumberland farmers, George and Matthew Culley, likewise tracked the course of the war in terms of its likely consequences for the market in agricultural produce. Responding to news of the assassination of Tsar Paul and the British victory at Copenhagen in 1801, they noted that these '*wonderfull* and *astonishing*' events would effect a dramatic change 'not only in pollitics [*sic*] but agricultural matters'. The opening of the Baltic to British trades, they predicted, would see the price of grain drop and that of beef rise.[91]

There were, however, moments when the human, rather than the economic, costs of the war were foregrounded, most notably in the outpouring of grief that accompanied the death of Admiral Nelson in 1805. As recent scholarship has shown, Nelson's appeal extended across a wide range of social groups. The admiral hero's physical vulnerability and romantic entanglements allowed women to construct a more accessible model of public patriotism that was sympathetic to the conflicting claims of public duty and personal emotion.[92] For the middling ranks, Nelson's ascent from comparatively humble origins provided a potent example of social mobility, whilst, to the devout, his carefully crafted reputation for personal piety made him an acceptable Christian hero.[93] Finally, his compassion and loyalty to his subordinates made him an icon for the ordinary people: a 'screen upon which all those who had fought in the war machine ... could project their own experience, identifications and desires for recognition'.[94]

Not all participated in the instant apotheosizing of Nelson that followed his death. Jane Taylor confessed herself unable to reconcile the glorification of martial endeavour with her non-conformist principles, arguing that the 'greatest hero' was the man who was 'able to despise public honours for the sake of private usefulness'.[95] Most accounts of the death of Nelson, however, stressed the spontaneous, sincere outpouring of emotion that was at once personal and collective. Charles Fothergill recorded that 'I as an individual could not restrain my tears on the occasion' and described how the assembled company at a Yorkshire inn had alternated between drunken cheers at the great victory and mass sobbing 'at the loss of the great Nelson'.[96] The liberal dissenter, Lucy Aikin described similarly mixed emotions and scenes of mass weeping, reporting that even the 'hard-headed underwriters at Lloyds' had, upon hearing the news, 'one and all burst into tears'. She further noted that 'many private streets were not lighted up at all, so much did sorrow prevail over triumph. No windows, it is said, were broken and some of the mob cried out, "What light up because Nelson is killed?"'[97]

As Aikin's reference to window-breaking indicates, British victories were often the occasion for scenes of riot and disorder. The insistence that the Battle of Trafalgar should be marked by deferential mourning rather than the customary revelry of victory celebrations was part of a general effort to bring patriotic celebrations under elite control. In reality, the aftermath of Trafalgar saw the usual outbreaks of disorder and window-breaking amongst the urban 'mob'. As Timothy Jenks suggests, these competing versions of 'victory culture' underscore the social tensions which ran through wartime patriotism, even in moments of apparent unanimity. In his guise as a popular hero, Nelson could be used to advance plebeian claims for access to the patriotic public sphere, the exclusivity of which the loyalist elite were anxious to maintain.[98] Although the death of Nelson raised particular questions about the appropriate tone of the victory celebrations, urban illuminations were a source of contention throughout the wars. Elite mistrust of organized patriotic festivities, which were uncomfortably reminiscent of revolutionary spectacles across the channel, meant that the decision to illuminate was often represented as a response to pressure from below.[99] The irony that it was those most likely to suffer the hardships of war who were most clamorous for illuminations, perplexed radical commentators: 'what affects me with the greatest pain and sorrow' complained a contributor to the *Belfast Monthly Magazine* 'is that the people whose countless thousands are the victims, ... participate in these ill-devised inauspicious scenes of triumph, and are ready to break your windows if you do not illuminate.'[100] While some believed that such public rejoicings played an important role in 'uniting the people in one common cause',[101] for many others victory illuminations were experienced not as a harmonious display of cross-class unity but as a disruptive occasion for plebeian excess. During the illuminations to mark Admiral Lord Howe's victory over the French fleet, Anna Larpent complained that she and her family were kept awake for two nights, so great was the uproar outside their house.[102] For some, it was only the threat of 'mob' violence, rather than any patriotic fervour, that prompted them to display the obligatory victory candles in their windows. After the announcement of Napoleon's abdication in 1814, Christian Dalrymple of Musselburgh, near Edinburgh, noted that 'it was thought prudent to illuminate even in the country'.[103]

To contain such disruptive outbursts, civic elites attempted to substitute more controlled public ritual for the riotous festivity of illuminations. In Bury St Edmunds, a town meeting was held on the signing of the Treaty of Amiens in March 1802, 'to determine on the properest [sic] mode of *mak[in]g the common people to rejoice on the General Day of Thanksgiving* otherwise than by an Illumination in the Town'. The celebrations eventually decided upon were carefully choreographed to demonstrate the leadership role of the propertied classes. The Aldermen and Corporation led a procession through the town, accompanied by the Volunteer corps, followed by a series of socially exclusive events: a 'Peace ball' and a ticketed dinner at the Assembly rooms.[104]

In Bury St Edmunds and elsewhere, much of the responsibility for organizing victory celebrations devolved upon local elites. Britain's governors displayed a notable reluctance to promote a more formalized, state-sanctioned victory culture. This was partly due to the long-standing association between 'nationalist' or patriot positions and oppositional politics, and the problematic relationship between secular nationalism and the British confessional state.[105] Consequently, the closest the British government came to promoting state nationalism was through the established church, and in particular through the Thanksgiving services that marked major military triumphs in combination with the days of fasting and humiliation on which the Protestant nation sought atonement for its sins. Added to the annual services commemorating the thwarting of the 'gunpowder plot' and William III's triumph in 1688–1689, these days of fasting and thanksgiving connected the events of the war to the established calendar of the Protestant nation. In diaries from this period, the most commonly transcribed commentaries on the war were taken from sermons preached on these occasions, and could range from brief notes of the biblical passages upon which the sermon was based to more extensive accounts of its arguments.[106] Harking back to the public thanksgiving at the defeat of the Spanish Armada in 1588, these state-appointed days of sacred commemoration and atonement also drew upon a 'Tudor' model of 'elect nationhood', in which British Protestants were encouraged to view themselves as the successors to the Israelites of the Old Testament, whose trials and providential deliverances were evidence of God's benevolent design for his 'chosen people'.[107]

Providential explanations were notoriously convoluted: British victories were interpreted as proof of the nation's elect status and French successes as evidence of a divine and beneficent plan that would in time reveal itself, whilst the dangers of national complacency were constantly warned against. After hearing a Thanksgiving sermon that presented such a tortuous interpretation of recent events, John Ramsay of Ochtertyre complained that it was a 'farrago which wanted concatenation', so tedious and fatiguing that it had brought on a painful case of rheumatism.[108] Yet perhaps more than ideas about national character, or the intrinsic liberty of freeborn Britons, providentialist religious discourse provided a crucial language through which civilians understood the interpenetration of individual and national fates during the wars. Personal providentialism, which encouraged individuals to read God's will in the events of their lives, and national providentialism, which stressed God's role in international affairs, could thus become intertwined.[109] The conflation of self and nation through providentialist discourse is a recurring feature in the diaries of the Yorkshire landowner, William Vavasour, evident in his repeated use of the collective 'we'. 'We have much reason to be thankful to providence', he wrote at the end of 1805, 'Napoleon the great and invincible as he appears can no longer transgress the bounds which Omnipotence has prescribed to his power than the sea can pass its limits against the will of its Maker.'[110] By emphasizing the role of personal piety and prayerful supplication in securing the nation's continued existence, even those who were unable to take arms to defend the nation or fight the French abroad could under-stand themselves as actively contributing to the common weal. Such an interpretation clearly appealed to the diarist who noted with approval his minister's Thanksgiving day injunction that, 'a nation can only be such as the individuals are who compose it and therefore we must lead a life deserving of God's goodness'.[111]

Although providentialism was a language shared by all Protestant sects in the British Isles, the fact that Thanksgiving and fast days were appointed by the government invariably alienated many Protestant dissenters, who saw these occasions as the product of an unholy alliance between church, state and aggressive militarism. On fast days, Britons were supposed to spend their time in devout prayer and contemplation, and to refrain from pleasurable indulgence and conducting business. Dissenters' refusal to observe these fasts, evident in the shops that remained open, was often remarked upon by their Anglican compatriots, exposing a clear division in the wartime nation.[112] A recent study stresses the inclusive nature of national thanksgivings and their capacity to bridge confessional divides, noting that Thanksgiving sermons were preached in both Roman Catholic and dissenting chapels.[113] However, this overlooks the fact that many dissenting ministers used fast-day and Thanksgiving sermons to critique the war and were often deeply opposed to the idea of 'rejoicing' at the nation's military successes. On the Thanksgiving to mark the anniversary of the peace in 1802, for instance, the Unitarian minister Robert Aspland, determined 'to speak freely' and preached that the war had been an 'enormous sin'.[114]

The potential for Thanksgiving days to act as an occasion for contestation rather than consensus can be illustrated by the following lines transcribed by the non-conformist bookbinder John Davies, of Ystrad, Wales, which had been pasted upon the door of his parish church on the day of Naval Thanksgiving to mark Admiral Nelson's victory at the Nile:

> Vile Hereticks are these your pranks
> To murder men and give God thanks
> Vain Hypocrites proceed no further
> For God accepts no thanks for murder.[115]

On the occasion of the National Thanksgiving day for the victory over the Dutch fleet at Camperdown, the previous year, 1797, David Cragg a radical Quaker and yeoman farmer from north Lancashire, entered a very similar epigram in his memorandum book alongside a scathing condemnation of the triumphalist endorsement of a 'bloody and pompous war'.[116] Another variation on these lines was supposedly etched by Robert Burns with his diamond stylus on the windowpane of a Scottish tavern, possibly following the celebrations for Admiral Jervis' victory in 1794.[117] With their aggressive repudiation of the notion that the carnage and bloodshed of battle could be a cause for 'rejoicing', these lines contested the claim that British victories could unite the nation in a collective experience of 'burning joy'. Yet, paradoxically perhaps, their mysterious appearance on a window pane in Dumfries, inscribed in a memorandum book in Lancashire, and pasted onto the door of a church in Cardiganshire, suggests how these apparently unconnected, local and personal expressions of opposition were unconsciously operating within a broader Britannic context.[118]

Conclusion

Upon the declaration of peace in 1814, Joseph Rogerson noted in his diary, with a touch of regret, 'Now as the wars all over people seem to want something to talk about.'[119] On the same day, the Rev. John Stonard reflected with a similar wistfulness, 'Surely there never will be any more news as long as we live ... The Papers will be as dull as a ledger and Politics insipid as the white of an egg.' Deprived of the 'violent excitements' they had recently experienced, people, he predicted, would soon begin to tire of peace.[120] While this nostalgia for a war that had only just ended may seem surprising, the fact that the conflict lasted more than two decades meant that for many Britons war had become normality. Importantly, in these early (and premature) reflections on the end of an era, it is the shared experience of reading and talking about war that is foregrounded.

As 'a thing to talk of' war can be understood as bringing Britons together in a shared conversational community; this should not, however, be taken as evidence of an unproblematic or widely shared militarist nationalism. While collective rejoicings at military successes were often represented as unifying the national body, these celebrations also revealed underlying fractures in the wartime nation, as the middling and upper ranks tried to assert control over plebeian 'excesses' and Protestant dissenters abstained from Thanksgiving and fast-day rituals. Efforts to encourage a unified response to military threats and achievements could, inadvertently, produce the opposite result: lurid invasion scenarios designed to encourage vigilance could result in panic and insecurity, while over-confident assessments of the nation's defensive powers risked giving rise to complacency. The association of ideas that for some observers of naval warships or military reviews led to pleasing reflections on the nation's proud history, could equally set in train quite a different set of reflections on the futility and horrors of war. The diverse and sometimes contradictory ways in which the British 'home front' was encouraged to imagine conflict meant that the meanings and interpretations of war were persistently open to contestation.

Conclusion: A Waterloo Panorama

Books on the battlefield

In the weeks and months following the battle of Waterloo, flocks of British tourists descended upon the battleground. Having followed from afar the contests that ravaged the continent, here was an opportunity to encounter the tangible remnants of battle, to experience with greater immediacy both the glory and destruction of war. In keeping with the era's vertiginous sense of the past rapidly receding beneath the wheels of history, Waterloo was soon subject to accelerated historicization. Tourists hastened to see it before it vanished into the realm of the distant and unknowable past. Once there, however, many were struck by the sheer quantity of books and loose pages that lay scattered amongst the detritus of war and 'literally whitened the surface of the earth', as one observer put it. These were letters, pages of novels and bibles, and sheets of music that had fallen from soldiers' knapsacks. Many of the tourists could not resist making their own inscriptions on this famous site. On the walls of the *Hotel de la Belle Alliance*, where Wellington's meeting with the Prussian General Blücher marked the victory of the coalition forces, James Simpson and his travelling companion inscribed a verse from *The Vision of Don Roderick* (1811), Walter Scott's patriotic tribute to Wellington's Peninsular success.[1]

The superimposition of print and manuscript texts on the sites of battle reflects a pervasive sense among battlefield travellers that the vivid realities of war were already obscured by the rapid accumulation of historical and narrative frames. Over the following century these layers of text continued to accumulate: Waterloo alone generated more eye-witness accounts than any other British battle prior to World War I.[2] A new understanding of the relationship between text and experience was one of the paradoxical products of the Revolutionary and Napoleonic wars. Despite being the most written about conflict in British history, the latter stages were marked by an emerging insistence on the authority of the eye witness, a consequence of the developing unease with the imaginative and pleasurable consumption of war. While it had long been acceptable for poets to use 'fancy' or 'imagination' to transport their readers to the battlefield, in *Childe Harold's Pilgrimage* (1812–1818), Lord Byron, who had travelled to Spain during the Peninsular campaign, would present himself as an actual observer of the battles he described. It was only through first-hand experience of the battlefield, he implied, that war could properly be apprehended.[3]

The imperative to 'bear witness' drove tourists across the channel, but any authority their accounts could assert had to yield to the superior claims of those who were present in Brussels *during* the battle. The presence of British civilians in such close proximity to the site of conflict is, of course, one of the memorable features of Waterloo. One of the best-known literary accounts of the battle, William Makepeace Thackeray's *Vanity Fair* (1847–1848) does not venture to describe events on the battlefield. Instead, the entire campaign is filtered through the experiences of the women left behind in Brussels. The assembled Britons were a mixture of fashionable but impecunious families who had decamped to Brussels on the outbreak of peace in 1814 in the quest for cheaper living on the continent, and curious travellers who had travelled to Flanders in the hope of being close (though not, probably, as close as they ultimately proved to be) to the site of an imminent and climactic contest between Napoleon and the Coalition forces. Added to this was the usual train of soldiers' wives, as well as a contingent of officers' wives for whom the accessibility and relative comfort of Brussels afforded an opportunity to accompany their husbands without enduring the hardships and deprivations of a military campaign.

The majority of British civilians in Brussels did not witness first-hand the fighting that took place between the 16th and 18th of June, but the battle was terrifyingly present nonetheless: the cannonading was clearly audible, while the scale of the slaughter would have been readily apparent as wounded and dying soldiers were carried back into the city. In the weeks and months following the battle, those who had been present in Brussels were quick to draw on their privileged positions as eyewitnesses to distinguish their accounts from the many narratives of the campaign and battlefield published by the 'Waterloo pilgrims' who had travelled to Brussels after the victory. Charlotte Anne Eaton, who had arrived at Ostend to begin an ill-timed tour of the continent with her brother and sister just a week before the battle, published a hugely successful 'Circumstantial detail' of Waterloo by a 'Near Observer' in August 1815 and a more extended account of her experiences in Brussels in 1817. Acknowledging the many other works that had appeared on the subject, Eaton nevertheless asserted the superiority her own narrative could claim as an eyewitness report:

> The Author must be permitted most earnestly to disclaim all idea of entering into competition with the writers whose talents and genius have

been so well displayed in describing the battle and the field of Waterloo. But they were not, like the Author of this Narrative, on the spot at the time these glorious events took place.[4]

Georgiana Capel, the young daughter of one of the foremost families in Brussels and niece to Lord Uxbridge who commanded the allied cavalry troops at Waterloo, similarly drew on her first-hand knowledge of the battle to critique Walter Scott's poetic rendering of the contest *The Field of Waterloo* (1815). Writing from Brussels in November 1815, Capel declared that she was 'enraged' by the poem and ridiculed both its pretensions to sublimity and the exaggerated description it gave of the battlefield. 'The fact is', she wrote to her grandmother, 'Scott came to Brussels with the intention of writing a Poem, *par consequence* it is very flat & not altogether correct, for certainly he must have been dreaming when he bestowed *Towers* upon the Farm of Hugoumont'.[5]

Georgiana Capel was not alone in finding Scott's poetry unequal to the task of memorialization. In contrast to the critical and commercial success Scott's celebratory mode of war poetry had garnered during the Peninsular campaign, his versification of Waterloo attracted a much more hostile critical reception, reflecting a widespread belief that the battle defied literary representation.[6] Explaining British poets' failure to do justice to Waterloo, the literary journal, *British Critic,* attributed this to the momentous nature of the victory which meant that the 'grandeur of reality overpowers the faint gleam of fiction'.[7] Accounts of Waterloo by civilian spectators repeatedly stressed their proximity to this 'reality'. The true horrors (and grandeur) of war, they maintained, could not be understood by a nation providentially exempted from its destructive forces. Yet, while invoking the authority of experience, civilians continued to reach for familiar cultural and literary narratives with which to frame that experience. Napoleon's fantastical and unanticipated reappearance on the European political stage brought to the fore once again the theatrical metaphors that had pervaded the imagined invasion scenarios of 1803–5. When news of Napoleon's escape from Elba reached Brussels in April 1815, the Whig MP Thomas Creevey quizzed the Duke of Wellington on the intentions of 'the *Manager* Buonaparte' and the nature of his forthcoming 'piece'.[8] Despite the perceived shortcomings of Scott's efforts to versify a modern battle, his earlier historical chivalric romances continued to exert their influence on personal narratives of Waterloo. The deeds of British valour performed there were, according to Charlotte Anne Eaton, 'more like the tales of chivalry and romance than the events of real life, or civilized ages'.[9] Eaton's was one of many accounts to instantly historicize the battle, claiming that such an epochal event could only be fully comprehended through the long lens of history. On a twilight visit to the graves of British officers buried near the battleground, Georgiana Capel drew upon an even earlier depiction of chivalric Celtic warriors, James Macpherson's *Poems of Ossian* (1761) to evoke the pervasive melancholy of the scene, conjuring up 'dim ghosts' who defended the tombs of these 'slumbering Heroes' as she moved across the burial field.[10]

The romantic contemplation in which both Eaton and Capel engaged as they traversed the battlefield was not so different from the conduct of those British officers who revisited the sites of battles in which they had fought, detailed in Chapter 3. They too meditated upon the glory and tragedy of warfare and the transience of human existence, modulating, in the process, the rawness of their experiences into something which could be reflected upon from a distance. The Gothic mode in which officers' accounts of combat and campaign were often written also framed civilians' accounts of Waterloo. Capel wrote of the flocks of birds of prey hovering above the open graves and the caps filled with congealed blood that lay upon the ground.[11] Eaton described her horror at the sight of a human hand reduced almost to a skeleton reaching out from one of the battlefield's mass graves: an instance of 'battlefield gothic', that fixation upon a single arresting detail so common in soldiers' narratives.[12] The language of providentialism that had provided one of the dominant frameworks for British domestic discourse about the wars was deployed by soldiers and civilians alike in the wake of Waterloo. These references ranged from the Duke of Wellington's allusion to personal providence ('the finger of providence was upon me and I escaped unhurt') to a cavalry officer, writing shortly after the battle, who saw in the British victory a providential design 'to humble the military pride and break the spirit of [the French] nation'.[13] The gulf which the new emphasis on the experiential knowledge of combat opened up between civilians and combatants was, in part, closed by this shared language for understanding and narrating war. For British officers, an ability to communicate their experiences of war in a language intelligible to civilian audiences was proof that they could move seamlessly between civilian and military worlds. Indeed, so proficient were they at this work of translation that Capel professed her longing to hear an officer's account of the battle 'in their own language, not *womanised*'.[14]

If these narratives of Waterloo tell us something about the relative lack of friction between the military and civilian worlds by the end of the wars, they can also shed light on how personal experiences of war were woven into a broader fabric of collective identities. For Georgiana Capel the victory at Waterloo was a distinctly aristocratic achievement and more particularly a source of familial pride. Her uncle, Lord Uxbridge's, gallantry during the battle was widely celebrated: his amputated leg had been buried with a headstone on the battlefield and would become a site of pilgrimage. In Georgiana's letters to her grandmother, Lord Uxbridge's mother, the reflected glory they derived from their male relative's heroism was a constant theme and she excitedly reported on the high regard in which Lord Uxbridge was held by the Belgians and the portraits and memorabilia that were produced in his honour. Describing a snuff box engraved with Uxbridge's portrait which she had seen in a local shop, Capel confessed that she longed to write upon it, 'I have the honour of being the Earl's niece'.[15] By trumpeting the heroic exploits of her uncle, Capel bolstered the aristocracy's claim to be a dutiful service elite and drew upon a long-established model of aristocratic female patriotism that centred upon the promotion of dynastic honour. Waterloo, according to this interpretation, was the victory of a particular class, for whom the wars had consolidated their prestige and affirmed their heroism.[16]

For Charlotte Eaton, by contrast, the victory at Waterloo was a national victory. In her published narrative she adopted a public and national persona clearly signalled by its titular claim to have been written 'by an Englishwoman'. Eaton's conception of national identity encompassed more than identification with England alone. Although born in the north of England, Eaton's father was Scottish, and she lived for many years in Scotland. She consequently expressed a particular affinity with the Highland regiments who had fought at Waterloo and paid tribute to their good behaviour, good humour and gallantry. While Eaton was quick to point out the tragic cost of victory, she nevertheless advanced a conception of British patriotism in which the nation's military prowess was understood as both the most important component of British national identity and the guarantor of all the other elements upon which British pre-eminence rested. In response to those who might query what Britain had gained from years of war and bloodshed, Eaton was insistent that national glory alone was sufficient to justify these sacrifices:

> Glory is the highest, the most lasting good. Without it, extent of empire, political greatness, and national prosperity are but a name, without it, they can have no security... Fortune may change; arts may perish; commerce may decay; and wealth and power, and dominion and greatness may pass away – but glory is immortal and indestructible.[17]

National glory, Eaton was keen to stress, rested upon more than the heroic actions of the British army's aristocratic leaders. At Waterloo, she wrote, 'every private soldier acted like a hero', and in her reflections on the domestic suffering of these soldiers' wives and mothers, she suggested how British glory also depended upon women's sacrifices.

By elaborating such an expansive vision of British patriotism, one which transcended rank and gender, Eaton was able to stake her own claim to a share in this national glory, a claim that was enhanced by her experience as an eyewitness to this momentous British victory. 'I returned to my country', she concluded, 'after all the varying and eventful scenes through which it had been my lot to pass more proud than when I left it of the name of AN ENGLISHWOMAN'.[18] Eaton and Capel's accounts of Waterloo drew on a shared literary repertoire; they diverged, however, in their interpretation of the victory's significance and whether it supported an inclusive or exclusive national narrative. It was a question that would be much contested in the decades that followed.

After Waterloo

In the immediate aftermath of Waterloo the massive fiscal–military state that had developed over the course of nearly a century of warfare with France and the relatively buoyant economy it had sustained contracted sharply with devastating effects.[19] The sudden withdrawal of government demand for provisions, materials and manpower produced an immediate slump in both manufacturing and agriculture. Simultaneously the British armed forces demobilized, discharging over 300,000 soldiers and sailors into a society marked by severe economic distress and high unemployment. For those with a commission, peacetime meant half pay, which was in fact usually closer to a quarter of full army pay, and an end to hopes of promotion without purchase. Many found employment in the domestic civil and imperial administration or in officering the new police forces: the Royal Irish Constabulary, established in 1814, or Peel's Metropolitan Police Force, founded in 1829. Ordinary soldiers meanwhile were eligible for a pension of up to 1s a day, a sum calculated as sufficient to keep the soldier from outright beggary but not to support a life of idleness. The fates of these veterans remain relatively under researched. A significant proportion appear to have become handloom weavers, or agricultural labourers, employment that required little skill or capital but left them vulnerable to post-war economic depression.[20] While John Cookson's recent study of Scottish military pensioners has modified the received image of the discharged soldier as permanently alienated from his home society, a widespread perception of the soldier as a socially disruptive and criminal force, nonetheless, remained. The post-war period witnessed a surge in prosecutions for crimes against property and petty crimes such as vagrancy and failure to support illegitimate children.[21] In 1815 a Select Commission on Mendicancy was established to investigate the large numbers of military veterans that had become beggars.[22] Perhaps unsurprisingly, many of the veterans who returned from war to an uncertain future joined the mass platform agitations between 1816 and Peterloo in 1819. Ex-service men were also prominent in the failed attempt at a general uprising in England and Scotland in 1820. Former drill sergeants instructed members of the radical reform movement in military marching and formation, while a range of symbolic imagery and practices derived from the army – martial music, drums and flags – was also appropriated by radicals. This form of militarized display was crucial in reconfiguring the image of mass protest, distancing it from earlier eighteenth-century associations with the disorderly 'mob' or 'crowd'.[23]

The conjunction of mass demobilization, economic depression and a popular clamour for political reform, in part, determined how the wars were publicly commemorated. Despite the sacrifices that had been made by those fighting overseas, as well as the nation in arms at home, the conflict would not, it soon became clear, be officially memorialized as a 'people's war'. This continued a pattern that had been established in the preceding decades. During the wars, the Pantheon at St Paul's Cathedral had become the principal site for the commemoration of the nation's military heroes, the Christian setting counterbalancing any perceived resemblance to the patriotic militarism of the French Revolutionary regime. The criteria for post-war memorialization stood in similar conservative contrast to that of the French. Whereas the French republic and empire had erected tablets and monuments commemorating the distinguished service of men from all ranks, in Britain official recognition of personal heroism was restricted to the elite. Naval and army commanders and, occasionally, the highest-ranking junior officer to fall in a battle, achieved apotheosis in the cool marble of the 'Temple of British Fame', but there were fewer than half a dozen representations of ordinary soldiers and sailors and no monuments commemorating their sacrifices.[24] After the defeat of Napoleon, parliament voted £300,000 for the erection of monuments to Trafalgar and Waterloo that would represent all who had fallen in the French wars. Continued contests over the inclusiveness of national commemoration, however, meant that neither project came to fruition. Charles Watkin Williams Wynn MP had proposed that the new national memorial be inscribed with the name of all servicemen who had died in the wars but, as Holger Hoock notes, celebrating ordinary soldiers and sailors in outdoor memorial art could easily be perceived as contentious in a period of political protest and social unrest.[25] There would be no English national war monument until the construction of Marble Arch between 1827 and 1833. The original plans included decorative friezes depicting scenes from the battle of Waterloo and the life of Nelson and celebrated George IV's 'fantasy-victory' over Napoleon.[26] The arch embodied a memory of the wars that was loyalist, exclusive and dedicated to the aggrandizement of monarchical authority.

Scotland and Ireland moved with greater alacrity to commemorate the wars. In Edinburgh, the foundation stone of the national monument on Calton Hill was laid during George IV's visit in 1822, though it remained unfinished when the money ran out in 1828. Conflict between Scottish Tories, who sought to promote Scotland's martial heritage, and Whigs, keen to celebrate the nation's civic and intellectual achievements, meant that the monument, originally intended to commemorate the sacrifices of soldiers and sailors, also became a shrine to the nation's literary and artistic worthies.[27] In Ireland, the commemoration of the wars assumed a religiously exclusive character. The martial heroism of the Protestant Ascendancy was memorialized in St Patrick's cathedral, where the colours of the Irish regiments were displayed alongside plaques commemorating Anglo-Irish officers. The foundation stone for Nelson's pillar was laid in 1809 and work began on the Wellington testimonial in 1817, erected in symbolic proximity to the vice-regal lodge in Phoenix Park, the seat of British power in Ireland. There were no monuments to the ordinary Irish Catholics who had served under both Nelson and Wellington.

That is not to say that the contributions of the rank and file went completely unacknowledged. The Waterloo sermons preached after the victory and each year on its anniversary were often in aid of the fallen and their relatives and typically paid tribute to the ordinary soldier's courage.[28] The Waterloo medal became the first campaign medal to be awarded to all those, regardless of rank, who had served in a military campaign, to the great indignation of Peninsular war veterans whose long service had gone unacknowledged. The veterans of the Peninsular war would eventually find their champion in the politically liberal Sir William Napier, whose six-volume *History of the Peninsular War* (1828–1840) provided a controversial, bottom-up history of the wars that was sympathetic to the rank and file. Napier vigorously defended the character of the British private. The claim that his courage derived from 'a phlegmatic constitution uninspired by moral feeling' was, Napier insisted, a 'stupid calumny'. In perhaps the most famous passage from the *History* he went on to observe that: 'Napoleon's troops fought in the brightest fields, where every helmet caught some gleam of glory; but the British soldier conquered under the cold shade of the aristocracy; no honours awaited his daring; no dispatch gave his name to the applauses of his countrymen; his life of danger and hardship was uncheered by hope, his death unnoticed'.[29]

The outpouring of military memoirs from the other ranks in the decades after Waterloo can be explained, in part, by the public appetite for tales of war, but must also be understood in light of this official reluctance to incorporate the ordinary soldier into the hegemonic narrative of British military triumph. Some, though by no means all, of these soldier memoirists proved alert to the valence of particular modes of war writing. During the wars, many officers, as noted in Chapter 3, had been at pains to insist upon the sensitivity of their responses to the horror and sublimity of war, displays of sensibility which worked to tighten the sympathetic bonds between the military and civilian worlds, while simultaneously emphasizing the gulf between the feeling officer and his unfeeling men. Full acknowledgment of the ordinary soldier's sacrifices and sufferings required a recognition that he was indeed a feeling being. This set the tone for many of the narratives from the other ranks. The *Journal of a Soldier of the Seventy-first or Glasgow Regiment* published in 1819 marks, as Neil Ramsey observes, a turning point in the development of the military memoir and the construction of the ordinary soldier as an object of sympathy. The *Journal* was hugely successful; it sold three thousand copies and went through several editions. It presented the private soldier as 'equally susceptible of every feeling of pain, and more exposed to hardships and privations, than the commanders', while providing a moving account of a soldier's sensibility progressively dulled by exposure to war's horrors.[30] It was not a military *bildungsroman,* nor did it have the episodic, whimsical quality of the picaresque, rather it told a tale of suffering and disillusionment that resonated with the political radicalism of the post-war years. Indeed, Leigh Hunt quoted extensively from the *Journal* in his satirical attack on the Duke of Wellington, 'The Dogs' (1822).[31]

The Journal of a Soldier inspired many other privates, including soldiers from the same regiment, to venture into print. A significant proportion was committed to celebrating the virtuous character of the rank and file and their 'constancy under daily sufferings and privations', while exposing instances of cruelty on the part of the officer class.[32] Labouring-class soldier's writing thus came to form a dissident tradition at odds with the 'pleasure culture of war' that persisted through the nineteenth century.[33] The contrast between the lavish expressions of grief and solemn commemoration accorded to commanding officers who had died on campaign, and the obscurity in which the ordinary soldiers who shared their fate were left to languish was a recurring trope in soldiers' autobiographies. Just as Private William Wheeler used his letters to memorialize those of his comrades who went unacknowledged in the military gazettes, so too, many military memoirs raised a textual monument to the ordinary soldier, the act of naming helping to individuate those whose deaths had been treated in the mass. When Edward Costello of the Rifle Brigade published his narrative in 1841, he acknowledged that he was adding to an already oversupplied market in soldiers' memoirs, but defended his contribution on the grounds that he wished to 'raise a cypress' to the memories of his gallant comrades who were unable to tell their own stories:

> the never to be forgotten Tom Crawley...Long Tom of Lincoln, once one of the smartest of our regiment, now the forlorn bone-picker of Knightsbridge...Wilkie, Hetherington, Plunkett and many others of those humbler heroes, conquerors in such well contested fields as Rodrigo, Badajos, Salamanca, and Waterloo &c. whose exploits form the principal attraction in this volume and whose stubborn spirits and perforated bodies formed the key-stones for the fame of our immortal Wellington, whose standard might have found a sandy support but for the individual bravery of the soldiers of his invincible divisions.[34]

Here, Costello reminded his readers that the sacrifices of his comrades and the mangled bodies of the rank and file formed the unacknowledged foundations, or – in what may have been an oblique reference to Marble Arch – the 'key-stones' for the official monuments commemorating their military leaders.

Yuval Noah Harari attributes the proliferation of military memoirs from the other ranks to transformations in the perception of the ordinary soldier, who went from being 'mere extras' in the culture of war to 'chief heroes'.

As soldiers came to be seen as thinking and feeling beings, so the reading public became increasingly willing to listen to their stories.[35] This, however, overlooks the contest over the meaning and interpretation of the wars in which these memoirs were imbricated; the hegemonic narrative of the wars in Britain had by no means positioned ordinary soldiers as 'chief heroes'. Some officers went so far as to challenge the rank and file's claims on the sympathy of the British public. Capt. George Wood, writing in the preface to his narrative of life as a subaltern officer, declared that one of the principal intentions of his memoir was to correct the impression created by the recent flood of memoirs that it was the rank and file who had endured the most severe hardships during the wars. 'Persons in the situation which I had the honour to fill in the Army during the most eventful period of my Country's struggles', he claimed, 'were no less exposed to pains and privations than those placed under them; besides having to contend with the mental anxiety arising from a much greater degree of responsibility'.[36] Wood sought to reinstate a hierarchy of feeling, in which the officer not only shared in his men's hardships, but felt them more acutely. Two memoirs published around the same time as Wood's, Moyle Sherer's *Recollections of the Peninsula* (1823) and George Gleig's *The Subaltern* (1826), similarly sought to refocus attention on the experiences of subaltern officers. Together, they promoted the idea that the subaltern officer was the proper object of the reading public's sympathetic identification. Insofar as the history of the subaltern officer could be taken to represent the middle classes' contribution to the war effort, these memoirs offered a more inclusive narrative of the wars. Unlike many of the memoirs from the other ranks, however, they did not fundamentally question the purpose of the war, the military hierarchy or the status quo.[37]

Re-reading the 'Chelsea Pensioners'

In recent years it has become something of a cliché to hold up David Wilkie's 1822 painting *Chelsea Pensioners Reading the Gazette of the Battle of Waterloo* as a metonym of the broader processes of identity formation at work in this period. Yet the painting is so richly suggestive of the variety of themes considered in this book that it is worth revisiting. Painted at the behest of the Duke of Wellington, it depicts the aged veterans of the wars of the eighteenth century alongside younger soldiers fresh from the Napoleonic campaigns enrapt as they read the Extraordinary Gazette announcing Wellington's victory. In an influential reading of the painting, Linda Colley identifies it as a 'perceptive interpretation of both the variety and roots of Britishness' and the mass British patriotism that emerged from the struggles against France.[38]

This was a patriotism that transcended rank, age, sex and ethnicity, as communicated by the inclusion of representatives from across the four nations of the British Isles and the empire: a Welsh horseman, a Highland soldier,

Sir David Wilkie, *Chelsea Pensioners receiving the Gazette Announcing the Battle of Waterloo* (c. 1819). Yale Centre for British Art, Paul Mellon Collection. B1974.3.24

even a black military bandsman. However, as Nicholas Rogers has recently pointed out, Wilkie's painting cannot be taken as an ideologically innocent representation of recent British history. It was, after all, commissioned by the Duke of Wellington in 1816. Wellington had originally requested a scene of old soldiers reminiscing about their military adventures, but in 1820, at a moment when Wellington's support for the government crackdown on the post-war radical movement had seen him sink in popularity, Wilkie decided to make his patron's victory the focal point. For Rogers the painting is not a reflection of a unified mass patriotism that emerged from the wars; it is the product of a much more contested terrain, 'a deliberate intervention by Wilkie to resuscitate his patron's fortune when people were beginning to debate what the war effort had been all about'.[39]

The painting is, to be sure, an idealized and ideologically inflected image of wartime unity. Chelsea pensioners were rigorously scrutinized to ensure that they were men of 'good character'. As a subject they were far removed from the discontented, demobilized soldiery that had, in the years after Waterloo, gravitated towards radical politics.[40] Yet, while the painting is idealized, it is by no means unaware of the ambiguities of wartime patriotism. As a representation of pan-Britannic unity, it deftly illustrates the interlocking identities which the army was able to encompass as it promoted both regimental and supra-national loyalties: on the left of the central group a figure holds aloft a set of regimental colours; listening to the news is a sergeant from the 42nd regiment who swells with pride at Wellington's tribute to the courage of this Highland regiment.[41] As this study has suggested, encounters with fellow soldiers from diverse cultural, religious and linguistic backgrounds could give concrete shape to the legislative abstraction that was the United Kingdom. The army was not a crucible of Britishness, insofar as it did not strive to impose a single, unitary identity on its recruits. What it provided was a flexible and, in an important sense, specifically military identity. It also offered a relatively tolerant environment for Catholic soldiers, or at least one in which overt expressions of Protestantism were discouraged; for Irish soldiers it may have offered a welcome refuge from more rancorous sectarian tensions at home. The divergent trajectories of Scottish and Irish martial unionism can be traced, in part, to the success with which soldiers' and sailors' personal experiences were woven into the national narratives of their respective countries. From the 1840s, the exploits of Irish soldiers in the Napoleonic wars would be celebrated in the comic novels of Charles Lever, the regimental histories of William Grattan, and various histories of the campaigns by William Hamilton Maxwell, but no image of Irish martial unionism was elaborated as powerful as that produced for Scotland by Walter Scott or Col. David Stewart of Garth. As the nineteenth-century commentator, Alexander Somerville, observed, 'it was the writing quite as much as the fighting of the Scottish regiments that distinguished them'.[42]

Wilikie's painting, at Wellington's behest, explicitly linked the victory of Waterloo to the series of eighteenth-century wars against France. But the French, or the enemy 'other', do not figure prominently. There is none of the crude xenophobia of Hogarth's *The Gates of Calais* (1748) or Thomas Rowlandson's *The Contrast* (1792). The centripetal energy that binds this group together does not derive from a violent Francophobia. Indeed it is likely that the veterans depicted by Wilkie would have felt some sympathy with Napoleon's troops who had fought hard and suffered greatly at Waterloo. As we have seen, the lineaments of Britishness were chiselled out as much in abrasive encounters with the army's allies in the Peninsula as in more violent encounters with the French on the battlefield. Moreover, a binary model cannot fully do justice to the complexly calibrated ways in which soldier-travellers mapped national and ethnic boundaries as they traversed Europe and the globe. A sense of belonging to a shared zone of civilization often united the British and their French opponents during these years, particularly when confronted with others whom they perceived to stand outside the boundaries of civility, whether Spanish *guerrillas* or Irish rebels. For British prisoners of war in France, continued adherence to a transnational code of honour meant that relations between captor and captive remained reasonably amicable. The protean character of the French nation as it transformed from absolute monarchy, to republic to empire further diminished the extent to which it could act as a stable foil to the British national character.

What Wilkie's painting privileges, then, is a form of identity developed not through 'othering' but through 'blending'. The focal point of the image is the gazette; it is this which has drawn this diverse group together, in the same way that it allowed people across the British Isles to experience the victory at Waterloo as a national event. Indeed, it was the inclusion of the Waterloo gazette that enabled Wilkie to transform what was originally intended as a genre painting – a scene of everyday life in the style of seventeenth-century Dutch art – into a history painting, a memorial to an epic battle. It is the newspaper that yokes together the quotidian and the historical. The arrival of the laurel-decked mail coach bearing the extraordinary gazette was a dominant topos in civilian memories of the wars; the symbol of these conflicts' modernity became itself an object of nostalgia.[43] By focusing not on fighting, but on reading and writing, Wilkie's painting also poses an important question about what it means to *experience* war, underlining once again the mediated character of the British experience. The gazette, as we have seen, was one of a number of different texts that shaped the civilian perception of war. Though written in Wellington's typically laconic style, the Waterloo despatch so thrilled the artist Benjamin Robert Haydon that he read and re-read the gazette until he had it off by heart.[44] Soldiers too understood that it was partly through the gazette that the chaotic experience of battle would begin to acquire meaning. As one officer wrote the day after Waterloo, 'The name of the place I do not know, *you will see it in the Gazette*, and it will be remembered by Europe as long as Europe is Europe'.[45] With its restrained diction and formulaic locutions, the gazette promoted a particular reading of war. The carnage of the battlefield was rendered as 'our immense loss' and victory measured not in the numbers of the enemy slain, but in the numbers of cannon captured (a hundred and fifty according to the Waterloo despatch). The 'particular mentions' of units that had distinguished themselves upheld a notion of soldierly identity and military honour that was expressed and affirmed through the regiment, while the gazette lists of killed and wounded, precisely ordered according to rank, reaffirmed military hierarchies: the ordinary soldier's wife who in Wilkie's painting anxiously scans the gazette will not discover there her husband's fate.

In the period 1793 to 1815 Britons, both military and civilian, drew on a range of different narrative frameworks and traditions to make sense of their experiences of war: Gothic tales provided a vocabulary with which soldiers could describe their fear and sense of dislocation, while providential narratives connected together individual and national fates. Personal experience, in turn, exerted pressure on dominant narratives, as subaltern officers' aspirations to masculine independence were undermined by the experience of military subordination and imagined invasion scenarios were rewritten in the light of actual French landings. A shared narrative of the sublimity and spectacle of war helped to bridge the division between the military and the domestic public, but such narratives could also have an exclusionary function, as they were used by the officer class to differentiate themselves from the unfeeling rank and file. The same imagining of conflict could result in radically divergent interpretations of war: narratives that urged the domestic population to imagine the horrors of war on one's own soil could easily slide into a critique of national bellicosity. New frameworks for understanding war emerged in this period, but older conceptions of war as a conflict between kings and princes rather than contending peoples remained influential. As I hope to have shown here, to understand how war was experienced and understood in this period we need to attend to these complex interactions between autobiographical experience and collective discourses, inclusive and exclusive narratives, and emerging and residual modes of interpretation.

Notes

Introduction

1. Revd James Little's Diary of the French Landing in 1798. Royal Irish Academy, Dublin, 3.B.51, f.14.
2. Winston Churchill, *The Second World War, Vol. 5: Closing the Ring* (Boston: Houghton Mifflin, 1985 [1951]), 377.
3. Diary of Anna Larpent, 3 March 1797. *A Woman's View of the Drama, 1790–1830: The Diaries of Anna Margaretta Larpent in the Huntingdon Library* (Marlborough: Adam Matthew, 1995 [Microfilm]).
4. George Steiner, *In Bluebeard's Castle. Some Notes towards the Re-definition of Culture* (London: Faber, 1971), 19.
5. Irene and Alan Taylor (eds), *The Secret Annexe: An Anthology of the World's Greatest War Diarists* (Edinburgh: Canongate, 2004); James Treadwell, *Autobiographical Writing and British Literature, 1783–1834* (Oxford: Oxford UP, 2005).
6. On the emergence of new forms of autobiographical war writing in this period see Yuval Noah Harari, *The Ultimate Experience: Battlefield Revelations and the Making of Modern War Culture, 1450–2000* (Basingstoke: Palgrave Macmillan, 2008) and Neil Ramsey, *The Military Memoir and Romantic Literary Culture, 1780–1835* (Aldershot: Ashgate, 2011).
7. Military historians will already be familiar with the rich collections of letters and diaries from these wars, many of which have been published in popular editions. Yet, as John Cookson notes, despite the ample material which is available and its potential to illuminate themes of broader relevance to the study of Georgian society 'its harvest by historians ... has hardly begun'. John E. Cookson, 'Regimental Worlds: Interpreting the Experience of British Soldiers during the Napoleonic Wars', in Alan Forrest, Karen Hagemann and Jane Rendall (eds), *Soldiers, Citizens and Civilians: Experiences and Perceptions of the Revolutionary and Napoleonic Wars, 1790–1820* (Basingstoke: Palgrave Macmillan, 2009), 24.
8. The process through which ordinary men and women across Europe increasingly understood themselves as participants in history and consequently came to value their own personal testimonies is brilliantly explored in Peter Fritzsche, *Stranded in the Present: Modern Time and the Melancholy of History* (Cambridge MA: Harvard UP, 2004).
9. Clive Emsley, *British Society and the French Wars, 1793–1815* (London: Macmillan, 1979), 4.
10. The argument for a 'new' British history that would neither falsely equate English history with the history of the British Isles, nor fragment into insular national histories of Wales, Scotland and Ireland was first outlined by J.G.A. Pocock in 1975. It is only in the last two decades, however, that historians of the eighteenth century have begun to engage fully with this project. J.G.A. Pocock, 'British History: A Plea for a New Subject', *Journal of Modern History*, 47 (1975), 601–21.
11. Linda Colley, *Britons: Forging the Nation, 1707–1837* (London: Vintage, 1996 [1992]), 5, 9.

12. There is a now a sizeable and ever-growing literature that engages with the core arguments presented in *Britons*. Some of the key works include: J.C.D. Clark, 'Protestantism, Nationalism, and National Identity, 1660–1832', *Historical Journal*, 43, 1 (2000), 249–276; Ian McBride and Tony Claydon, 'The Trials of the Chosen Peoples: Recent Interpretations of Protestantism in Britain and Ireland', in Ian McBride and Tony Claydon (eds), *Protestantism and National Identity: Britain and Ireland, c.1650–1850* (Cambridge: Cambridge UP, 1998), 3–32; Terry Brotherstone, Anna Clark and Kevin Whelan (eds), *These Fissured Isles: Ireland, Scotland and British History, 1798–1848* (Edinburgh: John Donald, 2005); Stephen Conway, *The British Isles and the War of American Independence* (Oxford: Oxford UP, 2000); Stephen Conway, *War, State and Society in Mid Eighteenth-Century Britain and Ireland* (Oxford: Oxford UP, 2006); John Cookson, *The British Armed Nation, 1793–1815* (Oxford, 1997); Austin Gee, *The British Volunteer Movement, 1794–1814* (Oxford: Clarendon, 2003); Robin Eagles, *Francophilia in English Society, 1748–1815* (Basingstoke: Macmillan, 2000); Stuart Semmel, *Napoleon and the British* (New Haven and London: Yale UP, 2004).

13. Gerald Newman, *The Rise of English Nationalism: A Cultural History, 1740–1830* (New York: St Martin's Press, 1987); Hugh Cunningham, 'The Language of Patriotism, 1750–1914', *History Workshop Journal*, 12, 1 (1981), 8–33.

14. Semmel, *Napoleon and the British*.

15. For a discussion of the problematic position of Ireland in Colley's thesis see Kevin Whelan, 'Ireland, Scotland and Britain in the Long Eighteenth Century', in Brotherstone, Clark and Whelan (eds), *These Fissured Isles*, pp. 43–60 and Thomas Bartlett, 'Britishness, Irishness and the Act of Union', in Dáire Keogh and Kevin Whelan (eds), *Acts of Union: Causes, Contexts and Consequences* (Dublin: Four Courts, 2001), 243–58.

16. On Ireland's contribution to the British war effort see Cookson, *British Armed Nation*, chapter 6, 153–181.

17. David Bell, *The First Total War: Napoleon's Europe and the Birth of Modern Warfare As We Know It* (Boston: Houghton Mifflin, 2007).

18. Colley, *Britons*, 265, 303. On the relationship between gender, war and politics in this period see Stefan Dudink and Karen Hagemann, 'Masculinity in Politics and War in the Age of Democratic Revolutions, 1750–1850', in Stefan Dudink, Karen Hagemann and John Tosh (eds), *Masculinities in Politics and War: Gendering Modern History* (Manchester: Manchester UP, 2004), 3–21 and Karen Hagemann, Gisela Mettele and Jane Rendall (eds), *Gender, War and Politics: Transatlantic Perspectives, 1775–1850* (Basingstoke: Palgrave Macmillan, 2010).

19. On the absence of studies of martial masculinity grounded in autobiographical experience see Karen Harvey, 'The History of Masculinity, circa 1650–1800', *Journal of British Studies*, 44 (2005), 296–311, 308.

20. Carolyn Steedman, 'Inside, Outside, Other: Accounts of National Identity in the 19th century', *History of the Human Sciences*, 8, 4 (1995), 59–76, 60.

21. See, for example, Marjorie Morgan, *National Identities and Travel in Victorian Britain* (Basingstoke: Palgrave Macmillan, 2001); Martin Daunton and Rick Halpern (eds), *Empire and Others: British Encounters with Indigenous Peoples, 1600–1850* (Philadelphia: University of Pennsylvania Press, 1999).

22. Benedict Anderson, *Imagined Communities: Reflections on the Origin and Spread of Nationalism* (London: Verso, 1991 [1983]).

23. Steedman, 'Inside, Outside, Other', 61.

24. Mary Favret, *War at a Distance: Romanticism and the Making of Modern Wartime* (Princeton, NJ: Princeton UP, 2009).

25. See Stephen Conway, 'War and National Identity in the Mid-Eighteenth-Century British Isles', *English Historical Review* (September, 2001), 864–893, 876–877; Colley, *Britons*, 332–33.
26. The classic critique is Joan Scott, 'The Evidence of Experience', *Critical Inquiry* 17 (Summer, 1991), 773–797, 793. For a response to Scott see Kathleen Canning, 'Feminist History after the Linguistic Turn: Historicizing Discourse and Experience', *Signs: Journal of Women in Culture and Society*, 4, 19 (1994), 368–405. The implications of Scott's criticisms for the definition and analysis of war experience and its narration are considered in some depth in Alan Forrest, Karen Hagemann and Jane Rendall, 'Introduction', *Soldiers, Citizens and Civilians. Experiences and Perceptions of the Revolutionary and Napoleonic Wars, 1790–1820* (Basingstoke: Palgrave Macmillan, 2009), 6–12.
27. Michael Roper, 'Between Manliness and Masculinity: The "War Generation" and the Psychology of Fear in Britain, 1914–1950', *Journal of British Studies*, 44 (April, 2005), 343–363, 345.
28. Penny Summerfield, *Reconstructing Women's Wartime Lives. Discourse and Subjectivity in Oral Histories of the Second World War* (Manchester; New York: Manchester UP, 1998); Carol Acton, *Grief in Wartime: Private Pain, Public Discourse* (Basingstoke: Palgrave Macmillan, 2007).
29. Kathleen Wilson, *The Island Race: Englishness, Empire and Gender in the Eighteenth Century* (London: Routledge, 2003), 3. See also, Etienne Balibar, 'The Nation Form: History and Ideology', in Etienne Balibar and Immanuel Wallerstein (eds), *Race, Nation, Class, Ambiguous Identities* (London and New York: Verso, 1991), 86–106, 93.
30. For an illuminating analysis of the politics of commemoration in British Napoleonic war memoirs see Ramsey, *The Military Memoir*.
31. This is in contrast to, for example, Stephen Conway's four-nation study of the impact of the American War of Independence, which uses other sources, including newspapers very fruitfully as the basis for comparison. Conway, *The British Isles and the War of American Independence*.
32. For a critique of this approach to the history of combat see John A. Lynn's 'Requiem for the Universal Soldier' in John A. Lynn, *Battle: A History of Combat and Culture from Ancient Greece to Modern America* (Boulder CO; Oxford: Westview Press, 2003), xiii–xxvi.
33. See, for example, Samuel Hynes, *The Soldiers' Tale: Bearing Witness to Modern War* (London: Pimlico, 1998).

1 Narrating War

1. Hesther Piozzi, Brynbella to John Lloyd, London, 14 June 1804. National Library of Wales [NLW], Aberystwyth, Wigfair Papers, MS12421D, 56.
2. Lieutenant John Christopher Harrison, Colchester Barracks, to his father, 20 November 1807. National Army Museum [NAM], London, 8008–56.
3. On the development of the British Post Office in the late eighteenth century see Susan E. Whyman, *The Pen and the People. English Letters Writers, 1660–1800* (Oxford: Oxford UP, 2009), 57–8.
4. Harari, *The Ultimate Experience*; Bell, *The First Total War*.
5. Fritzsche, *Stranded in the Present*, 41.
6. M. Hewitson, '"I Witnesses": Soldiers, Selfhood and Testimony in Modern Wars', *German History*, 28, 3 (2010), 310–25.

7. The description of ego-documents as 'kaleidoscopic fragments' that resist resolution into a single picture, or story, of wartime subjectivity comes from James Hinton, *Nine Wartime Lives. Mass Observation and the Making of the Modern Self* (Oxford: Oxford UP, 2010), 200.

8. The literature on this subject is extensive and continually expanding. Key works include: Paul Fussell, *The Great War and Modern Memory* (Oxford: Oxford UP, 1975); Hynes, *The Soldiers' Tale* and Hynes, 'Personal Narratives and Commemoration', in Jay Winter and Michael Sivan (eds), *War and Remembrance in the Twentieth Century* (Oxford: Oxford UP, 1998), 205–20; Joanna Bourke, *An Intimate History of Killing: Face-to-Face Killing in Twentieth Century Warfare* (London: Granta, 1999). On First World War letters see Jessica Meyer, *Men of War: Masculinity and the First World War in Britain* (Basingstoke: Palgrave Macmillan, 2009) and Michael Roper, 'Maternal Relations: Moral Manliness and Emotional Survival in Letters Home during the First World War', in Stefan Dudink, Karen Hagemann and John Tosh (eds), *Masculinities in Politics and War. Gendering Modern History* (Manchester: Manchester UP, 2004), 295–316 and Michael Roper, *The Secret Battle: Emotional Survival in the Great War* (Manchester: Manchester UP, 2009).

9. This relative neglect has begun to be addressed, see Bell, *First Total War*; Harari, *The Ultimate Experience*; and Ramsay, *The Military Memoir*. Some of the generic features of French Napoleonic war narratives are discussed in Alan Forrest, *Napoleon's Men: The Soldiers of the Revolution and Empire* (London: Hambledon, 2002) and Philip Dwyer, 'Public Remembering, Private Reminiscing: French Military Memoirs and the Revolutionary and Napoleonic Wars', *French Historical Studies*, 22, 2 (Spring, 2010), 231–58.

10. Michael C. Nelson, 'Writing during Wartime: Gender and Literacy in the American Civil War', *Journal of American Studies*, 31 (1997), 43–68, 43.

11. See for example Jürgen Habermas, *The Structural Transformation of the Public Sphere: An Inquiry into a Category of Bourgeois Society*, trans. Thomas Burger (Cambridge MA: MIT Press, 1992), 49–50; Elizabeth Heckendorn Cook, *Epistolary Bodies: Gender and Genre in the Eighteenth Century Republic of Letters* (Stanford CA, Stanford UP, 1996).

12. Dror Wahrman, *The Making of the Modern Self: Identity and Culture in Eighteenth-Century England* (New Haven: Yale UP, 2004), 182.

13. Rev. Thomas Cooke, *The Universal Letter Writer: or, New Art of Polite Correspondence* (London, 1795), 74, 96.

14. Ibid., 96.

15. Martha Hanna similarly notes the influence of nineteenth-century letter-writing manuals and the conversational intimacy they encouraged on French letters from the front during World War I. Martha Hanna, 'A Republic of Letters: The Epistolary Tradition in France during World War I', *American Historical Review*, 108, 5 (2003), 1338–61.

16. William Wilkinson to his wife, Sally, 9 September 1807, Minotaur, Copenhagen. London, National Maritime Museum [NMM], WIL/1/6.

17. William Wilkinson to his wife, Sally, 15 February 1809, HMS Christian, Torbay. London, NMM, WIL/1/23. In her examination of correspondence between husbands and wives in Germany during WWI, Christa Hämmerle identifies similar pleas for greater epistolary intimacy from soldiers serving at the front to their wives, which, she suggests, may indicate a reversal of poles in the dialogue of the sexes. Christa Hämmerle, '"You Let a Weeping Woman Call you Home?" Private Correspondences during the First World War in Germany', in Rebecca Earle (ed.), *Epistolary Selves: Letters and Letter Writers, 1600–1945* (Aldershot: Ashgate, 1999), 152–82, 161.

18. See, for example, John Mills' letter to his mother, Puebla, 21 April 1810. Ian Fletcher (ed.), *For King and Country: The Letters and Diaries of John Mills, Coldstream Guards, 1811–1814* (Staplehurst: Spellmount, 1995), 30.
19. Philip Hay to his mother, Toulon, 1 December 1793. NAM, 6707–13.
20. John E. Cookson, 'Regimental Worlds: Interpreting the Experience of British Soldiers during the Napoleonic Wars', in Forrest et al., *Soldiers, Citizens and Civilians*, 23–42, 32. Clive Emsley suggests an even lower average literacy rate amongst the rank-and-file of between 25–30 per cent. Emsley, *British Society and the French Wars*, 172.
21. David Latimer Wright, Weeley Barracks, 1804. NAM, 7205–2.
22. David Latimer Wright, Portsmouth, 23 July 1808. NAM, 7205–2. On the complicated bureaucracy that military families had to negotiate in order to claim the bequests of bereaved relatives see Patricia Y. Lin, 'Extending her Arms: Military Families and the Transformation of the British State, 1793–1815' (University of California, Berkeley: Unpublished PhD thesis, 1997), 170–7.
23. Janet Gurkin Altman, 'Women's Letters in the Public Sphere', in Elizabeth C. Goldsmith and Dena Goodman (eds), *Going Public: Women and Publishing in Early Modern France* (London and Ithaca: Cornell UP, 1995), 100.
24. See for example William Wright Knox to his brother, Isle of Leon, 1 July 1811. Public Record Office Northern Ireland [PRONI], Belfast. TS 1125/3. 'Some Letters from Spain Written by an Officer', 38.
25. J.C. Harrison to his father, Colchester, 20 November 1807, NAM, 8008–56.
26. Lieutenant George Hennell, 3 leagues east of Valladolid to his brother, 5 August 1812. Michael Glover (ed.), *A Gentleman Volunteer: The Letters of George Hennell from the Peninsular War, 1812–1813* (London: Heineman, 1979), 27.
27. Mary Favret, 'War Correspondence: Reading Romantic War', *Prose Studies*, 19, 2 (1996), 173–85, 178.
28. John Aitchison, Sanquinada, 12 September 1810. W.F.K. Thompson (ed.), *An Ensign in the Peninsular War: The Letters of John Aitchison* (London: Joseph, 1994), 111.
29. Timothy Jenks, *Naval Engagements: Patriotism, Cultural Politics and the Royal Navy, 1793–1815* (Oxford: Oxford UP, 2006), 14–22.
30. MS diary of William Paterson, Portugal, 31 March 1813. NAM, 8211–162, 1.
31. William St Clair, *The Reading Nation in the Romantic Period* (Cambridge: Cambridge UP, 2004), 232–3.
32. 'Journal of Edwin Griffith'. Glover (ed.), *From Corunna to Waterloo*, 7.
33. Hynes, *The Soldiers' Tale*, 25.
34. For a brief discussion of the possibility of identifying combat trauma in soldiers prior to its medical classification in the twentieth century see Edgar Jones, 'Historical Approaches to Post-Combat Disorders', *Philosophical Transactions of the Royal Society*, 361 (2006), 533–42, 534–5.
35. John Mills to his mother, Fuentes de Onoro, 8 May 1811. Fletcher (ed.), *For King and Country*, 34–5.
36. On the difficulties of defining trauma see Cynthia Caruth, 'Unclaimed Experience: Trauma and the Possibility of History', *Yale French Studies*, 79 (1991), 181–92, 181.
37. Dominick La Capra, *History in Transit: Experience, Identity, Critical Theory* (Ithaca; London: Cornell University Press, 2004), 122.
38. Daniel Gordon, 'The City and the Plague in the Age of Enlightenment', *Yale French Studies*, 92 (1997), 67–87, 86–7. Michael C. Nelson observes of the 'unwritability topos' in war-texts that in 'its assertion that every admission of the inadequacy of description is the most profound comment on war ... [it] aggrandizes the important teller by linking him to war stories past and future'. Nelson, 'Writing during Wartime', 62.

39. Wright Knox to his brother, Lisbon, 11 Jan 1810, 'Some Letters from Spain', 21–2.
40. Bell, *The First Total War*.
41. Harari, *The Ultimate Experience*, 125.
42. Journal of John Mills, 18 October 1812. Fletcher (ed.), *For King and Country*, 244; Anon, *Narrative of a Private Soldier, in One of His Majesty's Regiments of Foot. Written by Himself. Detailing many Circumstances Relative to the Irish Rebellion in 1798, the Expedition to Egypt in 1801; and Giving a Particular Account of his Religious History and Experience* (Glasgow, 1819), 105.
43. John Rous, Mongualde, 15 March 1813. Ian Fletcher (ed.), *A Guards Officer in the Peninsular: The Peninsular War Letters of John Rous, Coldstream Guards, 1812–1814* (Tunbridge Wells: Spellmount, 1992), 50.
44. Dr George Birch to Robert Deans, HMS Royal Sovereign off Toulon, 13 June 1808. Letterbook of Robert Deans, NMM, LBK 9. As William St Clair notes, these works and others such as *Robinson Crusoe* and *Gulliver's Travels* formed the canon of eighteenth century prose fiction. St Clair, *The Reading Nation in the Romantic Period*, 130.
45. David McNeil, *The Grotesque Depiction of War and the Military in Eighteenth-century English Fiction* (Newark: University of Delaware Press, 1990), 94–5.
46. On the key elements of the Gothic novel see Angela Wright, *Gothic Fiction: A Reader's Guide to Essential Criticism* (Basingstoke: Palgrave Macmillan, 2007).
47. Roger N. Buckley (ed.), *The Napoleonic War Journal of Captain Thomas Henry Browne, 1807–1816* (London: Bodley Head for the Army Records Society, 1987), 58.
48. Diary of Captain Edward Hodge, October 1808–March 1809. NAM, 7202–33, 26–31.
49. William Wheeler, Madrid, 23 August 1812. B.H. Liddell Hart (ed.), *The Letters of Private Wheeler, 1809–1828* (Aldestrop: Windrush, 1993 [1951]), 94.
50. William Wheeler, 20 April 1814. Hart (ed.), *The Letters of William Wheeler*, 149–51. In *Gil Blas*, the eponymous hero strongly suspects that a rabbit fricassee served in a Spanish inn is a 'cat, dressed up as the double of a rabbit'. Alain René Le Sage, *The Adventures of Gil Blas of Santillane*, trans. Tobias George Smollett (New York, 1820 [1749]), vol. 2, 303. A similar scene referring back to the original episode in *Gil Blas* can also be found in Tobias Smollet, *The Adventures of Peregrine Pickle* (Philadelphia, 1825 [1751]), vol. 2, 92.
51. On the influence of the picaresque on working-class and military autobiography see Mary Jo Haynes, *Taking the Hard Road: Life Course in French and German Workers' Autobiographies in the Era of Industrialization* (Chapel Hill, NC: University of North Carolina Press, 1995), 34–5; Carolyn Steedman, *The Radical Soldier's Tale: John Pearman, 1819–1908* (London; New York: Routledge, 1988), 41; and David M. Hopkin, 'Storytelling, Fairytales and Autobiography: Some Observations on Eighteenth and Nineteenth-century French Soldiers' and Sailors' Memoirs', *Social History*, 29 (2004), 186–98.
52. William Wheeler, Brussels, 8 April 1815. Hart (ed.), *Letters of Private Wheeler*, 160.
53. Robert Brown, *An Impartial Journal of a Detachment from the Brigade of Foot Guards, Commencing 20th February 1793 and Ending 9th May 1795* (London, 1795), 246–7.
54. A contrast can be drawn here with nineteenth-century middle-class autobiographical writing, in which life stories are often plotted along a steadily ascending line. Maynes, *Taking the Hard Road*, 33.
55. See, for example, Sergeant William Stephenson 'A Short Account of the March of the 3rd or King's Own Dragoons thro' Portugal and Spain...Giving the Exact History of Each Day's March'. London, NAM, 6807–215–4.

56. See, for example, Richard Johnson, 'Journal of the HMS Thalia, Remarks &c. 1795–1800'. NMM, JOD/11.
57. Emsley, *British Society and the French Wars*, 172.
58. Yuval Noah Harari, 'Military Memoirs: A Historical Overview of the Genre from the Middle Ages to the Late Modern Era', *War in History*, 14, 3 (2007), 289–309, 300.
59. See, for example, MS Memoirs of an Unidentified Soldier of the 38th Foot, NAM, 7912–21; Anon, *Narrative of a Private Soldier, in One of His Majesty's Regiments of Foot*.
60. Linda Colley, 'Going Native, Telling Tales: Captivity, Collaborations and Empire', *Past & Present*, 168, 1 (2000), 170–93 and Linda Colley, *Captives: Britain, Empire and the World, 1600–1850* (London: Jonathan Cape, 2002).
61. Joe Snader, *Caught between Two Worlds: British Captivity Narratives in Fact and Fiction* (Lexington, KY: University Press of Kentucky, 2000).
62. On the literary components of the British captivity narrative see Linda Colley, 'Perceiving Low Literature: The Captivity Narrative', *Essays in Criticism*, 3 (2003), 199–217.
63. Thomas O'Neill, *An Address to the People of the United Kingdoms of Great Britain and Ireland, Containing an Account of the Sufferings of Thomas O'Neill, a British Officer, While Confined in the Prisoner of the Concierge, at Paris ... and ... during his Second Imprisonment as a Prisoner at War* (London, 1806), 1. See also Lord Blayney, *Narrative of a Forced Journey through Spain and France as a Prisoner of War in the Years 1810 to 1814* (London, 1814).
64. See, for example, Edward Boys, *Narrative of a Captivity and Adventures in France and Flanders between the Years 1803 and 1809 by Capt. Edward Boys, R.N.* (London, 1827).
65. The Journal of John Robertston, 1807–1811, 21 Jan 1807. NMM, JOD/202, 30. On the lament tradition in American prisoner of war narrative, drawn from the books of Samuel, Chronicles and Lamentations, see Robert C. Doyle, *Voices from Captivity: Interpreting the American POW Narrative* (Lawrence, Kansas: University Press of Kansas, 1994), 61–2.
66. On biblical reading and journal-keeping as a source of consolation in Robinson Crusoe see Eric Jager, 'The Parrot's Voice: Language and Self in Robinson Crusoe', *Eighteenth-Century Studies*, 21, 3 (1988), 316–33.
67. Blayney, *Narrative of a Forced Journey*, vol. 1, 341.
68. 'An Evening's Contemplation in a French Prison' transcribed by John Robertson, 'Journal of John Robertson', 27 February 1809. NMM, JOD/202, 197. Robertson's journal identifies the author as a H.P. Haughton. The poem, however, was published in 1814 with an attribution to G.F. Palmer 'a sailor who has been confined six years in different French prisons'. *The Universal Magazine of Knowledge and Pleasure*, March 1815, 227–8. Compare with Sterne's portrait of an imagined captive: 'I took a single captive, and having first shut him up in his dungeon, I then look'd through the twilight of his grate door ... I beheld his body half wasted away with long expectation and confinement ... he had seen no sun, no moon in all that time – nor had the voice of friend or kinsman breathed through his lattice – his children – But here my heart began to bleed'. Laurence Sterne, *A Sentimental Journey*, ed. Ian Jack and Tim Parnell (Oxford: Oxford UP, 2003 [1768]), 61.
69. The image of Britain as an island prison or fortress isolated from the Continent was a common trope in British writing from this period. See, for example, Christopher Bellew to Christopher Dillon Bellew, 30 March 1804: 'Confined & imprisoned in

these islands at present, we have no foreign news, except what the enemy chooses to give us'. National Library of Ireland [NLI], Dublin. Bellew Papers, MS 27127.

70. Historians of twentieth-century wars have fruitfully used such sets of correspondence to explore the interaction of differing modes of perception and experience between the home and the front line. See, for example, Hämmerle, 'You Let a Weeping Woman Call You Home', 157.

71. In 1795 a concessionary rate of one penny per letter was introduced for seamen, non-commissioned officers and private soldiers. Peter B. Boyden, 'The Postal Service of Wellington's Army in the Peninsula and France, 1809–1818', in Alan J. Guy (ed.), *The Road to Waterloo: The British Army and the Struggle against Revolutionary and Napoleonic France* (Stroud: Sutton, 1990), 149–54, 150.

72. Martha Freer to Edward Freer, Knipton, 1809 in Norman Scarfe, 'Letters from the Peninsula: The Freer Family Correspondence, 1807–1814', *Transactions of the Leicestershire Archaeological Society*, 29 (1953), 8

73. Anne Murray Keith to Jeremiah Hill, Balcarres, 2 October 1793. National Library of Scotland [NLS], Edinburgh, MS 3524/40.

74. Harriet Elliot to her father Sir Gilbert Elliot, Minto, 18 December 1809. Edinburgh, NLS, MS 11099/46.

75. Irina Paperno, 'What Can be Done with Diaries?' *The Russian Review*, 63 (2004), 561–73, 565.

76. Lynn Z. Bloom, '"I Write for Myself and Strangers": Private Diaries as Public Documents', in Suzanne L. Bunkers and Cynthia A. Huff (eds), *Inscribing the Daily: Critical Essays on Women's Diaries* (Amherst: University of Massachusetts Press, 1996), 23–37, 25. On the typical details included in such eighteenth- and nineteenth-century diary entries, see Laurel Thatcher Ulrich, *A Midwife's Tale: The Life of Martha Ballard Based on Her Diary, 1785–1812* (New York: Knopf, 1991), 8.

77. Louise P. Carter, 'British Women during the Revolutionary and Napoleonic Wars, 1793–1815: Responses, Roles and Representations' (University of Cambridge, D.Phil. thesis, 2005), 157.

78. See Cynthia Huff, 'Textual Boundaries: Space in Nineteenth-Century Women's Manuscript Diaries', in Bunkers and Huff, *Inscribing the Daily*, 123–38, 125.

79. *The Lady's British Diary for the Year 1806* (London, 1806), 130–2; *The Ladies Daily Companion for the Year of Our Lord 1807* (Canterbury, 1807), 1. Centre for Kentish Studies, Maidstone. Knatchbull MS, U951/F24/4–5.

80. Michael Paris locates the development of a 'pleasure culture of war' in this period. According to Paris, distanced from the brutal reality of war civilians were increasingly able to enjoy its vicarious excitements. Michael Paris, *Warrior Nation: Images of War in British Popular Culture, 1850–2000* (London: Reaktion, 2000), 26. The phrase 'pleasure culture of war' was originally used by Graham Dawson to describe developments in the later nineteenth century. See Graham Dawson, *Soldier Heroes: British Adventure, Empire and the Imagining of Masculinity* (London: Routledge, 1994).

81. Diaries of Fanny C. Knatchbull (neé Austen, changed her name to Knight in 1812 and married Sir Edward Knatchbull in 1820), 1804–1809. Centre for Kentish Studies, Maidstone, Knatchbull MS U951/F24, 1–9.

82. See for example the diaries of Tatton Sykes, 1793–1794. Sykes family papers, Hull University Archives, Hull, DDSY102/27–28.

83. Diary of Alured Punchen 1802, Centre for Kentish Studies, U145 F18.

84. Matthew McCormack, 'Liberty and Discipline: Militia Training Literature in Mid-Georgian England', in Catriona Kennedy and Matthew McCormack (eds), *Soldiering in Britain and Ireland, 1750–1850: Men of Arms* (Basingstoke: Palgrave Macmillan, 2012), 159–78.

85. St Clair, *Reading Nation in the Romantic Period*, 225–8.
86. See for example, Diaries of Christian Dalrymple, 28 November 1798; 20 April 1803; 31 July 1803; 20 October 1803; 20 February 1805. NLS, Newhailes papers, MS 25459–60; Diaries of Thomas Pattenden, 8 March 1797; 7 March 1798; 29 November 1798; 27 February 1799. East Kent Archives, Dover, DO/ZZ1/1–3; Transcription of part of a Thanksgiving day sermon preached by Dr Horseley, Lord Bishop of Saint Asaph on the 5th of December 1805 in the Commonplace Book of Thomas Salisbury of Denbigh, NLW, MS 9669E.
87. Andrew Cambers, 'Reading the Godly and Self-Writing in England, circa 1580–1720', *Journal of British Studies*, 46 (October, 2007), 796–825.
88. Diary of Mary Cobb (neé) Blackburn, n.d. [March 1793?]. East Kent Archives Centre, Dover. RU/126/1, vol. 1.
89. W.F. Cobb (ed.), *Memoir of the Late Francis Cobb Esq. Of Margate Compiled from His Journals and Letters* (Maidstone, 1835).
90. Diary of Mary Cobb, 1795–1799, East Kent Archives Centre, Dover. RU/126/1, vol. 3.
91. Diary of William Vavasour, 17 August 1810. West Yorkshire Archive Service, Leeds. Weston Hall MS, WYL639/445.
92. Reinhart Koselleck, *Futures Past: On the Semantics of Historical Time* (Cambridge MA; London: MIT Press, 1985), chapter 14, 255–76.
93. Pieter Fritzsche, 'The Case of Modern Memory: Review Essay', *The Journal of Modern History*, 73, 1 (March, 2001), 87–117, 94–99; James Chandler, *England in 1819: The Politics of Literary Culture and the Case of Romantic Historicism* (Chicago: Chicago UP, 1998).
94. Fritzsche, *Stranded in the Present*, 83.
95. John Brewer, 'Reconstructing the Reader: Prescription, Texts, and Strategies in Anna Larpent's Reading', in James Raven, Helen Small and Naomi Tadmor (eds), *Practice and Representation of Reading in England* (Cambridge: Cambridge UP, 1996), 227–45 and Marilyn Morris, 'Negotiating Domesticity in the Journals of Anna Larpent', *Journal of Women's History*, 22, 1 (Spring, 2010), 85–106.
96. Diary of Anna Larpent, 8 May 1793; 20 Feb 1793.
97. Diary of Anna Larpent, 23 June 1815.
98. Diary of Anna Larpent, 12 April 1802.

2 Becoming Soldiers and Sailors

1. William Thornton Keep to his mother, Winchester, 7 November 1808. Ian Fletcher (ed.), *In the Service of the King: The Letters of William Thornton Keep, at Home, Walcheren and the Peninsula, 1808–1814* (Staplehurst: Spellmount, 1997), 17.
2. Keep to his mother, Winchester, 7 November 1808; 20 November 1808. Fletcher (ed.), *In the Service of the King*, 17–21.
3. David Roberts, *The Military Adventures of Johnny Newcome: With an Account of his Campaign on the Peninsula and in Pall Mall...* (London, 1815); Alfred Burton (pseud. John Mitford), *The Adventures of Johnny Newcome in the Navy; a Poem in Four Cantos* (London, 1818).
4. Forrest, *Napoleon's Men*, 4–10.
5. Karen Hagemann, 'German Heroes: The Cult of Death for the Fatherland in Nineteenth-Century Germany', in Dudink et al. (eds), *Masculinities in Politics and War*, 116–34; Ute Frevert, *A Nation in Barracks: Modern Germany, Military Conscription and Civil Society*, trans. Andrew Boreham with Daniel Brückenhaus (Oxford: Berg, 2004), 9–46.

6. Karen Hagemann and Jane Rendall, 'Introduction: Gender, War and Politics, 1775–1830', in Hagemann et al. (eds), *Gender, War and Politics,* 1–40, 17.
7. G.A. Steppler, 'The British Army on the Eve of War', in Guy (ed.), *The Road to Waterloo,* 4.
8. N.A.M. Rodger, *The Command of the Ocean: A Naval History of Britain, 1649–1815* (London: Allen Lane, 2004), 639.
9. Clive Emsley, *The Longman Companion to Napoleonic Europe* (London: Longman, 1993), 138.
10. David Gates, 'The Transformation of the British Army, 1783–1815', in David G. Chandler and Ian Beckett (eds), *The Oxford History of the British Army* (Oxford: Oxford UP, 1994), 133–7.
11. Rodger, *Command of the Ocean,* 442–3, 497.
12. Nicholas Rogers, *The Press Gang: Naval Impressment and Its Opponents in Georgian Britain* (London and New York: Continuum, 2007), 5.
13. N.A.M. Rodger, 'Honour and Duty at Sea, 1660–1815', *Historical Research,* 75, 190 (2002), 425–47, 426.
14. J.A. Houlding, *Fit for Service: The Training of the British Army 1715–1795* (Oxford: Oxford UP Reprints, 2000 [1981]), 100, 104. The purchase system would not be abolished until 1871.
15. Richard Glover, *Peninsular Preparation: The Reform of the British Army, 1795–1809* (Cambridge: Cambridge UP, 1963), 146, 153.
16. Charles M. Clode, *The Military Forces of the Crown,* 2 vols (London, 1869), vol. 2, 608, quoted in Richard Holmes, *Redcoat: The British Soldier in the Age of Horse and Musket* (London: Harper Collins, 2002), 159.
17. See Stana Nenadic, 'The Impact of the Military Profession on Highland Gentry Families, c. 1730–1830', *The Scottish Historical Review,* 85, 1 (April 2006), 75–99, 93.
18. Houlding, *Fit for Service,* 100.
19. Letter from Lt John Mills, 20 May 1810. Ian Fletcher (ed.), *For King and Country: The Letters and Diaries of John Mills Coldstream Guards, 1811–1814* (Staplehurst: Spellmount, 1995), 144.
20. Colley, *Britons,* 198.
21. Rodger, *Command of the Ocean,* 508.
22. Michael Lewis, *A Social History of the Navy, 1793–1815* (London: George Allen & Unwin, 1960), 31, 36.
23. Rodgers, *Command of the Ocean,* 513.
24. Glover, *Peninsular Preparation,* 215.
25. Gates, 'Transformation of the Army', 147.
26. Patricia Y.C.E. Lin, 'Extending her Arms: Military Families and the Transformation of the British State, 1793–1815' (Unpublished PhD thesis, University of California, Berkeley, 1997).
27. Cookson, 'Regimental Worlds', 33.
28. Rodger, *Command of the Ocean,* 492.
29. Denver Brunsman, 'Men of War: British Sailors and the Impressment Paradox', *Journal of Early Modern History,* 14 (2010), 9–44, 35.
30. On the contrast between French and British soldiers see Matthew McCormack, *The Independent Man. Citizenship and Gender Politics in Georgian England* (Manchester: Manchester UP, 2005). On the popular image of the soldier's life see Cookson, *British Armed Nation,* 111.
31. See Gillian Russell, *The Theatre of War: Politics, Performance and Society, 1793–1815* (Oxford: Clarendon, 1995), 12.
32. Ramsey, *Military Memoir,* 124.

33. On the navy in British culture and society during this period see Margarette Lincoln, *Representing the Royal Navy, British Sea Power, 1750–1815* (Aldershot: Ashgate, 2002); Kathleen Wilson, 'Nelson and the People: Manliness, Patriotism and Body Politics', in David Cannadine (ed.), *Admiral Lord Nelson Context and Legacy* (Basingstoke: Palgrave Macmillan, 2005), 49–66.
34. Colley, *Britons*, 195.
35. Jane Austen, *Mansfield Park*, ed. Kathryn Sutherland (Harmonsworth: Penguin, 1996 [1814]), 92.
36. John Barrell, *The Birth of Pandora and the Division of Knowledge* (Basingstoke: Macmillan, 1992), 64.
37. Mary Wollstonecraft, *A Vindication of the Rights of Woman*, ed. Sylvana Tomaselli (Cambridge: Cambridge UP, 1995 [1792]), 84, 92.
38. Holmes, *Redcoat*, 139. See also Scott Hughes Myerly, *British Military Spectacle from the Napoleonic Wars through the Crimea* (Cambridge MA: Harvard UP, 1996), 53–66.
39. Myerly, *British Military Spectacle*, 56, 59, 64.
40. Anon., *Memoirs of a Sergeant: The 43rd Light Infantry during the Peninsular War* (Gloucestershire, 2005 [1835]), 21.
41. Ann Kussmaul (ed.), *The Autobiography of Joesph Mayett of Quainton, 1783–1839* (Buckinghamshire Record Society, 1986), 24.
42. Colley, *Britons*, 330.
43. Mary Jo Maynes, *Taking the Hard Road: Life Course in French and German Workers' Autobiographies in the Era of Industrialization* (Chapel Hill, 1995), 11–12.
44. Cookson, *British Armed Nation*, 111–12.
45. William Surtees, *Twenty-Five Years in the Rifle Brigade* (Blackwood: Edinburgh, 1833), 2.
46. Anon., *Journal of a Soldier of the Seventy-First or Glasgow Regiment, Highland Light Infantry from 1806 to 1815* (Edinburgh, 1819), 8. Joseph Donaldson similarly related how, before deciding to join the army, he had been shunned by the local community. Joseph Donaldson, *Recollections of the Eventful Life of a Soldier* (Philadelphia, 1845), 40.
47. T.W. Moody (ed.), 'An Irish Countryman in the British Navy, 1809–1815', *Irish Sword*, 4 (1960), 229–30.
48. Myerly, *British Military Spectacle*, 54.
49. Edward Jones to Robert Owen Jones, 3 February 1815 and 2 January 1816. National Library of Wales, Aberystwyth, Glansevern MS, 2258, 2264.
50. William Wilkinson to Sally Wilkinson, 19 December 1807. NMM, WIL/1/12.
51. Harry Ross-Lewin, *With the Thirty-Second in the Peninsular and Other Campaigns by Harry Ross-Lewin of Ross Hill, Co Clare*, ed. John Wardell (Dublin, 1904), 1.
52. On the role of the soldier hero in imaginings of boyhood masculinity see Graham Dawson, *British Adventure, Empire and the Imagining of Masculinities* (Routledge, Oxford, 1994).
53. Ross-Lewin, *With the Thirty-Second*, 4.
54. McCormack, *The Independent Man*, 1.
55. E. Barker to S. Homfray, 18 July 1800. Quoted in Rodger, *Command of the Ocean*, 386.
56. George Ridout Bingham, Burgos, to his mother, 3 October 1812. NAM, 6807–163–2.
57. David A. Bell, *The First Total War: Napoleon's Europe and the Birth of Modern Warfare as We Know It* (Houghton Mifflin: New York, 2007) and Ute Frevert, *A Nation in Barracks: Modern Germany, Military Conscription and Civil Society*, trans. Andrew Boreham with Daniel Brückenhaus (Berg: Oxford and New York, 2004).

58. Frevert, *A Nation in Barracks*, 3; Louis A. Zurcher Jr, 'The Sailor Aboard Ship: A Study of Role Behaviour in a Total Institution', *Social Forces*, 43, 3 (1965), 389–400.
59. Cookson, *British Armed Nation*, 184.
60. Wright Knox, Colchester Barracks to William Knox, 18 November 1808. 'Some letters from Spain Written by an Officer'. PRONI, TS 1125/3, 4.
61. Wright Knox, 5 December 1808. 'Some letters from Spain', Wright Knox, 5 December 1808, PRONI, TS 1125/3, 5.
62. Myerly, *British Military Spectacle*, 42.
63. Lt. David Powell 'Some Account of a Campagne [*sic*] in 1794', NLI, MS 1577.
64. William Thornton Keep, Berry Head to Sam Keep, 12 August 1812, Fletcher (ed.), *In the Service of the King*, 84.
65. William Thornton Keep to his mother, 6 April 1812, Fletcher (ed.), *In the Service of the King*, 83.
66. See Karen Harvey, 'Men Making Home: Masculinity and Domesticity in the Eighteenth Century', *Gender & History*, 21, 3 (November, 2009), 520–40.
67. On bachelors, domesticity and masculinity in Georgian England see Amanda Vickery, *Behind Closed Doors: At Home in Georgian England* (New Haven: Yale UP, 2011), 49–82.
68. William Thornton Keep to Sam Keep, Berry Head, 12 August 1812, Fletcher (ed.), *In the Service of the King*, 84. In her account of male bonding in World War I, Joanna Bourke suggests that the development of intimate male friendships was stimulated by the absence of women. Joanna Bourke, *Dismembering the Male: Men's Bodies, Britain and the Great War* (London: Reaktion, 1996), 133.
69. Roger N. Buckley, *The Napoleonic War Journal of Captain Thomas Henry Browne, 1807–1816* (London: Bodley Head for the Army Records Society, 1987), 67.
70. Samuel Lumsden, Eastbourne to William Lumsden, Waterford, 23 April 1813. Belfast, PRONI, D/649/1–16.
71. George Woodberry, 'The Idle Companion of a Young Hussar during the Year 1813', 8 August 1813, NAM, 6807/267, 204.
72. Anon., *Narrative of a Private Soldier, in One of His Majesty's Regiments of Foot. Written by Himself. Detailing Many Circumstances Relative to the Irish Rebellion in 1798, the Expedition to Egypt in 1801; and Giving a Particular Account of his Religious History and Experience* (Glasgow, 1819).
73. See Anon., *Journal of a Soldier of the 71st, or Glasgow Regiment, Highland Light Infantry 1806–1815* (Edinburgh, 1819), 14 and Joseph Donaldson, *Recollections of the Eventful Life of a Soldier* (Philadelphia, 1845), 52.
74. Anon., *Narrative of a Private Soldier*, 16.
75. Donaldson, *Recollections*, 52.
76. The term 'docile bodies' is taken from Michel Foucault's account of the development of a disciplinary society in which he identified the military as the forerunner of later disciplinary institutions. Michel Foucault, *Discipline and Punish. The Birth of the Prison* (Penguin: London, 1979), 135–69.
77. See definition of 'discipline' in Charles James, *A New and Enlarged Military Dictionary or Alphabetical Explanation of Technical Terms* (London, 1805).
78. Anon., *Journal of a Private in the 71st*, 14.
79. Lynn, *Battle: A History of Combat*, 125
80. Ibid., 77.
81. Glover, *Peninsular Preparation*, 118.

82. Captain T.H. Cooper, *A Practical Guide for the Light Infantry Officer, Comprising Valuable Extracts from All the Most Popular Works on the Subject...* (London, 1806), xvi.
83. See Arthur N. Gilbert, 'Military and Civilian Justice in Eighteenth Century England: An Assessment', *The Journal of British Studies*, 17, 2 (1978), 41–65.
84. Donaldson, *Recollections*, 102.
85. Cookson, 'Regimental Worlds', 33.
86. William Wheeler, 13 February 1809 and 20 June 1809. Hart (ed.), *Letters of Private Wheeler,* 15, 21.
87. Penelope Corfield, *Power and the Professions in Britain, 1700–1850* (London: Routledge, 1995), 192.
88. Gates, 'Transformation of the Army', 141.
89. Samuel Lumsden, Eastbourne to William Lumsden, 23 April 1813. PRONI, D/649/2.
90. Bell, *First Total War.*
91. Rodger, 'Honour and Duty at Sea', 427.
92. Carroll Smith-Rosenberg, 'The Republican Gentleman: The Race to Rhetorical Stability in the New United States', in Dudink, Hagemann and Tosh (eds), *Masculinities in Politics and War*, 64.
93. The shift from politeness, with its emphasis on the social aspect of gentlemanly behaviour, to the concept of 'manliness' and a greater stress upon men's inner, individual character can be located even later in the early to mid Victorian period. See John Tosh, 'Gentlemanly Politeness and Manly Simplicity in Victorian England', *Transactions of the Royal Historical Society*, 12 (2002), 455–72.
94. James Penman Gairdner, London to his father, 10 September 1810. NAM, 7011-21-1.
95. Matthew McCormack, 'Dance and Drill. Polite Accomplishments and Military Masculinities in Georgian Britain', *Cultural and Social History*, 8, 3 (2011), 315–30.
96. Russell, *Theatres of War*, 3.
97. Rodger, 'Honour and Duty at Sea', 436–437; Arthur N. Gilbert, 'Law and Honour among Eighteenth-Century British Army Officers', *Historical Journal*, 19 (1976), 75–87.
98. William Thornton Keep to his mother, Berry Head, 10 September 1812. Fletcher (ed.), *In the Service of the King*, 92–3.
99. Donna T. Andrew, 'The Code of Honour and its Critics: The Opposition to Duelling in England, 1700–1850', *Social History*, 5 (1980), 409–34.
100. Letter from William Thornton Keep, Berry Head, 10 September 1812. Fletcher (ed.), *In the Service of the King*, 94.
101. Diary of Lt. John Aitchison, 26 March 1811. W.F.K. Thompson (ed.), *An Ensign in the Peninsular War. The Letters of John Aitchison* (London: Michael Joseph, 1981), 11.
102. W.C. Coles, Elvas, to his brother John Coles, Hampshire, 19 December 1808, NAM., London, 6807/419–2.
103. Anna Clark, *Scandal: The Sexual Politics of the British Constitution* (Princeton NJ; Oxford: Princeton UP, 2004), 148–76.
104. W.C. Coles, Lisbon to John Coles, Hants, 14 January 1810, N.A.M., 6987/419–2.
105. W.C. Coles, Bristol to John Coles, Hants, 21 April 1808, N.A.M., 6807/419–2.
106. N.A.M. Rodger, *The Wooden World: An Anatomy of the Georgian Navy* (London: Fontana, 1988), 15.

107. Edward Mangin, 'Some Account of the Writer's Situation as Chaplain in the British navy' in Rear-Admiral H.G. Thursfield (ed.), *Five Naval Journals, 1797–1817* (Navy Records Society: London, 1951), vol. 91, 31.

108. Isaac Land, *War, Nationalism and the British Sailor, 1750–1850* (New York: Palgrave Macmillan, 2009), 35.

109. Greg Dening, *Mr Bligh's Bad Language: Passion, Power and Theatre on the Bounty* (Cambridge: Cambridge UP, 1992), 19.

110. Mangin, 'Some Account of the Writer's Situation...', 16.

111. Ibid., 32.

112. Rodger, *Wooden World*, 23.

113. 'Journal of Robert Mercer Wilson', July 1805, in Thursfield (ed.), *Five Naval Journals*, 129.

114. Ibid., 245.

115. Ibid., 130–1. The importance of occupational identity and the opportunity to display and develop one's sea-craft in muting impressed sailors' resentments against the navy are discussed in Brunsman, 'Men of War', 9–44.

116. Land, *War, Nationalism, and the British Sailor*, 34.

117. James Lowry, *Fiddlers and Whores: The Candid Memoirs of a Surgeon in Nelson's Fleet*, ed. John Millyard (London: Chatham, 2006 [1807]), 31. The pranks and tricks played upon 'greenhorns' or 'Johnny Newcomes' are also detailed at length in Burton, *The Adventures of Johnny Newcome in the Navy*, 18–19.

118. For a reference to the ceremony being performed upon crossing the Tropic of Cancer see 'Journal of Robert Clarke, HMS Swiftsure', January 1815, in Thursfield (ed.), *Five Naval Journals*, 474.

119. On the crossing the line ceremony see Dening, *Mr Bligh's Bad Language*, 76–80.

120. For an ethnological analysis of the ceremony see Simon J. Bronner, *Crossing the Line: Violence, Play, and Drama in Naval Equator Traditions* (Amsterdam: Amsterdam UP, 2006).

121. Dening, *Mr Bligh's Bad Language*, 77.

122. 'Journal of Robert Clarke, HMS Swiftsure', January 1815, in Thursfield (ed.), *Five Naval Journals*, 474.

123. Founded in 1733 as the Naval academy, it acquired the title 'Royal' in 1773, and was renamed the Royal Naval College in 1806. Lewis, *A Social History of the Navy*, 142–9.

124. The many ways in which these official regulations were circumvented are detailed in Lewis, *A Social History of the Navy*, 149–77.

125. William Rennie to his father John Rennie, 4 March 1810; 27 Sept 1811. National Library of Scotland, Edinburgh. Rennie Papers, MS 19933, F33, 56.

126. William Rennie to his father John Rennie, 22 December 1811. NLS, Rennie Papers, MS19933, F94.

127. Rodger, *The Wooden World*, 273–81.

128. Mangin, 'Some Account of the Writer's Situation...', 34; 'Diary of Samuel Grant, Purser, 30 August 1798. National Maritime Museum, London, GRT/6; 'Journal of Robert Clarke, HMS Swiftsure', 3 January 1815, in Thursfield (ed.), *Five Naval Journals*, 467.

129. William Rennie, 28 June 1814. NLS, Rennie Papers, MS19933, F152.

130. Henry Ross-Lewin, *With the Thirty-Second in the Peninsula and Other Campaigns*, ed. John Wardell (Dublin, 1904), 39.

131. The best account of the political and administrative dimensions of pan-Britannic military recruitment is Cookson, *British Armed Nation*.

132. Ronald Krebs provides a comprehensive critical survey of the various approaches to this topic. Ronald R. Krebs, 'A School for the Nation? How Military Service Does Not Build Nations, and How it Might?', *International Security*, 28, 4 (2004), 85–124. See also Barry R. Posen, 'Nationalism, the Mass Army and Military Power', *International Security*, 18, 2 (1993), 80–124.

133. David Bell, for example, observes that the army was probably the most successful instrument of national integration available to French republicans David Bell, *The Cult of the Nation in France: Inventing Nationalism 1680–1800* (Cambridge MA; London: Harvard UP, 2001), 201.

134. Laurence Brockliss, 'The Professions and National Identity', in L.W.B. Brockliss and David Eastwood (eds), *A Union of Multiple Identities: The British Isles, c.1750–c.1850* (Manchester: Manchester UP, 1997), 9.

135. In 1811 England made up 57 per cent of the United Kingdom population, Scotland 10 per cent, and Ireland 33 per cent meaning that Scotland was the most over-represented nation in the army, whilst England was slightly under-represented. Cookson, *British Armed Nation*, 126–7.

136. Ian McBride, *Eighteenth-Century Ireland: The Isle of Slaves* (Dublin: Gill & Macmillan, 2009), 186–7.

137. See Robert Clyde, *From Rebel to Hero: The Image of the Highlander, 1745–1830* (East Linton: Tuckwell, 1995), 150–80.

138. Cookson, *British Armed Nation*, 129. Despite the prominent role played by the Highland soldier in Scotland's martial and British identity, recruitment from Highland areas would gradually decline during the wars with Lowlanders outnumbering Highlanders in many regiments.

139. Andrew MacKillop, *'More Fruitful than the Soil': Army, Empire and the Scottish Highlands* (East Linton: Tuckwell, 2000), esp. chapter 7, 204–233.

140. See, for example, Charles O'Neil, *Private O'Neil: The Recollections of an Irish Rogue of HM 28th Regt* (Leonaur, 2007 [first published as *The Military Adventures of Charles O'Neil* (1851)], 12; Edward Costello, *Adventures of a Soldier: Written by Himself Being the Memoirs of Edward Costello* (London, 1852, 2nd edn), 2; Anon., *Memoirs of a Sergeant* (Stroud: Nonsuch, 2005 [1835]), 19.

141. Cookson, *British Armed Nation*, 176.

142. Ruan O'Donnell, 'Liberty or Death': The United Irishmen in New South Wales, 1800–4', in Thomas Bartlett, David Dickson, Dáire Keogh and Kevin Whelan (eds), *The 1798 Rebellion: A Bicentenary Perspective* (Dublin: Four Courts, 2003), 607–19, 609.

143. J. R. Western, 'Roman Catholics Holding Military Commissions in 1798', *English Historical Review*, 70, 276 (1955) 428–32; E.M. Spiers, 'Army Organisation and Society in the Nineteenth Century', in Tom Bartlett and Keith Jeffery (eds), *A Military History of Ireland* (Cambridge: Cambridge UP, 1997), 335–358, 341.

144. Sam Scott, 'The French Revolution and the Irish Regiments in France', Hugh Gough and David Dickson (eds), *Ireland and the French Revolution* (Dublin: Irish Academic Press, 1990), 14–27, 19.

145. Diary of Captain P.R. Jennings, 27 March 1802, NAM, 8301–203. On the Catholic 'underground gentry' see Kevin Whelan, *The Tree of Liberty: Radicalism, Catholicism and the Construction of Irish Identity, 1760–1830* (Cork: Cork UP, 1996), 3–58.

146. Diary of Captain Peter R. Jennings, n.d., n.p.

147. See Stephen Conway, 'Christians, Catholics, Protestants: The Religious Links of Britain and Ireland with Continental Europe, c. 1689–1800', *English Historical Review*, 126, 509 (2009), 833–862, 857.

148. Diary of Captain Peter R. Jennings, n.p, n.d.
149. Cookson, 'Regimental Worlds', 51.
150. Watkin Tench, Brest, 9 November 1794. Watkin Tench, *Letters from Revolutionary France: Letters Written to a Friend in London Between the Month of November 1794, and the Month of May 1795*, ed. Gavin Edwards (Cardiff: Cardiff UP, 2001 [1796]), 11–13.
151. Philip J. Haythornthwaite, *The Armies of Wellington* (London: Brockhampton, 1998), 48.
152. Charles James, *The Regimental Companion Containing the Relative Duties of Every Officer in the British Army* (London, 1800), 2 vols, vol. 1, 59.
153. Diary of Lieutenant Thomas Powell, 22 May 1793. N.A.M. 7607–45.
154. Taylor White to his mother, 21 November 1793. NAM, 7612–100.
155. Buckley (ed.), *Napoleonic War Journal of Captain Thomas Henry Browne*, 25.
156. William Wheeler, 26 August 1809 and February 1811. Hart (ed.), *Letters of William Wheeler*, 37, 47.
157. Geoff Quilley, 'Duty and Mutiny: The Aesthetics of Loyalty and the Representation of the British Sailor c. 1789–1800', in Philip Shaw (ed.), *Romantic Wars: Studies in Culture and Conflict, 1793–1822* (Aldershot: Ashgate, 2000), 80.
158. James Stanier Clarke, *Naval Sermons Preached on Board His Majesty's Ship the Impeteux...* (London, 1798), 172.
159. Letterbook of Robert Deans, HMS Royal Sovereign, May 1809. N.M.M. LBK 9.
160. Lincoln, *Representing the Royal Navy*, 12.
161. Richard Johnson, 'Journal of the HMS Thalia, Remarks & c. 1795–1800'. N.M.M., JOD/11. Copies of patriotic ballads can also be found in George Gould, 'Journal, HMS Mercury, 1800–1802', N.M.M. JOD/47.
162. W.C. Coles, Monte Video to Chas. Coles, Hants, 27 July 1807, N.A.M., 6807/419.
163. Laurence Brockliss, 'The Professions and National Identity', in Laurence Brockliss and David Eastwood (eds), *A Union of Multiple Identities: The British Isles, c.1750–c.1850* (Manchester: Manchester University Press, 1997), 9–28, 9.
164. William Thornton Keep, Berryhead to his mother, 14 January 1812. Fletcher (ed.), *In the Service of the King*, 76.
165. William Wheeler, Berryhead Barracks, 20 June 1809. Hart (ed.), *Letters of Private William Wheeler*, 21.
166. Cookson, 'Regimental Worlds', 51.
167. Donaldson, *Recollections*, 49.
168. Anon., *Journal of a Soldier of the 71st*, 16.
169. Wheeler, before Antwerp, 26 August 1809 and near Eschellar, 17 August 1813. Hart (ed.), *Letters of William Wheeler*, 37, 123.
170. See for instance Andrew Ross's letter declining an application from an Irish gentleman for a ensigncy in the Reay Fencible Highlanders in preference for Scottish officers 'who understand the language and are accustomed to the dress of the corps'. Major Andrew Ross to Michael Grace Esq., 2 August 1798. NAM, 6406–22. The memoir of William Grattan of the Connaught Rangers relates an anecdote concerning a young Gaelic-speaking private in his regiment, who, upon being asked a question in English by General Mackinnon, could only answer him in Irish. William Grattan, *Adventures with the Connaught Rangers, 1809–1814*, ed. Charles Oman (London: Greenhill, 2003), 126.
171. Alexander MacKinnon, 'The Battle of Holland' (Blàr na h-Òlaind), in Ronald Black (ed.), *An Lasair: Anthology of 18th Century Scottish Gaelic Verse* (Edinburgh: Berlin, 2001), 355.
172. Anon., *Memoirs of a Sergeant*, 21.

173. Donaldson, *Recollections*, 71.
174. Lieutenant George Woodberry, MS Journal 'The Idle Companion of a Young Hussar during the year 1813'. NAM, 6807–267.
175. William Keep, 17 July 1809. Fletcher (ed.), *In the Service of the King*, 36.
176. Lincoln, *Representing the Royal Navy*, 5.
177. Rodger, *Command of the Ocean*, 498.
178. Hugh O'Neill, Barletta to Mrs Magennis, Co. Down, 24 October 1798. PRONI, T/1880/2.
179. William H. Hamilton, HMS Orquixo to his father, 12 October 1805. Thursfield (ed.), *Five Naval Journals*, 375.
180. Robert Wilson's Journal, July 1808. Thursfield (ed.), *Five Naval Journals*, 239.
181. Michael Snape, *The Redcoat and Religion: The Forgotten History of the British Soldier from the Age of Marlborough to the Eve of the First World War* (London: Routledge, 2006), 91–2, 161.
182. Ibid., 94, 148.
183. George Ridout Bingham, Almofala, 8 January 1813. NAM, 6807–163/3.
184. Snape, *The Redcoat and Religion*, 161.
185. In March 1811, an Irish MP, Parnell, raised the issue in the House of Commons, noting that despite general orders exempting Catholics from attending Protestant services, this policy was continuously neglected and abused. 'Debate on the Mutiny Bill – Catholic soldiers', 11 March 1811. Thomas C. Hansard, *Parliamentary Debates, 1803–1811* (1812), vol. 19, 350–6. On conflict in the Irish militia over compulsory attendance at Protestant services see Thomas Bartlett, 'Indiscipline and Disaffection in the French and Irish Armies during the Revolutionary Period', in Gough and Dickson (eds), *Ireland and the French Revolution*, 179–99, 188; Snape, *The Redcoat and Religion*, 161.
186. O'Neil, *Private O'Neil*, 38.
187. Snape, *The Redcoat and Religion*, 161.
188. Snape, *The Redcoat and Religion*, 123; On Picton's address see Grattan, *Adventures*, 17.
189. James Kemmis to Thomas Kemmis, 31 July 1800 and 15 May 1813. NLI, Kemmis Papers, 15139 ff. 6, 9.
190. John Green, *The Vicissitudes of a Soldier's Life* (Louth, 1827), 21–2. Rifleman Benjamin Harris recorded a similar instance of sectarian violence amongst a group of freshly recruited 'hot-headed Paddies' of the 95th regiment. Christopher Hibbert (ed.), *The Recollections of Rifleman Harris: As Told to Henry Curling* (Moreton-in-Marsh: Windrush, 1996), 6–7.
191. See Tony Claydon and Ian McBride 'Introduction: The Trials of the Chosen Peoples: Recent Interpretations of Protestantism and National Identity in Britain and Ireland', in Ian McBride and Tony Claydon (eds), *Protestantism and National Identity. Britain and Ireland, c.1650–1850* (Cambridge: Cambridge UP), 3–32.
192. Snape, *The Redcoat and Religion*, 145–50.
193. Anon., 'MS memoir of unidentified soldier of 38th Foot, 1808–1815'. N.A.M., 7912–21, 18.
194. Edmund Burke, *Reflections on the Revolution in France* (London, 1790), 68–9.
195. William Wheeler, Spithead, 9 February 1811. Hart (ed.), *Letters of Private Wheeler*, 46.
196. Robert Barrie, Portsmouth to his mother, 31 October 1811. N.M.M. BIE/1.
197. Robert Wilson's Journal, September 1806 and July 1808. Thursfield (ed.), *Five Naval Journals*, 144, 237.
198. Cookson, 'Regimental Worlds', 33–5.

199. Cooper, *Practical Guide for the Light Infantry Officer*, xxii.
200. William Wheeler, Blatchington Barracks, 25 March 1816. Hart (ed.), *Letters of Private Wheeler*, 195.
201. See, for example, the court martial of Lieutenant Lawson Huddlestone, 14 March 1811 in Charles James, *A Collection of the Charges, Opinions, and Sentences of General Courts Martial; As Published by Authority, from the Year 1795 to the Present Time* (London, 1820), 368–70.
202. Haythornthwaite, *Armies of Wellington*, 54.
203. William Keep to his Father, on board HMS *Illustrious*, 28 July 1809. Fletcher (ed.), *In the Service of the King*, 43.
204. Cookson, 'Regimental Worlds', 45.
205. Lieutenant George Woodberry, 27 Jan 1813. 'The Idle Companion of a Young Hussar during the Year 1813'. NAM, 6807–267, 8.
206. Captain George Ridout Bingham to his mother, field of action, near Talavera, 19 July 1809. NAM, 6807–163, TS, vol. 1, 53.
207. J.C. Harrison to his father, Azambuja, 29 November 1810. NAM, 8008–56.
208. Alan Forrest, *Soldiers of the French Revolution* (Durham NC: Duke UP, 1990), 28–9.
209. Cookson, *British Armed Nation*, 121–2.
210. Cookson, *British Armed Nation*, 171.
211. Andrew MacKillop, 'For King, Country and Regiment?: Motive and Identity within Highland Soldiering, 1746–1815', in Steve Murdoch and Andrew MacKillop (eds), *Fighting for Identity: Scottish Military Experience, 1550–1900* (Leiden: Brill, 2002), 185–212.
212. For example, John Kincaid of the Rifle Brigade, while declaring his preference for mixed regiments, concluded 'I love to see a national corps, and hope that the British army is never without one'. John Kincaid, *Tales from the Rifle Brigade* (Barnsley: Pen & Sword, 2005 [1830, 1835]), 293.
213. Thomas Browne, 1 March 1808. Buckley (ed.), *Napoleonic War Journal of Captain Thomas Henry Browne*, 73.
214. Lt James Penman Gairdner, 20 November 1812. Diaries of James Penman Gairdner, NAM 6902–5, vol. 1.
215. Regimental order noted in Lt. George Woodberry, 17 March 1813. 'The Idle Companion of a Young Hussar During the Year 1813', NAM 6807–267.
216. MacKillop, 'For King, Country and Regiment?', 194.
217. Charles James, *A New and Enlarged Military Dictionary, or, Alphabetical Explanation of Technical Terms…* (London, 1802), 'Rogue's March', n.p.
218. William Wheeler, Horsham Bks. 17 Feb 1810. Hart (ed.), *Letters of Private William Wheeler*, 41.
219. William Keep, on board HMS *Illustrious*, 28 July 1809. Fletcher (ed.), *In the Service of the King*, 43.
220. William Wheeler, 5 August 1809. Hart (ed.), *Letters of Private William Wheeler*, 28.
221. Robert Roswell Palmer, 'Frederick the Great, Guibert, Bülow: From Dynastic to National war', in Peter Paret (ed.), *Makers of Modern Strategy: From Machiavelli to the Nuclear Age* (Princeton NJ: Princeton UP, 986), 91–122, 92.

3 Combat and Campaign

1. MS Memoir of Lt G. J. Sullivan, October 1812–September 1813. NAM, 7504–17, 3.
2. Paul Fussell, *The Great War and Modern Memory* (Oxford: Oxford UP, 1975), 8. Though, as some scholars of the First World War have noted, the collective story

of disillusionment tends to rest on a selection of canonical war memoirs, which are not necessarily representative of most soldiers' experience. Samuel Hynes, *The Soldiers' Tale. Bearing Witness to Modern War* (London: Pimlico, 1998), 103–5.

3. Philip J. Haythornthwaite, *The Armies of Wellington* (London: Brockhampton, 1998), 236.
4. Ensign Augustus Frederick Dobree, 'A Journal of the Campaign in Spain in the Years 1808–09'. NAM, 6807–148–1, 4.
5. Kevin Foster, *Fighting Fictions: War, Narrative and National Identity* (London: Pluto, 1999), 12.
6. Fussell, *Great War and Modern Memory*, 7.
7. Bell, *Total War*, 7.
8. Harari, *The Ultimate Experience*.
9. Ibid., 213–31.
10. Haythornthwaite, *Armies of Wellington*, 203.
11. William Wheeler, Fontarabia, 14 June 1814. Hart (ed.), *Letters of Private William Wheeler*, 153.
12. Kincaid, *Tales from the Rifle Brigade*, 275.
13. MS Diary of Captain Commissary John Charleton, Corps of Royal Artillery Drivers 22 Oct 1808–24 Jan 1809. NAM, 8009–50.
14. Journal of Lt and Adjutant John Hunt. NAM, 6807, 11.
15. Mary Favret has pointed to the metaphorics of weather in Romantic literature's treatments of these wars. While she sees this as a method of bringing a distant war home, this example suggests how it also shaped combatants' more immediate experience of war. Mary Favret, 'War in the Air', *Modern Language Quarterly*, 65, 4 (2004), 57–77.
16. Rory Muir, *Tactics and the Experience of Battle in the Age of Napoleon* (New Haven and London: Yale UP, 1998), 6.
17. Gareth Glover (ed.), *From Corunna to Waterloo: The Letters and Journals of Two Napoleonic Hussars, 1801–1816* (London: Greenhill, 2007), 164.
18. 'Diary of John Aitchison, 21 July' in W.F.K. Thompson (ed.), *An Ensign in the Peninsular War: The Letters of John Aitchison* (London: Penguin, 1981), 175.
19. James Beattie, *Dissertations Moral and Critical: On Memory and Imagination. On Dreaming. The Theory of Language. On Fable and Romance* (London, 1783), 610, 615.
20. William Wheeler, San Il de Fonson, 3 August 1812. Fletcher (ed.), *In the Service of the King*, 86.
21. Thomas Henry Browne, 13 June 1813. Buckley (ed.), *Journal of Thomas Henry Browne*, 209.
22. Sir Walter Scott quoted in Simon Bainbridge, *British Poetry and the Revolutionary and Napoleonic Wars: Visions of Conflict* (Oxford: Oxford UP, 2003), 124.
23. Harari, *Ultimate Experience*, 170–1.
24. According to Major-General Blayney 'instead of mere automatons put in motion by a power of whose principles they are ignorant, every French soldier reasons on the movements of the army he belongs to, and says what *he* would have done in such a case. I have been often surprised at the shrewd observations and theoretical knowledge of some of the private men'. Lord Blayney, *Narrative of a Forced Journey through Spain and France as a Prisoner of War in the Years 1810 to 1814* (London, 1814), 113.
25. See, for example, John Aitchison's tribute to the 'coolness' of British soldiers during the Battle of Talavera. John Aitchison, 14 September 1809. Thompson (ed.), *Letters*, 57.
26. Haythornthwaite, *Armies of Wellington*, 204.

27. William Wheeler, near West Zuburg, 5 August 1809. Hart (ed.), *Letters of Private William Wheeler*, 30.
28. See, for example, William Freer's account of the battle of Almeida in Norman Scarfe, 'Letters from the Peninsula: The Freer Family Correspondence, 1807–1814', *Transactions of the Leicestershire Archaeological Society*, 29 (1953), 18.
29. John Mills, Quintana del Puente, 14 September 1812. Ian Fletcher (ed.), *For King and Country: The Letters and Diaries of John Mills, Coldstream Guards, 1811–1814* (Staplehurst: Spellmount 1995), 223.
30. George Hennell, before Badajoz, 5 April 1812. Glover (ed.), *Gentleman Volunteer*, 19.
31. Elaine Scarry, *The Body in Pain. The Making and Unmaking of the World* (Oxford: Oxford UP, 1985).
32. Kathleen Canning, 'The Body as Method? Reflections on the Place of the Body in Gender History', *Gender & History*, 11, 3 (1999), 499–513.
33. Muir, *Tactics and the Experience of Battle*, 9.
34. George Hennell, San Estevan, 8 July 1813. Glover (ed.), *Gentleman Volunteer*, 102.
35. Verses written by Alexander Marshall, 1806. NLS, MS 15371, 29.
36. Anon., *Journal of a Soldier of the 71st*, 97.
37. Nelson's wounded body, as Kate Williams argues, was also key to his popularity amongst British women. Kate Williams, 'Nelson and Women: Marketing, Representations and the Female Consumer', in David Cannadine (ed.), *Admiral Lord Nelson: Context and Legacy* (Basingstoke: Palgrave Macmillan, 2005), 67–91, 80.
38. John Mills, Escorial, 29 August 1812. Fletcher (ed.), *Letters*, 210.
39. Keegan, *Face of Battle*, 189.
40. Mrs Clay to Mrs Freer, n.d., *Freer Letters*, 22.
41. Philip Shaw, *Waterloo and the Romantic Imagination* (Basingstoke: Palgrave Macmillan, 2002), 25; Mary A. Favret, 'Coming Home: The Public Spaces of Romantic War', *Studies in Romanticism*, 33, 4 (Winter, 1994), 539–48.
42. Captain Phillips, 26 March 1801. NAM, 8011–40.
43. Lt George Woodberry, 'The Idle Companion of a Young Hussar during the Year 1813'. NAM, 6807–267, 182.
44. Woodberry, 'Idle Companion', 181.
45. Browne, 28 July 1813. Buckley (ed.), *Journal of Thomas Henry Browne*, 231.
46. Wheeler, St Jean de Luz, 28 November 1813. Hart (ed.), *Letters of Private William Wheeler*, 144.
47. Joanna Bourke, *An Intimate History of Killing: Face-to-Face Killing in Twentieth Century Warfare* (London: Granta, 2000).
48. George Graham, 4 May 1794. National Archives of Scotland [NAS], Edinburgh, GD29/2097/16.
49. Wheeler, Salamanca, 10 December 1812 and St Jean de Luz, 21 Nov 1813. Hart (ed.), *Letters of Private William Wheeler*, 103, 137.
50. Muir, *Tactics and the Experience of Battle*, 229.
51. Keegan, *Face of Battle*, 188.
52. Lt George Woodberry, 'Idle Companion'. NAM, 6807–267, 121.
53. Maximillian E. Novak, 'Gothic Fiction and the Grotesque', *Novel: A Forum on Fiction*, 13 (1979), 50–67.
54. Journal by Lieutenant John Hunt, 1799, NAM, 6807–55, 14.
55. George Hennell, 3 Leagues East of Valladolid, 5 August 1812. Glover (ed.), *Gentleman Volunteer*, 27.
56. Woodberry, 'Idle Companion', 6 August 1813, 202.

57. Keep, Pass of Maya, 17 September 1813. Fletcher (ed.), *In the Service of the King*, 169.
58. Philip Shaw, '"Shocking Sights of Woe": Charles Bell and the Battle of Waterloo', in John Bonehill and Geoff Quilley (eds), *Conflicting Visions: War and Visual Culture in Britain and France, c. 1700–1830* (Aldershot: Ashgate, 2005), 198–9.
59. Louise P. Carter, 'British Women during the Revolutionary and Napoleonic Wars, 1793–1815: Responses, Roles and Representations' (Unpublished DPhil, Cambridge, 2005), 175.
60. Journal of Major Alexander Crosby Jackson, 15 September 1799. NAM, 7010–13.
61. Tobias Smollett, *The Adventures of Ferdinand Count Fathom* (London: Penguin, 1990 [1753]), 52. Keep, HMS *Hero*, 8 October 1812. Fletcher (ed.), *In the Service of the King*, 102; 'Copy of an Account of Colonel Ponsonby's Sufferings at the Battle of Waterloo, February 1822', NLI, MS 15555.
62. Sarah Knott, 'Sensibility and the American War of Independence', *American Historical Review*, 109, 1 (2004), 19–40.
63. George Hennell, Alcala, 28 October 1812. Glover (ed.), *Gentleman Volunteer*, 54.
64. Hennell, Badajoz, 5 April 1812. Glover (ed.), *Gentleman Volunteer*, 19.
65. Thomas Henry Browne, Buckley (ed.), *Napoleonic War Journal*, 198.
66. Wheeler, St Jean de Luz, 24 Nov 1813. Hart (ed.), *Letters of Private William Wheeler*, 142.
67. Willington Shelton, 18 March 1814. Letters of Willington Shelton, NAM, 7312–82.
68. Anon., *Journal of a Soldier*, 105.
69. Bourke, *Intimate History of Killing*, 142.
70. Wheeler, Passages, 2 September 1813. Hart (ed.), *Letters of Private Wheeler*, 125.
71. Haythornthwaite, *Armies of Wellington*, 226.
72. Jackson, 'Journal of the Campaign in Holland', 1.
73. In 1802 Charles James' *Military Dictionary* defined 'Le Moral' as a term 'frequently used by the French' to express the prepossession or assurance which we feel in conscious superiority. Charles James, *A New and Enlarged Military Dictionary, or, Alphabetical Explanation of Technical Terms* (1802), n.p.
74. Diary of John Aitchison, 23 September 1812. Thompson (ed.), *Ensign in the Peninsular War*, 202.
75. John Cook and Robert Burnham, 'Nicknames of British units during the Peninsular wars', <ww.napoleon-series.org/military/organization/c_nickname.html> accessed 14 October 2011.
76. Ian F.W. Beckett, *Discovering English County Regiments* (Risborough: Shire, 2003), 87, 90.
77. Letter from George Ridout Bingham to his mother, Olivenza, 7 August 1812, NAM, 6807–13–1, 80.
78. Woodberry, 'The Idle Companion of a Young Hussar', NAM, 6807–26, 16, 156, 230.
79. Diary of Capt. P.R. Jennings. NAM, 8301–203, 6–7.
80. Captain Archibald Armstrong 'Description of the Battle of Talavera', NLI, O'Hara Papers, MS 20368.
81. Alexander Gellen, 12 March 1808. NAM, 8002–5.
82. For a detailed analysis of Highland soldiers' responses to and absorption of 'martial race' ideology in the later nineteenth century see Heather Streets, *Martial Races: The Military, Race and Masculinity in British Imperial Culture, 1857–1914* (Manchester: Manchester UP, 2004), 190–224.

83. Alexander MacKinnon, 'The Battle of Holland' (Blàr na h-Òlaind), in Donald Black (ed.), *An Lasair. Anthology of 18th century Scottish Gaelic Verse* (Edinburgh: Birlinn, 2001), 355.

84. On military service and Highland identity see Andrew MacKillop, '*More Fruitful Than the Soil': Army, Empire and the Scottish Highlands, 1715–1815* (East Linton: Tuckwell Press, 2000), 204–33.

85. Keep, near Vittoria, 22 June 1813. Fletcher (ed.), *In the Service of the King*, 148.

86. Katherine Turner, *British Travel Writers in Europe 1750–1800: Authorship, Gender and National Identity* (Aldershot: Ashgate, 2001), 18.

87. Colley, *Britons*.

88. Bell, *Total War*, 265.

89. This can be contrasted with twentieth century approaches to warfare, where military establishments experimented to varying degrees with the concept of 'hate training'. Bourke, *Intimate History of Killing*, 152–5.

90. Thomas Henry Browne, 28 July 1813. Buckley (ed.), *Journal of Thomas Henry Browne*, 229.

91. W.C. Coles, 5 August 1810. NAM, 6807–419–2.

92. Thomas Henry Browne, *Journal of Thomas Henry Browne*, 134, 241.

93. William Wheeler, Fontarabia, 20 April 1814. Hart (ed.), *Letters of Private Wheeler*, 149–51.

94. John Westcott, 'Journal of a Campaign in Portugal'. BL, Add MS, 32468, 128.

95. On French soldiers' attitudes towards the Peninsula see Alan Forrest, *Napoleon's Men: The Soldiers of the Revolution and Empire* (London and New York: Hambledon Continuum, 2002), 124–6.

96. 'Journal of Major Edwin Griffith. Glover (ed.), *From Corunna to Waterloo*, 84.

97. William Keep, Flushing, 11 September 1809. Fletcher (ed.), *In the Service of the King*, 58.

98. John Aitchison, 1 August 1809. NLS, Rennie Papers, MS 19932, ff 177.

99. Peter Mandler, *The English National Character: The History of an Idea from Edmund Burke to Tony Blair* (New York and London: Yale UP, 2006), 30. Though often identified as the personification of Englishness, the figure of John Bull was also sometimes invoked to represent a broader British national character. See Tamara L. Hunt, *Defining John Bull: Political Caricature and National Identity in late Georgian England* (Aldershot: Ashgate, 2003), 121–69.

100. Verses transcribed in the diary of Lt James Penman Gairdner, March 1813. NAM, 7101–20.

101. Edwin Griffith, 3 August 1813. Glover (ed.), *From Corunna to Waterloo*, 171.

102. Woodberry, 'Idle Companion', 1813, 207.

103. Gillian Russell, *The Theatres of War: Politics, Performance and Society, 1793–1815* (Clarendon: Oxford UP, 1995).

104. William Thornton Keep, Toro, 3 June 1813. Fletcher (ed.), *In the Service of the King*, 143.

105. John Aitchison, Diary, 21 July 1812. Thompson (ed.), *Ensign in the Peninsular War*, 176.

106. Col. J.C. Harrison, 8 September 1807. NAM, 8008–56.

107. Russell, *Theatres of War*, 77.

108. Charles Chambers, 4 September 1807, 'A Brief Chronological Journal of Remarkable Occurrences on board His Majesty's Fireship Prometheus'. British Library, Add MS, 37014, 46.

109. Fussell, *The Great War*, 197.

110. E.P. Thompsom, 'Patrician Society, Plebeian Culture', *Journal of Social History*, 7, 4 (1974), 382–405; Russell, *Theatres of War*, 18–19.
111. Fussell, *The Great War*, 199.
112. Keep, Fontarabia, 20 March 1814. Fletcher (ed.), *In the Service of the King*, 203.
113. James Penman Gardiner, 31 December 1813, Diaries of James Penman Gardiner. NAM, 6902–5, vol. 2.
114. John Rous, 16 April 1814. Ian Fletcher (ed.), *A Guards Officer in the Peninsula* (Tunbridge Wells: Spellmount, 1992), 111.
115. On the wars' affirmation of elite dominance see Colley, *Britons*, 205.
116. William Wheeler, St. Andia, 1 January 1814. Hart (ed.), *Letters of Private William Wheeler*, 148.

4 Travellers in Uniform

1. Anna Maria Elliot, 27 Feb 1810. National Library of Scotland, Edinburgh. Minto Papers, MS 11099/66.
2. On the role of travel in the construction of identities see Brian Dolan, *Exploring European Frontiers: British Travellers in the Age of Enlightenment* (Basingstoke: Palgrave Macmillan, 2000); Marjorie Morgan, *National Identities and Travel in Victorian Britain* (Basingstoke: Palgrave Macmillan, 2001).
3. Samuel Broughton, *Letters from Portugal, Spain and France, 1812–1814* (Stroud: Nonsuch, 2005 [1815]).
4. On the popularity of travel literature see St Clair, *Reading Nation* (Cambridge: Cambridge UP, 2004), 233–4.
5. George Robert Gleig, *The Subaltern: A Chronicle of the Peninsular War* (Barnsley: Leo Cooper, 2001 [1825]), 129.
6. See Charles Edsaile, *The Peninsular War* (London: Penguin, 2003), 20–1.
7. George Ridout Bingham to his mother, Rio Major, 17 April 1809. NAM, 6807–163.
8. Throughout the wars British soldiers were also actively engaged in a series of campaigns in India. However, as the majority of these troops belonged to the East India Company and the campaigns were linked only indirectly to the Revolutionary and Napoleonic wars they are not included here.
9. The term 'contact zone' is borrowed from Mary Louise Pratt. Though she uses it to refer to the spaces of colonial encounter, it can also be usefully applied to British–European encounters in this period. Mary Louise Pratt, *Imperial Eyes: Travel Writing and Transculturation* (London: Routledge, 1992), 6.
10. Memoir of Lt G. J. Sullivan written in the years 1812–14. National Army Museum, 7504–17, 17.
11. J. Maynard, 6 July 1813. NAM, 8807–52.
12. Anon., *Journal of a Soldier of the Seventy-First*, 88.
13. George Rosen, 'Nostalgia: a "Forgotten" Psychological disorder', *Psychological Medicine*, 5 (1975), 340–54; Forrest, *Napoleon's Men*, 41.
14. Andrew Duncan, *Medical Commentaries … Collected and Published by Andrew Duncan* (London and Edinburgh, 1787), 343–9.
15. Diary of Thomas Peacoke, 31 June 1801. NAM, 8209–28.
16. William Keep to his mother, Flushing, 18 September 1809. Fletcher (ed.), *In the Service of the King*, 61.
17. See, for example, William Freer, 10 August 1811. *Freer Letters*, 22.

18. See Charles Chambers, 'Journal of Remarkable Occurrences on board His Majesty's Fireship the Prometheus', 29 August 1807. BL, Add MS, 37014. Anon., *Memoirs of a Sergeant* (Stroud: Nonsuch, 2005 [1835]), 154.
19. John Mills to his mother, Pinhel, 25 December 1811. Fletcher (ed.), *For King and Country*, 94.
20. I am very grateful to Andrew Bamford for having produced these estimates in answer to a query from Gavin Daly and myself. Andrew Bamford, 'A Computation of the Number of British Troops Deployed to the Peninsular Theatre, 1808–1814', <http://www.napoleon-series.org/military/organization/Britain/Strength/c_ Strength1814.htm>accessed 10 July 2012.
21. Jeremy Black, *The British Abroad: The Grand Tour in the Eighteenth Century* (Stroud: Sutton, 2003), 76–7.
22. Walter Scott quoted in Diego Saglia, 'War Romances, Historical Analogies and Coleridge's *Letters on the Spaniards*', in Philip Shaw (ed.), *Romanticism and War: Studies in Culture and Conflict, 1793–1822* (Aldershot: Ashgate, 2000), 142.
23. William Keep to his mother, Coria, 2 April 1813. Fletcher (ed.), *In the Service of the King*, 138.
24. 'Diaries of James Penman Gardiner', 8 August 1812. NAM, 6902–5.
25. Lt G. J. Sullivan, 'Account of Service in Peninsula, 1812–1814'. NAM, 7504–17, 37.
26. John Westcott, 'Journal of the Campaign in Portugal'. British Library, Add MS, 32468, 7.
27. 'Diary of Captain Edward Hodge', 13 December 1808. NAM, 7202–3, 11.
28. John Mills to his mother, 11 June 1811. Fletcher (ed.), *For King and Country*, 40; Letter from Captain G.H. Percival, Puebla to Mrs Charles Drummond, 2 June 1811, NAM, 8208–8.
29. George Ridout Bingham, 10 March 1810. NAM, 6807–163.
30. John Rous to his mother, near Bercianos, 28 May 1813. Fletcher (ed.), *A Guards Officer in the Peninsula*, 59.
31. William Wheeler, Lisbon, 13 March 1811. Hart (ed.), *Letters of Private William Wheeler*, 49.
32. On dirt as a symbolic signifier of otherness see Adeline Masquelier, 'Dirt, Undress and Difference: An Introduction', in Adeline Masquelier (ed.), *Dirt, Undress and Difference: Critical Perspectives on the Body's Surface* (Bloomington Ind.: Indiana UP, 2005), 6.
33. Diary of William Paterson, 1812–1813. NAM, 8211–162, 16–17.
34. William Keep to his mother, Coria, 2 April 1813. Fletcher (ed.), *In the Service of the King*, 137.
35. See, for example, John Westcott, 'Journal of the Campaign in Portugal by John Westcott Late Master of the Band First Battalion 26th Cameronian Regiment of Foot'. BL, MS 32468, 17.
36. William Wheeler, Madrid, 23 August 1812. Hart (ed.), *Letters of Private William Wheeler*, 94. Wheeler referred here to *The History of the Inquisition* published anonymously in Dublin in 1798. See Ana Hontanilla, 'Images of Barbaric Spain in Eighteenth-Century British Travel Writing', 37, 1, *Studies in Eighteenth-Century Culture*, 119–143, 130.
37. On anti-Catholicism and the Gothic novel see Robert Miles, 'Europhobia: The Catholic Other in Horace Walpole and Charles Maturin', in Avril Horner (ed.), *European Gothic* (Manchester: Manchester UP, 2002). For a discussion of the Gothic and eighteenth-century literary representations of Spain see Diego Saglia, *Poetic*

Castles in Spain: British Romanticism and Figurations of Iberia (Amsterdam; Atlanta GA: Rodopi, 2000), 40–52.
38. 'Journal of Lt. George Woodberry', 25 August 1813 and 14 July 1813. NAM, 6807–267, 182, 212.
39. William Wheeler, Penamacore, 28 December 1812. Hart (ed.), *Letters of Private William Wheeler*, 72.
40. Hibbert (ed.), *Recollections of Rifleman Harris*, 46.
41. Anon., *Memoirs of a Sergeant*, 128.
42. Diary of Captain P.R. Jennings, 15 December 1806, NAM, 8301–203.
43. Grattan, *Adventures*, 9.
44. McBride, *Eighteenth-Century Ireland. The Isle of Slaves*, 229.
45. According to a letter published in *Cobbett's Weekly Political Register* in 1810, Bartholomew Crotty, President of the Irish College at Lisbon, had even petitioned General Sir John Moore to allow the college's priests to accompany the army as it marched into Spain. 'Catholic claims', *Cobbett's Weekly Political Register*, 13 January 1810.
46. Charles O'Neill, *Private O'Neil: The Recollections of an Irish Rogue* (Leonaur, 2007 [1851]), 104.
47. William Thornton Keep to his mother, Casas de Gomez, 9 January 1813. Fletcher (ed.), *In the Service of the King*, 121; George Woodberry, 'Idle Companion', 8 March 1813. NAM, 6807–267, 49.
48. Thomas Hodge, 'Diary of Captain Edward Hodge (7th Light Dragoons) During the Corunna Campaign, October 1808–March 1809', 21 November 1808. NAM, 7202–33, 16.
49. John Rous to his mother, Sotresquedo, 12 June 1813. Fletcher (ed.), *A Guards Officer in the Peninsula*, 61.
50. Edwin Griffiths, 24 January 1809, Glover (ed.), *From Corunna to Waterloo*, 93.
51. Broughton, *Letters from Portugal, Spain and France*, 71.
52. Pratt, *Imperial Eyes*, 57–64.
53. John Aitchison to his father, Badajoz, 6 December 1809. Thompson (ed.), *An Ensign in the Peninsular War*, 71.
54. George Woodberry, 'Idle Companion', 25 February 1813, NAM, 6807–267, 35.
55. George Hennell to his brothers, Aldea Nueva de Figueira, 30 May 1813. *A Gentleman Volunteer*, 73.
56. Hontanilla, 'Images of Barbaric Spain', 122.
57. Saglia, *Castles in Spain*, 43.
58. Diary of Captain Edward Hodge, 21 December 1809. NAM, 7202–33.
59. Rev. Samuel Briscoe, 14 March 1810. NAM, 2002–05–03.
60. W.C. Coles, 28 February 1810. NAM, 6807–419.
61. John Aitchison to his father, Castello de Vide, 27 May 1812. Thompson (ed.), *An Ensign in the Peninsular War*, 157.
62. George Woodberry, 'Idle Companion', 6 June 1813. NAM, 6807–267, 135.
63. See J.G.A. Pocock, *Virtue, Commerce and History: Essays on Political Thought and History, Chiefly in the Eighteenth Century* (Cambridge: Cambridge UP, 1985).
64. On the fractious relationship between British and Spanish forces see Edsaile, *The Peninsular War*, 153–4, 211–12.
65. John Aitchison to his father Celorico, 20 June 1810. Thompson (ed.), *Ensign in the Peninsular War*, 101.
66. John Mills, Los Santos, 25 March 1812. Fletcher (ed.), *For King and Country*, 126.
67. William Coles, 1 April 1810, NAM, 6087–419.

68. Diary of William Paterson, NAM, 8211–162, 149.
69. Kathleen Wilson, *The Island Race: Englishness, Empire and Gender in the Eighteenth Century* (London: Routledge, 2003), 24–5.
70. Revd Samuel Briscoe, 14 March 1810. NAM, 2002–05–03.
71. William Coles, 4 January 1810, NAM, 6807–419–2.
72. Haythornthwaite, *The Armies of Wellington*, 214.
73. Jonathan Leach, *Rough Sketches of an Old Soldier* (London, 1831), xi–xii.
74. On West Indian Creole society in the eighteenth-century English imaginary see Wilson, *Island Race*, 129–68.
75. Leach, *Rough Sketches*, 20–1.
76. Michael Durey (ed.), *Andrew Bryson's Ordeal: An Epilogue to the 1798 Rebellion* (Cork: Cork UP 1998), 81–3.
77. See for example, the letters of Andrew Francis Barnard an officer who served in the West Indies between 1795 and 1796. PRONI, Hervey/Bruce Papers, D/1514/1/31, 33.
78. Thomas Henry Browne, 29 December 1808. Buckley (ed.), *Journal of Thomas Henry Browne*, 92.
79. Roxann Wheeler, *The Complexion of Race: Categories of Difference in Eighteenth-Century Culture* (Pennsylvania: University of Pennsylvania Press, 2000), 3–6.
80. John Millyard (ed.), *Fiddlers and Whores: The Candid Memoirs of a Surgeon in Nelson's Fleet by James Lowry* (London: Chatham, 2006), 39, 84.
81. Thomas Walsh, *Journal of the Late Campaign in Egypt: Including Descriptions of that Country* (London, 1803), 235.
82. Donald Malcolm Reid, *Whose Pharaohs? Archaeology, Museums and Egyptian National Identity from Napoleon to World War I* (Berkeley, CA; London: University of California Press, 2002), 31.
83. Eitan Bary-Yosef, '"Green and Pleasant Lands": England and the Holy Land in Plebeian Millenarian Culture, 1790–1820', in Kathleen Wilson (ed.), *A New Imperial History: Culture, Identity and Modernity in Britain and the Empire, 1660–1840* (Cambridge: Cambridge UP, 2004), 260–80.
84. Anon., *Narrative of Private Soldier in one of his Majesty's Regiments of Foot…and giving a particular account of his Religious History and Experience* (Glasgow, 1819), 72, 83, 114.
85. Lowry, *Memoirs*, 62.
86. Colin Kidd, 'Ethnicity in the British Atlantic world, 1688–1830', in Wilson (ed.), *A New Imperial History*, 260–77.
87. Reid, *Whose Pharaohs?* 28.
88. Lowry, *Memoirs*, 64. On the shifting emphasis in European constructions of the East from religious to more secular markers of difference see M.E. Yapp, 'Europe in the Turkish Mirror', *Past & Present*, 137 (November, 1992), 134–55, 152.
89. Capt. Exham Vincent, 'Memorandum of Occurrences from 30th July 1800 to the Surrender of Egypt September 1801'. NAM, 7611–24, 31.
90. Lowry, *Memoirs*, 67.
91. Anon., *Narrative of a Private Soldier*, 115, 152.
92. George Ridout Bingham, 29 April 1809; 10 August 1809; 21 September 1812. NAM, 6807–13, 11, 64, 92.
93. For a discussion of the picturesque in English travel writings on Wales, Scotland and Europe see Morgan, *National Identities and Travel*, 69–72.
94. W.C. Coles, 29 May 1810. NAM, 6807/419, vol. 2.

95. John Westcott, 'Journal of the Campaign in Portugal by John Westcott Late Master of the Band 1st Battalion 26th Cameronian Regiment of Foot' British Library Add MS, 32468, 205.

96. George Ridout Bingham, 30 December 1810. NAM, 6807–13, vol. 1, 103.

97. William Keep to his mother, on the lines before Flushing, 13 August 1809. Fletcher (ed.), *In the Service of the King*, 50.

98. Snape, *Redcoat and Religion*, 146.

99. Thomas Henry Browne, 30 August 1807. Buckley (ed.), *Journal of Thomas Henry Browne*, 54.

100. J. C. Harrison, 8 September 1807. NAM, 8008–56.

101. Private Alexander Gellen, 12 March 1808. NAM, 8002–5.

102. Of course this mental topography was shaped in part by the particular settings of the British theatre of war. Had their campaigns taken them through Poland and Russia, this North/South civilizational axis may well have been supplemented by another dividing Western from Eastern Europe.

103. John Rous to his mother, St Jean de Luz, 14 November 1813. Fletcher (ed.), *A Guards Officer in the Peninsula*, 87.

104. William Freer, 23 February 1814, *Freer Letters*, 35.

105. Diary of James Penman Gardiner, 17 February 1814. NAM, 6902–5.

106. Edwin Griffith, 25 April 1814. Glover (ed.), *From Corunna to Waterloo*, 218

107. Edwin Griffiths, 25 April 1814. Glover (ed.), *From Corunna to Waterloo*, 218.

108. James Penman Gairdner, 30 May 1814. NAM, 6902–5.

109. On aristocratic cosmopolitanism in the eighteenth century see Gerald Newman, *The Rise of English Nationalism* (New York: St Martin's, 1987), 21–47; Robin Eagles, *Francophilia in English Society, 1748–1815* (Basingstoke: Macmillan, 2000).

110. See Peter Mandler, *The English National Character: The History of an Idea from Edmund Burke to Tony Blair* (New Haven; London: Yale UP, 2006), 27–38.

111. Diary of Captain John Charleton, 20 January 1809. NAM, 8009–50.

112. John Wardell (ed.), *With 'The Thirty-Second' in the Peninsular and other Campaigns by Harry Ross-Lewins of Ross Hill, Co. Clare* (Dublin, 1904), 220.

113. Lowry, *Memoirs*, 168, 178.

114. Lowry, *Memoirs*, 182.

115. Anon., *Narrative of a Soldier in the 71st*, 229.

116. The impact of demobilization remains an understudied area, some suggestion of the hardship and poverty experienced by disbanded soldiers and sailors can be found in Douglas Hay, 'War, Dearth and Theft in the Eighteenth Century: The Record of the English Courts', *Past and Present*, 95 (May 1982), 117–60, 139–40.

117. See for example William Keep to his mother, Plymouth, 17 April 1814. Fletcher (ed.), *In the Service of the King*, 205.

118. Edwin Griffiths, 8 February 1809. Glover (ed.), *From Corunna to Waterloo*, 96.

5   Prisoners of War

1. Lines written in the notebook of Samuel Oakes, Royal Marines. NAM, 7407–5–1.

2. See Michael Lewis, *Napoleon and his British Captives* (London: George Allen & Unwin, 1962).

3. Clive L. Lloyd, *A History of Napoleonic and American Prisoners of War, 1756–1816: Hulk, Depot and Parole* (Suffolk: Woodbridge, 2007), 21–3.

4. Geoffrey Best, *Humanity in Warfare: The Modern History of the International Law of Armed Conflicts* (New York: Weidenfeld and Nicholson, 1980), 31–74; Gavin Daly, 'Napoleon's Lost Legions: French Prisoners of War in Britain, 1803–1814', *History*, 89, 295 (2004), 361–80.

5. Black, *The British Abroad*, 171–4.

6. [Henry Lawrence], *A Picture of Verdun, or the English detained in France...from the Portfolio of a Détenu* (London, 1810), 2 vols, vol. 1, 2.

7. Bell, *Total War*, 143.

8. Daly, 'Napoleon's Lost Legions', 371.

9. Daly, 'Napoleon's Lost Legions', 367.

10. There was a precedent for Napoleon's edict. In 1793 when the British navy had entered Toulon, the French government ordered the arrest of all Britons then in France, but this order had been rescinded in 1795 and the captives freed. Lewis, *Napoleon and his British Captives*, 21.

11. Lewis, *Napoleon and his British Captives*, 48.

12. Lewis, *Napoleon and his British Captives*, 51.

13. Alon Rachamimov, *POWs and the Great War: Captivity on the Eastern Front* (Oxford and New York: Berg, 2002), 57.

14. Lawrence, *Pictures of Verdun*, 75–80.

15. Edward Boys, *Narrative of a Captivity, Escape and Adventures in France* (London, 1827), 41.

16. Lewis, *Napoleon and his British Captives*, 54–5.

17. On Prisoner of War 'event scenarios' see Robert C. Doyle, *Voices from Captivity: Interpreting the American POW Narrative* (Lawrence, KS: University Press of Kansas, 1994), chapter 4.

18. Such fears of personal dishonour were not as acute for those taken prisoner between 1793 and 1815 as it would later be for First World War POWs who, steeped in the 'cult of the offensive', deemed it a failure of patriotic manliness to be captured unwounded. See Rachamimov, *Captivity on the Eastern Front*, 44–5, 146. Samuel Hynes has similarly observed that 'an odour of disgrace still hangs over many prisoners' stories'. Hynes, *The Soldiers' Tale*, 232.

19. Boys, *Narrative of a Captivity*, 6.

20. Boys, *Narrative of a Captivity*, 8.

21. 'Journal of the late Captain Joseph Bull', Dublin, Trinity College Dublin (TCD), MS 3764, 2.

22. Lawrence, *Pictures of Verdun*, vol. 1, 18

23. Lawrence, *Pictures of Verdun*, 43.

24. Maria Cope, 'Memoirs of Captivity in France'. NLI, MS 1718, part II, 17.

25. Boys, *Narrative of a Captivity*, 8.

26. Peter Bussell, 25 February 1806, *The Diary of Peter Bussell, 1806–1814*, ed. G.A. Turner (London: Peter Davies, 1931), 5. See also, Farrell Mulvey, *Sketches of the Character, Conduct and Treatment of the Prisoners of War at Auxonne, Longwy &c. from the Year 1810 to 1814* (London, 1818), 21.

27. Bussell, 30 December 1812, *Diary of Peter Bussell*, 175.

28. Verses transcribed in notebook of Samuel Oakes, Royal Marines. NAM, 7407-5-1.

29. Bussell, 22 April 1809, *Diary of Peter Bussell*, 84. For further examples of petitions from prisoners of war to the British government and of the general sense of abandonment expressed by members of the merchant navy in particular see

William Story, *A Journal Kept in France, During a Captivity of More than Nine Years...* (Sunderland, 1815), 97–9.

30. Lewis, *Napoleon and his British Captives*, 45–7.
31. Boys, *Narrative of a Captivity*, 17.
32. Boys, *Narrative of a Captivity*, 93.
33. Bussell, 25 October 1808, *Diary of Peter Bussell*, 74.
34. Bussell, 17 February 1811, *Diary of Peter Bussell*, 142.
35. Journal of John Robertson, 5 August 1808. National Maritime Museum, Greenwich, JOD/202, 141.
36. Bussell, 14 March 1810, *Diary of Peter Bussell*, 117.
37. A similar combination of stasis and loss of trust in official reports has been used to explain the proliferation of rumours and superstitions in the First World War trenches. See March Bloch, *The Historian's Craft* (Manchester: Manchester UP, 1992 [1954]), 89.
38. The comet of 1811 would prompt similar speculations amongst the prisoners of war. See journal of John Robertson, July 26 1807 and 14 September 1811, NMM, JOD/202, 74, 430.
39. Lawrence, *Pictures of Verdun*, 90.
40. See, for example, Gerald H. Davis, 'Prisoner of War Camps as Social Communities in Russia: Krasnoyarsk, 1914–1921', *Eastern European Quarterly*, 21, 2 (1987), 147–160; Francis D. Cogliano, '"We All Hoisted the American Flag": National Identity among American Prisoners in Britain During the American Revolution', *Journal of American Studies*, 31 (1998), 19–37; and Hynes, *The Soldiers' Tale*, 238.
41. Lawrence, *Pictures of Verdun*, 65.
42. Lewis, *Napoleon and his British Captives*, 119.
43. Lawrence, *Pictures of Verdun*, 125; 'Memoirs of Maria Cope', vol. 2, 27.
44. Lawrence, *Pictures of Verdun*, 97.
45. Ibid., 15.
46. Ibid., 18–19
47. Rev. R.B. Wolfe, *English Prisoners in France, Containing Observations on Their Manners and Habits* (London, 1830), 6.
48. Lawrence, *Pictures of Verdun*, vol. 1, 107–8.
49. See, for example, Alan Kidd, 'Philanthropy and the "Social History" Paradigm', *Social History*, 21 (1996), 180–92; Sarah Lloyd, 'Pleasing Spectacles and Elegant Dinners: Conviviality, Benevolence and Charity Anniversaries in Eighteenth-Century London', *Journal of British Studies*, 41, 1 (2002), 23–57.
50. Edward Reilly Cope to his father William Cope, Valenciennes, 10 August 1809. NAM, 8511–15.
51. Bussell, 25 December 1807, *Diary of Peter Bussell*, 58.
52. Diary of William (or Thomas Dixon?), 1 May 1807. NAM, 2005–07–04, 13.
53. On plebeian funeral culture and associations see Thomas Laqueur, 'Bodies, Death and Pauper Funerals', *Representations*, 1, 1 (1983), 109–31.
54. 'Journal of John Robertson', 26 February 1808; 26 July 1809. NMM, JOD/202, 102, 227.
55. 'Journal of John Robertson', 5 August 1808. NMM, JOD/202, 141.
56. Mulvey, *Sketches of the Character, Conduct, and Treatment of the Prisoners of War*, 25.
57. Wolfe, *English Prisoners in France*, 81–3.
58. Bussell, 29 May 1807, *Diary of Peter Bussell*, 49. See also Diary of Thomas (or William) Dixon, 29 May 1808, NAM, 2005–07–04, 46.

59. Boys, *Narrative of a Captivity*, 85. Francis Cogliano, in his study of American POWs interned in Britain during the War of Independence, identifies similar affirmations of American revolutionary identity amongst the captive communities. Cogliano, 'We All Hoisted the American Flag', 19–37.

60. Bussell, 4 June 1812, *Diary of Peter Bussell*, 164.

61. Story, *Journal kept in France*, 28.

62. Mulvey, *Sketches of the Character, Conduct, and Treatment of the Prisoners of War*, 22–3.

63. Benedict Anderson, *Imagined Communities: Reflections on the Origin and Spread of Nationalism* (London: Verso, 1991), 6.

64. [H.P. Houghton?], 'An Evening's Contemplation in a French Prison, or an Humble Imitation of Mr Grey's Elegy in a Country Church Yard', in 'Diary of Thomas (or William?) Dixon', n.d., NAM, 2005–07–04, 77.

65. 12 September 1806, *Diary of Peter Bussell*, 40; 'Journal of John Robertson', 26 February 1811, NMM, JOD/202, 400.

66. 'Journal of John Robertson', 17 March 1807, NMM, JOD/202, 36.

67. 'Journal of John Robertson', 1 October 1809, NMM, JOD/202, 262.

68. 'A Sketch Stuck up in Answer to the Committee's order', 'Diary of Thomas (or William?) Dixon', 15 July 1808, NAM, 2005–07–04, 53.

69. 'Journal of John Robertson', March 26 1807, NMM, JOD/202, 45.

70. Bussell, 21 December 1808, *Diary of Peter Bussell*, 78. Bussell's sentiments on this occasion were echoed by John Robertson. 'Journal of John Robertson', 24 December 1808, NMM, JOD/202, 177.

71. 'Diary of Thomas (or William?) Dixon', 19 June 1808, NAM, 2005–07–04, 99.

72. See John C. Gallagher, *Napoleon's Irish Legions* (Carbondale and Edwardsville: Southern Illinois Press, 1993), 38.

73. Bussell, 7 January 1810, *Diary of Peter Bussell*, 114.

74. Ibid., 21 April 1810, 120.

75. 'A Few Remarkable Occurances [*sic*] in Rhyme which Happened in Arras Citadel 1807', in 'Journal of John Robertson', NMM, JOD/202, 59.

76. 'Journal of John Robertson', 17 March 1809, NMM, JOD/202, 311.

77. Lowry, *Fiddlers and Whores*, 94.

78. As argued by Bell, *Total War*.

79. 'The Journal of Joseph Bull', TCD, MS 3764, 7.

80. 'The Journal of Joseph Bull', TCD, MS 3764, 7.

81. Blayney, *Narrative of a Forced Journey Through Spain and France*, 43, 66.

82. Boys, *Narrative of a Captivity*, 35.

83. Jeffrey Prendergast, 'The Prisoner of War, or, an Account of the Circumstances of a Captivity in France during the Years 1794–1795. Originally Written as a Letter to His Mother', MS memoir. NAM, 8003–122, 6.

84. 'Journal of Joseph Bull', TCD, MS 3764, 3; 'Diary of Lt. Robert Melville, 1812–1814'. NAM, 7902–5.

85. 'Journal of Joseph Bull', TCD, MS 3764, 19.

86. 'Journal of John Robertson', 17 Jan 1810, NMM, JOD/202, 299.

87. Bussell, 2 May 1809, *Diary of Peter Bussell*, 87.

88. Prendergast, 'Prisoner of War', 18.

89. Bussell, 17 December 1812, *Diary of Peter Bussell*, 173.

90. Bussell, 10 April 1813, *Diary of Peter Bussell*, 179–80.

91. Story, *Journal Kept in France*, 80.

92. Mulvey, *Sketches of the Character, Conduct, and Treatment of the Prisoners of War*, 24.

93. Watkin Tench, Brest-water, 7 December 1794. Gavin Edwards (ed.), *Letters from Revolutionary France: Letters Written to a Friend in London Between the Month of November 1794, and the Month of May 1795* (Cardiff: University of Wales Press, 2001 [1796]), 23.
94. Tench, Quimper, 2 March 1795, *Letters from Revolutionary France*, 65.
95. Stuart Semmel, *Napoleon and the British* (New Haven and London: Yale UP, 2004), 7–9.
96. Tench, Quimper, 2 March 1795, *Letters Written from Revolutionary France*, 71.
97. 'Journal of Joseph Bull', TCD, MS 3764, 6, 8.
98. 'Journal of Joseph Bull', TCD, MS 3764, 20.
99. Bussell, 2 October 1813, *Diary of Peter Bussell*, 187.
100. Ibid., 21 December 1812, 174.
101. Ibid., 1 January 1811, 137.
102. Tench, May 1795, *Letters from Revolutionary France*, 125.
103. Blayney, *Narrative of a Forced Journey*, 78.
104. 'Journal of Joseph Bull', TCD, MS 3764, 17.
105. Lawrence, *Picture of Verdun*, 110–11.

6 Citizen-Soldiers

1. John Marsh, 1795, Brian Robins (ed.), *The John Marsh Journals: The Life and Times of a Gentleman Composer* (Stuyvesant NY: Pergamon, 1998), 575–80.
2. For a more detailed discussion of Marsh's journals and his varied accomplishments and interests see John Brewer, *The Pleasures of the Imagination: English Culture in the Eighteenth Century* (London: Harper Collins, 1997), 531–72.
3. R.J. Morris, 'Voluntary Societies and British Urban Elites, 1780–1850', *The Historical Journal*, 26, 1 (1983), 95–118.
4. See Jon Newman, '"An Insurrection of Loyalty": The London Volunteer Regiments' Response to the Invasion Threat', in Mark Philp (ed.), *Resisting Napoleon: The British Response to the Threat of Invasion* (Aldershot: Ashgate, 2006), 75–91, 81.
5. John Marsh, May 1795, Robins (ed.), *John Marsh Journals*, 577.
6. The phrase 'addition of mass' is John Cookson's. Cookson, *The British Armed Nation*, 14.
7. J.R. Western, *The English Militia in the Eighteenth Century: The Story of a Political Issue, 1660–1802* (London: Routledge, 1965), 127–61.
8. J.E. Cookson, 'Service without Politics? Army, Militia and Volunteers during the American and French Revolutionary Wars', *War in History*, 10 (2003), 381–397, 383.
9. Emsley, *British Society and the French Wars*, 53.
10. Western, *The English Militia*, 223.
11. Ibid., 245–71.
12. Wheeler, Maidston, 12 April 1809. Hart (ed.), *Letters of Private Wheeler*, 17.
13. Thomas Bartlett, 'An End to Moral Economy: The Irish Militia Disturbances of 1793', *Past and Present*, 99 (1983), 41–64.
14. Henry McAnally, *The Irish Militia 1793–1816: A Social and Military Study* (Dublin and London: Clonmore and Reynolds, 1949), 114.
15. McAnally, *The Irish Militia*, 146.
16. R.M. Sunter, 'The Problems of Recruitment for Scottish Line Regiments during the Napoleonic Wars', *Scottish Tradition*, 26 (2001), 56–68, 58.

17. Cookson, *The British Armed Nation*, 105.
18. Marquess of Yester to Duke of Portland, 8 September 1797. National Library of Scotland, Edinburgh, Yester Papers, MS 7099.
19. *Caledonia Mercury*, 26 August 1797.
20. Cookson, *The British Armed Nation*, 101.
21. For the earlier interpretation of the Volunteers as an extension of loyalists associations see Robert R. Dozier, *For King, Constitution and Country: The English Loyalists and the French Revolution* (Lexington KY: University Press of Kentucky, 1983). Revised accounts of the movement can be found in J.E. Cookson, 'The English Volunteer Movement of the French Wars, 1793–1815: Some Contexts', *Historical Journal*, 32 (1989), 867–91; Austin Gee, *The British Volunteer Movement 1794–1814* (Oxford: Oxford UP, 2003).
22. Gee, *Volunteer Movement*, 2.
23. Colley, *Britons*, 308.
24. Gee, *Volunteer movement*, 71.
25. Cookson, 'English Volunteer Movement', 868; Gee, *Volunteer Movement*, 68–9.
26. Colley, *Britons*, 315.
27. Thomas Bartlett, '"A Weapon of War as Yet Untried": Militarisation and Politicisation in Ireland, 1780–1820', *Culture et Pratiques en France et en Irelande* (Paris, 1988), 135.
28. William Wordsworth, 'To the Men of Kent, October 1803', *The Poetical Works of William Wordsworth* (London, 1840), 6 vols, vol. 3, 197.
29. Cookson, *The British Armed Nation*, 213.
30. G. Strickland, York to Francis Cholmeley at Bransby, 3 October 1803. M.Y. Aschroft (ed.), *To Escape the Monster's Clutches: Notes and Documents Illustrating the Preparations in North Yorkshire to Repel the Invasion Threatened by the French from 1793* (Northallerton: North Yorkshire County Council, 1977), 71.
31. Revd Robert Elliot, 22 September 1803. NLS, Minto Papers, MS 11085/83.
32. Anne Murray Keith to Jeremiah Hill, 6 June 1798. NLS, MS 3524.
33. Emma Vincent McLeod, 'A City Invincible? Edinburgh and the War Against Revolutionary France', *British Journal for Eighteenth Century Studies*, 23 (2000), 153–66.
34. *Caledonian Mercury*, 27 February 1797.
35. Jessie Harden to her sister, 10 July 1803. National Library of Scotland, MS 8870 (2), Doc. 205, 133. My italics.
36. George Home, Edinburgh, 23 March 1795. National Archives of Scotland, GD267/1/18/14.
37. Anne Cholmeley, Bransby to Francis Cholmeley, 21 August 1803. Ashcroft (ed.), *To Escape the Monster's Clutches*, 71.
38. Peter Haddon, Leeds to William Spencer Stanhope, London, 29 April 1804. Bradford, Bradford Central Library, Spencer Stanhope Papers, Sp St/6/1/119.
39. John Cookson distinguishes between Volunteering as an expression of active loyalty and this more limited national defence patriotism, which involved a personal commitment to the nation only against a visible adversary. Cookson, *The British Armed Nation*, 211–13.
40. Christopher Kelly Bellew, 5 January 1797. NLI, MS 27135 (9).
41. John Marsh, 3 May 1797 and 2 September. Robins (ed.), *John Marsh Journals*, 666, 717.
42. Emsley, *British Society and the French Wars*, 102.
43. Anna Maria Elliot, 21 November 1803. NLS, Minto Papers, MS 11755(38).

44. Diary of Sir Christopher Courtney, 26 Feb 1798. Hull, Hull University Archives, Courtney Family of Beverley Papers, DDX/60.
45. Ann Kussmaul, *The Autobiography of Joseph Mayett of Quainton (1783–1839)* (Aylesbury: Buckhinghamshire Record Society, 1986, no. 23).
46. Catherine Cholmeley, 16 August 1803. *To Escape the Monster's Clutches*, 70.
47. William Vavasour, 16 July 1798; 5 September 1803. Diaries of William Vavasour, Weston Hall, Otley, Yorkshire. Leeds, West Yorkshire Archive Service, WYL/639/445. On the use of public shaming to enforce displays of loyalty see Jon Newman, 'An Insurrection of Loyalty', 85.
48. Mark Philp, 'Introduction: The British Response to the Threat of Invasion, 1797–1815', in Mark Philp (ed.), *Resisting Napoleon: The British Response to the Threat of Invasion, 1797–1815* (Aldershot: Ashgate, 2006), 7.
49. Duncan Ban MacIntyre, 'Song of the Gazette' translated from Gaelic by Angus Macleod in Angus Macleod, *The Songs of Duncan Ban MacIntyre* (Edinburgh: Oliver & Boyd, 1952), 379.
50. Western, *The English Militia*, 314.
51. For a more detailed discussion of Jane Austen's treatment of the militia see Tim Fulford, 'Sighing for a Soldier. Jane Austen and Military Pride and Prejudice', *Nineteenth-Century Literature*, 57, 2 (2002), 153–78.
52. Letters from Reginald Heber to his brother Richard Heber, September to October 1804. R.H. Cholmondeley (ed.), *The Heber Letters, 1783–1832* (London: Batchworth Press, 1950), 146–55.
53. Joseph Farrington, 5 August 1803. Kenneth Garlick and Angus Macintyre (ed.), *The Diary of Joseph Farrington* (New Haven and London: Yale UP, 1979), vol. 6, 2094.
54. Diary of Sir Christopher Courtney, 29 Dec 1793. Hull University Archives, DDX/60, vol. 3.
55. Matthew McCormack, 'Rethinking Loyalty in Eighteenth-Century Britain', *Journal for Eighteenth-Century Studies*, 35, 3 (September, 2012), 407–21.
56. 19 August 1803. NLS, Minto Papers, MS 11085/82.
57. Neil Ramsey, 'Making Myself a Soldier: The Role of Soldiering in the Autobiographical Work of John Clare', *Romanticism*, 13, 2 (2007), 177–88, 179.
58. Kussmaul (ed.), *Autobiography of Joseph Mayett*, 35.
59. Simon Bainbridge, *British Poetry and the Revolutionary and Napoleonic Wars. Visions of Conflict* (Oxford: Oxford UP, 2003), 134–5.
60. Walter Scott, Summer 1803. H.J.C. Grierson (ed.), *The Letters of Sir Walter Scott, 1787–1807* (London: Constable & Co, 1932), 188–9.
61. Walter Scott, 17 November 1797. *Letters of Sir Walter Scott*, 80.
62. Thomas Hodges, 1793, Harrow. Centre for Kentish Studies, Maidstone, Twisden MS, U49/C13/128.
63. Diary of Christopher Courtney, 28 August 1798. Hull University Archives, Papers of Courtney family of Beverley, DDX/60, vol. 4.
64. Ralph Creyke, 22 November 1803. *To Escape the Monster's Clutches*, 73.
65. Diary of William Vavasour, 9 April 1799. WYAS, Weston Hall Ms, WYL639/398.
66. Adam Ogilvie, Brauxholm to John Rutherford, 6 September 1799. NLS, Rutherford of Edgerston Papers, Acc. 7903/3.
67. John Marsh, 5 February 1800. Robins (ed.), *John Marsh Journals*, 685.
68. Yester to Dundas, 7 April 1798. NLS, Yester Papers, MS 7099, f55.
69. Kevin B. Linch, 'A Citizen and Not a Soldier: The British Volunteer Movement and the War against Napoleon', in Alan Forrest, Karen Hagemann and Jane Rendall

(eds), *Soldiers, Citizens and Civilians: Experiences and Perceptions of the French Wars, 1790–1820* (Basingstoke: Palgrave Macmillan, 2008), 303–10.

70. Diary of Christopher Courtney, 22 October 1800. Hull University Archives, Courtney family papers, DDX/60, vol. 4.
71. John Marsh, 1795, Robins (ed.), *John Marsh Journals*, 578–9.
72. Narcissus Batt 'Yeomanry Memorandum, 1814'. Belfast Yeomanry Order Book, 1803–1810. PRONI, D/3221/1
73. Cookson, 'English Volunteer Movement', 876–7.
74. Letters from Reginald Heber to his brother Richard Heber September to October 1804 in Cholmondeley (ed.), *Heber Letters*, 146–55.
75. Jessie Harden, 4 November 1803. NLS, Harden Journals, MS 8870 (2), Doc 206, 175.
76. Colley, *Britons*, 276.
77. For a more extensive discussion of these issues see Louise P. Carter, 'British Women during the Revolutionary and Napoleonic wars: Responses, Roles and Representations' (Unpublished D.Phil: University of Cambridge, 2005).
78. Wilson, *The Island Race*, 97.
79. Journals of Christian Dalrymple of Newhailes, January to May 1804. NLS, Newhailes Papers, MS 25460.
80. 4 October 1803, *Belfast Newsletter*.
81. Wilson, *The Island Race*, 107.
82. Louise P. Carter, 'British Women during the Revolutionary and Napoleonic Wars', 93–110.
83. Mark Hallett and Jane Rendall, *Eighteenth-century York: Culture, Space and Society* (York: Borthwick Institute, 2003), ix.
84. Journal of Miss Ewbank of York, 1803. NLS, MS 9481, p. 29. I am very grateful to Dr Jane Rendall for drawing this account to my attention.
85. Journal of Miss Ewbank of York, 15 May 1804. NLS, MS 9481, 59.
86. On the gradual exclusion of women from the British army over the course of the nineteenth century see Myra Trustram, *Women of the Regiment: Marriage and the Victorian Army* (Cambridge: Cambridge UP, 1984).
87. Anna Walker, 11 July 1804. 'The Diary of Mrs Walker'. PRONI, T/1565/1, 125.
88. Rebecca Leslie to Mrs Stewart, 12 July 1798. PRONI, Stewart of Killymoon Papers, D/3167/A/14.
89. Anna Walker, 16 August 1803. 'The Diary of Mrs Walker'. PRONI, T/1565/1, 72.
90. On wives' incorporation into their husband's work see Janet Finch, *Married to the Job* (London: Allen and Unwin, 1983).
91. Anna Walker, 16 May 1805, PRONI, 'The Diary of Mrs Walker', T/1565/1, 159. Rebecca Leslie, PRONI, Stewart of Killymoon Papers, D/3167/3/A/18, 121.
92. Anna Walker, 20 October 1803, 'The Diary of Mrs Walker'. PRONI, T/1565/1, 135.
93. Rebecca Leslie to Elizabeth Stewart, 23 July 1798. PRONI, Stewart of Killymoon Papers, D/3167/3/A/18.
94. Anna Walker, 1 August 1805. 'The Diary of Mrs Walker'. PRONI, T/1565/1, 173.
95. On the Britannicization of the Irish garrison and the reduction in the proportion of Irish troops see Cookson, *Armed Nation*, 155. On women and the imperial garrison in India see Sara Suleri, *The Rhetoric of English India* (Chicago: Chicago UP, 1992), 75–9.
96. Rebecca Leslie, 7 June 1798. PRONI, Stewart of Killymoon Papers, D/3167/3/A/10.
97. 'Diary of Anne Walker', 28 July 1803. PRONI, T/1565/1, 67.

98. Rebecca Leslie, 7 June 1798; 22 June 1799. PRONI, Stewart of Killymoon Papers, D/3167/3/A/10.
99. Rebecca Leslie, 31 July 1798. PRONI, Stewart of Killymoon Papers, D/3167/3/A/19.
100. Rebecca Leslie, 12 July 1798, 12 July 1798 and 14 August 1798. PRONI, Stewart of Killymoon D/3167/3/A/14, 23.
101. 'Diary of Anne Walker', 13 September 1805. PRONI, T/1565/1, 181.
102. Thomas Bartlett, 'Britishness, Irishness and the Act of Union', in Dáire Keogh and Kevin Whelan (eds), *Acts of Union: the Causes, Contexts and Consequences of the Act of Union* (Dublin, 2001), 248.
103. 'Diary of Anne Walker', 2 May 1802. PRONI, T/1565/1, 9.
104. Rebecca Leslie, 27 December 1801; 21 March 1803. PRONI, D/3167/3/A/18, 59, 66.
105. Rebecca Leslie, 28 December 1798. PRONI, D/3167/3/A/38.
106. Maria Edgeworth, 'Castle Rackrent', in Marilyn Butler (ed.), *Castle Rackrent and Ennui* (Harmondsworth: Penguin, 1992 [1801]), 122.
107. McAnally, *The Irish Militia*, 244.
108. Ibid., 126. In reality, as Cookson suggests, it is likely that many of the affrays between Irish militia regiments stemmed from antipathies arising from strong regional attachments. Cookson, *The British Armed Nation*, 171.
109. Colley, *Britons*, 332.
110. The role of the soldier in the transmission of British folktales, ballads and customs presents a potentially fruitful avenue through which militia service's impact on the diffusion of local culture could be measured. On the soldier as a disseminator of folk customs in French culture see David Hopkin, 'La Ramée: The Archetypal Soldier as an Indicator of Popular Attitudes to the Army in Nineteenth-Century France', *French History*, 14, 2 (2000), 115–49, 121.
111. Elaine McFarland, 'Scotland and the 1798 Rebellion: The Limits of 'Common Cause', in Thomas Bartlett, David Dickson, Dáire Keogh and Kevin Whelan (eds), *1798: A Bicentenary Perspective* (Dublin: Four Courts Press, 2003), 570; Katrina Navickas, *Loyalism and Radicalism in Lancashire, 1798–1815* (Oxford: Oxford UP, 2009), 6.
112. John Marshall, May 1805; 27 June 1811. National Library of Scotland, MS 15371, 26, 63.
113. James Radford, 4 May 1797. E.F. Radford (ed.), *Two Military Men. The Letters of father and Son, 1794–1816* (Durham: Roundtuit, 2006), 20.
114. A.R.H. Baker and M. Billinge, *Geographies of England: The North-South Divide, Material and Imagined* (Cambridge: Cambridge UP, 2004).
115. Kussmaul (ed.), *Autobiography of Joseph Mayett*.
116. James Oakes, 19 October 1798. Jane Fiske (ed.), *The Oakes Diaries. Business Politics and the Family in Bury St Edmunds, 1778–1827* (Suffolk: Boydell Press for the Suffolk Records Society, 1990), vol. 1, 369.
117. 'Diary of Mary Anne Ffolliot', 16 August 1813. PRONI, D/1995.
118. James Oakes, 13 September 1796. Fiske (ed.), *Oakes Diaries*, vol. 1, 336.
119. Diary of Anna Margaretta Larpent, 29 August 1793.
120. Bell, *Total War*.
121. Anon., *Narrative of a Private Soldier in his Majesty's 92nd Regiment of Foot: Written by Himself* (Glasgow, 1819), 14.
122. Archibald McLaren, *A Minute Description of the Battles of Gorey, Arklow and Vinegar Hill...* (Dublin, 1798), 39.

123. Anon., *Narrative of a Private Soldier*, 26.

124. Col. David Leslie, 12 December (no year). NAS, GD26/9/524.

125. Diary of Thomas Law Hodges, 17 March 1799. BL, Add MS, 40,166, ff. 68. See also Lt David Powell 'Account of a Campagne [*sic*] in the County of Cork, Flanders and Brebant', March 1794. NLI, MS 1577, 17.

126. Montagu Burgoyne, 9 September 1812 to Major O'Hara. NLI, O'Hara Papers, MS 20,311(6).

127. Etienne Balibar, 'The Nation Form: History and Ideology', in Etienne Balibar and Immanuel Wallerstein (eds), *Race, Nation, Class: Ambiguous Identities* (London; New York: Verso, 1991), 95.

128. Sir Francis Wood to his wife, Lady Anne Wood, Clonmell, 30 April 1799. Borthwick Archives, University of York. Halifax Papers, A2.7.2.

129. Diary of Thomas Law Hodges, 8 Feb 1799. BL, Add MS 40,166, f.68, 31.

7   Bringing the War Back Home

1. S.T. Coleridge, *Fears in Solitude, Written in 1798, during the Alarm of an Invasion, to Which are Added, France, an Ode; and Frost at Midnight* (London, 1798), 5–6.

2. See, for example, Karen Hagemann, 'Occupation, Mobilization, and Politics: The Anti-Napoleonic Wars in Prussian Experience, Memory and Historiography', *Central European History*, 39 (2006), 580–610, 586.

3. For Germany see Ute Planert, 'From Collaboration to Resistance: Politics, Experience, and Memory of the Revolutionary and Napoleonic Wars in Southern Germany', *Central European History*, 39 (2006), 676–705. For a revisionist account of popular resistance to the French elsewhere in Europe see, Charles Esdaile (ed.), *Popular Resistance in the French Wars: Patriots, Partisans and Pirates* (Basingstoke: Palgrave Macmillan, 2005).

4. On the role of the print culture and the press in constructing the nation as an 'imagined community' see Benedict Anderson, *Imagined Communities: Reflections on the Origins and Spread of Nationalism* (London, 1991).

5. Mark Rawlinson, 'Invasion! Coleridge, the Defence of Britain and the Cultivation of the Public's Fear', in Philip Shaw (ed.), *Romantic Wars: Studies in Culture and Conflict, 1793–1822* (Aldershot: Ashgate, 2000), pp. 110–137, p. 115.

6. [William Cobbett], *A Warning to Britons against French Perfidy and Cruelty* (London, 1798).

7. Mark Philp, 'Introduction: the British Response to the Threat of Invasion, 1797–1815', in Mark Philp (ed.), *Resisting Napoleon: The British Response to the Threat of Invasion* (Aldershot: Ashgate, 2006), 8.

8. H.F.B. Wheeler & A.M. Broadley, *Napoleon and the Invasion of England: The Story of the Great Terror* (Stroud: Nonsuch, 2007 [1908]), 443.

9. Semmel, *Napoleon and the British*, 51–63.

10. 'John Bull in a Dream or the Effects of Uncertainty' (London, 1803). British Museum, Prints and Drawings, 1985, 0119, 176.

11. Philp, 'Threat of Invasion', 13.

12. Mark Jones, 'Alarmism, Public-Sphere Performatives, and the Lyric Turn: or, What is 'Fears in Solitude' Afraid of?', *Boundary 2*, 30, 3 (2003), 67–105.

13. Jessie Harden, 4 November 1803. NLS, Harden Journals, MS 8870 (2), 175.

14. Wheeler and Broadley, *Napoleon and the Invasion of England*, 306–7.

15. B. Howard, n.d. [1797?]. National Library of Wales, Wigfair Papers, NLW MS 12437E, 10.
16. Anon., *The False Alarm: a Narrative of the Lighting of the Border Beacons in 1804* (Jedburgh, 1869).
17. George Culley to John Welch, Eastfield, 1 February 1804. Anne Orde (ed.), *Matthew and George Culley: Farming Letters, 1798–1804* (Suffolk: Surtees Society Publications, 2006), vol. 210, 583.
18. Martha McTier to her brother William Drennan, Belfast, n.d. 1798. Jean Agnew (ed.), *Drennan-McTier Letters* (Dublin: Irish Manuscripts Commission, 1999), 3 vols, vol. 2, 390.
19. Joseph Farington, 17 July 1803. Garlick and Macintyre (eds), *Diary of Joseph Farington*, vol. 6, 2082.
20. George Home to Patrick Home, Edinburgh, 28 October 1803. NAS, Home-Robertson of Wedderburn papers, GD/267/8/.
21. George Culley to John Welch, 1 August 1803. Orde (ed.), *Farming Letters*, 507.
22. Mrs H.C. Knight, *Jane Taylor. Her Life and Letters* (London, 1880), 38–9. On the Colchester evacuations see also Wheeler and Broadley, *Napoleon and the Invasion of England*, 349.
23. Geoff Quilley, 'Duty and Mutiny', 94.
24. Christopher Bellew to Christopher Dillon, Dublin 1797. NLI, Bellew of Mt Bellew Papers, MS 27127, 6.
25. Samuel Oakes, 9 May 1797. Fiske (ed.), *Oakes Diaries*, vol. 1, 349.
26. Diary of Anna Larpent, 10 May 1797.
27. G.M. Macaulay, 23 July 1797. *The War Diary of a London Scot, 1796–7*, ed. MacKenzie (Paisley: A. Gardner, 1916), 186.
28. The credibility of this account has been questioned in a recent history of the Fishguard landing, where it is identified as the probable product of local myth-making. J.E. Thomas, *Britain's Last Invasion: Fishguard 1797* (Stroud: Tempus, 2007), 149–56. However, reports that women and children dressed in red flannels had been mustered along the cliffs were already in circulation just a few days after the landing. See Ann Knight, Haverford West, 28 February 1797. NLW, Aberystwyth. MS 13209D, 3.
29. Gwyn A. Williams, *The Search for Beulah Land: The Welsh and the Atlantic Revolution* (London: Croom Helm, 1980), 130.
30. Richard Fenton, *A Historical Tour through Pembrokeshire* (London, 1811), 9. See also letter from H. Mathias to Lord Milford, 1798 in David Salmon, 'The French Invasion of Pembrokeshire in 1797: Official Documents, Contemporary Letters and Early Narratives', *West Wales Historical Records*, vol. 14 (1929), 129–206, 170.
31. *An Authentic Account of the Invasion by the French Troops, on Carrig Gwasted Point, Near Fishguard* (Haverfordwest, 1842), 16.
32. *An Authentic Account of the Invasion*, 6.
33. Thomas Knox, *Some Account of the Proceedings That Took Place on the Landing of the French near Fishguard on the 22nd February 1797…* (London, 1800).
34. For this interpretation see Thomas, *Britain's Last Invasion*, 115–24.
35. Gwyn A. Williams, 'Beginnings of Radicalism', in T. Hebert and G.E. Jones, *The Remaking of Wales in the Eighteenth Century* (Cardiff: University of Wales Press, 1988), 126.
36. John Henry Manners Rutland, *Journal of a Tour Through North and South Wales and the Isle of Man* (London, 1805).

37. Guy Beiner, *Remembering the Year of the French. Irish Folk History and Social Memory* (Madison Wis; London: University of Wisconsin Press, 2007), 129.
38. 'Rev. James Little's Diary of the French Landing 1798'. RIA, 3.B.51, f. 2.
39. 'Diary of Revd. Little', f. 82.
40. 'Diary of Revd. Little', f. 42.
41. I consider Stock's narrative in greater depth in '"Our Separate Rooms": Bishop Stock's Narrative of the French invasion of Mayo, 1798', *Field Day Review*, 5 (2009), 94–107.
42. Joseph Stock, *A Narrative of What Passed at Killala in the County Mayo and the Parts Adjacent during the French Invasion in the Summer of 1798 by an Eyewitness* (London, 1800), 16, 17, 34.
43. See, for example, John Barrell, *The Spirit of Despotism: Invasions of Privacy in the 1790s* (Oxford: Oxford UP, 2006), 220–42.
44. Stock, *Narrative*, 160.
45. Journal of Robert French, September 1797. NLI, MS 4922.
46. Philp, *Resisting Napoleon*, 9.
47. Blanchard Jerrold, *The Life of George Cruikshank in Two Epochs* (Chicheley, 1971[1882]), 29.
48. Diary of Anna Larpent, 27 August 1793.
49. Michael Paris, *Warrior Nation: Images of War in British Popular Culture, 1850–2000* (Reaktion: London, 2005). The phrase 'pleasure culture of war' was originally used by Graham Dawson to describe developments in the later nineteenth century, Graham Dawson, *Soldier Heroes: British Adventure, Empire and the Imagining of Masculinity* (London: Routledge, 1994).
50. John Henry Manners (5th Duke of Rutland), *Journal of a Tour round the Southern Coasts of England* (London, 1805).
51. 'Journal of a Tour through Kent in 1809', Maidstone, Centre for Kentish Studies, U2402 F1.
52. Diaries of Thomas Pattenden, May 1800. Dover, East Kent Archives DO/ZZ1/1–3.
53. Diary of John Sills, 28 July 1809. Centre for Kentish Studies, U/442/Z6/1–3.
54. William Cobbett, *The Life and Adventures of Peter Porcupine, with a Full and Fair Account of all His Authoring Transactions* (Philadelphia, 1796), 17–18.
55. Richard Heber, Cornwall, to his aunt, Elizabeth Heber, 29 October 1800 in Cholmondeley (ed.), *The Heber Letters*, 127–8.
56. Bainbridge, *British Poetry and the Revolutionary and Napoleonic Wars*.
57. St Clair, *The Reading Nation*, 227.
58. Elizabeth Ham, *Elizabeth Ham by Herself, 1783–1820*, ed. Eric Gillet (London, 1945), 52.
59. John Housman, 'Tour of England', *The Monthly Magazine* (September, 1798), vol. 6, 193.
60. Samuel Bamford, *Early Days* (London: Simpkin, Marshall & Co, 1849), 244–5.
61. John Cookson, *The Friends of Peace: Anti-war Liberalism in England, 1793–1815* (Cambridge: Cambridge UP, 1982), 54.
62. Letter from John Templeton to William Tennent n.d. [1815?]. PRONI, Tennent Papers. D/1748, 301/1.
63. Betty T. Bennett (ed.), *British War Poetry in the Age of Romanticism: 1793–1815* (New York; London: Garland, 1976).
64. On the origins of the British Peace movement in this period see Martin Ceadel, *The Origins of War Prevention: The British Peace Movement and International Relations, 1730–1854* (Oxford: Oxford UP, 1996), 166–221 and Cookson, *Friends of Peace*.

65. Rawlinson, 'Invasion', 133.
66. *Caledonian Mercury*, 16 March 1793; 4 April 1793.
67. John Marsh, 7 March 1800. Robins (ed.), *John Marsh Journals*, 708.
68. Anna Larpent, 23 August 1793.
69. Ibid., 13 May 1795.
70. A.D. Harvey, *English Literature and the Great War with France: An Anthology and Commentary* (London: Nold Jonson, 1981), 135.
71. Lady Charlotte Bury, 23 July 1814. Charlotte Bury, *Diary Illustrative of the Times of George Fourth...* (London, 1839), 4 vols, vol. 2, 8.
72. Thomas de Quincey, *The English Mail-Coach and Other Essays* (London: JM Dent & Sons, 1961), 19.
73. Eviatar Zerubavel, 'The Standardization of Time: A Sociohistorical Perspective', *American Journal of Sociology*, 88, 1 (1982), 1–23, 6.
74. Battlefield dispatches can thus be understood as crucial to that sense of national simultaneity that Benedict Anderson has identified as a key hallmark of the modern nation Anderson, *Imagined Communities*, 22–36.
75. Timothy Jenks, *Naval Engagements: Patriotism, Cultural Politics, and the Royal Navy, 1793–1815* (Oxford: Oxford UP, 2006), 14–20.
76. De Quincey, *English Mail-Coach*, 24.
77. Mary A. Favret, 'Coming Home: The Public Spaces of Romantic War', *Studies in Romanticism*, 33 (Winter, 1994), 1.
78. Jenks, *Naval Engagements*, 15.
79. 'Diary of Joseph Rogerson', 16 August 1809, in W.B. Crump (ed.), *The Leeds Woolen Industry 1780–1820* (Leeds: Thoresby Society, 1931), 100. My italics.
80. Jane Taylor, Colchester, 20 December, 1805. *Memoirs, Correspondence and Poetical Remains of Jane Taylor* (London, 1841), 53, 55.
81. George M. Macaulay, 6 December 1796; 3 March 1797. Mackenzie (ed.), *War Diary of a London Scot*, 108, 137.
82. See for example Samuel Oakes record of Admiral Jervis' victory over the Spanish Fleet in 1797. Samuel Oakes, 4 March 1797. Fiske (ed.), *The Oakes Diaries*, vol. 1, 343.
83. The commonplace book of Thomas Salisbury of Denbigh, for instance, contains numerous extracts from battle gazettes. Salisbury also compiled a chronology of 'Gallant achievements during the war with France from 1792 to 1801 by the British and their allies'. 'Commonplace Book of Thomas Salisbury of Denbigh', NLW, MS 9669E. Joseph Farington, 18 August 1812, Garlick and Macintyre (eds), *Diary of Joseph Farington*, vol. 12, 4185–97.
84. Diary of Joseph Rogerson, 16 August 1809, Crump (ed.), *Leeds Woolen industry*, 100.
85. Major Greenwood, 'British Loss of Life in the Wars of 1794–1815 and in 1914–1918', *Journal of the Royal Statistical Society*, 105, 1 (1942), 1–16.
86. Both these figures are based upon estimations of excess mortality from disease and therefore an even higher number would have actually died over the course of the wars. Greenwood, 'British Loss of Life', 5.
87. On grief as a dominant experience of the First World War see Jay Winter, *Sites of Memory, Sites of Mourning: The Great War in European Cultural History* (Cambridge: Cambridge UP, 1995), 224.
88. Betty T. Bennett, 'Introduction', *British War Poetry*, 14. The pervasive presence of the war widow in British art and literature in this period has been the subject of much recent discussion. See for example, Mary Favret, 'Coming Home', 539–48;

Stephen C. Behrendt, "'A Few Harmless Numbers": British Women Poets and the Climate of War, 1793–1815', in Shaw (ed.), *Romantic Wars*, 13–36.

89. Emsley, *British Society and the French Wars*, 135.
90. 'Diary of Joseph Rogerson', 20 December 1808. Crump (ed.), *The Leeds Woolen Industry*, 90.
91. George and Matthew Culley to John Welch, 18 April 1801. Orde (ed.), *Farming Letters*, 145–6.
92.See Kate Williams, 'Nelson and Women: Marketing, Representations and the Female Consumer' in David Cannadine (ed.), *Admiral Lord Nelson: Context and Legacy* (Basingstoke: Palgrave Macmillan, 2005), 67–89.
93. Jenks, *Naval Engagements*, 186–97.
94. Kathleen Wilson, 'Nelson and the People: Manliness, Patriotism and the Body Politic', in Cannadine (ed.), *Admiral Lord Nelson*, 63.
95. Jane Taylor, Colchester, 20 December 1805, *Memoirs*, 55.
96. Charles Fothergill, 8 November 1805 in Paul Romney (ed.), *The Diary of Charles Fothergill, 1805. An Itinerary to York, Flamborough and the North-Western Dales of Yorkshire* (Leeds: Yorkshire Archaeological Society, 1984), 218.
97. Lucy Aikin to her mother, Stoke Newington, November 1805 in Philip Hemery Le Breton (ed.), *Memoirs, Miscellanies and Letters of the Late Lucy Aikin* (London, 1864), 81.
98. Jenks, *Naval Engagements*, 225. In Dublin, William Drennan also reported the widespread breaking of windows during the Trafalgar illuminations. William Drennan, Dublin to Martha McTier, 10 November 1805, *Drennan-McTier Letters*, vol. 3, 388.
99. Following Admiral Lord Howe's victory on the 'Glorious First of June 1794', *The Times* reported that the happy news 'brought out mobs demanding illumination'. *The Times*, 12 June 1794.
100. *Belfast Monthly Magazine*, vol. 11, (September, 1813), 183.
101. Joseph Farington, 7 July 1813. Garlick and Macintyre (eds.), *Diary of Joseph Farington*, vol. 12, 4388.
102. Diary of Anna Larpent, 11 and 12 June 1794.
103. Diary of Lady Christian Dalrymple, 15 April 1814. NLS, Newhailes Papers, MS 25459.
104. Samuel Oakes, March 30, May 7 and May 8, 1801. Fiske (ed.), *Diaries of Samuel Oakes*, vol. 2, 19–20. My italics.
105. Linda Colley, 'Whose Nation? Class and National Consciousness in Britain 1750–1830', *Past and Present*, 113 (November, 1986), 97–117.
106. See for example: Diaries of Christian Dalrymple, 28 November 1798, 20 April 1803, 31 July 1803, 20 October 1803, 20 February 1805. NLS, Newhailes papers, MS 25459–60; Diaries of Thomas Pattenden, 8 March 1797, 7 March 1798, 29 November 1798, 27 February 1799. East Kent Archives, DO/ZZ1/1–3; Transcription of part of Thanksgiving day sermon preached by Dr Horsley, Lord Bishop of Saint Asaph on the 5th of December 1805 in the Commonplace Book of Thomas Salisbury of Denbigh, NLW, MS 9669E.
107. Tony Claydon and Ian McBride, 'The Trials of the Chosen Peoples: Recent Interpretations of Protestantism and National Identity in Britain and Ireland', in Tony Claydon and Ian McBride (eds), *Protestantism and National Identity: Britain and Ireland, c. 1650–1850* (Cambridge: Cambridge UP, 1998), 10–11.
108. John Ramsay, 15 December 1805, in Barbara L.H. Horn, *Letters of John Ramsay of Ochtertyre, 1799–1812* (Edinburgh: Scottish History Society, 1966), 172.

109. On the relationship between these two discourses of providentialism in the United States see Nicholas Guyatt, *Providence and the Invention of the United States, 1607–1876* (Cambridge: Cambridge UP, 2007).
110. Diary of William Vavasour, December 1805. WYAS, Weston Hall MS.
111. Diary of Thomas Pattenden, 29 November 1798. East Kent Archives, DO/ZZ1/1.
112. See for example, Samuel Oakes 25 March 1796. Fiske (ed.), *Diaries of Samuel Oakes*, vol. 1, 327.
113. Laurence Brockliss, John Cardwell and Michael Moss, 'Nelson's Grand National Obsequies', *English Historical Review*, 121, 490 (2006), 162–182, 181.
114. Robert Aspland, Newport, to his father, June 4 1802. Brook Aspland, *Memoir of the Life, Works and Correspondence of the Rev. Robert Aspland, of Hackney* (London, 1850), 121.
115. Diary of John Davies, Ystrad, 1796–99. NLW, MS 12850A, 109.
116. Katrina Navickas, 'The Cragg Family Memorandum Book: Society, Politics, and Religion in North Lancashire during the 1790s', *Northern History*, 42, 1 (March, 2005), 151–162, 155.
117. 'Ye hypocrites! Are these your pranks?/To murder men, and give God thanks?/ Desist for shame! Proceed no further:/God won't accept your thanks for Murther'. The epigram entitled 'On a Thanksgiving for a National Victory', was first published with an attribution to Burns in 1834, and has long been included in Burns anthologies. More recently, it has been suggested that the lines were adapted by Burns from an earlier verse *Four Lines Put in the Basin of the Tron Church on the Thanksgiving Day for Perth and Preston, 17th June 1716*. See Andrew Noble and Patrick Scott Hogg (eds), *The Canongate Burns* (Edinburgh: Canongate, 2003), 987.
118. There is evidence of similar verses cropping up outside churches on the days appointed for national Thanksgiving. In January 1798, the *Cambridge Intelligencer* published a much longer anonymous poem, found, the paper claimed, in 'St Peter's church yard in Colchester' which began 'Rejoice ye Pharisees! And sing/ the glories of your Church and King...with pure hands present to God,/Your tatter'd trophies, drench'd in blood'. Lynda Pratt, 'Naval Contemplation: Poetry, Patriotism and the Navy, 1797–99', *Journal of Maritime Research*, 2, 1 (2000), 84–105.
119. Diary of Joseph Rogerson, 15 April 1814. Crump (ed.), *Leeds Woollen Industry*, 163.
120. Rev. John Stonard to Richard Herber, East Malling, 15 April 1814. Cholmondeley (ed.), *The Heber Letters*, 267.

Conclusion: A Waterloo Panorama

1. James Simpson, *A Visit to Flanders in July 1815, Being Chiefly an Account of the Field of Waterloo, with a Short Sketch of Antwerp and Brussels* (Edinburgh, 1816 [8th edn]), 107.
2. As Stuart Semmel observes: 'Early journeys to Waterloo had been self-guided affairs, patched together by travellers who had few published sources besides newspaper battle accounts through which to filter what they saw. With the passing of time it became increasingly less possible to feel that one was viewing the naked battlefield. Too many layers of mediation had sprung up to separate the tourist from the historical landscape'. Stuart Semmel, 'Reading the Tangible

Past: British Tourism, Collecting and Memory after Waterloo', *Representations*, 69 (Winter, 2000), 9–37, 26. The accounts considered here, however, suggest that this layer of mediation was already in place during the early phase of Waterloo tourism and, indeed, can also be identified in eye-witness accounts of the battle itself. John Keegan, *The Face of Battle: A Study of Agincourt, Waterloo and the Somme* (London: Pimlico, 2004 [1976]), 119.

3. Bainbridge, *British Poetry and the Revolutionary and Napoleonic Wars*, 170–9.
4. Charlotte Anne Eaton, *Narrative of a Residence in Belgium During the Campaign of 1815; and of a Visit to the Field of Waterloo. By an Englishwoman* (London, 1817), iii–iv.
5. Georgian Capel to Lady Uxbridge, November 1815. George Charles Henry Victor Paget, Marquess of Anglesey (ed.), *The Capel Letters: Being the Correspondence of Lady Caroline Capel and Her Daughters with the Dowager Countess of Uxbridge from Brussels and Switzerland 1814–1817* (London: Jonathan Cape, 1955), 150.
6. Philip Shaw, *Waterloo and the Romantic Imagination* (Basingstoke: Palgrave, 2002), 53.
7. *British Critic*, 6 (1816), 611.
8. Journal of Thomas Creevey, Brussels, 22 April 1815. John Gore (ed.), *Thomas Creevey's Papers, 1793–1838* (Harmondsworth: Penguin, 1985 [1948]), 127.
9. [Charlotte Anne Eaton] *The Battle of Waterloo Containing the Series of Accounts Published by Authority, British and Foreign, with Circumstantial Details Relative to the Battle...* (London, 1816 [8th edn]), Xxxix.
10. Georgiana Capel to Countess Uxbridge, August 1815. Paget (ed.), *Capel Letters*, 137.
11. Georgiana Capel to Countess Uxbridge, July 1815 and August 1815. Paget (ed.), *Capel Letters*, 128 and 137.
12. Eaton, *Narrative of a Residence in Belgium*, 285. On this 'gothic intrusion' in the description of Waterloo see Shaw, *Waterloo and the Romantic Imagination*, 76.
13. Duke of Wellington to Lady Frances Webster, 19 June 1815. Duke of Wellington (ed.), *Supplementary Despatches and Memoranda of Field Marshal, Arthur Duke of Wellington* (London, 1863), vol. 10; From a letter quoted in Jeremy Black, *Waterloo: The Battle that Brought Down Napoleon* (London: Icon, 2011), 178.
14. Georgiana Capel to Countess Uxbridge, August 1815. Paget (ed.), *Capel Letters*, 131.
15. Georgiana Capel to Countess Uxbridge, July 1816, Ibid., 168.
16. On the role of the Napoleonic wars in securing the continued dominance of the British aristocracy see Colley, *Britons*, 192. On women's contribution to the promotion of dynastic honour see Judith S. Lewis, *Sacred to Female Patriotism: Gender, Class and Politics in Late Georgian Britain* (New York and London: Routledge, 2003).
17. Eaton, *Narrative of a Residence in Belgium*, 346–7.
18. Eaton, *Narrative of a Residence in Belgium*, 351.
19. See Philip Harling and Peter Mandler 'From "Fiscal-Military" State to Laissez-Faire State, 1760–1850', *Journal of British Studies*, 32 (January, 1993), 44–70; Norman Gash, 'After Waterloo: British Society and the Legacy of the Napoleonic wars', *Transactions of the Royal Historical Society*, 5th series, 28 (1978), 145–57.
20. Gash, 'After Waterloo', 150.
21. J.E. Cookson, 'Early Nineteenth-Century Scottish Military Pensioners as Homecoming Soldiers', *Historical Journal*, 52, 2 (2009), 319–341; Joanna Innes, 'Prisons for the Poor: English Bridewells, 1555–1800', in Francis Snyder and Douglas Hay (eds), *Labour, Law and Crime: An Historic Perspective* (London, 1987), 108.

22. J.W.M. Hichberger, *Images of the Army: The Military in British Art, 1815–1914* (Manchester: Manchester UP, 1988), 141.
23. Gash, 'After Waterloo', 151–2; Nick Mansfield, 'Military Radicals and the Making of Class, 1790–1860', in Catriona Kennedy and Matthew McCormack (eds), *Soldiers and Soldiering in Britain and Ireland, 1750–1850: Men of Arms* (Basingstoke: Palgrave Macmillan, 2012), 57–75.
24. Holger Hoock, *Empires of the Imagination: Politics, War and the Arts in the British World, 1750–1850* (London: Profile, 2010), 132–61.
25. Hoock, *Empires of the Imagination*, 161.
26. Hoock, *Empires of the Imagination*, 367–8.
27. J.E. Cookson, 'Scotland's National Monument, 1816–1828', *Scottish Tradition*, 24 (1999), 3–12; J.E. Cookson, 'The Edinburgh and Glasgow Duke of Wellington Statues: Early Nineteenth-Century Unionist Nationalism as a Tory Project', *Scottish Historical Review*, 83, 1 (2004), 23–40.
28. Rev. Edward Patteson, *A Sermon Delivered in the Parish Church of Richmond in Surrey, on Sunday the 30th day of July, on Behalf of the Families of Those Who Fell or Who Were Disabled in the Battle of Waterloo or in the Other Arduous Conflicts of the Present Campaign* (London, 1815), 27.
29. Sir William Francis Patrick Napier, *History of the War in the Peninsula and in the South of France, from the Year 1807 to the Year 1814* (Brussels, 1839), vol. 2, 164.
30. Ramsey, *Military Memoir*, 125.
31. Ibid., 113.
32. See, for example, Anon., *Vicissitudes in the Life of a Scottish Soldier, Written by Himself* (London, 1827), v.
33. Ramsey, *Military Memoir*, 133.
34. Edward Costello, *The Adventures of a Soldier; or, Memoirs of Edward Costello* (London, 1841), vii.
35. Harari, *The Ultimate Experience*, 190–3.
36. Capt. George Wood, *The Subaltern Officer. A Narrative. By Captain George Wood of the Line* (London, 1825), vii.
37. Ramsey, *Military Memoir*, 65.
38. Colley, *Britons*, 386–7.
39. Nicholas Rogers, *The Press Gang: Naval Impressments and Its Opponents in Georgian Britain* (London; New York: Continuum, 2007), 105.
40. Hichberger, *Images of the Army*, 142–3.
41. For a key to and explanation of the painting see Allan Cunningham, *The Life of Sir David Wilkie with His Journals, Tours and Critical Remarks on Works of Art; and a selection from His Correspondence* (London, 1843), vol. 2, 76.
42. Alexander Somerville quoted in Andrew MacKillop, 'For King, Country and Regiment?: Motive and Identity within Highland Soldiering, 1746–1815', in Murdoch and MacKillop (eds), *Fighting for Identity*, 185.
43. See, for example, *Autobiographic Recollections of George Pryme: Edited by his daughter* (Cambridge and London, 1870), 53. Thomas de Quincey, *The English Mail-Coach and Other Essays* (London: Dent, 1961[1849]); James Pagan, Aliquis, Robert Reid et al., *Glasgow, Past and Present Illustrated in Dean of Guild Court Reports and in the Reminiscences and Communications of Senex, Aliquis, J.B. &c.* (Glasgow, 1851), 2 vols, vol. 1, 113.
44. Tom Taylor (ed.), *Life of Benjamin Robert Haydon, Historical Painter, from His Autobiography and Journals* (London, 1853), 3 vols, vol. 1, 277–8.
45. Lieutenant C.W. Short to his mother, Nivelle, 19 June 1815, NAM, 7702–05.

Bibliography

Manuscript collections

England

Borthwick Institute Archives, University of York, York.

A2.7.2 Halifax Papers, Letters of Sir Francis Wood to his wife Lady Anne Wood, 1798–1800.

Bradford, Bradford Central Library.

Sp St/6/1/119 Spencer Stanhope Papers, correspondence between Walter Spencer Stanhope and Peter Haddon, 1775–1815.

British Library, London.

Add MS 32468 John Westcott, 'Journal of the Campaign in Portugal by John Westcott Late Master of the Band 1st Battalion 26th Cameronian Regiment of Foot'.

Add MS 37014 Charles Chambers, 'A Brief Chronological Journal of Remarkable Occurrences on Board His Majesty's Fireship Prometheus'.

Add MS 40166 Diary of Thomas Law Hodges, 1798–1799.

Centre for Kentish Studies, Maidstone.

U145 F18 Diary of Alured Punchen, 1802.

U/442/Z6/1–3 Diary of John Sills, 1809–1821.

U2402 F1 Journal of a Tour through Kent in 1809.

U951/F24 Knatchbull MS Diaries of Fanny C. Knatchbull, 1804–1809.

East Kent Archives, Dover.

DO/ZZ1/1–3 Diaries of Thomas Pattenden.

RU/126/1 Diaries of Mary Cobb (neé) Blackburn, 1792–1802.

Hull University Archives, Hull.

DDSY102/27–28 Sykes Family Papers, Diaries of Tatton Sykes, 1793–1794.

DDX/60 Courtney Family of Beverley Papers, Diary of Sir Christopher Courtney, vols 3 & 4, 1787–1803.

National Army Museum, London.

2002–05–03 Letters associated with Rev. Samuel Briscoe, 1809–1825.

2005–07–04 Diary of William (or Thomas Dixon?), 1806–1811.

6406–22 Letterbooks of Col. Andrew Ross, 1796–1805.

6707–13 Letters of Philip Hay, 1793–1795.

6807–55 Journal by Lieutenant and Adjutant John Hunt of the 7th Light Dragoons. During the Regiment's absence on the Expedition to North Holland in the year 1799.

6807–148–1 Ensign Augustus Frederick Dobree, 'A Journal of the Campaign in Spain in the Years 1808–09'.

6807–419 Letters of William Coles, 1806–1817.

6807–163–2 Letters of George Ridout Bingham.

6807–215–4 Sergeant William Stephenson 'A Short Account of the March of the 3rd or King's Own Dragoons thro' Portugal and Spain ... Giving the Exact History of Each Day's March'.

6807–267 George Woodberry, 'The Idle Companion of a Young Hussar during the Year 1813'.

6902–5 Diaries of James Penman Gairdner, 3 vols, 1811–1815.

7010–13 Journal of Major Alexander Crosby Jackson, 1798–1826.

7101–20 Verses transcribed in the diary of Lt. James Penman Gairdner, March 1813.

7202–33 Diary of Captain Edward Hodge, October 1808–March 1809.

7205–2 Letters of David Latimer Wright.

7407–5–1 Notebook of Samuel Oakes, Royal Marines.

7504–17 MS Memoir of Lt G. J. Sullivan, October 1812–September 1813

7607–45 Diary of Lieutenant Thomas Powell, 1790–1795.

7611–24 Capt. Exham Vincent, 'Memorandum of Occurrences from 30th July 1800 to the Surrender of Egypt September 1801'.

7612–100 Documents relating to Taylor White, 7th Light Dragoons, 1793–1794.

7702–05 Lieutenant C.W. Short to his mother, Nivelle, 19 June 1815.

7912–21 MS Memoirs of an Unidentified Soldier of the 38th Foot, 1808–1815.

8002–5 Letter of Private Alexander Gellen, 92nd foot, 12 March 1808.

8003–122 Jeffrey Prendergast, 'The Prisoner of War, or, an Account of the Circumstances of a Captivity in France During the Years 1794–1795. Originally Written as a Letter to his Mother'.

8008–56 Letters of J.C. Harrison.

8009–50 Diary of Captain Commissary John Charleton, Corps of Royal Artillery Drivers 22 October 1808–24 January 1809.

8011–40 Letters of James Brown and related documents, 1798–1801.

8209–28 Diary of Thomas Peacocke, 1800–1801.

8211–162 Diary of William Patterson.

8301–203 Diary of Captain P. R. Jennings.

8511–15 Letterbook associated with Edward Reilly Cope, Loyal Irish Fencibles, 1797–1809.

8807–52 Maynard Papers.

National Maritime Museum, London.

BIE/1 Letters from Rear-Admiral Robert Barrie to his family, 1797–1812.

GRT/1–11 Diaries of Samuel Grant, Purser, 1793–1803.

JOD/11 Richard Johnson 'Journal of the HMS Thalia, Remarks &c. 1795–1800'.

JOD/202 The Journal of John Roberston, 1807–1811.

JOD/47 George Gould, 'Journal, HMS Mercury, 1800–1802'.

LBK/9 Letterbook of Robert Deans.

WIL/1 Letters of Commander William Wilkinson.

West Yorkshire Archive Service, Leeds.

WYL639/445 and 398 Weston Hall MS, Diaries of William Vavasour 1797, 1798–1827.

Ireland

National Library of Ireland, Dublin.

MS 1577 Lt David Powell 'Some Account of a Campagne in 1794'.

MS 15139 Kemmis Papers, Letters to Thomas Kemmis from his brother Major General James Kemmis, 1774–1819.

MS 1718 Maria Cope, 'Memoirs of Captivity in France, 1803–1813'.

MS 4922 Journal of Robert French, 1797–1799.

MS 20368 O'Hara Papers, Captain Archibald Armstrong 'Description of the Battle of Talavera'.

MS 20311 O'Hara Papers, Letters to Major Charles King O'Hara relating to the Sligo Militia.

MS 27127 Bellew Papers, Letters of Christopher Bellew, 1784–1803.

MS 27135 Bellew Papers, Letters from Chrisopher Kelly Bellew to Michael Bellew, 1788–1797.

Public Record Office Northern Ireland, Belfast.

D/3221/1 Belfast Yeomanry Order Book, 1803–1810.

D/649/1–16 Letters of Samuel Lumsden to Edward Lumsden, 1813–1818.

D/1514/1/31, 33 Hervey/Bruce Papers Letters of Andrew Francis Barnard, 1795–1796.

D/1748/B/1 Correspondence of William Tennent, 1783–1832.

D/1995 Diary of Mary Anne Ffolliot, 1809–1827.

D/3167/A Stewart of Killymoon Papers, Letters of Rebecca Leslie to Elizabeth Stewart, 1798–1799.

T 1125/3 William Wright Knox 'Some Letters from Spain Written by an Officer, 1808–1813'.

T/1565/1 Diary of Mrs Ann Walker, 1802–1807.

T/1880/2 Letter of Hugh O'Neill, Barletta to Mrs Magennis, Co. Down, 24 October 1798.

Royal Irish Academy, Dublin.

3.B.51 Revd James Little's Diary of the French Landing in 1798.

Trinity College Dublin, Dublin.

MS 3764 Extracts from the Journal of the late Captain Joseph Bull.

Scotland

National Library of Scotland, Edinburgh.

MS 25458–60 Newhailes Papers, Journals of Christian Dalrymple of Newhailes, 1798–1816.

MS 3524 Letters of Ann Murray Keith to Jeremiah Hill, 1769–1808.

MS 7099 Yester Papers, Letterbook of the 7th Marquess concerning defence in case of invasion, 1794–98.

MS 7903/3 Rutherford of Edgerston Papers.

MS 8870 (2), Harden Journals, Journal of Jessy Harden (neé Allan), 1801–1811.

MS 9481 Journal of Miss Ewbank of York, 1803–1805.

MS 11085 Minto Papers Letters of Rev. Robert Elliot, 1781–1814.

MS 11099 Minto Papers Letters of Anna Maria Elliot, 1804–1820.

MS 15371 Marshall Papers, 1790–1815.

MS 19933 Rennie Papers Letters of William Rennie.
MS 25458–60 Diaries of Christian Dalrymple, Newhailes Papers, 1798–1816.

National Archives of Scotland, Edinburgh.

GD26/9/524 Letters of Capt. John Leslie.
GD29/2097 Letters from Lieutenant George E. Graham, 1793–1799.
GD267 Home-Robertson of Wedderburn, letters to Patrick Home of Wedderburn, 1785–1806.

Wales

National Library of Wales, Aberystwyth.

MS 2258, 2264 Glansevern Papers, Letters of Edward Jones to Robert Owen Jones, 1815, 1816.
MS 9669E Commonplace Book of Thomas Salisbury of Denbigh.
MS12421D Wigfair Papers.
MS 12850A Diary of John Davies, Ystrad, 1796–1799.
MS 13209D Letters from Ann Knight to her father, 1797.

Newspapers and Periodicals

British Critic
Belfast Monthly Magazine
Belfast Newsletter
Caledonian Mercury
The Universal Magazine of Knowledge and Pleasure
The Monthly Magazine
The Times

Printed primary sources

Publishers not supplied for works before 1850.
Agnew, Jean (ed.), *Drennan-McTier Letters* (Dublin: Irish Manuscripts Commission, 1999), 3 vols, vol. 2.
An Authentic Account of the Invasion by the French Troops, on Carrig Gwasted Point, Near Fishguard (Haverfordwest, 1842).
Anon., *Narrative of a Private Soldier, in One of His Majesty's Regiments of Foot. Written by Himself. Detailing Many Circumstances Relative to the Irish Rebellion in 1798, the Expedition to Egypt in 1801; and Giving a Particular Account of his Religious History and Experience* (Glasgow, 1819).
Anon., *Journal of a Soldier of the Seventy-First or Glasgow Regiment, Highland Light Infantry from 1806 to 1815* (Edinburgh, 1819).
Anon., *Vicissitudes in the Life of a Scottish Soldier, Written by Himself* (London, 1827).
Anon., *Memoirs of a Sergeant in the 43rd Light Infantry during the Peninsular War* (Stroud: Nonsuch, 2005 [1835]).
Anon., *The False Alarm; A Narrative of the Lighting of the Border Beacons in 1804* (Jedburgh, 1869).
Ashcroft, M.Y. (ed.), *To Escape the Monster's Clutches: Notes and Documents Illustrating the Preparations in North Yorkshire to Repel the Invasion Threatened by the French from 1793* (Northallerton: North Yorkshire County Council, 1977).

Aspland, Brook, *Memoir of the Life, Works and Correspondence of the Rev. Robert Aspland, of Hackney* (London, 1850).

Austen, Jane, *Mansfield Park*, ed. Kathryn Sutherland (Harmonsworth: Penguin, 1996 [1814]).

Bamford, Samuel, *Early Days* (London: Simpkin, Marshall & Co, 1849).

Bayne, Alicia (ed.), *Autobiographic Recollections of George Pryme. Edited by his daughter* (Cambridge and London, 1870).

Bennett, Betty (ed.), *British War Poetry in the Age of Romanticism, 1793–1815* (New York; London: Garland, 1976).

Black, Ronald (ed.), *An Lasair. Anthology of Eighteenth-Century Scottish Gaelic Verse* (Edinburgh: Berlinn, 2001).

Blayney, Andrew Thomas Lord, *Narrative of a forced journey through Spain and France as a Prisoner of war in the years 1810 to 1814* (London, 1814).

Boys, Edward, *Narrative of a Captivity and Adventures in France and Flanders between the Years 1803 and 1809 by Capt. Edward Boys, R.N.* (London, 1827).

Broughton, Samuel, *Letters from Portugal, Spain and France, 1812–1814* (Stroud: Nonsuch, 2005 [1815]).

Brown, Robert, *An Impartial Journal of a Detachment from the Brigade of Foot Guards, Commencing 20th February 1793 and Ending 9th May 1795* (London, 1795).

Buckley, Roger N. (ed.), *The Napoleonic War Journal of Captain Thomas Henry Browne, 1807–1816* (London: Bodley Head for the Army Records Society, 1987).

Burke, Edmund, *Reflections on the Revolution in France, and on the Proceedings of Certain Societies in London Relative to That Event* (London, 1790).

Burton, Alfred (pseud. John Mitford), *The Adventures of Johnny Newcome in the Navy; A Poem in Four Cantos* (London, 1818).

Bury, Charlotte, *Diary Illustrative of the Times of George Fourth...* (London, 1839).

Bussell, Peter, *The Diary of Peter Bussell, 1806–1814*, ed. G.A. Turner (London: Peter Davies, 1931).

Cholmondeley, R.H. (ed.), *The Heber Letters, 1783–1832* (London: Batchworth Press, 1950).

Churchill, Winston, *The Second World War, Vol. 5: Closing the Ring* (Boston: Houghton Mifflin, 1986).

Clarke, John Stanier, *Naval Sermons Preached on Board His Majesty's Ship The Impeteux: In the Western Squadron, During its Services off Brest* (London, 1798).

Cobb, W.F. (ed.), *Memoir of the Late Francis Cobb Esq. of Margate Compiled from His Journals and Letters* (Maidstone, 1835).

Cobbett, William, *The Life and Adventures of Peter Porcupine, with a Full and Fair Account of all His Authoring Transactions* (Philadelphia, 1796).

——, *A Warning to Britons against French Perfidy and Cruelty* (London, 1798).

Coleridge, S.T., *Fears in Solitude, Written in 1798, During the Alarm of an Invasion, to Which Are Added, France, an Ode; and Frost at Midnight* (London, 1798).

Cooke, Rev. Thomas, *The Universal Letter Writer: or, New Art of Polite Correspondence* (London, 1795).

Cooper, Captain T. H., *A Practical Guide for the Light Infantry Officer, Comprising Valuable Extracts from All the Most Popular Works on the Subject ...* (London, 1806).

Costello, Edward, *Adventures of a Soldier: Written by Himself being the Memoirs of Edward Costello* (London, 1852 [2nd edn]).

Cunningham, Allan, *The Life of Sir David Wilkie with his Journals, Tours and Critical Remarks on Works of Art; and a Selection from his Correspondence* (London, 1843).

De Quincey, Thomas, *The English Mail-Coach and Other Essays* (London: JM Dent & Sons, 1961).

Denning, R.T.W. (ed.), *The Diary of William Thomas of Michaelston-Super-Ely, Near St Fagans Glamorgan, 1762–1795* (Cardiff: South Wales Record Society, 1995).

Donaldson, Joseph, *Recollections of the Eventful Life of a Soldier* (Philadelphia, 1845).

Duncan, Andrew, *Medical Commentaries...Collected and Published by Andrew Duncan* (London and Edinburgh, 1787).

Durey, Michael (ed.), *Andrew Bryson's Ordeal: An Epilogue to the 1798 Rebellion* (Cork: Cork UP 1998).

Eaton, Charlotte Anne, *The Battle of Waterloo Containing the Series of Accounts Published by Authority, British and Foreign, with Circumstantial Details Relative to the Battle...* (London, 1816 [8th edn]).

——, *Narrative of a Residence in Belgium During the Campaign of 1815; and of a Visit to the Field of Waterloo. By an Englishwoman* (London, 1817).

Edgeworth, Maria, 'Castle Rackrent', in Marilyn Butler (ed.), *Castle Rackrent and Ennui* (Harmondsworth: Penguin, 1992 [1801]).

Fenton, James, *A Historical Tour through Pembrokeshire* (London, 1811).

Fiske, Jane, (ed.), *The Oakes Diaries: Business Politics and the Family in Bury St Edmunds, 1778–1827* (Suffolk: Boydell Press for the Suffolk Records Society, 1990).

Fletcher, Ian, (ed.), *A Guards Officer in the Peninsular: The Peninsular War Letters of John Rous, Coldstream Guards, 1812–1814* (Tunbridge Wells: Spellmount, 1992).

——, *For King and Country: The Letters and Diaries of John Mills, Coldstream Guards, 1811–1814* (Staplehurst: Spellmount, 1995).

——, *In the Service of the King: The Letters of William Thornton Keep, at Home, Walcheren and the Peninsula, 1808–1814* (Staplehurst: Spellmount, 1997).

Garlick, Kenneth and Angus Macintyre (eds), *The Diary of Joseph Farrington* (New Haven and London: Yale UP, 1979).

Glover, Michael (ed.), *A Gentleman Volunteer: The Letters of George Hennell from the Peninsular War, 1812–1813* (London: Heineman, 1979).

——, *From Corunna to Waterloo: The Letters and Journals of Two Napoleonic Hussars. Major Edwin Griffith and Captain Frederick Philips. 15th (King's) Hussars, 1801–1816* (London: Greenhill, 2007).

Gore, John (ed.), *Thomas Creevey's Papers, 1793–1838* (Harmondsworth: Penguin, 1985 [1948]).

Grattan, William, *Adventures with the Connaught Rangers, 1809–1814*, ed. Charles Oman (London: Greenhill, 2003).

Green, John, *The Vicissitudes of a Soldier's Life* (Louth, 1827).

Grierson, H.J.C. (ed.), *The Letters of Sir Walter Scott, 1787–1807* (London: Constable & Co, 1932).

Ham, Elizabeth, *Elizabeth Ham by Herself, 1783–1820*, ed. Eric Gillet (London, 1945).

Hansard, Thomas C., *Parliamentary Debates, 1803–1811* (1812), vol. 19.

Hart, B.H. Liddell (ed.), *The Letters of Private Wheeler, 1809–1828* (Aldestrop: Windrush, 1993 [1951]).

Hibbert, Christopher (ed.), *The Recollections of Rifleman Harris: As Told to Henry Curling* (Moreton-in-Marsh: Windrush, 1996).

Horn, Barbara L.H., *Letters of John Ramsay of Ochtertyre, 1799–1812* (Edinburgh: Scottish History Society, 1966).

James, Charles, *The Regimental Companion Containing the Relative Duties of Every Officer in the British Army* (London, 1800), 2 vols.

——, *A New and Enlarged Military Dictionary, or, Alphabetical Explanation of Technical Terms...* (London, 1802).

——, *A New and Enlarged Military Dictionary or Alphabetical Explanation of Technical Terms* (London, 1805).

——, *A Collection of the Charges, Opinions, and Sentences of General Courts Martial; As Published by Authority, from the Year 1795 to the Present Time* (London, 1820).

Kincaid, John, *Tales from the Rifle Brigade* (Barnsley: Pen and Sword, 2005 [1830, 1835]).

Knight, Mrs H.C. (ed.), *Jane Taylor. Her Life and Letters* (London, 1880).

Kussmaul, Ann (ed.), *The Autobiography of Joesph Mayett of Quainton, 1783–1839* (Cambridge: Buckinghamshire Record Society, 1986).

Larpent, Anna, *A Woman's View of the Drama: The Diaries of Anna Margaretta Larpent in the Huntingdon Library* (Marlborough: Adam Matthew Publications, 1995, Microfilm).

Lawrence, Henry, *A Picture of Verdun, or the English Detained in France...from the Portfolio of a Détenu* (London, 1810), 2 vols.

Leach, Jonathan, *Rough Sketches of an Old Soldier* (London, 1831).

Le Breton, Philip Hemery (ed.), *Memoirs, Miscellanies and Letters of the Late Lucy Aikin* (London, 1864).

Le Sage, Alain René, *The Adventures of Gil Blas of Santillane*, trans. Tobias George Smollett (New York, 1820 [1749]), 2 vols.

Lowry, James, *Fiddlers and Whores: The Candid Memoirs of a Surgeon in Nelson's Fleet*, ed. John Millyard (London: Chatham, 2006 [1807]).

Macaulay, G.M., *The War Diary of a London Scot, 1796–7*, ed. W.C. MacKenzie (Paisley: A. Gardner, 1916).

Macleod, Angus, *The Songs of Duncan Ban MacIntyre* (Edinburgh: Oliver & Boyd, 1952).

Mangin, Edward, 'Some Account of the Writer's Situation as Chaplain in the British Navy', in Rear-Admiral H.G. Thursfield (ed.), *Five Naval Journals, 1797–1817* (London: Navy Records Society, 1951), vol. 91.

Manners, John Henry (5th Duke of Rutland), *Journal of a Tour Round the Southern Coasts of England* (London, 1805).

——, *Journal of a Tour through North and South Wales and the Isle of Man* (London, 1805).

Moody, T.W. (ed.), 'An Irish Countryman in the British Navy, 1809–1815: The Memoirs of Henry Walsh' [2 parts], *Irish Sword*, 4 & 5 (1960 & 1961), 149–56; 228–245.

Mulvey, Farrell, *Sketches of the Character, Conduct and Treatment of the Prisoners of War at Auxonne, Longwy &c. from the Year 1810 to 1814* (London, 1818).

Napier, Sir William Francis Patrick, *History of the War in the Peninsula and in the South of France, from the Year 1807 to the Year 1814* (Brussels, 1839).

O'Neil, Charles, *Private O'Neil: The Recollections of an Irish Rogue of HM 28th Regt (London: Leonaur, 2007 [first published as The Military Adventures of Charles O'Neil [1851]).

O'Neill, Thomas, *An Address to the People of the United Kingdoms of Great Britain and Ireland, Containing an Account of the Sufferings of Thomas O'Neill, a British Officer, while Confined in the Prisoner of the Concierge, at Paris...and...during his Second Imprisonment as a Prisoner at War* (London, 1806).

Paget, George Charles Henry Victory [Marquess of Angelsey] (ed.), *The Capel Letters: Being the Correspondence of Lady Caroline Capel and her Daughters with the Dowager Countess of Uxbridge from Brussels and Switzerland 1814–1817* (London: Jonathan Cape, 1955).

Patteson, Revd Edward, *A Sermon Delivered in the Parish Church of Richmond in Surrey, on Sunday the 30th day of July, on Behalf of the Families of Those Who Fell or Who Were Disabled in the Battle of Waterloo or in the Other Arduous Conflicts of the Present Campaign* (London, 1815).

Radford, E.F. (ed.), *Two Military Men: The Letters of Father and Son, 1794–1816* (Durham: Roundtuit, 2006).

Roberts, David, *The Military Adventures of Johnny Newcome: With an Account of His Campaign on the Peninsula and in Pall Mall* (London, 1815).

Robins, Brian (ed.), *The John Marsh Journals: The Life and Times of a Gentleman Composer* (Stuyvesant NY: Pergamon, 1998).

Rogerson, Joseph, 'Diary' in W.B. Crump (ed.), *The Leeds Woolen Industry 1780–1820* (Leeds: Thoresby Society, 1931).

Romney, Paul. (ed.), *The Diary of Charles Fothergill, 1805: An Itinerary to York, Flamborough and the North-Western Dales of Yorkshire* (Leeds: Yorkshire Archaeological Society, 1984).

Ross-Lewin, Harry, *With the Thirty-Second in the Peninsular and Other Campaigns by Harry Ross-Lewin of Ross Hill, Co Clare*, ed. John Wardell (Dublin, 1904).

Scarfe, Norman (ed.), 'Letters from the Peninsula. The Freer Family Correspondence, 1807–1814', *Transactions of the Leicestershire Archaeological Society*, 29 (1953).

Simpson, James, *A Visit to Flanders in July 1815, Being Chiefly an Account of the Field of Waterloo, with a Short Sketch of Antwerp and Brussels* (Edinburgh, 1816 [8th edn]).

Smollett, Tobias, *The Adventures of Peregrine Pickle* (Philadelphia, 1825 [1751]), 2 vols.

Sterne, Laurence, *A Sentimental Journey*, ed. Ian Jack and Tim Parnell (Oxford: Oxford UP, 2003 [1768]).

Stock, Joseph, *A Narrative of What Passed at Killala in the County Mayo and the Parts Adjacent during the French Invasion in the Summer of 1798 by an Eyewitness* (London, 1800).

Story, William, *A Journal Kept in France, during a Captivity of More than Nine Years* (Sunderland, 1815).

Surtees, William, *Twenty-Five Years in the Rifle Brigade* (Edinburgh: Blackwood, 1833).

Taylor, Alan and Irene Taylor (eds), *The Secret Annexe: An Anthology of the World's Greatest War Diarists* (Edinburgh: Canongate, 2004).

Taylor, Jane, Memoirs, *Correspondence and Poetical Remains of Jane Taylor* (London, 1841).

Taylor, Tom (ed.), *Life of Benjamin Robert Haydon, Historical Painter, from his Autobiography and Journals* (London, 1853).

Tench, Watkin, *Letters from Revolutionary France: Letters Written to a Friend in London Between the Month of November 1794, and the Month of May 1795*, ed. Gavin Edwards (Cardiff: University of Wales press, 2001 [1796]).

Thompson, W.F.K. (ed.), *An Ensign in the Peninsular War: The Letters of John Aitchison* (London: Joseph, 1994).

Thursfield, Henry George (ed.), *Five Naval Journals, 1797–1817* (Navy Records Society: London, 1951), vol. 91.

Walsh, Thomas, *Journal of the Late Campaign in Egypt. Including Descriptions of that Country* (London, 1803).

Wellesley, Arthur [Duke of Wellington] (ed.), *Supplementary Despatches and Memoranda of Field Marshal, Arthur Duke of Wellington* (London, 1863), vol. 10.

Wolfe, Revd R.B., *English Prisoners in France, Containing Observations on Their Manners and Habits* (London, 1830).

Wollstonecraft, Mary, *A Vindication of the Rights of Woman*, ed. Sylvana Tomaselli (Cambridge: Cambridge UP, 1995 [1792]).

Wood, Capt. George, *The Subaltern Officer. A Narrative. By Captain George Wood of the Line* (London, 1825).

Wordsworth, William, *The Poetical Works of William Wordsworth* (London, 1840), 6 vols, vol. 3.

Select bibliography of secondary sources

Anderson, Benedict, *Imagined Communities: Reflections on the Origin and Spread of Nationalism* (London: Verso, 1991 [1983]).

Bainbridge, Simon, *British Poetry and the Revolutionary and Napoleonic Wars: Visions of Conflict* (Oxford: Oxford UP, 2003).

Bartlett, Thomas, 'Britishness, Irishness and the Act of Union', in Dáire Keogh and Kevin Whelan (eds), *Acts of Union: Causes, Contexts and Consequences* (Dublin: Four Courts, 2001), 243–58.

Bartlett, Thomas, David Dickson, Dáire Keogh and Kevin Whelan (eds), *The 1798 Rebellion: A Bicentenary Perspective* (Dublin: Four Courts, 2003).

Bartlett, Thomas and Keith Jeffery (eds), *A Military History of Ireland* (Cambridge: Cambridge UP, 1997).

Bell, David, *The First Total War: Napoleon's Europe and the Birth of Modern Warfare As We Know It* (Boston: Houghton Mifflin, 2007).

Black, Jeremy, *The British Abroad: The Grand Tour in the Eighteenth Century* (Stroud: Sutton, 2003).

Bourke, Joanna, *Dismembering the Male: Men's Bodies, Britain and the Great War* (London: Reaktion, 1996).

——, *An Intimate History of Killing: Face-to-Face Killing in Twentieth Century Warfare* (London: Granta, 1999).

Brockliss, Laurence, 'The Professions and National Identity', in Laurence Brockliss and David Eastwood (eds), *A Union of Multiple Identities: The British Isles, c.1750-c.1850* (Manchester: Manchester University Press, 1997), 9–28.

Brotherstone, Terry, Anna Clark and Whelan, Kevin (eds), *These Fissured Isles: Ireland, Scotland and British History, 1798–1848* (Edinburgh: John Donald, 2005).

Cannadine, David (ed.), *Admiral Lord Nelson: Context and Legacy* (Basingstoke: Palgrave Macmillan, 2005).

Clyde, Robert, *From Rebel to Hero: The Image of the Highlander, 1745–1830* (East Linton: Tuckwell Press, 1995).

Cogliano, Francis D., '"We All Hoisted the American Flag": National Identity among American Prisoners in Britain During the American Revolution', *Journal of American Studies*, 31 (1998), 19–37.

Colley, Linda, *Britons: Forging the Nation, 1707–1837* (London: Vintage, 1996 [1992]).

——, *Captives: Britain, Empire and the World, 1600–1850* (London: Jonathan Cape, 2002).

Conway, Stephen, *The British Isles and the War of American Independence* (Oxford: Oxford UP, 2000).

——, 'War and National Identity in the Mid-Eighteenth-Century British Isles', *English Historical Review*, 116, 468 (September, 2001), 864–93.

——, 'Christians, Catholics, Protestants: the Religious Links of Britain and Ireland with Continental Europe, c. 1689–1800', *English Historical Review*, 125, 509 (2009), 833–62.

Cookson, John E., *The British Armed Nation, 1793–1815* (Oxford: Oxford UP, 1997).

——, 'Service without Politics? Army, Militia and Volunteers during the American and French Revolutionary Wars', *War in History*, 10 (2003), 381–97.

——, 'Regimental Worlds: Interpreting the Experience of British Soldiers during the Napoleonic Wars', in Alan Forrest, Karen Hagemann and Jane Rendall (eds), *Soldiers, Citizens and Civilians: Experiences and Perceptions of the Revolutionary and Napoleonic Wars, 1790–1820* (Basingstoke: Palgrave Macmillan, 2009), 23–42.

Daly, Gavin, 'Napoleon's Lost Legions: French Prisoners of War in Britain, 1803–1814', *History*, 89, 295 (2004), 361–80.

Dawson, Graham, *Soldier Heroes: British Adventure, Empire and the Imagining of Masculinity* (London: Routledge, 1994).

Dening, Greg, *Mr Bligh's Bad Language: Passion, Power and Theatre on the Bounty* (Cambridge: Cambridge UP, 1992).

Doyle, Robert C., *Voices from Captivity: Interpreting the American POW Narrative* (Lawrence, Kansas: University of Kansas Press, 1994).

Dudink, Stefan and Karen Hagemann, 'Masculinity in Politics and War in the Age of Democratic Revolutions, 1750–1850', in Stefan Dudink et al. (eds), *Masculinities in Politics and War: Gendering Modern History* (Manchester: Manchester UP, 2004).

Dwyer, Philip, 'Public Remembering, Private Reminiscing: French Military Memoirs and the Revolutionary and Napoleonic Wars', *French Historical Studies*, 22, 2 (Spring 2010), 231–58.

Eagles, Robin, *Francophilia in English Society, 1748–1815* (Basingstoke: Palgrave, 2000).

Emsley, Clive, *British Society and the French Wars, 1793–1815* (Basingstoke: Macmillan, 1979).

Favret, Mary, 'Coming Home: The Public Spaces of Romantic War', *Studies in Romanticism*, 33 (Winter, 1994), 539–48.

——, 'War Correspondence: Reading Romantic War', *Prose Studies*, 19, 2 (1996), 173–85.

——, *War at a Distance: Romanticism and the Making of Modern Wartime* (Princeton, NJ: Princeton UP, 2009).

Forrest, Alan, *Soldiers of the French Revolution* (Durham NC: Duke UP, 1990).

——, *Napoleon's Men: The Soldiers of the Revolution and Empire* (London: Hambledon, 2002).

Forrest, Alan, Karen Hagemann and Jane Rendall, 'Introduction', *Soldiers, Citizens and Civilians: Experiences and Perceptions of the Revolutionary and Napoleonic Wars, 1790–1820* (Basingstoke: Palgrave Macmillan, 2009), 6–12.

Foster, Kevin, *Fighting Fictions: War, Narrative and National Identity* (London: Pluto, 1999).

Fritzsche, Peter, *Stranded in the Present: Modern Time and the Melancholy of History* (Cambridge MA: Harvard UP, 2004).

Fussell, Paul, *The Great War and Modern Memory* (Oxford: Oxford UP, 1975).

Gash, Norman, 'After Waterloo: British Society and the Legacy of the Napoleonic wars', *Transactions of the Royal Historical Society*, 5th series, 28 (1978), 145–57.

Gee, Austin, *The British Volunteer Movement, 1794–1814* (Oxford: Clarendon, 2003).

Gilbert, Arthur N., 'Law and Honour among Eighteenth-Century British Army Officers', *Historical Journal* 19 (1976) 75–87.

——, 'Military and Civilian Justice in Eighteenth-Century England: An Assessment', *The Journal of British Studies*, 17, 2 (1978) 41–65.

Glover, Richard, *Peninsular Preparation: The Reform of the British Army, 1795–1809* (Cambridge: Cambridge UP, 1963).

Guy, Alan J. (ed.), *The Road to Waterloo: The British Army and the Struggle against Revolutionary and Napoleonic France* (Stroud: Sutton, 1990).

Hagemann, Karen, 'German Heroes: The Cult of Death for the Fatherland in Nineteenth-Century Germany', in Stefan Dudink, Karen Hagemann and John Tosh (eds), *Masculinities in Politics and War: Gendering Modern History* (Manchester: Manchester UP, 2004), 116–36.

Hagemann, Karen, Gisela Mettele and Jane Rendall (eds), *Gender, War and Politics: Transatlantic Perspectives, 1775–1850* (Basingstoke: Palgrave Macmillan, 2010).

Hämmerle, Christa, '"You let a weeping woman call you home?" Private correspondences during the First World War in Germany', in Rebecca Earle (ed.), *Epistolary Selves: Letters and Letter Writers, 1600–1945* (Aldershot: Ashgate, 1999), 152–82.

Harari, Yuval Noah, *The Ultimate Experience: Battlefield Revelations and the Making of Modern War Culture, 1450–2000* (Basingstoke: Palgrave Macmillan, 2008).

Hontanilla, Ana, 'Images of Barbaric Spain in Eighteenth-Century British Travel Writing', *Studies in Eighteenth-Century Culture*, 37, 1 (2008), 119–143.

Hoock, Holger, *Empires of the Imagination: Politics, War and the Arts in the British World, 1750–1850* (London: Profile, 2010).

Houlding, J. A., *Fit for Service: The Training of the British Army 1715–1795* (Oxford, Oxford UP Reprints, 2000 [1981]).

Hynes, Samuel, *The Soldiers' Tale: Bearing Witness to Modern War* (London: Pimlico, 1998).

Jenks, Timothy, *Naval Engagements: Patriotism, Cultural Politics and the Royal Navy, 1793–1815* (Oxford: Oxford UP, 2006).

Keegan, John, *The Face of Battle: A Study of Agincourt, Waterloo and the Somme* (London: Pimlico, 2004 [1976]).

Kennedy, Catriona, '"Our Separate Rooms": Bishop Stock's Narrative of the French Invasion of Mayo, 1798', *Field Day Review*, 5 (2009), 94–107.

Koselleck, Reinhart, *Futures Past: On the Semantics of Historical Time* (Cambridge MA: MIT Press, 1985).

Land, Isaac, *War, Nationalism and the British Sailor, 1750–1850* (New York: Macmillan, 2009).

Lewis, Michael, *A Social History of the Navy, 1793–1815* (London: George Allen & Unwin, 1960).

——, *Napoleon and his British Captives* (London: George Allen & Unwin, 1962).

Lincoln, Margarette, *Representing the Royal Navy, British Sea Power, 1750–1815* (Aldershot: Ashgate, 2002).

Lynn, John A., *Battle: A History of Combat and Culture from Ancient Greece to Modern America* (Boulder CO: Westview, 2003).

MacKillop, Andrew, *'More Fruitful than the Soil': Army, Empire and the Scottish Highlands* (East Linton: Tuckwell, 2000).

——, 'For King, Country and Regiment?: Motive and Identity within Highland Soldiering, 1746–1815', in Steve Murdoch and Andrew Mackillop (eds), *Fighting for Identity: Scottish Military Experience, 1550–1900* (Leiden: Brill, 2002), 185–212.

Mandler, Peter, *The English National Character: The History of an Idea from Edmund Burke to Tony Blair* (New York and London: Yale UP, 2006).

Maynes, Mary Jo, *Taking the Hard Road: Life Course in French and German Workers' Autobiographies in the Era of Industrialization* (Chapel Hill: North Carolina UP, 1995).

McAnally, Henry, *The Irish Militia 1793–1816: A Social and Military Study* (Dublin and London: Clonmore and Reynolds, 1949).

McBride, Ian and Tony Claydon, 'The Trials of the Chosen Peoples: Recent Interpretations of Protestantism in Britain and Ireland', in Ian McBride and Tony Claydon (eds), *Protestantism and National Identity: Britain and Ireland, c.1650–1850* (Cambridge: Cambridge UP, 1998), 3–29.

McCormack, Matthew, *The Independent Man: Citizenship and Gender Politics in Georgian England* (Manchester: Manchester UP, 2005).

McNeil, David, *The Grotesque Depiction of War and the Military in Eighteenth-century English Fiction* (Newark: University of Delaware Press, 1990).

Morgan, Marjorie, *National Identities and Travel in Victorian Britain* (Basingstoke: Palgrave Macmillan, 2001).

Myerly, Scott Hughes, *British Military Spectacle from the Napoleonic Wars through the Crimea* (Cambridge MA: Harvard UP, 1996).

Navickas, Katrina, *Loyalism and Radicalism in Lancashire, 1798–1815* (Oxford: Oxford UP, 2009).

Nelson, Michael C., 'Writing during Wartime: Gender and Literacy in the American Civil War', *Journal of American Studies*, 31 (1997), 43–68.

Nenadic, Stana, 'The Impact of the Military Profession on Highland Gentry Families, c. 1730–1830', *The Scottish Historical Review*, 85, 1 (April 2006), 75–99.

Newman, Gerald, *The Rise of English Nationalism: A Cultural History, 1740–1830* (New York: St Martin's, 1987).

Newman, Jon, '"An Insurrection of Loyalty": The London Volunteer Regiments' Response to the Invasion Threat', in Mark Philp, (ed.), *Resisting Napoleon: The British Response to the Threat of Invasion* (Aldershot: Ashgate, 2006), 75–91.

Paris, Michael, *Warrior Nation: Images of War in British Popular Culture, 1850–2000* (London: Reaktion, 2000).

Pratt, Mary Louise, *Imperial Eyes: Travel Writing and Transculturation* (London: Routledge,1992).

Quilley, Geoff, 'Duty and Mutiny: The Aesthetics of Loyalty and the Representation of the British Sailor c. 1789–1800', in Philip Shaw (ed.), *Romantic Wars: Studies in Culture and Conflict, 1793–1822* (Aldershot: Ashgate, 2000), 80–109.

Rachamimov, Alon, *POWs and the Great War: Captivity on the Eastern Front* (Oxford and New York: Berg, 2002).

Ramsey, Neil, *The Military Memoir and Romantic Literary Culture, 1780–1835* (Aldershot: Ashgate, 2011).

Rawlinson, Mark, 'Invasion! Coleridge, the Defence of Britain and the Cultivation of the Public's Fear', in Philip Shaw (ed.), *Romantic Wars: Studies in Culture and Conflict, 1793–1822* (Aldershot: Ashgate, 2000), 110–37.

Rodger, N.A.M., *The Wooden World: An Anatomy of the Georgian Navy* (London: Fontana, 1988).

——, 'Honour and Duty at Sea, 1660–1815', *Historical Research*, 75, 190 (2002), 425–47.

——, *The Command of the Ocean: A Naval History of Britain, 1649–1815* (London: Allen Lane, 2004).

Rogers, Nicholas, *The Press Gang: Naval Impressment and Its Opponents in Georgian Britain* (London and New York: Contiuum, 2007).

Russell, Gillian, *The Theatres of War: Politics, Performance and Society, 1793–1815* (Oxford: Clarendon, 1995).

Saglia, Diego, *Poetic Castles in Spain: British Romanticism and Figurations of Iberia* (Amsterdam; Atlanta GA: Rodopi, 2000).

Semmell, Stuart, 'Reading the Tangible past: British Tourism, Collecting and Memory after Waterloo', *Representations*, 69 (Winter, 2000), 9–37.

——, *Napoleon and the British* (New Haven and London: Yale UP, 2004).

Shaw, Philip (ed.) *Romanticism and War: Studies in Culture and Conflict, 1793–1822* (Aldershot: Ashgate, 2000).

——, *Waterloo and the Romantic Imagination* (Basingstoke: Palgrave Macmillan, 2002).

Snape, Michael, *The Redcoat and Religion: The Forgotten History of the British Soldier from the Age of Marlborough to the Eve of the First World War* (London: Routledge, 2006).

St Clair, William, *The Reading Nation in the Romantic Period* (Cambridge: Cambridge UP, 2004).

Steedman, Carolyn, *The Radical Soldier's Tale: John Pearman, 1819–1908* (London; New York: Routledge,1988).

——, 'Inside, Outside, Other: Accounts of National Identity in the Nineteenth Century', *History of the Human Sciences*, 8, 4 (1995), 59–76.

Thomas, J.E., *Britain's Last Invasion: Fishguard 1797* (Stroud: Tempus, 2007).

Wahrman, Dror, *The Making of the Modern Self: Identity and Culture in Eighteenth-Century England* (New Haven, 2004).

Western, J.R., *The English Militia in the Eighteenth Century: The Story of a Political Issue, 1660–1802* (London: Routledge, 1965).

Wheeler, H.F.B. & A.M. Broadley, *Napoleon and the Invasion of England: The Story of the Great Terror* (Stroud: Nonsuch, 2007 [1908]).

Wilson, Kathleen, *The Island Race: Englishness, Empire and Gender in the Eighteenth Century* (London: Routledge, 2003).

——, (ed.), *A New Imperial History: Culture, Identity and Modernity in Britain and the Empire, 1660–1840* (Cambridge: Cambridge UP, 2004).

Unpublished dissertations

Carter, Louise P., 'British Women during the Revolutionary and Napoleonic wars, 1793–1815: Responses, Roles and Representations', DPhil thesis, University of Cambridge, 2005.

Lin, Patricia Y., 'Extending her Arms: Military Families and the Transformation of the British State, 1793–1815', PhD thesis, University of California, Berkeley, 1997.

Index

Alexandria, battle of (1801), 84
American war (1775 –83), 38, 41, 115, 137, 140
Anderson, Benedict, 6–7, 126
Anti-Catholicism *see* Religion
Arras, prisoner of war depot, 24, 116, 120, 121, 124–5, 126–7, 128, 130, 131
Austen, Jane, 1, 28, 38, 144

Badajoz, storming of (1812), 16, 76, 178
Bainbridge, Simon, 174
Bamford, Samuel, 175
battle
  aftermath of, 79–81
  battlefield tourism, 187–90
  despatches, 75, 76, 78, 83, 178–80, 194, 199
  deaths in, 76, 77–8, 82, 179, 180
  see also deaths in war
  expression of fear before, 72–3
  killing, 78–9
  narratives of, 18–19, 74–81
  wounding, 76–77
Belfast, 105, 138, 147, 151–2, 164, 176, 182
Bell, David A., 4–5, 19, 46, 85, 90–1
Black Legend, the, 102
British army
  barracks, 5, 42–3, 44, 59, 60, 151, 153, 156, 171, 172
  commissions and promotion, 22, 35–6, 41, 55, 62, 65, 77, 81, 84, 192
  morale, 45, 71, 82–3
  and national integration, 53–63, 85, 198
  reading culture of, 19–22, 87, 96–7, 106
  recruitment to, 35, 39, 54–5
  reform of, 5, 36, 37, 46, 67
  reputation of, 38, 39, 84–5, 87–8
  uniforms, 42–3, 86

see also Ireland; masculinity; officers; regiment; religion; soldiers; Scotland; Wales
Britishness, 3–4, 7, 53–4, 56, 79, 84–5, 87–88, 94–6, 100, 102–3, 118–9, 125–9, 131–2, 156–7, 163, 166, 183–5, 191, 196–8
  see also John Bull; national identities
Burke, Edmund, 21, 63
Burns, Robert, 185
Byron, Lord George Gordon, 188

Cape St Vincent, Battle of (1797), 180, 185
Catholics and Catholicism *see* religion
Cervantes, Miguel de, 20, 96
chivalry, 33, 34, 74, 89, 96, 161, 174–5, 189–90
Church of England *see* religion
Church of Scotland *see* religion
Churchill, Sir Winston, 1
civilians,
  narratives of war, 25–31, 187–92
  mediated experience of war, 7, 11, 25, 31, 89, 160–61, 174–8, 180–1, 187, 199
  see also civilian mobilization; invasion threat; military-civilian relations; military tourism; prisoners of war; victory celebrations; war, pleasure culture of; war, opposition to
civilian mobilization, 135–159
  motivations, 139–40, 140–47
  challenges and tedium of, 136–7, 147–8
  women's contribution to, 148–54
  see also militia; Volunteers; Yeomanry
civilization, narratives of, 100–102, 103, 104, 109–11, 113
Clarke, Mary Anne, 48
class, 67, 88, 89, 144–5, 147, 148, 150, 175, 180, 181, 182
  middle classes, 9, 36, 48, 100, 111, 136, 181, 196

CPSIA information can be obtained
at www.ICGtesting.com
Printed in the USA
LVOW04*2011050516

486873LV00013B/221/P